The Ethnomusicologist

McGRAW-HILL BOOK COMPANY

New York   San Francisco   St. Louis   Düsseldorf   London   Mexico   Panama   Sydney   Toronto

The ETHNOMUSICOLOGIST

Mantle Hood

Institute of Ethnomusicology
University of California, Los Angeles

McGRAW-HILL SERIES IN MUSIC

William J. Mitchell, *Consulting Editor*

ATKISSON *Basic Counterpoint*

CHASE *America's Music*

CROCKER *A History of Musical Style*

CROCKER & BASART *Listening to Music*

HOOD *The Ethnomusicologist*

LERNER *Study Scores of Musical Styles*

RATNER *Harmony: Structure and Style*

RATNER *Music: The Listener's Art*

SALZER & SCHACHTER *Counterpoint in Composition*

WAGNER *Band Scoring*

WAGNER *Orchestration: A Practical Handbook*

This book was set in Fototronic Laurel by York Graphic Services, Inc., printed on permanent paper by Halliday Lithograph Corporation, and bound by Book Press. The designer was Ronald Q. Lewton. The original illustrations were prepared by Robert E. Berner. The editors were Robert P. Rainier and Ronald Q. Lewton. Charles A. Goehring supervised production.

The ETHNOMUSICOLOGIST

Printed in the United States of America.

Library of Congress catalog card number: 79-132344

34567890 HDHD 7987

07-029725-8

FOREWORD

TO BEST of present knowledge, most students come to ethnomusicology because they have heard and become interested in some music that has not been dealt with in the course of their formal studies. A few may have come from other disciplines or from reading the articles on musicology in journals, dictionaries, or encyclopedias of music. From these, they have probably gained the impression that ethnomusicology is a study *zu ethnographischen Zwecken,* as Guido Adler put it, that is, of non-European, "exotic" music. In his article "Ethnomusicology" in the *Harvard Dictionary of Music* (1969), Mantle Hood states categorically, "Ethnomusicology is an approach to the study of *any* music, not only in terms of itself but also in relation to its cultural context." He continues, "Currently the term has two broad applications: (1) the study of all music outside the European art tradition, including survivals of earlier forms of that tradition in Europe and elsewhere; (2) the study of all varieties of music found in one locale or region, e.g., the 'ethnomusicology' of Tokyo or Los Angeles or Santiago would comprise the study in that locality of all types of European art music, the music of ethnic enclaves, folk, popular and commercial music, musical hybrids, etc.; in other words, all music being used by the people of a given area."

Obviously, even as localities merge in an area, so areas merge in larger units until we have the universally accepted half-worlds, Western and non-Western. These in turn merge in the concept of the music of man as a whole that was inherent in the word "music" as applied to the bundle of traditions cultivated in a city, locality, or region. But is this not precisely the logical meaning of the word "musicology"? Linguistics is the study of all the languages of man. Astronomers do not limit their field to a single galaxy; nor do biologists, to insects with six legs. If the study of music is ever to enter into the increasingly interdisciplinary academic domain, it must have the "truly world-wide perspective" Professor Hood pleads for. The need for an ethnomusicology of the fine art of European music is as urgent as for that of any other "high culture." Ultimately, there would be no roles for separate studies, musicology and ethnomusicology; but there would still be a distinction between the musicological and ethnomusicological *approaches*, the first, to the thing in itself, the second, to the thing in its cultural context as one of quite a number of other contexts, physical, mathematical, logical, philosophical, aesthetic, moral, economic, political, religious.

The publisher's invitation to the author of the present volume was to write a textbook. His answer was that conditions do not justify such an undertaking, that there is no general agreement upon the nature of ethnomusicology—upon the scope, methods, and aims of the study—and hence no clear distinction between musicology and ethnomusicology, that ethnomusicologists are still pioneers, and that as in all pioneering it is the individual student, rather than an organized collective or profession, that blazes the paths, sets the pace, and creates the standards. He agreed, however, that the long-delayed upsurge of interest in the many musics of mankind called for broader and more comprehensive guidance— not so much of the few mature workers who will find their own ways, partly by intuition, partly by reason, partly by learning from each other, as of the majority of younger men and women who in the course of choosing careers have to consider not only what comes closest to their individual interests and abilities but also what are the conditions under which they must prepare themselves for and pursue their careers. *The Ethnomusicologist* is, then, to be regarded primarily as the student himself—what, as a beginner, he can find ethnomusicologists to be and what, if he goes through the training, he himself might be.

As of the 1970s we stand upon the threshold of a second epoch in the study of music. The first was dominated by Eric M. von Hornbostel. The learned man approached musics that were not his own as objectively as possible, at his desk, by analysis, transcription into conventional European notation, and comparative study of the field recordings and documentation of others, though increasingly of his own, as in the case of Bartók, Kunst, Lachmann, and others. The job was strictly nonparticipatory as far as the music studied was concerned. The epoch will go down in history as that of "Comparative Musicology" (*vergleichende Musikwissenschaft*). The second epoch got under way in the 1950s under the leadership of the author of the present volume. The "armchair" study, analysis, manual transcription, and comparative study of the first epoch was intensified by development of electronic music-writing in Norway, Sweden, Germany, Czechoslovakia, Israel, and the United States. But the distinguishing mark of the second epoch is the learning to *make*, that is, becoming reasonably participatory in, the music one is studying. We have realized that to the speech knowledge of music— that is, the knowledge sought and expressed in terms of a language—there must be added the music knowledge of music. Where speech knowledge fails, music knowledge can be gained only by the making of it. One does, after all, expect a foreign student of French or Chinese to be reasonably fluent in those languages. Candidates for the degree of doctor of philosophy in musicology are universally expected to be able to sing at least a nineteenth-century Lied in tune and to play with moderate proficiency at least one concert-type instrument. The ethnomusicologist of this book is, then, quite another person from the comparative musicologist of the first epoch—Béla Bartók and a few others were probably exceptions. Precept and objectivity have their place in learning, but there is more than one reason to believe that it is second to example. And in all example, the subjective element—at least, in the humanities—is as important as the objective. The example presented here is the author himself. In the final analysis it is he who is "The Ethnomusicologist" *par excellence*. He is already emulated by a number of promising young students. We shall be fortunate to whatever extent they achieve the rare combination of artist, scholar, and teacher that he is.

CHARLES SEEGER

To HAZEL

the dancer who will understand
how inevitable it always was
that we should walk this trail together

TABLE of CONTENTS

The Ethnomusicologist

INTRODUCTION

THE APPARENT OMISSION of a preface to this book is deceptive, since much of the material discussed in this and subsequent chapters might be considered prefatory in the rapidly developing field known as ethnomusicology—a field that has almost as many approaches and objectives as there are practitioners but has as yet no standard nomenclature, no generally recognized theories and certainly no theory of theories. There seems to be something about the term itself—"ethnomusicology"—that both repels and attracts. Some African and Asian scholars avoid the word entirely; others in the same parts of the world call themselves ethnomusicologists in the pursuit of studying their indigenous music. I know a young Japanese ethnomusicologist who is specializing in the music of India and a young German scholar who is concentrating on the traditions of Mexico. American ethnomusicologists seem to be involved with areas all over the globe, as well as with the music of the Amerindians, Anglo-American folk song, Negro spirituals, and even, to a limited extent, with the neglected field of American jazz. Cultural background, nationality, and "race" offer no particular clue to the identity of the ethnomusicologist.

WHAT'S IN A NAME?

The inventor of the term, Jaap Kunst, himself, was not too satisfied with his coinage but defended it on the grounds that it was a more accurate designation than "comparative musicology," a translation of the German *vergleichende Musikwissenschaft*. Comparative method, he reasoned, like historical, descriptive, analytical, critical, and synthetic methods, may be applied to all branches of scientific inquiry. For a time some broadly oriented Western scholars were hopeful that the prefix would eventually be dropped in the conviction that musicology ought to include the study of all kinds of music, everywhere. For a scholar like Frank Harrison, however, such breadth of inclusion carries implications of a new approach:

> The traditional enterprises of musicology can no longer be pursued *in vacuo*. For their ultimate meaning and value rest on their contribution to restoring silent music to the state of being once more a medium of human communication. Re-creation in any full sense cannot be divorced from the original function of the music, any more than a musical work from another society can be fully understood apart from its social context.
>
> Looked at in this way, it is the function of all musicology to be in fact ethnomusicology, that is, to take its range of research to include material that is termed "sociological." This view would still assume the basic importance of analytical and stylistic studies, but would look further than has been customary in investigating the various aspects of music as an expression of an individual in his social context.[1]

In time, this approach will be recognized as essential to the study of all music. Meanwhile, the label "ethnomusicology" has focused attention on the fact that the requirements of this approach go beyond the usual practice of either musicology or ethnology. This tag, whatever sensitive arguments might be raised against it, has had the positive effect of establishing the identity of a unique field of inquiry, so that today, at least in the United States, it is widely known and accepted (though not necessarily understood) by scholarly societies of other disciplines, the American Council of Learned Societies, university and college admin-

---

[1] Frank Ll. Harrison, "American Musicology and the European Tradition," in Frank Ll. Harrison, Mantle Hood, and Claude V. Palisca, *Musicology*, pp. 79–80. © 1963 by the Trustees of Princeton University. Reprinted by permission of Prentice-Hall, Inc., Englewood Cliffs, N.J.

istrators, American foundations, and various branches of the federal government. Notwithstanding the likely continuation of pedantic arguments over terminology, the prefix "ethno" will probably adhere to the root "music" and its suffix "ology" for some long time to come.[2]

In a field that requires the broadest possible interdisciplinary approach, it is not surprising that there are yet to be developed a set of standard theories and practices and a corresponding abstract nomenclature that can be understood and applied by representatives of the different disciplines. Professional membership in ethnomusicology is made up of scholars of the most diverse types of background, training, and experience. I am not referring to the individual whose principal claim to professionalism is a Nagra tape recorder and casual forays into various parts of the world as a "collector." Nor am I including the person whose singular drive is a recent flirtation with the Indian sitar. The casual collector *may* collect something of value; and a serious romance with an Indian sitar is likely to be a salutary affair in one way or another. But there is more to ethnomusicology than the possession of a professional tape recorder or a passion for Indian music. Important as they are, neither the collection of music nor the performance of it per se makes the practitioner any kind of "ologist." I have even met one or two individuals who call themselves ethnomusicologists because they own a fair sampling of commercial recordings.

Who is an ethnomusicologist? Are musicology and anthropology the qualifying disciplines for membership in this rapidly increasing tribe that appears to be self-generating through no recognized kinship system?

Jaap Kunst took his degree in law. Erich M. von Hornbostel was trained in psychology, and he was assisted by the physician Otto Abraham, whose chief interest was in the physiology of music. George Herzog's training included linguistics and folklore. In the recent historical past of this relatively young field, some of the principal pioneers have been trained in art history, physics, acoustics, archeology, biology, and so forth. It is true, however, that, when compared with other members of their respective disciplines, these professionals are highly exceptional in their devotion to the subject of music. In fact, the generative force that has produced this polyglot tribe *is* music.

One point is clear: The *subject* of study in the field of ethnomusicology is music. Essentially different but interdependent *approaches* to the subject might well include related studies in history, ethnography, folklore, literature, dance, religion, theater, archeology, etymology, iconography, and other fields concerned with cultural expressions. In addition to purely musical information, various

---

[2] Recently there have also developed such specialized branches of study as ethnobotany, ethnobiology, ethnolinguistics, and others.

3

objectives toward which the study leads might encompass a better understanding of two or more societies or individuals or groups within a society as to behavior; psychology; perception; system of values; artistic, aesthetic and philosophical standards; and so forth. And potentially there are a great number of possible *applications* of the knowledge gained about the subject that might involve national or international relations, economics, communications, labor relations, propaganda, protest, censorship, and many unsuspected areas of interest to the social and political scientists. Plausible approaches to, objectives in, and applications of such study are virtually unlimited. But the primary *subject* of study in ethnomusicology is *music*.

Currently, institutions of higher learning, especially in the United States, France, Germany, and some non-European countries such as Israel, Ghana, Nigeria, Japan, the Philippines, and Chile, are turning their attention to the development of training programs in ethnomusicology. The majority of these programs are centered in departments or schools of music; a few are located in departments of anthropology or in area-study research centers. Ideally, such programs include close cooperation with related disciplines in the humanities and social sciences as well as centers for area studies. *Institutional* responsibility for this kind of training and research and the concomitant concern for job placement represent a sharp break with the recent past. Formerly, training, research, and ultimate professional employment were entirely the *individual* responsibility of the devoted scholar, whatever disciplinary path he chose to follow. The sine qua non of successful studies in ethnomusicology—thorough training in music—was usually acquired outside his academic preparation. And ultimately his primary professional employment often had little or nothing to do with his principal interest, ethnomusicology.

Today the demand in colleges and universities in the United States for well-trained ethnomusicologists far exceeds the supply. And it appears likely that the shortage will become even more critical. A good program of training leading to the Ph.D. is necessarily long; existing programs cannot hope to supply competent graduates at the rapid rate that institutions are trying to add them to their staff. Scholars in the social sciences and the humanities have begun to recognize the unique contribution ethnomusicology is making to their own spheres of interest. The vanguard of such scholars, for the most part, is made up of those associated by common interests in a center for area studies, rather than of scholars confined to the more isolated departmental structure of the university or college. Much lip service has been paid to the importance of interdepartmental programs and interdisciplinary studies. In practice, however, there is very little activity of this sort outside the center for area studies or the institute of a subject discipline. There is very little evidence of any real communication among departments in the

4

humanities; the same can be said of departments in the social sciences. Scholarly intercourse among faculties and students of the humanities, social sciences, and the physical sciences is almost nil. Very recently, however, there are indications that various disciplines recognize this fact and are actively seeking ways to establish communication. One of the catalysts that may help to break down this insularity is the broad interdisciplinary character of a subject discipline like ethnomusicology. The current interest in this young maverick profession can only accelerate. Supply and demand, in my judgment, will be out of balance for some years to come. It is a seller's market.

WHAT'S IN A BOOK?

Before accepting the invitation to write some kind of book concerned with the field of ethnomusicology, I tried to determine the potential of reader audience in relation to brief outlines of some ten different books that appeared to be timely at this stage in the development of the field. I discussed these with advanced graduate students in music, anthropology, folklore, and linguistics; with various colleagues in ethnomusicology; and with scholars in other disciplines. Although there was a recognizable need for a "music-of-the-world" book, it was ruled out from the beginning as being an impossible assignment for any one author. In the course of discussion, the lack of standard terminology, theory, and practice made it clear that the usual type of textbook would be premature—in fact, for these reasons simply could not be written at this time. An exemplary monograph was considered for its value as a model, and it was agreed that this would make a welcome addition to the literature. But there were already a number of excellent monographs to provide models, and such an additional study might reach a relatively limited audience. A "contributions" type of book—that is, a survey of high points in the development of ethnomusicology—would be looking backward; and besides there were several worthy approaches in this direction already available.[3] Specific problems peculiar to the field seemed a good possibility: notation and transcription, recording techniques, the documentary film, instrumental classification, descriptive and analytical methods. But each of these, in view of current need, could hardly be justified as an individual study lifted out of the context of other closely related problems.

An outline for the tenth book developed in response to a number of considerations that at first glance appear to have a very casual relationship. Some

---

[3] Compare Alan Merriam, *The Anthropology of Music*, Northwestern University Press, Evanston, Ill., 1964; Bruno Nettl, *Folk and Traditional Music of the Western Continents*, Prentice-Hall, Inc., Englewood Cliffs, N.J., 1965; Bruno Nettl, *Theory and Method in Ethnomusicology*, Free Press, New York, 1964.

wag once defined ethnomusicology as the thing ethnomusicologists do, a truism that is not too enlightening. During the period of soul-searching in the quest for a good outline, I was asked to write an entry for the new edition of the *Harvard Dictionary of Music* under the heading "ethnomusicology." After several drafts submitted to my colleagues for criticism, the final version sent off to the press carried the definition about as far as our collective judgments could manage within the space limitations of a dictionary entry. It went a little farther than the brief definition mentioned above; by implication it even suggested, in the most general terms, a few of the basic things an ethnomusicologist does. But, understandably, it still leaves hanging the question, "What does the ethnomusicologist *really* do?"

Another link in this chain of deliberations came from constant association with students. Over the span of a dozen or so years of teaching, I have heard many of the same basic questions asked by succeeding generations of students. Answers to these questions, fitted together in some kind of logical order, might provide a useful text. I have also observed, however, that a whole range of even more vital questions are *not* asked, for the simple reason, I suppose, that the student who has not yet been out into the field is ignorant of the practical problems that stand between the thing to be done and actually doing it.

An added ingredient to this kettle of rumination came as the residue of a lot of reading. In trying to keep abreast with new publications, I had noticed that from the reader's viewpoint most books contained two basic orders of information: one, facts and figures collected from sources written by other scholars in various disciplines; the other, facts and figures derived from the author's own personal experience of getting on with the job. Quite a few of these books, but certainly not all, seemed to be rather fat in the first order of information (from book to book too often the same information) and noticeably lean in the second order of information. Now, it is true, scholarly documentation requires the security of a heavy dosage of secondary sources to shore up findings and conclusions based on the primary activities of the lone scholar. Do not misunderstand: I am not for a moment questioning the validity of this universally honored tradition; to the contrary, with one or two critical reservations I strongly support it. At the moment, however, I am trying to maintain the point of view of the reader who is not especially concerned with the preservation of the author's immaculate reputation but more with the substance of the matter at hand. In this reasonably uncritical posture, I have found that those passages of a book written directly out of the author's firsthand experience and observation achieve an immediacy of communication alongside of which the information from secondary sources is quite pale. Said another way, in the formative stages of this field of inquiry, the prime interest should be in what the ethnomusicologist is currently doing or aspiring to do or even in his half-formed questions that have not yet managed

6

to define his future doing. It is true, of course, that much can be learned from what he has already done, as long as we remember that it was done in the sociological, technological, and political climate of fifty years ago, twenty years ago, ten years ago—or even yesterday.

An unconscious contributor to part of the outline of this book is the steady stream of foreign and domestic visitors to the main Seminar in the Institute of Ethnomusicology at UCLA (University of California at Los Angeles). A few years ago, during the visit of some VIP (whose identity by now has been blurred by the sheer number of short-term visitors), those of us who meet for weekly debate—students and colleagues—suddenly realized that our discourse in English must sound to the visitor almost like a foreign language. In the course of many long deliberations, we had evolved, almost unconsciously, a fairly extensive vocabulary of high-level abstractions, which for the initiate permitted an efficient and rapid exchange of ideas that otherwise would require almost interminable, tedious explanation. In some instances, months of exploration and discussion lay behind the ultimate common usage of a single term. For the occasional visitor and for the student newly introduced to this arena of deliberation, our expedient nomenclature made rather heavy demands. By the same token, it represents an invaluable factor in "doing" that deserves wider dissemination.

A principal contributor to the outline of this book has been the ever-changing personnel and personality of the main Seminar itself. For those who have participated in the mixed pleasure and pain of our Wednesday afternoon discussions this will come as no surprise. One pristine theorem has emerged from our collective efforts. Given a group of "doers" that represents a wide diversity of backgrounds, training, and experience; given an immediacy of communication founded on mutual understanding of terminology, approaches, and objectives: the most abstract theories, the most specific practices, the widest range of speculations can be tested, evaluated, and recast in a much more substantial mold than any that might be fashioned by the isolated professional. It might appear to be self-evident that a group of scholars and advanced graduate students can apply critical method more successfully than any one member of the group. However, the person who has attended a number of congresses with their inevitable panel discussions and "structured" conference themes will agree, I believe, that both premises of our theorem are essential to a predictable result. Professionals in ethnomusicology the world over seem to have one hell of a time understanding one another's terms and objectives.

Although I have not attempted to determine the relative weight of the several observations that finally shaped the character of this book, all of them seem to point toward a particular need: a concrete exposition of the things an ethnomusicologist does, illustrated by specific examples drawn from firsthand experience. That experience includes about sixteen years of preoccupation with Indonesian studies, two field trips to Java and Bali, two to West Africa, and responsibility for a program of training and research in ethnomusicology since 1954, in which context I have had the privilege of prolonged contact with performing musicians from many parts of the world. I have tried to keep secondary sources at a minimum, using such materials when, to the best of my knowledge, they are not widely known in existing literature and seemed to offer the best solution in driving home a point. Within the classical tradition of scholarly documentation, perhaps it is a sign of human frailty that too often the reader's critical faculties are temporarily numbed the moment his attention is focused between quotation marks. I shall take refuge in the inherent "authority" of this device as little as possible.

Some of the things an ethnomusicologist does require aural examples if they are to be illustrated clearly. The three LP records accompanying this book comprise brief excerpts of pertinent recordings made or supervised by me in the field. From time to time, I shall ask the reader to hear particular examples illustrative of important points in the text.

It was stated in the first sentence that there are almost as many approaches and objectives in this field as there are practitioners. I have set down one of these approaches in the most forthright style I could muster in the expectation that it will be accepted as only one of a number of possibilities. By now the reader may have scanned the table of contents. Although I believe the subject headings are clear, a few words of warning may be in order about the inevitable bias that tends to be present in molding literary flesh to such a skeleton.

As ringleader of the many individuals who have participated in the main Seminar[4] I assume full—well, at least partial—responsibility for the circuitous

[4] It is impossible to acknowledge all who have contributed directly or indirectly to these continuing Seminars, but among them must be mentioned my colleagues: Charles Seeger (research musicologist), William Hutchinson (psychology of music), Leon Knopoff (physics, geophysics, musical composition), William Bright (linguistics, anthropology), David Morton (composition, ethnomusicology—Thailand), Leland Gralapp (art history), Klaus Wachsmann (ethnomusicology—Africa), Hormoz Farhat (composition, ethnomusicology—Iran), Boris Kremenliev (composition, ethnomusicology—the Balkans); and former graduates who now are involved with their own programs at other institutions, including especially Professors William P. Malm (University of Michigan), José Maceda (University of the Philippines), Tanjore Viswanathan (University of Madras), Robert Brown (California Institute for the Arts), Robert Garfias (University of Washington), Willem Adriaansz (University of Sydney), Ruby Ornstein (Brown University), Lois Anderson (University of Wisconsin), Sam Chianis (Binghamton University), Joseph Katz (Columbia University), Donn Borcherdt (deceased), Fred Lieberman (Brown University), Ricardo Trimillos (University of Hawaii), Atta Mensah (University of Zambia), Ben Aning (University of Ghana), Akin Euba (Ifé University, Nigeria), Esther Grebe (University of Chile). Members of the staff who have contributed to the Seminar materially and substantively are Michael Moore (recording technician), David Kilpatrick (assistant technician), Ann Briegleb (librarian), Sam Hileman and Dick Fitz-Gerald (Institute editors), Max Harrell (museum scientist), Hardja Susilo

8

route we have traveled together. And as author of this book I relieve the participants of any responsibility for the bias, viewpoint, and personal penchant with which any of our ideas held in common may be reported here. An essayist—and I believe that what you are reading is a kind of essay—is likely to be influenced, consciously or otherwise, by his total background and experience. If he is a good essayist, he tries to make an objective presentation of viewpoints that conflict with his own. But the problem of doing this with complete success is something like one man playing both sides of a chessboard. If ethnomusicology is what an ethnomusicologist does, then what he does must somehow relate to what he is. Therefore, a few vital statistics may be of some help in recognizing the random forces that have motivated the chess player. My undergraduate training was about equally divided between the humanities and the sciences. Extracurricular studies in music began about the age of six and have never stopped. The checkerboard (or chessboard) of professional activities in the continual process of breadwinning have included several fields of the arts, tooling engineering, and agricultural science. The first exposure to European societies was in the role of infantryman in World War II. Repeated exposures to European, Asian, and African societies have been as a recipient of several research grants. A prolonged involvement with jazz and with musical composition established a certain descriptive and analytical point of view long before the beginning of formal, academic training in music. There have been strong influences from teachers like Ernst Toch, Jaap Kunst, and Charles Seeger. Another factor, which does not show itself too readily in a curriculum vitae, is the compelling tendency to identify with and to establish an empathy for other human beings. Perhaps Kunst had such a trait in mind when he said, ". . . intuition and tact, one either has them or has them not, but they are indispensable if satisfactory results are to be obtained."[5] An abiding concern for other human beings, I believe, is an essential attribute of the person attracted to the field of ethnomusicology. Without it, he had better chart a different course.

SOCIETY AND ITS SCALE OF VALUES

TWO EXTREMES: THE UNITED STATES AND THE ISLAND OF BALI The attitudes of different societies and of different groups within a society toward the arts vary widely. The circumstances, underlying conditions, and motivations that

---

(lecturer in Indonesian music and technical translator), Tsun-Yuen Lui (lecturer in Chinese music and technical translator), Suenobu Togi (lecturer in Japanese music and dance and technical translator), Tjokorda Mas (lecturer in Balinese music and technical translator), Gayathri Rajapur (lecturer in Indian music), Robert Ayitee (lecturer in African music).

[5] Jaap Kunst, *Ethnomusicology*, 3rd ed., Martinus Nijhoff, The Hague, 1959, p. 20.

9

shape these attitudes are not always easy to discern. But a truly significant study of music or dance or theater cannot be isolated from its socio-cultural context and the scale of values it implies. For the sake of comparative illustration, we might look briefly at two contrasting examples with the assumption that the attitudes of all other societies fall somewhere between these two extremes: the United States and the island of Bali in Indonesia.

Suppose we start with a thumbnail sketch of the United States as it might be viewed from the outside looking in. The mainland of the United States covers an area about 2,000 by 3,000 miles, has a topography that includes high mountain ranges, broad fertile plains, and deserts, and has a climate that ranges from subtropical to temperate; the large land mass of the state of Alaska has a frigid climate, and the state of Hawaii is a chain of semitropical islands. The total population is about 200 million. The states of Alaska and Hawaii as well as several states on the mainland are relatively underpopulated, and two-thirds of the mainland population live in fewer than ninety metropolitan centers, the rest in rural areas. The oldest arrivals in the United States are the Eskimos and the American Indians; more recently arrived are the Polynesians of Hawaii; and the most recent arrivals, beginning in the sixteenth century but rapidly increasing in the nineteenth century, are a population majority of European descent and a considerable number of Asian, African, and mixed descent. Presently, there are many ethnic groups which show some tendency of being segregated as enclaves within the society, location usually being determined by earlier economic factors that, during the rapid growth of the country in the past century or so, attracted different segments of a worldwide labor force. Although it is considered a classless society, several different economic strata can be identified which in the large cities effect certain residential segregation based on income bracket. Nonetheless, the various races and ethnic groups that make up the society follow fairly homogeneous habits relating to creature comforts, taste, and implied standards of living, probably due to advanced technology, mass-media communication, skillful merchandising, and an efficient flow of interstate commerce. There is nearly a total separation of church and state, and the society enjoys religious freedom when this is not in conflict with the Bill of Rights, a national document guaranteeing certain rights reserved for the individual. In practice, racial discrimination and both implicit and explicit segregation abrogate some of these rights. The United States is governed by a type of indirect democracy. Beginning within the framework of the town meeting, its governmental structure expanded to a loose confederation of states and finally matured with the adoption of a constitution that united the states under a central federal agency comprised of an administrative branch, a judicial branch, and a congress representing the electorate. Through the years, as the machinery of government became increasingly complex, the relationship

10

between the people and the representatives elected to govern them has become increasingly indirect. At the base of its economy, the country has great wealth in natural resources; it has a well-developed agriculture, fisheries, forestry, heavy and light industries, and a vigorous national and international trade. Its citizens endorse compulsory education through the twelfth grade, encourage mass higher education through state taxation, private endowments, and some federal aid, and subsidize research in the social and physical sciences and to a lesser extent support creativity and a modicum of research in the arts and the humanities.

Bali is a tiny but culturally very important part of the Republic of Indonesia, a political unit of heterogeneous peoples living on some 3,000 islands that girdle the equator like a belt 1,700 miles wide and 3,000 miles long, running east from the tip of Southeast Asia. The island of Bali is about the size of the state of Rhode Island or (slightly larger than) the island of Majorca and has a population of fewer than 2 million. It is situated a few hundred miles south of the equator, and the temperature of its tropical climate varies little in the six-month alternation of dry and wet monsoons. Ringed by a fertile coastline and foothills it rises to a central area of high volcanic mountains. The Balinese are Malay-Polynesian stock that migrated from the mainland of Southeast Asia during the Neolithic period sometime between 2500 and 1500 B.C. There are two recognized strata of society, early arrivals known as the Bali Aga, now living in the mountainous regions, and late arrivals dwelling in the coastal areas and foothills. Most recently arrived are a small number of Chinese and Indian merchants and traders. Fishing, agriculture, and limited animal husbandry form the base of a self-sufficient economy. The majority of the population live in small rural villages; and, except for two urban centers, one in the north and one in the south, there is no electricity. There is complete freedom of religion, but almost the whole society is devoted to Balinese Hinduism, a form of religious worship originating in India and introduced to Bali from the neighboring island of Java where it had undergone several centuries of assimilation with indigenous forms of animism and ancestor worship. National policies of the central government in Djakarta have affected the social pattern of the Balinese very little beyond the enforcement of compulsory education and certain essentially restrictive controls effected by military and state officialdom. Local government is derivative of an ancient form of benevolent feudalism operating within the framework of Balinese Hindusim—the basis of the social structure—which results in little real discrimination among priest, prince, and commoner. In spite of a residual caste system, Bali has a communal society that includes group ownership of most land and group responsibility for a plethora of religious duties and obligations, for the welfare of the village, its temples, rice fields, and so forth. This complex but highly organized communal structure has produced a nearly classless society, totally committed to

11

the values and sanctions that have made religion a way of life. Education in the traditions of the society, existing apart from the formal requirements of national policy, is acquired through oral methods and strict imitation of the time-honored mores essential to Balinese Hinduism. The perpetuation of these traditions seems assured as long as this form of religious devotion continues. Aside from a small aristocracy and an even smaller number of white-collar workers in the two urban centers, the society has a relatively uniform standard of living and tastes.

Now let us make a cursory examination of the attitudes of these two societies toward the arts. Afterward, we might consider additional factors that could deepen the evaluation.

Viewed as a total society, the United States regards the arts as nonessential, low on its scale of values. The hero of the day is in orbit in outer space or tunneling into the bowels of the earth or exploring the ocean floor. The poet, the painter, the musician, the dancer, the writer, the actor manage a tolerable acceptance as nonessential members of an affluent society. Modern plumbing, electricity, and the full range of modern appliances, including hi-fi and television, are considered essential parts of the average man's household. He is a rare man indeed who foregoes any one of these items in order to afford a painting or sculpture or monetary contributions to the local civic symphony or amateur dance group or neighborhood theater group. It is true, there is a lively business in the popular arts: recordings of rock music and a variety of hybrids; paperback books on every imaginable subject from philosophy to pornography; reproductions of calendar and classical arts; TV productions of soap operas, horse operas, situation comedies, comic-strip series, science-fiction series; motion pictures with suggested audiences rated all the way from "family" to the "underground" variety which, like that of much current theater, seeks the sensationalism of public nudity and implicit or explicit sex acts. This heterogeneous assortment of popular arts is nominally supported by a majority of the population through the direct purchase of the product itself, tickets for admission, or leading brands of cigarettes, beauty aids, and automobiles.

Possession of a first and a second automobile has high priority over direct support of the arts. On the other hand, fairly recently some large public and private buildings have had a small, very small, percentage of their budgets reserved for murals or mosaics and outdoor sculpture, usually of an avant-garde style that communicates little with the general public and sometimes arouses civic controversy. Whatever the persuasion of the individual consumer of automobiles, television sets, and cosmetics, it can also be pointed out that dollar support of the arts, in one form or another, by private foundations, some institutions of higher learning, and benevolent individuals is probably greater in the United States than any other

12

country in the world. However, dollar support is not necessarily an index of consumer valuation in determining the attitude of a society toward the arts. Perhaps this generous funding from the top economic stratum can be considered a kind of "forced feeding."

It is indicative that within the federal government there is no "ministry of culture." The recently formed federal agencies called the National Endowment for the Arts and the National Endowment for the Humanities are a token response, with token budgets, to the hue and cry from some intellectual minorities that there is a gross imbalance between support of the arts and humanities and support of the sciences. Representatives in the Congress can be comfortable in the knowledge that their token response, after all, was made to only a slim minority of their constituency. Products of explicit value in this technological society tend to be measured in the most concrete terms—another landing on the moon, a superatomic arsenal, the (contraceptive) pill, imitation milk. It might be interesting to speculate whether the gradual acceptance of electronic music is an extension of this set of values to include an art form based on such reassuring tangibles as scientific know-how and technological gadgetry. The moot question is the extent to which approval is being won through a fascination with technology rather than the valid search for new aesthetic and artistic standards.

Just how essential is music to the functioning of this society? If it is true that the arts are a reflection of the times and society of which they are a part, how long will it be before electronic music replaces Mendelssohn's "Wedding March" or "Happy Birthday," assuming, for the sake of argument, that this new direction in music is indeed a reflection of the times.

But thus far we have been considering a type of music that represents a minuscule percentage of social acceptance. On the basis of current broad social acceptance, we might sooner expect weddings, birthdays, funerals, and religious devotion—about the only truly essential usage of music in this society—to be celebrated with a beatle style of music making. And indeed beatle-influenced rock music has had such a role. Or perhaps these residual evidences of a functional usage of music in American society, again using relative percentage of saturation as a guide, will be brought abreast of the times by the formulas of industrial psychology that have produced that monster Muzak for which every imaginable kind of consumer has built up a tolerance.

The native reader of American English may begin to bridle at this point, especially if he is a dedicated concertgoer, devoted to the theater, or a collector of original works of art. Since I count myself in this segment of American society, let me come to his defense by pointing out that the bridling reader and I belong to a very small, though admittedly not inconspicuous, group that could hardly

13

be thought of as representative of the total society. The champion of Anglo-American folk song might also be indignant, claiming that I have slighted or ignored an invaluable part of his heritage. Forgetting for the moment the "Anglo" ingredient in his argument, I have no quarrel with his value judgment; but again it represents a fractional percentage of society—unless he means to include all the hybrids like hillbilly, citybilly, rockabilly, and so forth. And then, of course, he is no longer referring to Anglo-American folk music but rather to a large and profitable slice of the commercial music business, which does have a sizable audience. "Folk" and "pop" music festivals draw enormous crowds.

Music and dance of the American Indian is little known or appreciated beyond the small number of users native to the tradition and a handful of my dedicated colleagues in ethnomusicology. Indian arts and crafts have a wider appeal, but the technological context in which they struggle to survive offers synthetic substitute materials and suffocates incentive with a bald and constant reminder that their use and function have become anachronistic. Traditional Polynesian arts are jealously guarded by a few Hawaiians who, perhaps wisely, protect the remnants of their culture from the millions of exotica seekers who come to the tropical paradise of tourism. Commercial hybrids of their arts manage a thriving business. The art of the Eskimo is highly prized by the private collector and by the museums; and, to a slight extent, it has developed a small market in reproductions. The oldest layers of American society—the Eskimo, the Indian, the Polynesian—have the most defenseless traditions in a technological age. The more recent arrivals from China and Japan, from Western Europe, the Balkans and the Near East—when these segments of society live in enclaves—manage to keep some semblance of their respective traditions as a reminder of their original heritage. But with each succeeding generation, this contact with a past identity becomes more tenuous.

African slaves in the southern United States managed to retain less of their African heritage than those who were settled in South America. And yet it was the American Negro's contribution to jazz that produced the blues and generated a style of music making that is truly a unique contribution from the United States. Jazz, with its many popular hybrids, has a large audience in American society and has won an international acceptance as well. This indigenous development in musical expression tends to be ignored by the small intellectual segment of society that supports the symphony orchestra and the chamber ensemble. Until very recently, American jazz has enjoyed more respectability abroad than in its own society. Capitalizing on the wide appeal of jazz, efforts to use it for international propaganda have usually been highly successful but sometimes have badly misfired.

In summary, aside from a certain entertainment and commercial value,

14

the arts in the United States are regarded as nonessential recreation or as ornamentation befitting an affluent mode of life.

The island of Bali, to the best of my knowledge, has more artists per capita than any other society. Here, where religion pervades every aspect of living, the creation and performance of music, dance, various forms of theater, sculpture, painting, and decoration are such an indispensable part of religious devotion that the arts, too, have become a way of life. Within the communal organization of Balinese society, the artist and his products are regarded as absolute essentials in the functioning of the community. Almost every performance or creation in the field of the arts is considered a kind of religious offering in which the dancer, the musician, or the carver is fulfilling all or part of his communal obligations. Music and dance and the literature on which they are based are fundamental to the constant round of religious rituals honoring major and minor temples and are equally essential in the assuagement of calamity, disaster, threat, pestilence—all the vicissitudes of life. From birth to death, the events that mark the personal, social, and religious life of the individual are celebrated under the panoply of Balinese traditional arts. The gamelan orchestra, the dance costumes and masks, the demons carved in stone that guard the entrances of local temples are as important to the life of the Balinese community as the surrounding rice fields that supply its food. There is no word in the Balinese language for "art"; the arts are such an organic part of living that there appears to be no need for such an abstraction.

Completely outside this rich sphere of Balinese tradition is a comparatively small commercial traffic with tourism. Inferior carvings and paintings, special performances of music and dance out of their proper context are served up for the eager tourist who predictably is overwhelmed by the exposure. One might speculate that when greater political and economic stability is achieved in Indonesia, tourism in Bali will reach considerable proportions and that a much greater commercialization of the arts will result. Even in the context of this eventuality, however, there will always remain two worlds of the arts in Bali: that of the tourist and that of the Balinese.

A deep commitment to the arts can also be seen at the national level. The central government of Indonesia has a ministry of education and culture and maintains cultural offices throughout Java and Bali as well as many of the Outer Islands. There is governmental support of conservatories devoted to training in the traditional arts as well as several academies that provide opportunities for graduates of the conservatories in advanced training and research in the arts. The traditional arts are programmed constantly by the national radio and are part of the curriculum in the public schools. From the poorest villager to the political elite, from the military to the university faculty, from the businessman to the

15

students of elementary and secondary schools, there is a knowledge of and often direct involvement in the arts. Such an attitude is typical of most of Indonesia's peoples.

In Bali it is the most concentrated. The arts rank at the very top of the scale of values and are considered essential to the Balinese way of life.

BEATLE MUSIC: "EVERYTHING ABOUT IT AFFECTS EVERYTHING ELSE" This brief examination of the attitudes of two different societies could be strengthened by consideration of a number of details. In seeking a deeper evaluation of the attitude of the United States toward the arts, it would be desirable to identify specific categories of the arts and the different segments of society with which they are associated. We should know the percentage of the total society that a given segment represents and should ascertain the various approaches needed in understanding the value that segment of society places on a specific form of art. If our task is limited to one segment of society and one type of artistic expression, the processes required are not too complex. However, in a reasonably unified society like the United States—unified in standards of living, taste, modes of transportation, commerce, communication—it is probably true that almost everything about it affects everything else to a greater or lesser degree. Therefore, a thorough evaluation of any one segment must take into account its interaction with the total society.

To illustrate the point, let us consider the development of beatle music in the United States. Beginning as an importation from Great Britain, this style of music had certain characteristics, both musical and nonmusical, that readily established communication with teen-agers in the United States who at this stage of the life cycle in this particular society are quite naturally in revolt against the mores of their elders. Distinctive hair style, dress, and abandon in body movements gave the teen-ager an identity that set him apart from older age groups. Homespun, candid lyrics, special lighting, and an exaggerated go-to-hell attitude made the identity more expansive. A simple instrumentation distinct from various kinds of jazz ensembles, a beat that teen-agers have described to me as being like "the heartbeat or the drive of an orgasm," a high dynamic level, a monotonous tempo— this musical configuration was an exclusive world of sound for the teen-ager that expressed his spirit of revolt in its diametrical contrast to the taste and habits of his elders.

The immense teen-age audience was quickly exploited by every conceivable entrepreneur and with such success that in a relatively short time beatle music began to affect other segments of society as well. Soon, dancing in beatle style was the "in" thing to do. The carefree movements of the teen-agers sometimes became clumsy, jerky, and desperately suggestive when the matrons and sexagenarians tried to imitate their youngsters. This idiom of music making invaded the singing commercials of radio and television, modified the style of commercial dance bands, raised the womens' hemline well above the knee, altered the clothing fashions of both sexes, and in many other ways provided a field day for numerous commercial enterprises.

What had begun as an exclusive realm of identity for the teen-ager became lost in the absorbing processes of commercial exploitation. So, he sought other ways of assuring his identity. The image deepened to include the use of halluci-natory drugs, love-ins, public nudity, light shows, the Indian sitar, beards and dirty bodies, communal sex orgies—the extreme fringes of the hippie world that were indicative of losing touch with reality.

In 1960, who would have thought that the amplified guitar—through the manipulations of clever management—would ever serve as the vehicle for such a social nightmare!

Thus far we have touched superficially several kinds of users and exploiters of beatle music. By now, it should be apparent that we need the help of the psy-chologist, sociologist, psychiatrist, physiologist, the medical profession, the brain research institute, experts in commercial marketing, and a host of others if we want to understand the conditions and motivations responsible for the attitudes of these several segments of society toward this kind of music. The *subject* of study, which we have not yet examined, is still music; but the *approaches* needed to comprehend the subject in its socio-cultural context are legion. The *objectives* of such a study could provide invaluable information about the psychology of the teen-ager in the United States and, in connection with the older generation, about the strong desire for social approval and the compulsive quest for eternal youth that plagues a number of Americans in their middle and declining years. Beatle music has also been exported to Africa and Asia. On a comparative basis, one of our objectives might be to learn the difference in response to this music among American, African, and Asian youth and among older generations as well. The *applications* of what we learn might be vital to the tycoons of commercial mar-keting, to the branches of our State Department concerned with the image we project abroad, to the political scientist who maintains sensitive contact with the political elites of foreign countries being exploited by the commercial music factories, to the home-based sociologist combating juvenile delinquency, to the President of the United States and his advisors in their concern over increasing crime in the large cities.

Any of these approaches, objectives, and applications should be based on a knowledge of the subject itself, beatle music. Its brief history and its effects on society mentioned above are only the gross aspects that show on the surface. So far as I am aware, no systematic study of the music is yet in progress. Answers

17

to some of the burning questions that are extramusical must certainly depend on answers to questions that are purely musical. Only a thorough research of the music itself can answer such basic questions as "What musical factors account for the immediate appeal of beatle music?" and "To what extent is the appeal nonmusical?"

At one point, the complete recorded repertory of the Beatles was used for comparative purposes in the Institute at UCLA in a study centered on the question "How do different societies and groups within them treat the element of time in relation to music?" Two points of interest emerged that can be compared with the teen-ager's own appraisal of the beat. It was learned that the basic pulse is slower than that of the average male heartbeat and of course even slower compared to that of the female. The measurement of tempo from beginning to end of a piece revealed that it consistently slows down—a feature not readily comparable to "the drive of an orgasm." However, perhaps the teenager's association of the beat with the heart pulse and sexual climax are suggested by additional musical factors: the heavy reinforcement of the beat by the ensemble of instruments, the relatively low pitch range, a particular quality of instrumental timbre, the monotony of the rhythm which even in the course of a slight ritard might induce a kind of hypnotic climax. It might be pertinent to study the harmonic rhythm; melodic formulas; melodic range; textual stereotypes and their relationship to different musical elements; instrumental tone quality including attack, decay, and release; the degree of technical articulation required of the performers; and so forth.

It would be important to have musical case histories for a number of the earlier successful performers to determine the extent to which a limited musical aptitude may be responsible for the simplicity of the style or whether the limited requirements in musicianship are incidental. The same source of information might lead to other genres of music that have contributed to the beatle style; and by comparison we might learn why the one has been so successful in communication and the degree to which its precursors were or were not successful with the same or different audiences.

Our evaluation of the attitude of the teen-ager would be more complete if we understood fully how he regards the performer. Is he merely accepted as a peer, regarded as a hero, or idolized as a mystical god? To gain perspective on this question we might want to compare the status of the beatle musician among teen-agers with the status of performers in the symphony orchestra or chamber ensemble among concertgoers. Does the segment of society that subscribes to the concert series regard the oboist or cellist as socially equal, superior, or inferior? Is the concertgoer likely to imitate his haircut, his clothes, copy his manner of walking and talking, ask for his autograph, tear buttons off his coat as a treasured

18

souvenir? How does the greater society reward the two types of musicians? Does it give the beatle group more money than the string quartet? How do you compare the relative value of these two types of musicians to their respective segments of society? to other members of the professional class of musicians? to the society as a whole?

As we observed earlier, the attitude of a society or groups within it toward the arts is not simple to discern. Perhaps that is why, in spite of Telstar and instantaneous international communication, the nations of the world remain remarkably ignorant of one another's scales of values. When we realize that some societies, like the one we examined briefly in Bali, would simply stop functioning if by some magical command the arts were suddenly withdrawn, we had better strive to understand why this is so. If we are not informed and appreciative of the importance of such matters, if we have no honest interest in or respect for the values another man holds dear, then how prepared are we to hold intercourse around the conference table with Indonesians, Vietnamese, Nigerians, Yugoslavs, Spanish Basques, American Indians?

THE CENTER FOR AREA STUDIES

Today many institutions of higher learning support research units organized on the basis of area studies. African study centers, Southeast Asian study centers, Latin American study centers, and many others are providing a concentration of interdisciplinary scholarship in the quest for a comprehensive knowledge of societies. The geographer, the historian, the political scientist, the agriculturist, the linguist, the ethnologist, the economist, the psychologist, the ethnomusicologist are learning that each of them has much to contribute to the others, that in one way or another all aspects of a social configuration are in constant interaction. Take, for example, some of the uses, functions, and symbolism of a natural material like bamboo. In Indonesia, bamboo may have significance for each of the scholars named above. It is used for the framework and walls in housing, cooking utensils, signaling instruments, musical instruments, ceremonial knives, decoration in religious ritual, shrines for the rice goddess, irrigation systems, toys, tools, poetic metaphors and similes, baskets and sunshades, weapons and shields, food, and so forth. The uses, functions, and symbolism of bamboo as musical instruments may be of real value to the linguist in his study of time depth or comparison of regional dialects. They may have significance that has not come to the attention of the ethnologist, the economist, the historian, the political scientist, the psychologist. In discussing bamboo with his colleagues in this context, the ethnomusicologist is likely to acquire as much information as he imparts.

These scholars are also aware that, although each of them speaks and

19

writes in a common language, they must bridge a certain technical vocabulary, if not jargon, in order to communicate with one another. The same English word in two different disciplines may have two different meanings. An awareness of the problem is itself a step toward the solution. And sometimes concrete terms useful in one discipline may make a valuable addition to the nomenclature of another discipline. The increasing tendency of borrowing terms promises ever greater interdisciplinary communication.

TWO MODES OF DISCOURSE   The ethnomusicologist, a newcomer to the area study center, faces a problem in communication with his colleagues that is different from that found in any other discipline. His discourse involves two languages: music and, let us say, English. Although all his colleagues read English, with some expected difficulties in technical terms and jargon, very few of them read music. Even the exceptional historian, political scientist, or ethnologist who undertakes to learn to read music (and it is really not difficult—ask any musician) is likely to be discouraged by the fact that the field has not yet developed standard theories, practices, and terminology. There is the added complication that the subject to which English discourse refers, music, is not only a different language, it is in fact a different *mode* of discourse. Transcriptions of music, even for those who can read them, are not the same as the aural discourse itself, that is, music; a transcription is valuable only when the reader compares it with a recording of the actual sounds in order to learn which elements are represented and which have resisted notation.

Among his obligations, therefore, the ethnomusicologist must learn to communicate not only with other ethnomusicologists but also with scholars in other disciplines, with university and college administrators, with foundations and governmental agencies, with a national and international community. No easy task in a field that is based on two modes of discourse.

Some scholars attempt to bypass the heart of the problem by bypassing the subject, music. They concentrate on the usage, function, and symbolism of music in society. These objectives in themselves are among the most important in the field; without a knowledge of these we would have little understanding of the music. There is a definite advantage in this approach. A description of usage, function, and symbolism can be communicated with minimal difficulty in the English language and with little or no reference to musical discourse per se. If, however, this sociological approach is not based on an analytical and stylistic study of the music being used in whatever symbolic function, then significant factors relating to usage, function, and symbolism may be missed or misunderstood.

Perhaps it is enough for the historian to know that two major tuning systems were developed in Java over a period of nearly 2,000 years, that this autochthonous development began with the importation of the Bronze-Iron Age shortly after the first century A.D., that the powerful Çailendras of the eighth century lent their name to one system but not the other, that the depiction of indigenous instruments in bas reliefs of this period was largely suppressed, that the power of music as a symbol of secular and religious authority in these times was feared, and so forth. He has learned something about historical development, technology, aesthetic preference, politics, and an implied struggle in power structure. None of these facts, however, could have emerged without the context of analytical and stylistic studies of the music itself.

If the aims of both ethnology and musicology are among the aims of one man—the ethnomusicologist—then he must learn to cope with two modes of discourse and the problems they pose in communication.

FIELD AND LABORATORY INSTRUMENTATION More than most other scholars in the humanities and social sciences, the ethnomusicologist is dependent on field and laboratory instrumentation. He could make no real inroads as a scientist until the fairly recent development of the broadcast quality, battery-operated tape recorder. The sound track, in many instances, is his only "music manuscript." Increasingly he has begun to depend on light and reasonably foolproof motion-picture cameras to document the social and cultural context of music, its interaction with performers, users, audience, community, and other art forms. He continues to push for the development of improved modes of "automatic notation," which by electronic means translate musical sounds from a tape recording into some form of objective display that eliminates the personal prejudice and aural bias naturally accumulated in the old methods of manual transcription.

The electronic age is his strongest ally—and at the same time his lethal enemy. The global dissemination of commercial music via radio, jukebox, television, and the motion picture is engulfing the weaker oral traditions of a number of societies. In the late 1930s, I lived for some time in Colorado. I was amazed to learn that the cowboys were avid readers of pulp-magazine cowboy stories. I have never learned whether anyone ever studied the extent to which these real cowboys were affected by the habits, language, manners, and bravado of the fictitious ones. It was my impression that a decided influence could be detected. Perhaps one day Africans, Asians, and American Indians will begin to imitate the fictitious celluloid accounts of their image in an effort to regain their identity. Of course, I exaggerate somewhat. But the fact remains that our technological age is destroying many of the traditional arts of the world at a much faster rate than the technological means of recording them for posterity can manage.

From the word "go" we have lost the race. And yet we must go on running.

21

THE LONG SHOT   If I have not already succeeded in discouraging the young aspirant to the field of ethnomusicology, let me try one more approach before we settle down to the business of getting the job done. In my late teens, at a time when I was quite seriously committed to the idea of becoming a writer, I had the privilege of getting to know such figures in the literary world as Ford Maddox Ford, Charles Rand Kennedy, Sherwood Anderson, Thomas Wolfe, and others. I was struck by the fact that each of them, in his own words, gave me the same advice. The writing game is lousy. It is filled with disappointment and frustration. Minor and major successes turn to dust in your hands. Be a banker, a lawyer, a politician, drive a truck. Do anything you are willing to put up with but avoid the writing game if you possibly can. If it turns out that you cannot exist without it, if writing is as essential to you as breathing, if abstinence from writing stifles your whole existence, then, of course, you *are* a writer.

If you have an insatiable appetite for all kinds of music, if you have a healthy curiosity about peoples and their customs, if you are sensitive to their values and feelings, if you have an unlimited capacity for hard work and frustration, then you *are* an ethnomusicologist in the making.

Incidentally, although the vignette about writing was intended as an example by analogy, the young aspirant to ethnomusicology might note well that a goodly part of the scholarly profession is spent in the role of writer.

The highlights touched on thus far are intended to give some indication of the breadth of the field of ethnomusicology. Such an orientation in the study of music includes approaches and objectives that relate to most disciplines in the humanities and social sciences. Both approach and objective are very much the concern of the ethnomusicologist; but, unless he is a rare species of superscholar, he will also have to rely on the researches and cooperation of his colleagues in various disciplines. There are many possible applications of the knowledge gained. These may not be a direct concern of the ethnomusicologist, but his broad experience with the subject qualifies him as an indispensable consultant.

The subject itself, some kind or kinds of music, is his primary concern. breadth and depth of possible subjects, their degree of generality or particularity, are almost infinite. The choice is his. He may undertake the description of an entire musical culture.[6] He may add to such an undertaking an analysis of the tradition.[7] He may concentrate on a single musical instrument[8] or on one

[6] William P. Malm, *Japanese Music and Musical Instruments*, Charles E. Tuttle Company, Rutland, Vt., 1959.
[7] Tran Van Khé, *La musique vietnamienne traditionelle*, Presses Universitaires de France, Paris, 1962.

style period of a single instrument.[9] His interest may narrow down to the output of a single composer[10] or the music of one type of social function.[11] In the other extreme, his experience and training may encourage him to attempt a worldwide view of music.[12]

It is the subject itself that dictates pertinent approaches and places emphasis on different scientific methods. A truly significant study is likely to include all of them: historical, descriptive, analytical, critical, synthetic, and comparative methods; the nature of the subject, of course, determines their relative emphasis. The amount of time the ethnomusicologist spends in the field, the laboratory, the library, and special archives is also indicated by the subject itself. These interdependent requirements in the study of music will also define the ultimate tasks of the ethnomusicologist at his writing desk and in the community at large.

Preceding all else is the training needed to achieve these goals.

---

[8] R. H. van Gulik, *The Lore of the Chinese Lute*, Monumentea nipponica monographs, no. 3, Sophia University, Tokyo, 1940.

[9] Willem Adriaansz, "The Kumiuta and Danmono Traditions of Japanese Koto Music," doctoral dissertation, UCLA, University Microfilms, Ann Arbor, 1965; in press, University of California.

[10] Nicholas Zinzendorf Nayo, "Akpalu and His Songs, A Study of Man and His Music," unpublished thesis for the Diploma in African Music, University of Ghana, 1964 (on file at the University of Ghana and at UCLA).

[11] Ben A. Aning, "Adenkum, a Study of the Music of Akan Female Bands," unpublished thesis for the Diploma in African Music, University of Ghana, no date (on file at the University of Ghana and at UCLA).

[12] Curt Sachs, *The Rise of Music in the Ancient World, East and West*, W. W. Norton & Company, Inc., New York, 1943.

Chapter One

MUSICAL LITERACY

IN THE SPRING of 1955, a young man about to receive his bachelor's degree in anthropology wrote to me. He described his undergraduate training, a program divided between anthropology and "some music courses," as being frustrating, a hybrid course of study that failed to satisfy his real interests. He said he was happy to hear that UCLA had a "department of ethnomusicology," and could he be admitted as a graduate student? My reply began by stating that we did not have a department of ethnomusicology but rather a program in the Department of Music leading to the A.B., M.A., and Ph.D. in music. After that opening, the three-page letter was an explanation of why this was so. For almost a month there was no response. Then about the time I had concluded that our B.S. in anthropology had been totally discouraged, I received a short note indicating he would enroll as an unclassified graduate student beginning with the summer session. He explained his delay in answering by saying my letter had given him a lot to think about. By now he has received his M.A. and Ph.D. in music with distinction and has established his own program in ethno-musicology at another major institution. The subject of my explanatory letter continues to give him—and all of us in ethnomusicology—a lot to think about.

It had to do with the business of earning a living.

WHO DOES THE HIRING?

Pioneering a program of training in ethnomusicology demands consideration of more than a hearty fare of ethnomusicological theory and practice. This specialized diet must be enriched by concoctions brewed from the question "Who is going to hire the graduate of such a program?" There are three probabilities: a department or school of music, a department of anthropology, or a split appointment between these two disciplines or one of them and a center for area studies.

Very few departments of music or anthropology will be able to afford the luxury of a faculty member who is qualified to teach only ethnomusicology. He will be expected to teach a reasonably wide range of subjects in addition to his field of speciality. Besides, if he has been narrowly trained, a department of music is likely to regard him as an anthropologist and a department of anthropology will tend to think of him as a musicologist. Although the split appointment is a possible solution, this mode of employment sometimes works a hardship on the employee. It is difficult enough to climb the academic ladder in one department; review and appraisal by two or three faculties add a number of complications.

What are the best prospects? New programs in ethnomusicology are springing up like mushrooms all over the United States. Most of them are being established in departments and schools of music in universities and colleges, large and small. Ethnomusicology has begun to affect the entire educative process in music. There is a tangible explanation for the trend.

After a long slumber and a period of incubation, music faculties have been awakened to the fact that their own exposure to music, the European art tradition, has been quite insular. Although not too many individuals among them have a serious resolve to "retool," it is commendable that most of them seek broader horizons for their students. Music educators are impatient to include authentic examples of non-Western music in the curriculum of elementary and secondary schools, and they are talking about the need for special institutes for teacher retraining. Music theorists are beginning to apprehend the requirements of a wider frame of reference. Some composers realize the vast potential of

25

resources that ethnomusicology makes available to them. One or two performers (and I predict that when the word gets out, their number will increase rapidly) have made the discovery that experience in the actual performance of non-Western music greatly increases their performance capabilities in Western music. With an eye on their own interests, a number of musicologists are taking a closer look at the methods used in ethnomusicology, thereby paying tribute to the ethnologist and sociologist. As the quotation from Frank Harrison indicated in the Introduction, the sociological approach to the study of music opens new vistas to the musicologist. Applied to the style periods of European music in history, such an approach gives the promise of a rich and deep reevaluation of existing stylistic studies.

This long-delayed but now burgeoning response has developed in less than a decade from remote curiosity to genuine enthusiasm. In retrospect, with the help of some well-placed propaganda by the ethnomusicologist and increasing frequency of exposure, it is not too surprising that musicians have begun to respond to all kinds of music. By analogy, what a dreary subject anthropology would be if, over the years, the study of man had been limited to the European!

What are the job qualifications expected of the graduate in ethnomusicology? Over the past eight or nine years I have had specific requests from departments of music looking for ethnomusicologists whose talents and training in Western music also qualify them for one of the following combinations: composition and theory, theory and literature, literature and performance (band or choral conducting), music librarianship, music education, piano pedagogy, and literature. In other words, opportunities for employment in the field of music require a candidate to have thorough training in Western music, including the usual emphasis on one or two areas within the discipline; his training and experience in ethnomusicology are considered a kind of highly desirable "bonus" that puts him ahead of other applicants if he is their peer as a Western musician. In the beginning, he will be expected to organize a survey course of the musical cultures of the world for the general student; his activities may possibly include an occasional offering of his area of speciality in ethnomusicology, with perhaps a performance course in conjunction with it. In time, as the interest and education of his colleagues, students, administration, and general community develop, he will probably spend more time teaching ethnomusicology and less time with Western subjects.

In addition to these breadwinning arguments, there is strong substantive support in the knowledge gained by broad training in the discipline of music. Musicology, the so-called science of music—that is, the application of scientific methods in talking and writing about music—is a product of the European tradition. It is true that musicology has been concerned chiefly with the literature of only one tradition. Within the limitations of this bias, however, the student of music can learn much of value which, with critical reevaluation, will serve as an indispensable foundation for his study of other musical traditions. Ernst Toch once told me that training in musicianship—learning to read music, sightsinging, music dictation, performance skills—is the ABCs of musical literacy. It enables musicians to talk to one another with reasonable intelligence and understanding. If musicianship is the key to basic literacy, then a broad acquaintance with music literature, West *and* East, is the mark of an educated musician. Of course before the Western-trained musician can extend his musical acquaintance beyond the literature of the European tradition, he must add to his skills the musical ABCs of other cultures—a topic that will be discussed at some length presently.

THE LONG, BUMPY ROAD TO ACADEMIA

By now, it must be apparent that the training of a student in ethnomusicology is necessarily long. If he is to be a literate musician, he must acquire a background as thorough as that of his fellow student specializing in the music of Bach, Beethoven, or Bartók. He must also negotiate specialized subjects and methods, learn one or more foreign languages beyond French and German, acquire some insight into sociological and linguistic methods, and spend one or two years conducting field work.

In time, it is possible that this long, bumpy road will be revamped into a modern six- or eight-lane highway. Two basic changes are needed. Departments and schools of music have much to learn from departments in the physical and applied sciences. In these departments, where the acquisition of new knowledge expands logarithmically every four or five years, the type and content of science courses are almost continually being changed and compressed. An undergraduate course in physics or mathematics today bears little resemblance to the courses of thirty or forty years ago. As the quantity of knowledge increases, course content is compressed to accommodate it. Undergraduate programs in music, on the other hand, tend to move in the opposite direction. Clinging to the basic pattern and emphasis established three or four decades ago, programs in music tend to proliferate instead of being compressed in order to accommodate new knowledge. The content of core courses now spread over four years of undergraduate training in Western music could and should be compressed to two years. The second basic change that will help smooth out and broaden the highway traveled by the student of music has to do with a change in emphasis. A disproportionate amount of undergraduate training is based on the music literature of the eighteenth and nineteenth centuries of the European tradition. Perhaps in time the literature of

27

this period, whose masterworks are sometimes referred to as "the hundred best tunes," will be given proper proportion by viewing it within the perspective of all music in the history of not only Western civilization but also non-Western civilizations as well.

FILLING IN THE HOLES

But rather than dream of superhighways, let us take a look at the prospective student in ethnomusicology. In terms of background and training, the typical student probably does not exist. Although he or she is likely to be a first- or second-year graduate student, as the subject becomes more widely known, there is a gradual increase in undergraduate interest. Some seniors, rarely freshmen or sophomores, manage to take a few courses in ethnomusicology as electives. The undergraduate survey and performance courses that they elect usually carry a sizable enrollment of general university students as well. The student who begins to acquire such a background at the undergradute level, of course, has an advantage over the graduate student who must fill in this training before he is ready to undertake seminars and individual research projects.

Not infrequently, the beginning graduate student has some "holes" in his undergraduate preparation in Western music. If his previous interests have centered on performance or music education, he is likely to be weak in his exposure to theory and literature. If his emphasis has been composition, he may have shunned earlier style periods of music in Western history. If he has had an orientation to Western musicology, he may need liberal refreshing in the skills of musicianship and performance. If his background has been principally in anthropology or folklore, he may be facing a special program that amounts to a distillation of the A.B. in music. Very few students of whatever background have sufficient skill in writing in the English language.

If he can write and if there are no holes in his Western music background, the graduate student is ready to become a "freshman" in ethnomusicology. Sometimes, however, the music major with a good solid foundation in the tradition of European art music encounters a different set of problems. Precisely because of his preparation in one tradition of music, he may have to work very hard during the first year of study in order to free himself from prejudiced "hearing" developed as a conditioning to the tempered tuning system; from theoretical notions about "perfect fourths, fifths and octaves"; from a narrow concept of consonance and dissonance; from bel canto and wide vibrato in tone quality; from ethnocentric concepts of melody, mode, scale, harmony, meter, rhythm, and so forth. Again

28

by analogy, if up to now the anthropologist had limited his study of man to the European, imagine the revisions he would have to make in theory and practice before facing the rest of the world!

"ONE EITHER HAS THEM OR HAS THEM NOT"

If it is difficult to describe the typical student in terms of background, it is relatively easy to identify certain traits of character and interests that tend to set him apart from some of his colleagues concentrating on other fields. He is inclined to be highly sensitive to other human beings, to respect their scales of values and their behavior, even if these are not compatible with his own. He is likely to have a latent or realized suspicion that everything in print about music is not necessarily true, even in some instances is necessarily not true. He has a healthy curiosity about the new and the unknown and a talent for stepping outside himself, or the self he thinks he is, long enough to take a sympathetic look at the unknown. His interests tend to be widespread, and he applies himself to them with intensity and enthusiasm, whether it is cooking or poetry or puppetry or stamp collecting. He has for the senior scholar an unabashed admiration, founded on the security of frequent differences of opinion with him. He has a deep love of the sheer sound and musicality of music, and he likes to make it. He is both a doer and something of a dreamer. He has strong tendencies toward romanticizing and a clear pragmatic streak that keeps him from losing his balance—most of the time. He has an analytical turn of mind but secretly half-believes in myths. He is very much an individual. Above all, his liking for music is closely tied to his liking for people; his interest in the one is inseparable from the other. He shows restraint in finding his way in new worlds and fans the flame of friendship gently with an intuitive avoidance of barging in where delicate values may be involved. In the most literal sense, he is a humanist attuned to the world of the arts.

These attributes are indispensable to field work; but as Kunst said about intuition and tact, "one either has them or has them not."

Not very many years ago, it was accepted that there were two kinds of ethnomusicologist, one who did field work and one who stayed at home to sort and sift materials collected by others. Today, we have a different view of the matter: it is assumed that one person does both jobs. In the days of recording on wax cylinders, A. H. Fox Strangways made this comment about the field worker:

> There are those who have the health, energy and personality, provided they have the time and the means, to go and collect material. It is hard to say which of these is the most important, but the right personality is the rarest. Without

the willing co-operation of the singers and dancers they will do little, and that willingness is only to be bought with unfeigned sympathy, inexhaustible curiosity, lively gratitude, untiring patience and a scrupulous conscience. It is easy to fake a tune till it fits a theory. It is easy to be content with a dozen specimens, and not to plough on and get the thirteenth which would have been worth them all. It is easy to think that it is we who confer the honour by collecting and recording, until a singer says, as she said to me, that she is not going to deliver her soul to a piece of wax which may get broken in the train.[1]

And Kunst anticipated the rationale of the current trend of training one person to work both in the field and at home:

It is precisely the variation between the two so diametrically opposed operations, in the field and in the study, which can make the life of an ethnomusicologist so rich and so eminently worth living. The man to whose lot it falls to be permitted the study of our science from both angles, may, indeed, consider himself lucky. He lives a "double life" in the right sense of the word; on the one hand a life of adventure: enjoying contact with strange peoples, experiencing the enchantment of penetrating into less known regions; on the other hand his scientific and esthetic inclinations find satisfaction in thorough, far-reaching analysis of the material collected, which, moreover, is so much more alive for him, having gathered it himself, than for others who receive the records, musical instruments and comments by mail or investigate them in a museum.[2]

In recent years it has become increasingly clear that the field worker and the home worker must be the same man, not only because of the added satisfaction and "aliveness" of the subject that Kunst speaks about but also because of the wide gap in communication between collector and someone else in the role of investigator. Even in Fox Strangway's day this problem was perceived, as the continuation of his discussion of the two types of workers reveals:

And there are those who sit at home and sift and sort. Materials come in from diverse places and very various minds. How much credence are we to attach to each? How are we to fill the lacunae? How reconcile contradictions? What advice is to be given to young collectors? The bare facts are not of much use without the ideas on which to string them, and the natural enthusiasm of the collector benefits by being set in the proper proportions.[3]

These questions underscore the handicap of the person whose work is confined to the laboratory and the desk, the researcher who lacks firsthand knowledge of the native context of his materials. But the handicap can also be reversed.

[1] A. H. Fox Strangways, "East and West," *Zeitschrift für vergleichende Musikwissenschaft*, vol. 1 (1933), quoted in Jaap Kunst, *Ethnomusicology*, 3rd ed., Martinus Nijhoff, The Hague, 1959, p. 20.

[2] Kunst, *Ethnomusicology*, op. cit., pp. 19–20.

[3] Fox Strangways, *loc. cit.*

Unless the collector is trained in the various requirements of the laboratory and has experience with the tedious problems of "stringing ideas on the bare facts," his mode of collection is likely to result in critical lacunae.

In considering the kind of training needed in order to meld field and laboratory methods into a unified field of theory and practice, we might return once more to our beginning graduate student. At the time he decides to enter a training program in ethnomusicology, to what extent has he defined his interests and objectives? To what degree is he aware of his personal motivations?

Answers to these basic questions are about as variable as the different student backgrounds considered earlier. Initially his interest may have been triggered by hearing some recordings of non-Western music or by attending a concert of Indian, Japanese, African, or some other type of music that he had never before encountered "live." If he fits our description of the typical student in his enthusiasm for the sheer sound and musicality of music, this initial exposure probably inspired him to collect some commercial recordings and even to visit the library to see what has been written on the subject. Sometimes with no more commitment than this the student is ready to seek advice. He is curious about the requirements of becoming an ethnomusicologist.

At this tender stage of interest, a long talk with an experienced counselor can make the difference between a false start and a firm beginning. It may help him realize that he has begun a difficult kind of soul-searching, a self-examination that involves personal motivation and objectives in relation to the cultural expressions and values of an alien society or a segment of his own society with which he has little or no identification. Let us invent such an interview and pose a few pertinent questions.

Suppose our student has become fascinated with the music of the Japanese koto. We can at least assure him that the first requirement in selecting a subject for research is unbounded enthusiasm. This, we gather, he has. Is he aware that there are several different types of koto, that there are distinct style periods of musical literature for the instrument, that the koto style of each period owes much to other genres of music of the time, that he may also have to become involved with the voice and shamisen, that important precursors are related to Japanese gagaku and Korean and Chinese relatives of the koto? We might inquire what he knows about the history of Japan, especially as it relates to music, dance, poetry, and various forms of theater. Has he been to Japan? Does he know the language? If not, what has he read in translation? What other art forms interest him in the culture? Has he tried creating haiku himself or only read and admired them in translation—or has he ever heard of this sophisticated poetic form? Has he any interest in bonsai? Or kendo? Has he ever compared the textile patterns of kimono designs from one period of Japanese history to those of another? What does he

31

admire about Japanese motion pictures? Landscape architecture, housing, pottery, calligraphy? How would he compare the Japanese novel with the English novel? Since all novels are involved with the problems and emotions of human beings, are Japanese problems and emotions likely to be the same as English ones? Are the emotions expressed in the same way? Are the solutions the same? Has he ever seen a stone garden? What does he make of all the bowing and scraping that formality demands in Japanese etiquette?

What genres and styles of Western music does he like? Who among Western composers are his favorites? Does he see any connection between these answers and his liking for Japanese koto? Does he know the literature of the Korean kayagum? The Chinese chin? How would he compare the musical styles of these two instruments with the koto? Is he aware of the musical antecedents from India that have influenced music in the Far East?

By this time, both student and counselor should have some idea of the depth of interest already established in the subject. Such questions are not designed to show the beginning student how little he knows or even how much there is to know but rather to suggest that, before he settles down to specialize on "an instrument," he take the time to make some acquaintance with the cultural context in which it belongs—and to take a look at other cultures from which the instrument and its literature derive. The beginner should be encouraged to sample even more widely than this; he should expose his ears to the spectrum of musical color spread round the globe. If in a reasonable time he returns to the Japanese koto and a fascination with the culture of which it is a part, then he is well on the way to shaping a specific program of study.

INTERNATIONAL MUSICIANSHIP

LEARNING TO HEAR The sampling process itself, to the extent it is based on listening to recordings, might begin with a suggested list from the counselor. But the student should be encouraged to roam as widely as local collections permit. He should take note of two extremes in his taste: the musical styles he is enthusiastic about and those that he dislikes. The grey areas in between are probably not so important in the beginning. He should return periodically to those musical traditions he *dislikes* in order to learn (1) whether he can begin to account for the basis of his dislike in concrete terms or (2) whether with repeated exposure his taste changes—that is, whether repetition allows him to perceive more. In this way, he is not only broadening the base of acquaintance with different musical expressions of the world but also refining, sensitizing, and liberalizing his aural perceptions.

But there should be more to sampling than just listening to recordings.

If one or more performance groups in non-Western music are available in the institution where he studies or among the ethnic enclaves found in many large cities, the student should be continually involved with them throughout his program of training. Attending a rehearsal as an auditor is more valuable for the purpose at hand than only listening to recordings of a given tradition, even though the recordings may represent higher standards than those attained by the local group. Recordings of music that is totally new to the listener place him at a great disadvantage. Over a good many years of listening, I have observed, always with the same sense of shock, the great difference between my aural impression of music heard on recordings and then heard for the first time live. The limitations of even the best high-fidelity recordings prompted me to publish the following note in the continuing series of LP recordings of non-Western music issued by the Institute:

> No field recording—nor studio recording, for that matter—can be considered a complete and accurate record of a musical performance. Under the very best circumstances, with one or multiple microphones, a recording is a selective transcription limited by the characteristics peculiar to a wide variety of equipment, the taste and experience of the collector, the acoustical hazards of the environment, and other variables that account for the difference between the live and the recorded musical experience. For this reason our series of I.E. Records makes available to the ethnomusicologist who has recorded in the field—often under the most difficult circumstances—refinements of sound engineering that allow him to improve the sound of his original recording, guided solely by his experience and taste, so that it may give a better simulation of reality.[4]

There is even a difference between the sound of live music—let us say a group from South India—on an American stage and in the home of one of the Indian musicians. It is difficult to determine the extent to which nonmusical factors in the environment affect the listener. Hearing Indian music among Indians in India, in the warm humid nights of Madras, where outdoors the indiscriminate street sounds are different from those of Detroit or San Francisco or Hong Kong, where the lingering odors of Indian cooking mingle with the piquancy of burning incense...the weightlessness of cotton clothing, the timelessness of an evening raga—how do you measure these effects of environment on the perception of Indian music?

I remember, during my student days, a particular selection on an LP recording of Indonesian music. By that time I had been hearing recordings and live performances of non-Western music for about twelve years. Furthermore, I

---

[4] Mantle Hood and Hardja Susilo, *Music of the Venerable Dark Cloud*, text accompanying the LP recording of Javanese Gamelan Khjai Mendung under the same title, IE Records, Stereo IER 7501, Institute of Ethnomusicology, UCLA, 1967, "Note" following the title page.

had been deeply immersed in the sounds of various kinds of Indonesian music for several years and had some limited experience as a performer in Javanese gamelan. I was convinced this liberal aural exposure had accomplished an ear training that enabled me to perceive any kind of music and to manage an aesthetic frame of reference that could shift as the example demanded—until I heard that little excerpt of Balinese kekawin.[5]

Kekawin in Bali is an ancient form of poetry sung by the priests. I returned to the recording many times. At this stage of the learning process, I had long since passed the point of disliking any kind of music, although I had, and still have, strong preferences. But this style of singing I could not cope with. It was evident that the problem had nothing to do with the skill or accomplishment of the singer, that is, he was not singing badly but in a style that gave me no point of orientation. In translation, the poetry was quite beautiful. But to refer to the performance as "music" I thought was stretching the term too far. The sound of this kekawin, to my ears at that time, was quite unpleasant. And yet I could sense the skill it required and surmised it was sung well and true to the style.

A few years later, I lived for some weeks in the puri, or palace, of Tjokorda Gdé Agung Soekawati in south Bali. One wall of the pavilion in which I slept also formed the wall of the temple courtyard next door. Every evening from about six-thirty to eight o'clock the priest sang kekawin. By the time I left Bali, my taste had changed so much—that is, I was able to perceive so much more through this exposure—that Balinese kekawin had become one of my favorite forms of unaccompanied voice. I am sure the enchanting setting and atmosphere helped disarm the rigid perceptual processes that earlier had blocked access to the recording. But most important, the performances were live and lasted nearly two hours. And I heard them night after night. Only then could I perceive the musical nuances and subtleties that complemented the poetic beauty characteristic of kekawin texts.

Perhaps the point is clear. No faculty is more important to the ethnomusicologist than his ability to hear without prejudice. He must develop an aural perception far greater than that demanded by any one musical tradition. His ear training should start at the beginning of his program and should never stop throughout his professional life.

LEARNING TO PERFORM: RHYTHM   Of course, the very best way to train the ear is by learning to sing and to play musical instruments yourself. Back to

[5] Hear further "Indonesia," ed. by Jaap Kunst, *The Columbia World Library of Folk and Primitive Music*, vol. 7, LP record, Columbia SL 210, Side 2, Band 1, Selection 25.

34

Ernst Toch's ABCs of musical literacy, *making* music is the most direct mode of music discourse. If there are no non-Western performance groups in the institution where the student is being trained (and there should be!), it is likely that a little diligent searching will uncover several in the community at large. We suffer from a lack of terms. By "non-Western" I mean "non-European-art-tradition." Greek folk music, Yugoslav, Mexican—any number of musical cultures provide excellent training for the process of ear stretching.

The student trained in Western music has some strongly conditioned limitations to overcome. Conventional Western training in musicianship produces a stunted growth in the perception and execution of rhythm and melody. This is probably due to the Western European preference for divisive rhythm and the ambiguous application of the theory of a tempered tuning system. Divisive rhythms are those based on a meter that has been derived through a process of dividing something large into something small. A whole note (o) can be divided into two half notes (♩ ♩) or four quarter notes (♩ ♩ ♩ ♩) or eight eighth notes (♪ ♪ ♪ ♪ ♪ ♪ ♪ ♪) or sixteen sixteenth notes (♬ ♬ ♬ ♬, etc.), and so forth. A dotted whole note (i.e., one and a half whole notes: o· = o + ♩) can be divided into three half notes (♩ ♩ ♩) or six quarter notes (♩ ♩ ♩ ♩ ♩ ♩). Half of these six quarters, with an appropriate pulse, may be a waltz (♩ ♩ ♩).

Additive rhythms, on the other hand, are based on a meter formed by adding unit groupings. Beginning with a small unit like the eighth note, we add one to make a group of two, add another to make three, add the two groups—two plus three—to make $\frac{5}{8}$ meter. Any odd or even number of units can be so grouped: $\frac{7}{8}$ (3 + 4 or 2 + 3 + 2, and so forth); $\frac{8}{8}$ (2 + 3 + 3 or 3 + 2 + 3 or 2 + 1 + 3 + 2), and so forth. The implied, though not necessarily executed, stress at the beginning of each group often relates to a dance step.

In my experience, professional performers whose training has been in divisive rhythm have a much less developed sense of time than those who have "grown up" with additive rhythm. It is almost impossible for the former to play additive rhythms with real precision, especially if several are performed simultaneously, such as, for example, the polyrhythms of Africa or the rhythmic improvisations of India performed against an asymmetric tala, or basic meter. Apparently, in the tradition of dividing something large into something small, precise time has given way to relative time. Within this tradition, on the other hand, excellent standards of ensemble performance, "playing together," have been developed by the string quartet. But even the Western string quartet has difficulty with the demands of additive polyrhythms; and orchestral ensembles, large or small, fall far below these standards.

35

Performers trained in additive rhythm, on the other hand, have no difficulty in playing divisive rhythm.

The student of ethnomusicology should be made aware that if he cannot tap out a particular rhythm and hold his own against other cross-rhythms or polyrhythms, he is probably not yet able to perceive the music, to hear it, when it is played by someone native to the tradition. And until he can hear the music he is studying, there is really not yet very much he can say about it as a scientist—an "ologist."

LEARNING TO PERFORM: PITCH His traditional training in pitch perception poses problems related to those encountered in rhythm. In much the same way that the European art tradition requires only a relative time sense, it also tolerates a surprising latitude in pitch discrimination. Two primary factors probably account for this. The first is the limitation of the octave to twelve pitches, the white and black keys of the piano, and the theory that the musical intervals between adjacent pitches are the same size. The second is an aesthetic preference for vibrato, that is, a greater or lesser fluctuation of pitch on sustained tones.

The first factor, the theory of equal temperament, has contributed to the development of a unified art tradition throughout the cultures of Western Europe. An Italian tenor can sing with a Dutch orchestra. Music composed for string quartet by a German can be played and understood by Frenchmen. It is true, there are subtle stylistic differences in performance practice that have established certain "nationalistic" musical traits. But all of the Western European art cultures speak, read, and write the same musical language. The theory of equal temperament applies with reasonable, but not absolute, accuracy in the tuning of keyboard instruments. Tempered tuning enables the keyboard performer to modulate from key to key, to transpose a piece from one starting pitch to any other and have it sound the same except for the difference that it is higher or lower. Wind players and string players are not so bound to this theory. The next time you hear a piano concerto listen carefully at the end of the orchestral exposition when the piano enters: if your perception of pitch is sensitive, you will feel the shock of two tuning systems colliding, nontempered and tempered. But Western audiences have built up a tolerance to accommodate this combination; in fact, few members of an audience are aware of the accommodation. The trio—piano, violin, and cello—can be more troublesome for some individuals. The theory of equal temperament, however, is not applied strictly even to the keyboard itself. Any piano tuner will tell you that he "stretches" the upper octaves.[6]

[6] *Stroboconn—Operation and Service Manual, Model GT-5*, Conn Corporation, Accessory Division, Elkhart, Indiana, 1964, p. 8.

The second factor, vibrato, is highly variable in application from one type of instrument or voice to another. It is an important aspect of performance style in the family of stringed instruments; it is almost entirely absent in the typical clarinet tone. All other wind instruments employ vibrato. To some extent, the "width" of vibrato varies from soloist to soloist. The fluctuations of some operatically trained voices may encompass a width of three or four semitones.[7] In some non-Western cultures, pitch discrimination is so refined that the Western operatic vibrato is misinterpreted by musicians of such societies as an indication that the singer has lost control of his voice.

The most highly developed sense of pitch discrimination I have encountered is among the Sundanese of West Java. Instruments used in various combinations are made up of those with bronze keys, gongs, a xylophone, flute, a plucked zither, drums, rebab (a bowed lute). Most of these ensembles include one or more vocalists. The instruments with fixed pitches—those with bronze keys, gongs, and xylophone—may be used in conjunction with any one of several tuning systems, for example, sléndro, pélog, mélog. Instruments with variable pitch, such as the flute and rebab, and the voice add to the fixed pitches of each tuning system what are known as vocal tones—pitches that are between those of the bronze keys. The tuning of the plucked zither may include some of these vocal tones. A Sundanese singer, rebab player, or flutist moves from one tuning system with its satellite vocal tones to another with complete ease and sure intonation. Borrowing pitches from one system to another is common, and in the past two decades the European twelve-tone system has been added to the pitch resources. I have not yet seen any studies of the total number of discreet pitches used by a Sundanese singer, but one evening in the summer of 1967 I spent an unforgettable three hours hearing all of the tuning systems of Sunda demonstrated by five female soloists accompanied by gamelan. It was startling at one point to hear the soloist move into the European tuning. The companion LP recording, Side I, Band 1, gives brief samplings of the five singers.

There are no value judgments implied in these observations. The remarkable accomplishments of the Sundanese singer makes her no better singer than her Western counterpart singing "Queen of the Night." It is simply a fact that the development of pitch has evolved in one direction in the European tradition and in many other directions in other parts of the world. If the student of ethnomusicology wants to perceive the music of other cultures, he must free himself from the conditioning of a single tradition—must train himself in international musicianship: ABC, ꦩꦤ ꦲꦤ ꦫꦤ ꦤ ꦲꦩ, ⌣ ʃ, and so forth.

[7] Carl E. Seashore, *Psychology of Music*, McGraw-Hill Book Company, Inc., New York, 1938, p. 44.

The aural part of this training should include practical studies in voice and in all four instrumental families: (1) idiophones (gongs, metallophones, xylophones, rattles, and so forth), (2) membranophones (drums, played with sticks, with hands, and a combination of the two), (3) chordophones (stringed instruments, preferably without frets), and (4) aerophones (wind instruments, preferably without keys, springs, and pads). As his performance skills increase, so will his comprehension of the musical norms of the tradition being studied.

VOCAL PRACTICE   One or two hints may be in order in the study of vocal practice. Methods of teaching voice in Western music probably have less standardization than all other areas of performance instruction. Yet two vocal teachers employing quite different methods may produce equally fine results. I claim no expertise in this field, but it appears to me that the one aspect of vocal training that is reasonably standard may be seen in the prescribed posture of the singer. No singer trained in the European art tradition ever slumps on stage as he negotiates an evening of Lieder. His posture is erect, his chest high and expanded, his head straight with his chin in, his mouth opens widely and his lips and tongue articulate in physical movements far greater than those required in normal speech.

In the vocal practices of some cultures, the required physical attitudes are quite different. Some years ago in attempting to learn to sing tjara Djawi, in a Javanese manner, I found that the most illusive aspects of the study related to the quality of the voice itself. Minimizing vibrato, hitting the right pitch, learning the phonology of the texts, executing microtonal ornaments—these problems responded to practice. But a true Javanese quality was difficult. One of my teachers willingly, but puzzled, submitted to an examination with a flashlight, so that I could watch the action of the tongue in relation to the teeth, the behavior of the uvular palate, and so forth. This helped some; but then I suddenly noticed that when he sang a high tone, he seemed to be violating all the rules of a correct physical attitude for a singer. His chin went out and up, his neck muscles tightened, a frown creased his forehead, so that he almost appeared to be in distress. When I tried imitating his appearance as I sang, there was an immediate change in the quality of my voice. From then on, I tried very hard to "look" Javanese in singing lessons.

INSTRUMENTAL PRACTICE   The approach to instrumental studies varies widely from culture to culture. But there are a few non-Western standard rules to be aware of between student and teacher. There is a unique characteristic of the American educative process that is likely to impede progress unless the student is consciously aware of the problem. In most educational institutions in the United States, classroom discussion, pointed and sometimes discursive questions from the students, and a strong desire for immediate comprehension all seem to spring from the basic question "Why?" In a much less formal role than that of the student in the European classroom, the American is impatient to know *why* thus-and-so is true or *why* he must do thus-and-so or whether there is not a *better* way of doing thus-and-so. In most cultures of the non-Western world, the study of music and dance depends on the processes of imitation and learning by rote. This is the principal modus operandi in Africa and Southeast Asia in those cultures that use no form of notation, depending entirely on oral tradition. But it is also an important aspect of the learning process in cultures of the Far East and South Asia that do use music notation. Whether the music under study has only an oral tradition or a written-oral tradition, the learning process does not include questions from student to teacher. It is not merely the possible connotation of disrespect, that the student is actually questioning the knowledge of the teacher, but also the fact that the tradition depends on nonverbal, musical imitation—true music discourse. The application of scientific methods in talking and writing about music is a European development. We Western musicians tend to be analytical, curious, intellectual, and, in the circumstance of learning to perform non-Western music, much too talkative. The best performers in non-Western cultures are unaccustomed to talking about music per se. Their traditional role is making music; and often the ultimate achievement for the performer is recognition that he has earned the right to be called a teacher. This does not mean that all non-European cultures lack theorists; quite the contrary, in fact, in a culture like India. But the theorist and the performer tend to live in different worlds. Sometimes this would appear to be the case in Europe, too; but here performer and theorist are much closer together, at least in their predilection for talking about music.

The teacher-performer of a non-Western culture is likely to start the beginner with a specific piece of music or a specific dance rather than with introductory exercises and graded studies. He may simply play the piece a few times and then ask the student to follow him. Let us consider examples from Indonesia and Africa. My first few lessons on the Javanese rebab were chaotic. The rebab has two strings with rather loose tension, a high bridge placed the width of "two fingers" from the top of the sound box on a gut head. There are no frets, and the strings are depressed somewhere in mid-air, but not to a fingerboard. The instrument is about $43\frac{1}{2}$ inches high and is held by the player who is seated cross-legged on a mat with the foot or spike of the instrument resting on the floor, so that the rebab is perpendicular to the floor or inclined slightly forward. A loose-haired bow about 21 inches long is tightened by the fourth finger of the right hand as it passes back and forth in a slight figure-eight motion from point to nut. These rudiments were learned from observation, not explanation. It took me some time to discover that there must be slightly more tension in the downbow

39

than the upbow and that the lower-pitched string, having the same gauge and length as the higher string and therefore less tension, requires slightly more tension from the fourth finger in both up and down bowing. Never having handled a bowed stringed instrument before, I occupied the first several months making accidental discoveries that most cellists might have known or surmised from the beginning. The piece itself, "Ladrang Wiludjeng," was a favorite beginner's piece because of its title: "ladrang" is the type of musical form and "wiludjeng" means "greetings" or "good health" or "good luck." What could be more appropriate for launching forth on a new study? After several years of learning rebab literature, I realized that "Ladrang Wiludjeng" was more demanding in its ornamentation than some of the "advanced" pieces I learned subsequently.

In my beginning instruction for the dance drum of Central Java, the batangan or tjiblon, I was only told to imitate the sounds made by the teacher while his hands struck the left and right heads of the instrument. Careful observation, highly stretched ears, and a lot of diligent effort finally began to evoke smiles of approval from the teacher—after many weeks of application.

In Ghana, an Ashanti master drummer provided a different mode of learning. After placing me, like a puppet, before the two large instruments that comprise the atumpan, pulling my legs farther apart, bending me over at the middle so the drumsticks fell naturally into position, correcting my grip on the sticks (he spoke no English and I no Twi), he walked around behind my back and began to tap out various rhythms on my left and right shoulders. These I was expected to transfer to the left and right drumheads before me. In retrospect, I believe the lessons progressed rather rapidly because there was no possibility of verbal communication between us.

Thus far, our consideration of training in international musicianship has been essentially extracurricular. Listening to recordings of non-Western music, to live performances and rehearsals, and participating as a performer should become constant habits of the student of ethnomusicology; and, like sleeping and eating, they should be considered essential energy-building habits for the sterner stuff of which academia is made. Perhaps a note of caution would not be amiss. Overeating and oversleeping are not conducive to good scholarship. The performance of non-Western music—for reasons that are not always obvious to the beginner—can be most seductive. The student will probably have to restrain his enthusiasm for new worlds of sound to the extent that he can reserve sufficient time and energy for a number of academic enterprises.

Before examining other requirements in international musicianship, let us return to the initial interview with the beginning student. Considering all that he must accomplish in the field of music, the graduate music major may be slightly apprehensive about what is expected of him in anthropology and linguistics. The student with a background in anthropology or folklore is likely to be even more concerned about requirements in music. A few years ago, in an essay that attempted a critical evaluation of ethnomusicology in the United States,[8] I mentioned a book by the famous biologist Alexis Carrel entitled *Man the Unknown*.[9] He had called attention to the trend toward overspecialization in the field of medicine and pointed out that this had led to serious inadequacies in diagnosis. Arguing that thorough diagnosis depends on a knowledge of the total man—physical, mental, spiritual, and social—he made the utopian proposal that a training program lasting twenty-five years be designed to produce an elite corps of super-diagnosticians. The exceptional candidates who could qualify for such training would be ready to begin practice about the age of fifty. Considering the pressure of our times—even though the student of ethnomusicology, too, could profit from a training program that would last until the age of fifty—we must seek another solution.

For some years, I have tried unsuccessfully to find courses in anthropology and linguistics that could make up a required core program for the student in ethnomusicology. Consultation with my colleagues in both fields plus my own personal experience with courses in their respective departments have revealed that even among selected courses only about 10 to 20 percent of the content has direct value for the ethnomusicologist. The exception is the occasional course offering in anthropology or linguistics by a person trained in or at least oriented toward ethnomusicology. Thus far the solution is a compromise at best. The student is encouraged to seek permission to audit portions of some courses and to take for credit those that fall clearly in the geographic area of his principal interest, once that has been defined. Departmental emphasis in *cultural* anthropology varies widely from one campus to another and must be appraised in terms of its usefulness to the ethnomusicology student. Of course, his exposure to the disciplines of anthropology and linguistics need not be limited to introductory courses; the student should—in fact, *must*—go on reading in these two fields for the duration of his professional life. In time, I suspect, he will become rather envious of his

---

[8] Mantle Hood, "Music, The Unknown," in Frank Ll. Harrison, Mantle Hood, and Claude V. Palisca, *Musicology*, Prentice-Hall, Inc., Englewood Cliffs, N.J., 1963, pp. 216–326.
[9] Alexis Carrel, *Man the Unknown*, Harper & Row, New York, 1935.

41

colleagues in these disciplines because of their tangible theories and terminology that allow discussion at a highly abstract level. But, in time, he also will begin to contribute toward the theory and nomenclature of his own field. Meanwhile, if he has learned to read the languages of these two disciplines, he has acquired a background that will enable him to collaborate with colleagues in these fields and to understand the especial significance of their researches for his own applications.

For the student with an undergraduate background in anthropology or folklore, a highly compressed program of study in Western music, designed to fill his particular needs, will teach him his ABCs and give him a musical literacy that amounts to the essence of an A.B. in music. Usually such a program is carried on jointly with beginning subjects in ethnomusicology. His horizon is wider, therefore, than that of some of his classmates in Western music. Sometimes this situation leads to interesting if not provocative discussions in the classroom and outside. This special program is simply teaching him to read and write in music. Like the music major who continues his readings in anthropology and linguistics, the special student must continue to widen his acquaintance with music literature for the rest of his life. Once we have a reading knowledge in a language—music is no exception—it is a rewarding pleasure to keep up the habit.

The student seeking an advanced degree in anthropology, linguistics, or folklore but oriented in his interests to ethnomusicology usually must content himself initially with less musical literacy than that of the music student in order to fulfill departmental requirements in his chosen discipline. He may have to settle for the ABCs and a few specialized courses in methodology.

FOREIGN LANGUAGES   Once the student has centered his interest on a particular musical culture and a particular genre of music, he must take stock of certain broad cultural requirements that are essential to his specialization. Foreign language probably heads the list. Any serious study of Japanese music must include a knowledge of the language. In some instances, it may be necessary to have some acquaintance with a lingua franca and a regional language as well. Indonesia is a case in point. The researcher in the field needs Bahasa Indonesia in moving around the islands and a regional language like Balinese, Javanese, Sundanese, Madurese, or what have you, in order to communicate in the language of his selected subject. Insofar as possible, the student should undertake the necessary language training before going to the field. If the study of a regional language is not available to him, then he faces the problems of learning in the field.

Frequently, I am asked by a student whether such-and-such a language or languages can be substituted for French and/or German in proceeding to the Ph.D. This is a very difficult question, one that almost has to be answered in response to the background and needs of the individual and the nature of his chosen subject. Perhaps for the very reason that a scientific approach to the study of music developed in Western Europe, the principal written literature in the field of ethnomusicology continues to be in English, French, and German. Furthermore, emphasis in these languages tends to follow a geographic pattern determined by former colonial possessions. French is the key language in certain areas of Africa, Southeast Asia, and Oceania. In Latin America, of course, most of the literature is in Spanish, some in German and in Portuguese. Any serious student of Indonesian culture must learn Dutch. In considering language substitutions such as Russian, Chinese, Japanese, Italian, Spanish, Portuguese, and so forth, we can point to large bodies of scholarly literature relating to cultural history that would appear to justify substitution more readily than, for example, a language like Ga, spoken in Ghana, or Minangkabau, spoken in Sumatra. The principal cultural studies of the former are published in English and of the latter in Dutch or English. It would be easy to say French and German, like sulphur and molasses in the spring, are good for a young man or woman and that additional language skills must be acquired as needed. My own language training formed a pattern dictated by expedience in the following sequence: Latin, French, German, Dutch, Indonesian, Javanese, and a smattering of a few regional languages. I confess that I am not very satisfied with the result. Sometimes I think I would gladly exchange my reading knowledge of any two of the first three for more fluency in the rest of them, until I visualize the void that would be left if I had no access to French or German publications—and a knowledge of Latin roots can be very handy. In the past few years in the company of some of my students I have begun to feel like an ignorant man without a knowledge of Japanese or Chinese.

Well, this line of speculation will take us right back to the superdiagnostician! In my opinion, the minimal language requirement for the Ph.D. is French and German with the rare possibility of one substitution by a language represented by an important body of literature. When necessary to the subject, a lingua franca and/or regional languages must be learned in addition.

When the student has selected his area and subject, he will want to consult with professors in art history, archeology, anthropology, theater, dance, comparative literature and religion, political science, history, and so forth, for suggested courses. Usually these faculty members are generous in their understanding of the load being carried by the student and will permit some auditing. Granted such permission, however, it is incumbent on the student to demonstrate that auditors can work as hard as "creditors."

AREA STUDIES   If the institution has a center for area studies complementing the student's chosen interest, most of the disciplines mentioned above will be represented. He should never miss a lecture, symposium, exhibition, film, or even social gathering, no matter what the specific subject or occasion. In the atmosphere of the area studies center, he will be surrounded by a variety of specialists all concerned with the same society that he must come to know thoroughly. A lecture by a historian, a panel discussion in the field of political science, a film or exhibition introduced by an art historian or archeologist, a dance demonstration, an analysis of traditional or modern literature—any of these is likely to provide information of importance to the ethnomusicologist.

Some years ago in the final stages of writing my dissertation on the subject of Javanese modal practices, I made a trip from Amsterdam to The Hague in order to attend a lecture given by an Indian sociologist. It was at Jaap Kunst's suggestion that I reluctantly interrupted my work and caught a train for The Hague. I was not uninterested in India or in sociology. But at this critical time, approaching a publisher's deadline and a fixed date for the doctoral promotion, was a casual lecture on Indian sociology worth the sacrifice of time and energy? What bearing could it possibly have on Javanese modal practice!

Within a few minutes after the lecturer began, I knew Kunst was right. I was learning a great deal about a people who had contributed much to the early history of Indonesia. The more I could understand about Indian society, the deeper my comprehension of the so-called Hindu-Javanese period and its lasting effects on Javanese society. Then suddenly the sociologist was speaking of raga in the clearest exposition I had ever heard. His explanation handed me the key to a comparison of raga and paṭet (Javanese mode) that greatly enhanced the final chapter of my dissertation.[10]

Although it may seem somewhat paradoxical, the greatest potential of the educative process at the graduate level is not to be found in *teaching* units (departments), in my judgment, but in organized *research* units like the centers for area studies or the institutes of subject disciplines. The interdisciplinary function and ultimately the viability of the research unit depends on the successful integration of teaching and research.

During his training and through the years of his professional life, the student of ethnomusicology must exert his own initiative in adding to the resources of his practice. His acquaintance with research activities in the academic world of the humanities and social sciences will have an important bearing on the success of his own career. In this regard, as suggested earlier, he holds a slight advantage

[10] See further Mantle Hood, *The Nuclear Theme as a Determinant of Paṭet in Javanese Music*, J. B. Wolters, Amsterdam, 1954, pp. 247–248.

over his colleagues in other fields of the humanities and the social sciences. That part of his research based on music discourse will be relatively inaccessible to them. With some diligent reading, on the other hand, the ethnomusicologist can secure a foundation for understanding the theories and practices of his colleagues in other fields. It is a stimulating and infinite vista that opens before him, limited only by his own time, energy, and resourcefulness.

A GUIDE TO READING

Universities and colleges that have an ethnomusicologist on the staff (and even a few that do not) require some guided reading among the standard works by pioneers in the field of ethnomusicology. Sometimes this requirement is part of a survey course in the musical cultures of the world, sometimes it is part of research methods and bibliography, sometimes it forms the basis of a pro-seminar. Several works provide a comprehensive guide to the publications of principal figures who have contributed to the brief historical past of this field. The most extensive coverage is to be found in the ample bibliography in Jaap Kunst's *Ethnomusicology*.[11] The student should endeavor to read everything he can lay hands on mentioned in that bibliography by such men as Erich M. von Hornbostel, George Herzog, Carl Stumpf, Alexander J. Ellis, and, of course, Kunst himself. A ready guide to the names of contemporary ethnomusicologists and some of their bibliographies is the international membership of the Society for Ethnomusicology and the journal, *Ethnomusicology*, published quarterly. An additional source, with some overlapping in membership, is the International Folk Music Council and its publications.

A PERSPECTIVE ON EARLY SOURCES   In terms of historical perspective, there is no need to repeat or even summarize what is readily available through the sources mentioned above. But a few words may help to give some perspective to the potential usefulness of numerous earlier publications. It is only in the past decade or so that the ethnomusicologist has begun to realize that his research must be based on at least a minimal competence in what I have been referring to as international musicianship. There have been one or two pioneers who recognized this fact some time earlier. In the preface to his book, *The Musical Instruments of the Native Races of South Africa*, first published in 1937, Percival R. Kirby remarked: "On...expeditions I frequently lived in native kraals, and participated in the musical performances of the people, the only way, in my

[11] Jaap Kunst, *Ethnomusicology*, and *Supplement to the Third Edition of Ethnomusicology*, Martinus Nijhoff, The Hague, 1960.

45

opinion, for a European observer to learn and understand the principles underlying native music."[12]

In retrospect, it would seem to be the obvious way of approaching the study of any music. But we must remember that ethnomusicologists publishing before World War II and its aftermath of rapidly emerging new and independent nations lived in an entirely different world. It had to be truly the exceptional European who would publicly demonstrate that he had something to learn from the peoples of a colonial possession by sitting down with them cross-legged on a mud floor to learn their native instrumental and vocal music or by joining them in their dances. For the most part, the intellectual and occasionally, as the exception, the aesthetic curiosity and interest of the early researcher had to be satisfied, under the most favorable circumstances, by observation and by questions put to the performer. Very often the questions themselves were inapplicable, stemming, as they did, from the conditioning of a totally different tradition, European art music. And very often the musicians and dancers being questioned were quite unaccustomed to verbalizing about their respective arts. In the least favorable circumstances, as Fox Strangways indicated, the researcher stayed at home puzzling over materials sent to him by someone else and pondering dusty specimens in a museum.

The era of early publications was totally different in another way. With studies provided by A. J. Ellis beginning in 1884,[13] the ethnomusicologist was given the cent system,[14] and he could measure non-Western intervallic structures as precisely as his ear and the limitations of the monochord would permit. But recording on wax cylinders and later on aluminum discs, with problems of consistency in the speed of a spring-wound drive mechanism and the bulk of equipment that hampered portage, was a serious handicap in attempting to capture the original sounds with anything approaching good fidelity. Very little documentation was attempted with the motion-picture camera. The technological developments of today represent a totally different world of equipment at the disposal of the ethnomusicologist.

[12] Percival R. Kirby, *The Musical Instruments of the Native Races of South Africa*, 2d ed., Witwatersrand University Press, Johannesburg, 1965, p. vii.

[13] Alexander J. Ellis, "Tonometrical Observations on Some Existing Nonharmonic Scales," assisted by Alfred Hipkins, *Proceedings of the Royal Society*, Nov. 20, 1884, pp. 368–385; and A. J. Ellis, "On the Musical Scales of Various Nations," *Journal of the Society of Arts*, vol. 33, no. 1688 (Mar. 27, 1885), pp. 485–527.

[14] An arbitrary division of the half step (the distance between any two adjacent keys on the piano) into 100 cents. All intervals on the piano, theoretically, are multiples of 100 cents; in non-Western cultures the intervals of tuning systems and scales tend to fall between these divisions; for example, seven half steps on the piano, the so-called interval of the fifth, equals 700 cents, while one form of Javanese fifth equals 678 cents.

With a few brilliant exceptions, the attitude of the researcher himself was also different from that of most ethnomusicologists today.[15] As a pioneer, he had at least transcended some of the bias and prejudice that led Berlioz to say, "The Chinese sing like dogs howling, like a cat screeching when it has swallowed a toad."[16] But, still, the early researcher was inclined to take a clinical view of the musical cultures of the non-Western world. He seemed not particularly concerned or interested in the fact that the music under study belonged to human beings, that it occupied an important place in their scale of values. He was caught up to some extent in the prevailing spirit near the end of the nineteenth century that regarded the world outside the European tradition as being curious, exotic, and more than a little quaint. He speculated on theories that involved the evolution of music, the very origins of music. With an understandable anxiety in finding himself exploring a totally strange and therefore mysterious culture, he sought to explain it all by measuring, in one way or another, its degrees of deviation from the standards of his own tradition. Sometimes he tried to explain its differences with the notion that all cultures go through the same evolution and that given time they will catch up to where we are now—perhaps. There was a great preoccupation in comparing (*vergleichende Musikwissenschaft*) every kind of music with every other kind of music—long before the things being compared were understood. This led to the fabrication of some wondrous theories that time has proven were founded more on fancy than on fact. Altogether, it was a glorious period that stimulated the imagination, and the imagination was called on rather often to fill in the unknown.

Notwithstanding the qualified value suggested by this brief overview,[17] early literature in the field of ethnomusicology still has much to offer. It is true that it is sometimes guilty of premature analytical and comparative conclusions based on generalities, compounded inaccuracies, and too little information. It indulges in oversimplifications and theories constructed on the bias of a European point of view. Nonetheless, these sources often develop an eloquent power of description that can open wide the windows of historical depth on traditions that have long since disappeared or have been almost unrecognizably altered. What is sometimes lacking in scientific methods and objectivity of viewpoint is offset

[15] Two very early exceptions were Charles Russell Day, *The Music and Musical Instruments of Southern India and the Deccan*, with an Introduction by A. J. Hipkins, Novello, Ewer and Co., London and New York, 1891; and Sir Francis Taylor Piggott, *The Music and Musical Instruments of Japan*, 1st ed., B. T. Batsford, London, 1893 (see especially Part I, pp. 1–75).

[16] Hector Berlioz, *A travers chants*, Paris, 1862, quoted in Richard Wallaschek, *Primitive Music*, Longmans, Green and Co., New York, 1893, p. 17.

[17] For a more extended examination of this early period, see further Mantle Hood, "Music, The Unknown," *op. cit.*

by the literary style of a liberally educated writer employing a keen sense of observation. Even the emptied shell of their imaginative theories tends to provide intriguing grist for the mills of speculation. What indeed is the true origin of music? What if Hornbostel did invent a theory like his cycle of blown fifths and then search for and select examples to support it?[18] It is still a fascinating idea—even though on the basis of present evidence it is untenable. Who knows what might emerge when sufficient accurate information is amassed? Perhaps a modification of Hornbostel's theory.

THE TIME LAG   Ultimately every published work—old, new, and in between—on the music and related arts of a given culture may provide an unexpected source of information that has value for the scholar. Of course, there is always a greater or lesser "ethnological lag" between the time field work occurs and the time a published account of it is finally off the press. I well remember with what anxiety I approached the shores of Java for the first time—after eight preparatory years of reading 2,000 years of cultural history, reported in publications spread over three centuries. What had changed? How much? Did the Javanese still take their music, dance, and theater as seriously as writers would have me believe? Would it be difficult to locate a performing gamelan? Did they still perform the famous shadow plays at wedding celebrations and circumcisions and to alleviate pestilence and disaster? Was there still such a thing as a dukun, a kind of witch doctor or medicine man? Did the Javanese still believe in magic power?

A CRITICAL APPROACH   In his general reading in the field of ethnomusicology, the student should cultivate a positive critical attitude, tempered by an awareness of the times in which the writer was working. Careful note should be made not only of what is said and how accurately it seems to be said, but also, more especially, of what is *not* said or what appears to be left unsaid. These are the lacunae, the blank areas of the subject. It is a wise author who if he does not know about an aspect of his subject simply fails to mention it. And it is the critical reader who discerns the omission. Sometimes the mention of one or another aspect of the subject is so fleeting or so general or, in the other extreme, so hopelessly complicated and involved in presentation that it, too, can be added to the list of omissions. Read in this way, publications on a given subject are likely to produce an impressive list of specific problems still to be explored, a list of

---

[18] See further the résumé study by Jaap Kunst, *Around von Hornbostel's Theory of the Cycle of Blown Fifths*, Koninklijke Vereeniging Indisch Instituut, Amsterdam, Publication LXXVI, vitgave van Het Indisch Instituut, Amsterdam, 1948.

what is unknown or not known to be true. For the enterprising student seeking a research topic this habit of reading has much to recommend it.

Another approach in the sphere of general reading should center on one book, let us say one that because of its subject has an especial appeal for the student. He will learn much about the subject, about research methods, about sources and lacunae, about the mechanics of writing, and about the author if he takes the time and trouble to consult the original context of every reference cited in text or footnote as well as the sources given in the bibliography. This approach, too, may suggest one or more research topics.

The acquisition of international musical literacy continues during a lifetime of varied professional activities. And musical literacy per se requires a critical examination of the problems encountered in transcription and notation.

Chapter Two
TRANSCRIPTION and NOTATION

NEAR THE BEGINNING of my studies with Jaap Kunst, he sat me down next to him early one morning, put several sheets of score paper in front of us, placed a recording on the turntable and told me we were going to take music dictation. It was an old recording of Javanese gamelan with male chorus and female soloist recorded at 78 rpm. He said we would concentrate first on the melodic line of the soloist. After playing it through twice, he returned the playhead once more to the outer edge of the disc and said, "Write until you lose the line, then we'll start over again." He had already indicated which pitches on the five lines and four spaces of the Western staff were to represent the near equivalents of the seven tones of the Javanese pélog tuning system.

We both sat there with our pencils poised while the introductory section of the piece was being played, then, remembering the phrase immediately preceding the entrance of the soloist, began to write as soon as the pe-sindènan, or solo part, commenced. After five or six notes of the melody I got stuck and raised my head. Kunst was still writing fluently and continued to do so for another fifteen or twenty seconds, while my musical face became redder and redder. He stopped, put the playhead down a few turns before the sindèn entrance, saying, "Always check what you've written from the beginning." I listened very intently to the replay, checked the half dozen notes I had written, found they were correct—and then got stuck in exactly the same place as before. My mentor went on checking his more extended notation and then added to his transcription another fragment fifteen or twenty seconds long.

By this time, I was beginning to feel like a pretty dull fellow. He stopped, went back to the entrance of the sindèn, and we repeated the procedure. This time, with great difficulty and acute misgivings, I managed to get something on paper at the troublesome spot and went on for another eight or ten notes before bogging down once again. Kunst was still writing and, by the time he stopped, had transcribed a sizable portion of the soloist's melody. We continued the process for about twenty minutes or so. By then my teacher had simply to follow the recording of the pesindènan from beginning to end, making an occasional slight correction as it played. In the same length of time, I had comparatively little to show for my anxious efforts. It was like facing an examination on a book I had never read. How could anyone take music dictation—very difficult dictation—so rapidly!

Sensing my distress, Kunst suggested we compare our transcriptions as far as I had gone. I was not only embarrassed by my meager results but also a bit uncomfortable in my suspicion that some of the details I had been struggling with were still not very accurately notated. I asked whether he would give me another ten or fifteen minutes to recheck more thoroughly what I had written by slowing down the speed from 78 rpm to $33\frac{1}{3}$ rpm. He nodded and went back to his desk. Then began the painstaking and aurally somewhat painful process of listening to the grunts and growls of Javanese gamelan and voice slowed down to a little less than half speed.

The recording presented more than the usual number of problems that confront the transcriber. Through a lot of usage, the disc had a disturbing amount of surface noise. The ensemble itself produced a very complicated texture in sound. A full Javanese gamelan has about thirty instrumentalists who perform on a variety of vertically or horizontally suspended bronze gongs of different sizes, an assortment of instruments with bronze keys—some with common trough resonators, some with individual bamboo or metal resonators, but all of them capable of a surprising sustaining power—a set of hand drums, sometimes a woodblock, a xylophone, one or two plucked zithers, a flute and a bowed lute (the rebab

51

described earlier). To this rich mixture of sonorities is added a male chorus of a dozen or more voices singing in unison, but with deliberate individuality expressed through variety of ornamentation. From one to three female soloists complete the ensemble.

The instrumentalists and singers perform according to a principle of orchestration that has been termed polyphonic stratification (see Illustration 2-1).[1] In this practice, between thirty and forty different melodic-rhythmic lines form distinct layers or strata of sound, each maintaining its own character in melodic contour, rhythmic idioms, and relative density (the number of musical events occurring within an arbitrary time span). The resultant of all these interdependent melodic-rhythmic lines is a very complex harmonic texture. Traditionally, the Javanese regard singers and instrumentalists as being of equal importance. Vocal entries are not accommodated by a reduction in the dynamic level of the gamelan, but instead the singers are expected to blend with the instrumental timbres, so that in effect the vocal lines are like silk threads woven among the slightly coarser texture of the polyphonic instrumental tapestry.[2]

For these reasons, the recording required great concentration in order to separate out the single strand of the female soloist's part. I struggled on for perhaps another half hour, finding that the slow speed revealed a number of mistakes in transcription. What I had been able to perceive at 78 rpm and what I now heard at 33⅓ rpm was sometimes the same, most of the time similar, and occasionally quite different. By this time, I was a little more confident of the accuracy of the notes on paper but still rather miserable in the realization that my preparation in music dictation had fallen far short of the mark. What had been for me an enjoyable and fluent skill applied to Western music began to look like a torturous exercise applied to Javanese music. My ego was completely deflated.

We might consider where our beginning graduate student probably stands in terms of training in this type of skill.

The music major is usually given training in musicianship during his freshman and perhaps sophomore years. By the end of his schooling in dictation, he is able to write out a simple four-part Bach chorale, a piano minuet, and similar

[1] For a more detailed explanation and illustrations of this practice, see the LP recording, *Music of the Venerable Dark Cloud*, and the accompanying text under the same title, IE Records, Stereo IER 7501, Institute of Ethnomusicology, UCLA, 1967, pp. 15–24.

[2] The commercial recording under discussion was made in the 1930s before singers and certain instrumentalists in Javanese gamelan had become aware of microphone technique. In this recording, the engineer had given only slightly more prominence to the voice than would be considered traditional. Since World War II, the spread of radio stations staffed by professional musicians has resulted in broadcasting and recording techniques that give exaggerated prominence to the voice, the rebab, and a few other principal instruments. Aside from broadcasts or recording sessions, however, the traditional practice still obtains today.

Illustration 2-1
"Sriredjeki" Keṇḍangan Ladrang Keṇḍang 2, Pélog Paṭet Nem, transcribed by Hardja Susilo; reprinted from Music of the Venerable Dark Cloud, *Institute of Ethnomusicology, UCLA, 1967.*

types of music that are not too demanding melodically, rhythmically, or harmonically. Then, in the normal course of events, he lays this skill on the shelf during his junior and senior years while he is occupied with more serious matters.

Probably because of the constant pressure of time in trying to cover the prescribed content of a course, few instructors in upper-division theory, literature, and composition get around to exercising the student's dictation muscles. Such exercise is even rarer at the graduate level. After a few years of neglect, the dictation muscles tend to become weak and flabby. If music dictation is not needed in conjunction with more mature studies, we might ask, "Why should the student be given such training in the first place?" A scholar reading a sixteenth-century manuscript would seem to have little need for skill in dictation. However, the better his facility at dictation the greater our assurance that he is able to "hear" what he is reading. In other words, the minimal advantage of skill in dictation can be justified as being on a par with sightsinging, performance, keyboard harmony, score reading, and related skills in basic musicianship.

Ideally, upper-division and graduate studies should continue to exercise and increase fluency in these basic skills. If the ideal does not obtain, then, when occasion demands, the neglected skill has to be pulled off the shelf, dusted off, and oiled up according to need.

There is better than an even chance that our beginning graduate student in ethnomusicology is rather rusty in music dictation. In the likelihood that his professors are preoccupied with more serious matters, he should take the initiative and add to his extracurricular program of playing, singing, and listening to non-Western music the habit of frequent sessions with one or two of his classmates in music dictation. Real fluency in dictation (like any other skill in music) is not acquired by taking a course but by forming the constant habit of practice.

MUSIC DICTATION: THE HORNS OF A DILEMMA

I told Kunst I was ready for the comparison of our two transcriptions as far as I had been able to carry out the assignment.

He began reading my notation but stopped short at the first trouble spot that had plagued me during the playing at 78 rpm and drew a circle around the cluster of five notes I had written. He showed me his version. The cluster was represented by a symbol for a turn placed over a single quarter note!

"This is much too detailed," he said. "Get the principal pitches down and don't worry about the ornamentation. Two many details obscure the flow of the melody. Your notation won't look the way it sounds."

Fortunately, I was studying with a most unusual European professor. If Kunst was shocked by my American educational prerogative of disagreeing with

54

the teacher, he gave no indication of it. I contended that without the details of ornamentation the line of the pesindènan might as well have been sung by an Anglo-American folk singer or even a virtuoso of German Lieder. The melodic details, I maintained, established its Javanese character, its distinctive identity. I had to admit, however, that Kunst's notation, more than mine, "looked the way it sounded" at 78 rpm.

This exercise in dictation illustrates a persistent problem in transcription that requires some further elaboration at this point—namely, how much detail is it essential to notate? And as we shall see later in the chapter, a number of related factors must also be taken into account: the nature and relative efficiency of notation in terms of the particular musical tradition it is meant to serve, the problems of applying Western notation to the music of other traditions, and the consideration of alternative approaches to the notation of non-Western music.

Through the years I have encountered accumulative evidence that the point of issue here—the relative importance of melodic-rhythmic detail—is a factor that deserves singular attention. Although I was not conscious of it at the time, this basic difference of opinion represents a classic difference in concept between the teachings of Hornbostel, whom Kunst emulated, and the practices of someone like George Herzog, a former pupil of Hornbostel, or more especially the meticulous transcriptions of Béla Bartók. These two approaches to transcription, one largely confined to principal pitches and the general flow of the melody and the other concerned with the most minute melodic and rhythmic details, are sometimes referred to as phonemic and phonetic types of transcription, respectively—terms rather loosely borrowed from the field of linguistics.[3]

PASSING THROUGH THE HORNS   Too often the different advantages of these two schools of notation have been debated as though they represent the horns of a dilemma in transcription practices. In fact, they should not be regarded as an "either-or" proposition but as the two extremes of a continuum in the basic problems of notation. Let us assume that Kunst's quarter note modified by a turn represents approximately the pitch D. We are reminded by the turn that it is not a plain D but one that is somehow ornamented. If we are interested in discovering how often the pesindènan uses plain D as opposed to an ornamented D or whether the usage of a plain or ornamented D depends on the occurrence of a particular principal pitch preceding or following it or whether these different usages are associated with certain structural points in the melody or special requirements of the text, and similar questions, then Kunst's phonemic repre-

[3] See further H. A. Gleason, Jr., *An Introduction to Descriptive Linguistics*, rev. ed., Holt, Rinehart, and Winston, Inc., New York, 1961, chap. 16.

sentation is adequate. On the other hand, if we want to know the different kinds of ornaments that can be used with D or the class or family of ornamentations of D that make it Javanese rather than an ornamented Greek D or a Japanese D or the extent to which these or different ornaments are used with other principal pitches or whether such ornaments are made up of principal pitches (carried by the bronze instruments) or vocal tones (which can be performed only by rebab, flute, and voice) or a combination of these, and similar precise questions, then we need a phonetic transcription that shows every detail.

Between these two extreme requirements, we could identify an almost infinite number of research questions which by their very nature indicate where emphasis must be placed along the G-S line of notation.

THE G-S LINE   Reference to the G-S line slipped out before I had intended to mention it. It is a term in constant use during the deliberations of the Wednesday Seminar at UCLA. Some years ago, we discovered that a principal cause for a breakdown in communication between students, between faculty members, and between student and faculty was a difference in points of reference. Realizing that the same research problem could be approached in the most general terms or in the most specific terms, we drew a long horizontal line on the blackboard and labeled one end of it "G" for "general" and the other end "S" for "specific."[4] Recognizing that any problem could be approached from either end of the line, we agreed that the ultimate objective lay somewhere in the middle of the line.

For example, it is interesting to know that many musical cultures use some form of five-tone tuning system. It is also interesting to learn that the Sundanese sléndro form includes the addition of as many as twelve vocal pitches and that they can be used only with careful regard for the regulations of mode (papaṭet) and submodes (surupan), the matter being further complicated by the practice of borrowing from other equally complex tuning systems. Neither item of information falls near the center of the G-S line, but an awareness that this location is our ultimate objective helps to place in perspective the facts presently known.

In time, we discovered that a vertical representation of the G-S line was also needed. Given an area of preoccupation somewhere along the horizontal G-S line, it was also necessary to establish the continuum from the general to the specific within that area of concern. Soon it became apparent that any segment of the vertical line might lead to other interesting G-S lines; so that in effect a G-S line generates other G-S lines in an infinite number of planes and directions. This will become more evident in the discussion of subsequent chapters.

___

[4] These are purely arbitrary designations which are meant to connote extremes, opposites, polarity, dichotomy, finite-infinite, general-particular, and the like.

Very often what appear to be sharp differences of opinion can be quickly resolved by reference to the different segments of the G-S line they occupy. It is a handy referent in connection with purely musical questions and also in consideration of ethnological problems, music examined in relation to its social and cultural context. In the course of some months of deliberation spent trying to redefine basic terms used in music so they would be valid in an international application, the G-S line was important not only in keeping our numerous approaches in proper perspective but also in recognizing some underlying theories that emerged. For example, much time was occupied in considering existing definitions of "mode." We discovered that there were quite a few in print among reliable and "authoritative" sources, and it was also interesting to note the different places they occupied on the G-S line. "Modo" was defined in such general terms as "a particular arrangement of small and large intervals" all the way down to the detailed requirements of the church modes. Some of them contradicted one another, some were confused or ambiguous in their employment of other terms, such as "scale," "tonic," "finalis," "disjunct and conjunct tetrachords," and so forth. And none of them could be applied on an international level. In fact, all of them taken together, contradictions aside, could not account for Indian raga, Javanese paṭet, Persian dastgah, and modal practices of other musical cultures well known to the members of the Seminar. After spending four or five months examining modal practices in various parts of the world, the Seminar was able to construct a definition, still being tested, that rests on the assumption that mode itself is a continuum, a theoretical G-S line. Thus far, we believe that there are certain minimal conditions that must obtain in musical practice before we can say a given music employs the concept of mode. Several musical traditions of Mexico seem to fulfill these minimal conditions. So much for the G end of the line. At the S end, we find complex and detailed concepts like those that govern the Indian raga or, in a different way, the Javanese paṭet. For the moment, we would have to place the Renaissance church modes somewhere in the middle of the mode continuum; but perhaps, as research methods continue to be refined, the church modes will move down the line closer to the modal practices of the Orient.

We might speculate briefly on the implications of the G-S line in establishing a continuum for certain musical practices that may show a correlation with social structure and/or human behavior. Two illustrations come to mind. The first arose in the course of the Seminar's interest in examining the ways in which different musical cultures handle the element of time in making music. Although the joint study is only well begun, several provocative discoveries suggest a possible correlation between the perception and usage of time in music and the relative independence or sense of communal obligation of the individual. As a working hypothesis, we might say that the greater the individual's sense of communal

57

obligation the more perceptive he is of time as a precise factor of music making. Examples studied thus far suggest that this correlation may exist as a continuum with, for example, Balinese and Javanese music making at one end and Western European music making at the other. In Bali, where Balinese Hinduism as the foundation of social structure has produced something approaching the ideal of communal spirit, we find the highest standards of ensemble performance known to me in any part of the world. Such standards are dependent on the keenest perception of time. In Java, where a similar religion persisted from the seventh to the sixteenth centuries and then nominally was superseded by Islam, the same sense of communal spirit seems to correlate with a different expression of keen perception of time in music making. Javanese musicians appear to have developed a sense of perfect time (in the sense that we speak of perfect pitch among Western musicians), so that the overall duration of an orchestral piece is always predictably the same in different performances. This is also true of long repeated sections within a piece. A sense of perfect time is also evident in another aspect of musicianship. Whereas in Bali the exacting requirements of rapid interlocking parts played by the ensemble prohibit any improvisation, in Java the very spirit of gamelan is based on group improvisation. Within the framework of precise time structures that govern the orchestral piece, the Javanese musician is so secure in his perception of time that he is expected to take subtle liberties in the basic pulse underlying the flow of his improvisation. At the other end of the countinuum, we have already mentioned certain difficulties Western musicians have with additive rhythms; and a comparison of different performances of the same piece by the same conductor (not to mention different conductors) reveals much less sensitivity to the notion of precise time. We need not review the social structure of this society or the relative independence characteristic of individual behavior. African examples studied would place them fairly close to the Indonesian end of the G-S line. The limited study of examples from China would tend to put them somewhere between the middle and the Indonesian end of the line.

The second example suggests a possible correlation between the principle of orchestration referred to as stratification and a hierarchical social structure. Various degrees of stratification are employed throughout Southeast Asia, in the traditional court music of the Far East, and among some societies of Africa. Beginning studies indicate that this too may lead to a theoretical continuum from complex to simple stratification correlated with the relative complexity of social structure.

Now let us consider some of the points touched on in the description of the lesson with Kunst.

If the material being studied exists as a single copy of a record or tape, it should be regarded as a unique manuscript to be housed in the rare book section of the archive or library. Countless repetitions required in making a transcription greatly damage the fidelity of the original. The transcriber *always* works from a dubbed copy.

Kunst insisted that the tedious chore of music dictation be undertaken early in the morning when the transcriber is physically and mentally fresh. The preliminary practice of listening through the whole piece several times provides an orientation to the gestalt of the form. During these initial playings, with one eye on the second hand of the clock, I find it useful to jot down in some kind of shorthand the occurrence of clearly recognizable sections.

The first objective is to get on paper a phonemic outline of the piece, remembering throughout the process Kunst's admonition, "Always check what you've written from the beginning." After a satisfactory phonemic outline has been made, the transcriber is ready to begin worrying out the phonetic details by reducing the speed of the playback. If he has elected to use an adaptation of Western notation, with appropriate diacritical markings to indicate deviations from Western standards of pitch, his phonemic transcription should be spaced several staves apart on the page. This permits corrections of the original phonemic line; added phonetic details can be placed on the empty staves below the original. Such a method is faster than constant erasing, and it furnishes essential information from which different composites can be made. It also provides a graphic record of the transcriber's perception at different speeds of playback. An accumulation of transcriptions in this form of "open score" will clearly indicate progress in the skill of dictation; beginning efforts compared to later ones should offer encouragement.

The completed draft of a phonemic-phonetic transcription might look something like Illustration 2-2. The ultimate advantage of this kind of data record comes in the flexibility it offers in representing different degrees of detail required in different contexts or applications—in what we might call the G-S line of communication. Although the subject of communication will be considered more fully in Chapter Eight, we might notice now the several levels of detail our notation yields. Each of these, in its own application, "looks the way it sounds," one of the most desirable features of a system of notation. Some examples: A study of ornamental practice intended for the specialist will require a phonetic version like Illustration 2-3. A study of cadence patterns might be shown as in Illustration 2-4. A study of the behavior of principal pitches in a modal hierarchy might be represented as in Illustration 2-5. A comparison of melodic contour might be based on our original phonemic version, corrected, Illustration 2-6. In order to show a detailed record of the actual performance heard on the recording, however, our efforts at music dictation must yield to the objective display of automatic notation produced in the laboratory by an electronic instrument like the Seeger Melograph

59

Illustration 2-2
Excerpt of matjapat sung by Mardoesari; phonemic-phonetic transcription showing different levels of detail in open score.

Illustration 2-3
Typical vocal ornaments used in matjapat.

Illustration 2-4
Typical cadence with neighbor tone and vocal tone shown in parentheses.

Illustration 2-5
Importance of principal pitches indicated by relative duration.

Illustration 2-6
Phonemic version corrected, and underlaid by melodic contour (rhythmic values based on Illustration 2-7).

60

Model C, Illustration 2-7. (Illustrations 2-2 through 2-7 may be heard on Side I, Band 2, of the accompanying LP recording; first at the normal speed of $7\frac{1}{2}$ ips [inches per second] and then for ease of identification at $3\frac{3}{4}$ ips.)

By now, it should be clear that among the broad requirements of international musicianship, the development of such skills as ear training, performance, and dictation are clearly the responsibility of the student. Certain problems encountered in the application of these skills require identification by the teacher. Recognition of chronic problems and awareness of their persistence should stimulate the student to be critical of chronic solutions. Ultimately the promise of better solutions is in the hands of succeeding generations of students.

Let us consider some problems in notation.

THE RELATIVE EFFICIENCY OF NOTATION

A chance conversation in 1961 with that ebullient singer of folk songs, Pete Seeger, stimulated speculation on a kind of reverse lend-lease in the field of notation. We were in attendance at a congress of the International Folk Music Council at Quebec City. One evening shortly after dinner, I sought a remote corner in the lounge of the congress headquarters to take advantage of a free half hour before the evening events began. For several months, I had been studying the Chinese chin with Tsun-Yuen Lui at UCLA and had brought with me on the plane to Canada the notation of a piece I was determined to memorize. I had been seated for some time totally preoccupied with reading and trying to retain Chinese notation when I felt someone looking over my shoulder.

Pete Seeger wanted to know when I had found time to learn to read Chinese. I assured him that the copy before me was only music notation, a beginner's piece I was trying to memorize. I told him how impressed I was with the economy and efficiency of the notation. He was curious to know how it worked. I explained that the tablature read down the page from right to left and that the symbols were composites of essential parts of different idiograms borrowed from the language. One composite symbol might indicate, for example, which of the seven strings was to be plucked, which finger of the right hand would do the plucking and whether the direction of the stroke was toward or away from the player, the point at which the string would be stopped by the left hand, which finger would do the stopping, and possibly an indication for playing in "harmonics" or for a special type of vibrato or a left-hand pizzicato (plucking). (See Illustration 2-8.) I also pointed out that the tablature gave no indication of duration, that the rhythm of the music was left to the choice of the individual performer, guided by his own feeling and sensitivity to the melody.

61

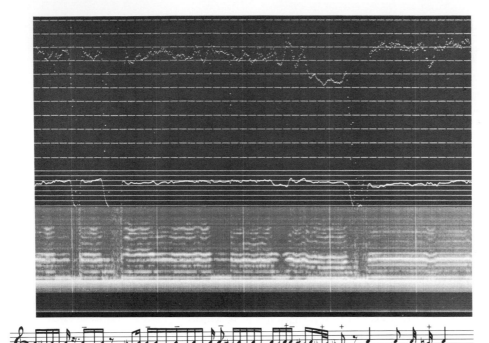

tan   ka - - - - - - bé - lan   Na - - - - - - - ra - - - - - - - - - - - - - pa - - - - - - - - - - - - - - -

Illustration 2-7
The upper portion of the Melogram shows the pitch line against equally spaced dashed lines representing the chromatic intervals of Western tuning (lapsed time from the beginning of one dash to the beginning of the next is $\frac{1}{10}$ second); the central portion of the display indicates loudness against a decibel standard represented by solid lines, the top indicating −0 db (decibels), the second line −6 db, the third line −12 db, and so forth; the lowest

Seeger was impressed. The notation used for his own special instruments, the five-string banjo and the guitar, is also a type of tablature. He told me that a number of techniques required on these instruments were not represented by the tablature but had to be indicated separately. He said the Chinese notation was much more complete. And then he added, "Why doesn't one of you musicologists make an adaptation of chin notation for the five-string banjo?"

Our mutual enthusiasm over the idea soon became sidetracked by the affairs of the congress. But perhaps, one day, someone will take his suggestion seriously. At least it should provide a refreshing exercise by juxtaposing the chronic problem, transcription of non-Western music, and the chronic solution, "doctored" Western notation. Meanwhile, I am inclined to accept Pete Seeger's judgment that the result holds promise of an improved notation for the banjo picker.

There are many forms of notation, both living and dead, known throughout the world of music. All established systems of music notation have developed in response to the particular requirements of the tradition they serve. They vary widely in their respective degrees of efficiency; but each one of them is sufficient unto its purpose or, when it ceases to be, is modified or discarded in favor of

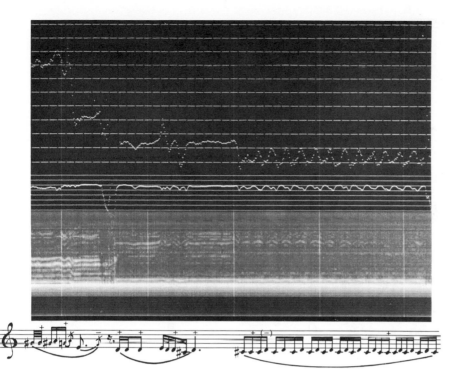

an improved system. Changes in a given music notation are not brought about so much by cultivation—that is, a conscious striving to improve the system for the sake of the system—as by change and innovation in the tradition of music making. In other words, a system of notation develops in direct response to the developments in musical expression. Conversely, if there is no notable change in the musical requirements, the notation does not change. An example of the former may be seen among the efforts of some contemporary composers (Illustrations 2-9 and 2-10) and of the latter in the long continuity of Jewish cantillation (Illustration 2-11).

What makes for an efficient system of notation? To insure clarity of representation, each symbol should stand for one and only one thing and should be capable of being combined in a variety of ways with other such symbols so that, theoretically, a system could be developed that would represent on paper all the specifications required to produce the sounds of a given tradition of music. The extent to which such a process can be carried out in a practical sense we can best determine by examining the relative efficiency of several types of notation.

We might begin by considering generally Kunst's comment that a notation

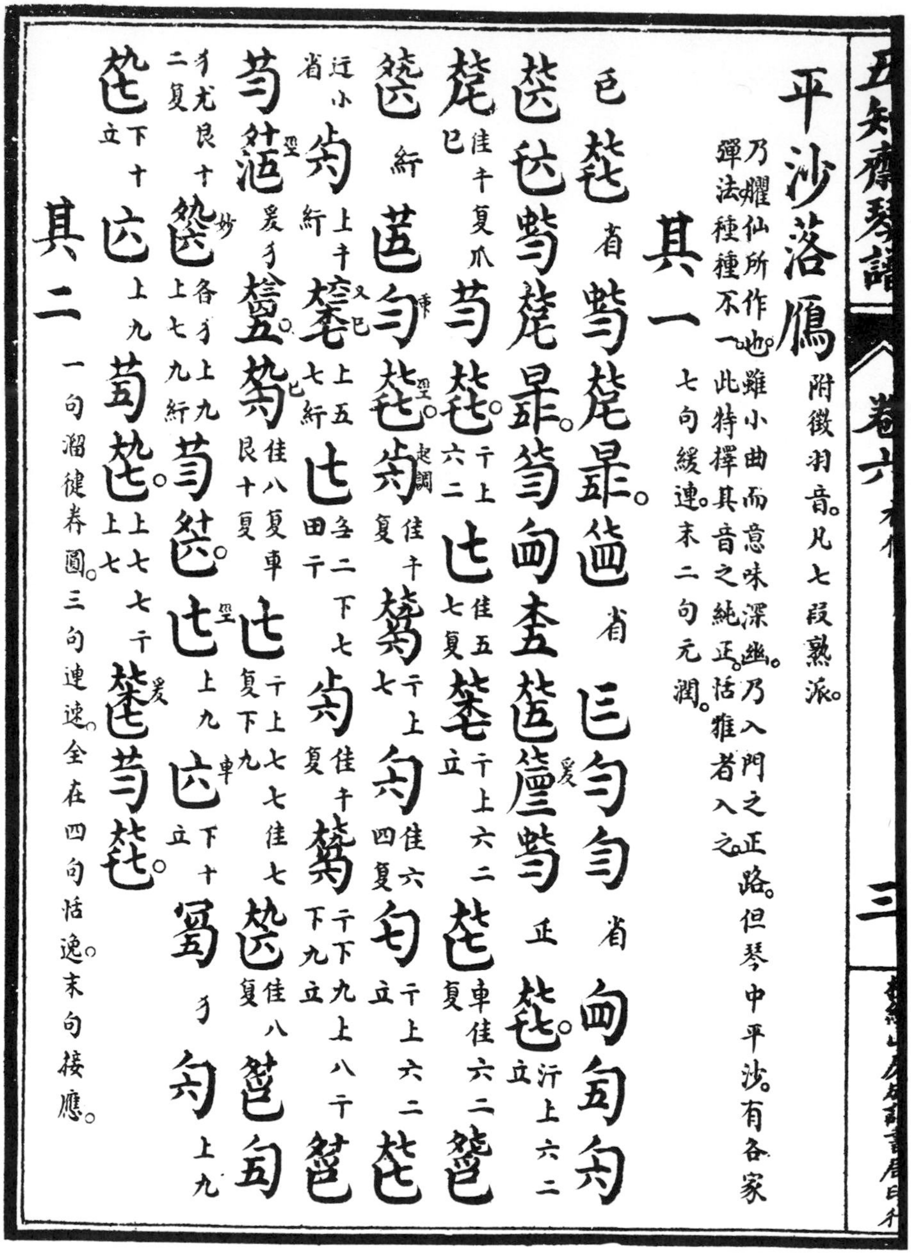
五知齋琴譜
卷六
平沙落雁 附徵羽音。凡七段熟派。
乃臞仙所作也。雖小曲而意味深幽。乃入門之正路。但琴中平沙。有各家彈法種種不一。此特擇其音之純正。恬雅者入之。七句緩連。末二句元潤。
其一
其二
一句溜健春圓。三句連速。全在四句恬逸。末句接應。

Illustration 2-8
"Teals on a Lonely Shore," for the chin, from Wu-chih-chai-ch'in-p'u, *compiled by Hsü Ch'i (ca. 1722).*

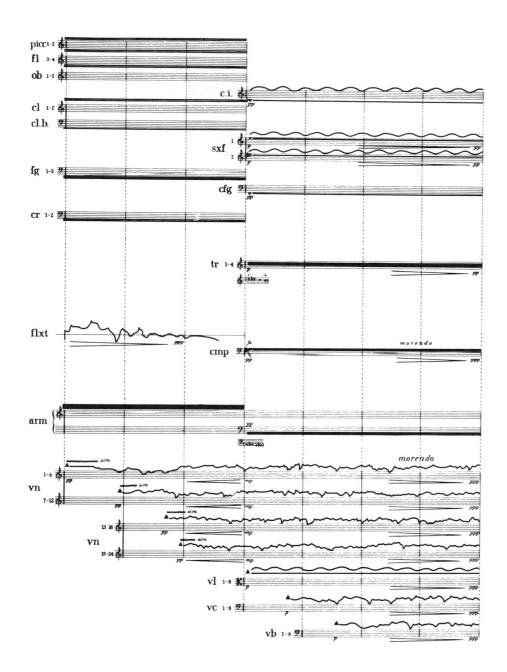

Illustration 2-9

An excerpt from Krzysztof Penderecki, De Natura Sonoris, Moeck Verlag, *Celle, Germany, 1966, p. 17.*

65

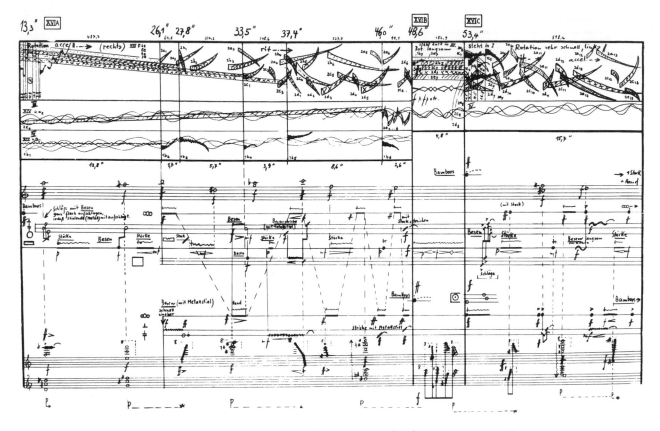

should look the way it sounds. That is, if the sound rises in pitch, the notation should rise toward the top of the staff or, if there is no staff as such, toward the top of the page. If the sounds begin to occur closer together in time, the notes should be placed closer together on the page. This, in fact, is the practice in standard Western notation, and for a Western musician accustomed to it, the notation looks the way it sounds—as far as it goes. Following this line of reasoning, we might expect louder notes to be larger[5] or printed in blacker ink than soft ones and the tone quality of a flute to be represented, for example, by various tints of yellow ink, the quality of the bassoon by shades of brown ink, the French horn by orange ink, the clarinet by blue ink. A few examples can be found that take this or some other equally definitive approach toward making the notation look the way it sounds. But different degrees of blackness and a variety of tints and shades of colored inks, it is generally agreed, require a very costly printing

Illustration 2-10
An excerpt from Karlheinz Stockhausen, Nr. 12 Kontakte, Universal Edition, London, 1966, p. 36.

[5] See, for example, the contemporary composition "Five Pieces for Shakuhachi," composed by Makoto Moroi, published by Ongakunotomo-sha, Tokyo, 1968.

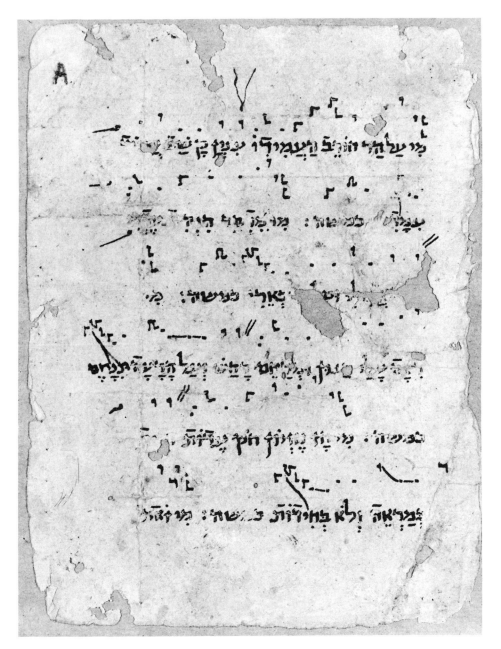

Illustration 2-11
A twelfth-century manuscript by Obadiah, the Norman, a proselyte well known in Jewish literature through his writings and through references in the works of others. Reproduced by special permission of the Library of the Jewish Theological Seminary.

67

process. Such a complex visual display is also difficult to read quickly. For practical reasons, the look of Western notation gives only a faint indication of the way it sounds.

The idea that a notation should look the way it sounds is subject to both a relative and a personal orientation. Probably no two readers will agree with my assignment of colors mentioned above—as, indeed, tomorrow neither might I. Some years ago, a colleague of mine who teaches composition showed me a "score" written by a young veteran of the Korean War who had applied for admission to the Department of Music. The notation was in the form of carefully drawn clusters of wavy lines which, the would-be student had assured him, represented precisely how he "heard" his composition. He had had no training in music and was denied admission. Since then, from time to time, I have been haunted by the possibility—remote, to be sure—that his meticulous wavy notation could have been an accurate representation of the sounds heard by an illiterate genius.

It may be a bit strained to debate whether musicians can tell "up" from "down," but we had better try to ascertain the extent to which the look of notation might be culturally determined. In Java, one occasionally meets an older musician whose hand falls when he speaks of a rising pitch and rises when he refers to a falling pitch. His point of reference is the rebab which, standing as it does in an upright position, must be stopped or fingered down the string to produce higher pitches and up the string to sound lower ones—like the cello or the double bass in the Western orchestra. Such a point of reference for the Western violinist and the flutist would be "toward and away" from the body, but with a left orientation for the violinist and a right orientation for the flutist. For the pianist, the point of reference would be both left and right. For the Indian violinist, who braces the scroll or peg-box end of the instrument against his heel while he sits cross-legged on a mat, the point of reference is reversed from that of the Javanese rebab player. For the performer on the Japanese koto or the Chinese chin, the proper orientation would be "away and toward," "up and down," "back and forth." For the Javanese bonang player, the point of orientation is constantly shifting. He is confronted by ten to fourteen bronze kettles arranged in two rows an octave apart in pitch. The row of female, or low-pitched, kettles is immediately before him and the row of male, or high-pitched, kettles is just beyond the female row; but the two rows are not laid out from left to right or from right to left in a sequence of high to low, nor are they consistent with one another. The kettles are given the most efficient placement to accommodate the movement of his two hands that sometimes stretch wide in playing octaves and sometimes work close together in rapidly moving melodies. The different pitched kettles, according to the frequency of their usage, are arranged in the most convenient location for the player. Sometimes, because of the modal hierarchy that governs pitch, a change of mode

KONSERVATORI
Karawitan Indonesia.   P A N G K U R   Balungan.
--H--   (Laras Pélog, Paṭet Barang)   (Djateng)

Keterangan:
            A = Titilaras dalam irama ke I
            B =   "   "   "   ke II
            C =   "   "   "   ke III
            D =   "   "   "   " bagian Ngelik.
            N6 = Kenong 6
            GN6 = Gong dan Kenong 6   ] = kembali ke [
            ˆ = Kempul
) = Kenong   ] =   "   "   [
            ( ) = Gong
            o = Keṭuk   ]] =   "   "   [[
            • = Kempjang

Buka: a. Rebab : lihat bagian Rebab.
            b. Gendèr :   "   "   Gendèr
            c. Bonang

                . 3 . 2   . 3 . 2   3 7 3 2   . 7 5 (6)

A.(Irama ke I)
        [3 2 3 7   3 2 7 6). N6
           • o •   ˆ   • o •
           7 6 3 2̂   5 3 2 7) N7
           • o •   • o •
           3 5 3 2̂   6 5 3 2) N6
           • o •   • o •
           5 3 2 7̂   3 2 7(6) GN6]
           • o •   • o •

B.(Irama ke II)
        [3   2   3   7   3   2   7   6) N6
           •   o   •   •   •   o   •
           7   6   3   2̂   5   3   2   7) N7
           •   o   •   •   •   o   •
           3   5   3   2̂   6   5   3   2) N6
           •   o   •   •   •   o   •
           5   3   2   7̂   3   2   7 (6) N6]]
           •   o   •   •   •   o   •

    Kalau akan pindah ke C (Irama ke III), dari Kenong ko-3
         irama diperlahan, menurut aba dari kenḍang. Titilarasnja:
       6 7 3̇ 2̇ 6 3 2 7̂ . 3 . 2 . 7 . 6 GN6
          •   o   •   •   •   o   •

from one piece to another is accommodated by a different arrangement of kettles. Two possible modal arrangements for the seven pitches of the pélog tuning system are shown in the example at the right.

The sequential arrangement of a notation usually follows culturally determined reading habits. Like the words on a printed page, Western notation reads from left to right across the page. Chinese notation for the chin follows the reading habits of its culture: down the page moving from right to left. One form of Javanese notation rendered in ciphers (Illustration 2-12) follows the normal reading habits of the people from left to right across the page. Another type, the so-called checkered script, or kraton (royal court), notation (Illustration 2-13) reads down the page from left to right. Neither form of Javanese notation, however, is used in performance since most of the musicians are involved in group improvisation. Notation in this instance serves merely as an archival record or, in very recent times, as a teaching aid in the conservatories devoted to gamelan studies.

$$\dot{4}\ \dot{6}\ \dot{5}\ \dot{3}\ \dot{2}\ \dot{1}\ \dot{7}$$
$$1\ 7\ 2\ 3\ 5\ 6\ 4$$

Player

$$\dot{4}\ \dot{6}\ \dot{5}\ \dot{3}\ \dot{2}\ 7\ \dot{7}$$
$$1\ \dot{1}\ 2\ 3\ 5\ 6\ 4$$

Player

Illustration 2-13
An example of Javanese
kraton (royal court) notation.

Illustration 2-14
"Greensleeves" in the Dorian
mode as rendered by Roderic
Knight. Since this mode is
most easily played on "e"
with the guitar, it is written
at that pitch level here for
ease of comparison with
Illustrations 2-16 through
2-20 and 2-27.

Let us consider further evidence that the look of notation and the sounds it represents tend to be relative and culturally determined by examining the well-known folk song "Greensleeves," as it might be represented in several different forms of notation. Illustration 2-14 shows one version of the modal melody in Western notation. In Illustration 2-15, the melody has been incorporated into an orchestral composition by the contemporary composer Ralph Vaughan Williams. Illustration 2-16 shows how the melody is notated in chords for the guitar. In the Southern states of the United States among the singing schools that use "shape-note" notation, the melody might appear as in Illustration 2-17. A type of modern guitar tablature is shown in Illustration 2-18. Illustration 2-19 shows the melody as it might have been notated in Spanish guitar tablature of the seventeenth century; and Illustrations 2-20 and 2-21, as it might have appeared in German lute tablature of the sixteenth century. Illustration 2-22 is a transcription in the tablature of the Chinese four-stringed lute known as the pipa, pictured in Illustration 2-23. Illustration 2-24 is a beginner's guide to the tablature for the pipa. Illustration 2-25 shows how the melody appears in Arabic cipher notation. In Illustration 2-26, the melody is given in tonic sol-fa (do re mi).

Theoretically, anyone—let us say a Laplander who communicates with his herd of reindeer by singing[6]—anyone willing to learn the meaning of these different musical symbols could reproduce the proper musical sounds. Actually, this is not true. Correct translation of the symbols into musical sounds depends

[6] See further Ragnwald Graff, "Music of the Norwegian Lapland," *Journal of the International Folk Music Council,* vol. 6 (1954), pp. 29–31.

Illustration 2-15

An excerpt from "Fantasia on Greensleeves," adapted from the opera "Sir John in Love," by Ralph Vaughn Williams. London: Oxford University Press. 1934.

*Illustration 2-16
The melody of "Green-
sleeves" including chord
notations for the guitar.*

faw sol law faw sol law me faw

*Illustration 2-17
"Greensleeves" written in
shape-notes. For other ex-
amples of this notation see
William Walker,* The South-
ern Harmony, and Musical
Companion, *published by
Nathan Whiting, New
Haven, 1835. The Revised
Edition (1854) is available
in reprint as* The Southern
Harmony Songbook, *Hastings
House, New York, 1939.*

73

Illustration 2-18
"Greensleeves" in a type of modern guitar tablature. The guitar version shown here and in Illustrations 2-19 and 2-20 is a modal adaptation of the arrangement for guitar by Theodore Norman, in Music for the Young Guitarist, *G. Schirmer, Inc., New York, 1966, p. 32. For other examples of this tablature, see Jerry Siverman,* The Folksinger's Guitar Guide, *Oak Publications, New York, 1962.*

Illustration 2-19
"Greensleeves" in seventeenth-century Spanish guitar tablature. Note that in this system the lines representing the strings are presented as if viewing them in a mirror, with the lowest on top, whereas in the modern tablature they are shown with the lowest string on the bottom. The tune is adapted slightly to accommodate the lack of the sixth string on the Spanish guitar. For other examples of this tablature, see Gaspar Sanz, Instruccion de Musica sobre la guitarra Espanola. *Reproducción en facsímil de los libros primero y segundo de la tercera edición (1674) y del libro tercero de la edición octava (1697); Institucion (Fernando el Catolico) de la EXCMA. Diputacion Provincial (C.S.I.C.) Zaragosa, España, 1952.*

74

tuning   A – d – g – b – e′ – a′

to play w/ guitar, lower g string 1/2 step to f♯

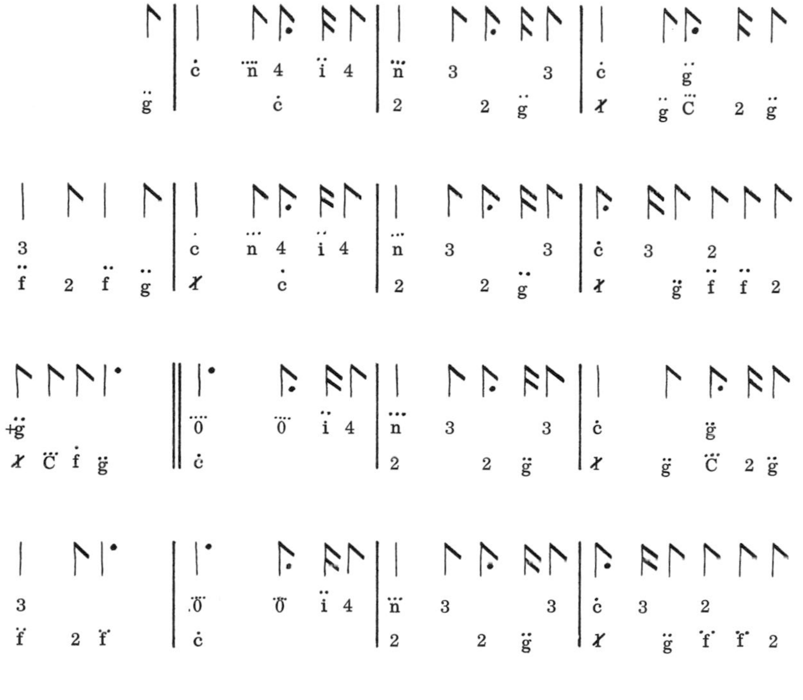

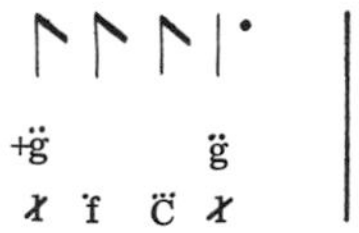

dots above letters indicate which finger is used

a plus sign before a letter indicates that it is sustained and

the rhythmic figure applies to other notes

Illustration 2-20
"Greensleeves" in sixteenth-
century German lute tablature. In this type there is a
separate symbol for each
position on each string (see
Illustration 2-21). For other
examples of this tablature,
see Hans Neusidler, "Ein
Newgeordent Künstlich Lau-
tenbuch, 1534," in Die Tab-
ulatur, Heft I, published by
Friedrich Hofmeister,
Hofheim am Taunus, 1965.

75

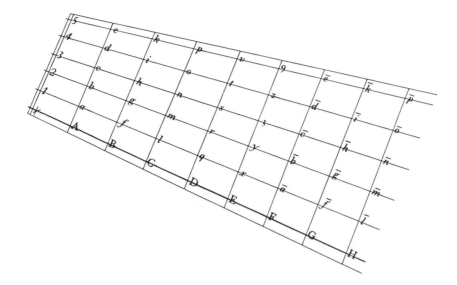

Illustration 2-21
A diagrammatic representation of the fingerboard for the sixteenth-century German lute tablature shown in Illustration 2-20.

on a familiarity with the oral tradition that supports them. A knowledge of the oral tradition is necessary because: (1) certain symbols may be ambiguous, that is, they may not fulfill our basic requirement for clarity of representation in an efficient system of notation; (2) in the course of development, each tradition has emphasized certain aspects of musical expression, and, reflecting this emphasis, its notation may have become too rigid to accommodate a variety of other practices known in actual performance.

The earliest notation used in the European medieval church was a system of neumes, a set of so-called polynomial symbols without reference to a staff with lines and spaces (Illustration 2-27). A polynomial symbol is one that represents several things; such a symbol still retained in modern Western notation is the turn (∿). Depending on the style period of the musical practice referred to, this might be performed several different ways.[7] The jazz musician's letter system is also a type of polynomial notation (Illustration 2-28). If the jazz musician is playing a harmonic instrument like the guitar, he must know how to break up the notes of the chord rhythmically and possibly carry a melody as well. If he is a trumpet player, the chordal notation is a reminder of the basic harmonic support for the melody he plays, which very likely includes other so-called passing tones not found in the basic chord. Very often this polynomial reminder is enough to meet the flexible requirements of jazz improvisation. In some instances, in fact, the soloist

[7] See further Willi Apel, *Harvard Dictionary of Music*, 1st ed., Harvard University Press, Cambridge, Mass., 1965, pp. 774–775.

*Illustration 2-22
"Greensleeves" arranged for the pipa by Tsun Yuen Lui. This tablature shows the melody in cipher notation in one column and, to the right of it, the plucking technique for the right hand. The fingerings for the left hand are not shown. (See also Illustration 2-24.)*

Illustration 2-23
Mr. Tsun Yuen Lui playing
the pipa.

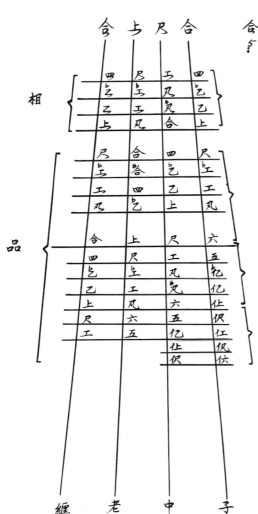

Illustration 2-24
This diagram of the finger-board of the pipa would be used by a beginner in learning the left-hand fingering positions for each pitch in the cipher notation.

1│3 . 4 5 $\overline{.6}$ 5│4 . 2 7 $\overline{.1}$ 2│3 . 1 1 $\overline{.7}$ 1

2 . 7 5 . 1│3 . 4 5 $\overline{.6}$ 5│4 . 2 7 $\overline{.1}$ 2│3 $\overline{.2}$ 1 7 5 7

1 . 1 1 . .‖7 . . 7 $\overline{.6}$ 5│4 . 2 7 $\overline{.1}$ 2│3 . 1 1 $\overline{.7}$ 1

2 . 7 5 . .│7 . . 7 $\overline{.6}$ 5│4 . 2 7 $\overline{.1}$ 2│3 $\overline{.2}$ 1 7 5 7

1 . . 1 . .‖

Illustration 2-25
"Greensleeves" in cipher nota-
tion, using Arabic numerals.

:r│f:—:s₁│l:—.t:l│s:—:m₁│d:—.r:m│f:—:r₁│r:—.d:r

│m:—:d₁│l₁:—:r│f:—:s₁│l:—.t:l│s:—:m₁│d:—.r:m│f:—.m:r│d:l₁:d

│r:—:r│r:—:—‖d':—:— ₁d':—.t:l│s:—:m ₁d:—.r:m│f:—:r₁│r:—.d:r

│m:—:d│l₁:—:— ₁d':—:— ₁d':—.t:l│s:—:m ₁d:—.r:m│f:—.m:r│d:l₁:d

│r:—:— ₁r:—:—‖

│ strong accent on letter following
₁ secondary accent
: unaccented
. divides space between above marks in half
— previous syllable sustained

Illustration 2-26
"Greensleeves" in the British
"tonic sol-fa" system of nota-
tion for amateur sightsinging.
The letters represent the syl-
lables do, re, mi, fa, sol, la,
ti, and the punctuation marks
show the rhythm and accent.
For explanations of the orig-
inal system developed by
Sarah Ann Glover in the
nineteenth-century, see
Sedley Taylor, A System of
Sight-Singing from the Established Musical Notation,
Based on the Principle of
Tonic Relation and Illus-
trated by Extracts from
Works by the Great Masters,
Macmillan and Co., London,
1890; and W. G. Whittaker,
"The Claims of Tonic Solfa,"
Part I, Music and Letters,
vol. 5, no. 4 (Oct. 1924),
pp. 313-321.

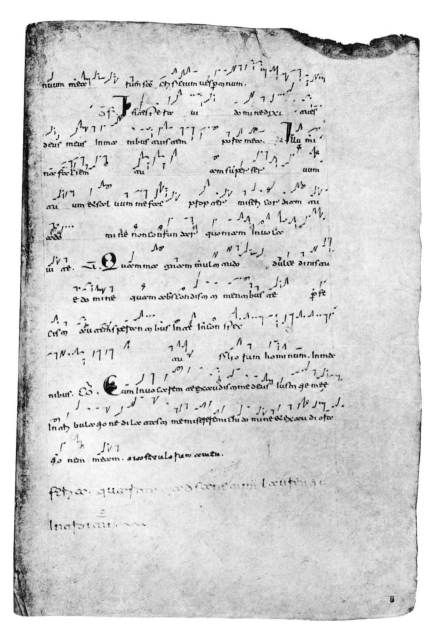

Illustration 2-27
Offertory "In te speravi," versicles "Illumina faciem" and "Quam magnam,"
and Communion "Cum invocarem," from Paleographie Musicale (pub. under
dir. of Dom Joseph Gajard, Moine de Solesmes), Société Saint-Jean L'Evangéliste,
Desclée et Cie, Tournay, Belgium, 1931, vol. 14, plate 71.

81

tends to avoid the notes of the chordal notation, leaving them to the supporting performers to supply.

Further ambiguity in Western notation is the so-called binomial symbol, which stands for two things. For example, the symbol 𝆮 ⌇⌇⌇⌇⌇, shown above the following half note, indicates a trill, a fluctuation between C and the note above it. Which note above it, C♯ or D? Does the trill begin with C, or the upper pitch? How fast should the fluctuations be? On which pitch does the trill end? Is there any kind of final stress or special release of the pitch? As our questions suggest, a proper realization of the trill requires a knowledge of the oral tradition surrounding it during a particular historical period of musical style.

The so-called monomial symbol stands for only one thing. A note head (○ or ●), a stem (|), a flag (♩), and a beam (━) are examples of monomial symbols. Although each represents only one thing, in different combinations they form composite symbols each of which stands for only one thing: a quarter note (♩), an eighth note (♪), two eighth notes (♫), a sixteenth note (♬), and so forth. Another symbol is the dot (·); it stands for half the time value of the symbol immediately preceding it: 𝅗𝅥. = 𝅗𝅥 + ♩ or ♩. = ♩ + ♪, and so forth.

The standard notation of Western art music has come a long way in its development from the neumes of the medieval church. The present system is primarily monomial, one symbol for one meaning, retaining only a small residue of earlier polynomial and binomial stages of its development. Within the framework of its essential monomial character, let us consider the relative efficiency of the system and the extent to which it depends on oral tradition.

As our "colorful" speculations a little earlier about Western notation may have suggested, the established form of notation gives no indication of different qualities of instrumental or vocal sounds beyond literary designations such as: violin, viola, cello, clarinet in B♭, clarinet in E♭, alto clarinet, and so forth; and soprano, mezzo-soprano, contralto, tenor, baritone, and bass. In such designations, the range of the instrument or voice is reasonably specific; but the character of tone quality, which has considerable variation within the two families of instruments mentioned as well as within the ranges of voice, is implied only in a general sense. The classification of operatic voices attempts to be more specific: dramatic soprano, lyric soprano, coloratura soprano, robust tenor, lyric tenor, dramatic tenor, basso profundo, basso cantante, basso buffo. However, no symbolic representation has been developed within the system for representing the timbre of either voice or instruments.

The indications for degrees of loudness are quite relative: *ppp, pp, p, mp, mf, f, ff, fff*—that is, from very soft to very loud. Sometimes the desperate composer resorts to: *ppppp* or *fffff*, to indicate he wants an effect that is *really* soft or earsplittingly loud. But how loud is forte (*f*)? What is the difference between mezzo-piano and mezzo-forte (*mp* and *mf*)? How do you compare the loudness of pianississimo (*ppp*) played by a string quartet and played by a 100-piece symphony orchestra? The expression of dynamics, at best, is relative to the context in which it is used.

General designations may be used to indicate tempo: very slow, slow, moderate, fast, very fast; or in Italian: grave, andante, moderato, allegro, presto—with the possibility of some tempos in between: largo, andantino, allegretto, prestissimo. A more precise indication of tempo, derived from the number of pulses per minute, may be added to these indications, for example, ♩ = 60. Sometimes, knowing that conductors or performers are not likely to be so precise, the composer will indicate: ♩ = 60–72. For the Javanese musician, by contrast, there is quite a difference between sixty and seventy-two pulses per minute guided, as he is, by a sense of perfect time and a musical structure, the product of polyphonic stratification, which itself has a built-in time factor. We shall have more to say about this presently.

The monomial symbols of Western notation are incapable of expressing certain durational subtleties in rhythm. Suppose we have five sixteenth notes played in the metrical time of one quarter note (♩ = ♬♬♪), but we want the duration of each successive sixteenth note to be slightly shorter than the one preceding it. About the only way to be sure the performer will understand the requirement is to do what I have just done: use an English sentence to explain it or, better still, if the composer is on hand at rehearsals, ask him to sing it. Something as common as the triplet, three notes in the time of two (♩ ♩ = ♩♩♩), has an oral prescription which says the three notes must *not* be of equal length in performance, that each note becomes successively shorter in duration.

Rhythmic subtleties in attack and duration can be expressed to some extent by special qualifying symbols. A quarter note might carry one of the following additional symbols: ♩ ♩ ♩ ♩ ♩ ♩ ♩. The first has a light attack, and the duration

is somewhat shorter than a quarter note but not as short as an eighth note (but somehow different from ♩ = ♩. ♪ ?). The second has a "strong" attack, and the

third an even stronger attack. The fourth indicates either that the note is fully sustained (shouldn't it be so normally?) and/or that the attack is "quite definite," but less definite than the second symbol suggests (!). The fifth symbol is neither as short as the first nor as long as the fourth (how long, then?). The sixth symbol calls for a strong attack that somehow is different from the second and third (a little shorter?). The last symbol, the fermata, tells the performer to sustain the note until the conductor or the consensus of the players indicates a release.

All these have become standard symbols used to qualify attack and duration. Interpretations of their precise meanings tend to vary somewhat among different performers. Perhaps at this point, however, we should bear in mind that any sound consists not only of attack and duration but also of release.

Certain types of aspirated release, for which there is no notation, are used by Western singers to create stress or accent for dramatic emphasis or to heighten an emotional effect.

The greatest variation in attack and release, however, occurs in relation to pitch. Western performers tend to slip and slide around somewhat in between the twelve pitches of the tempered tuning system, producing a range of microtonal intervals. But such performance has never developed into any kind of regulated aesthetic practice requiring graphic representation in the notation. There are some terms of reference to cover the situation, such as "portamento," "glissando," "slide," or a general term like "expressivo." But sometimes individual performers employ a sliding attack on a pitch or use slides in connecting pitches when there is no written prescription calling for their usage. The rigidity of the twelve-tone system and a preoccupation with the theory of equal temperament have produced an equally rigid notation in relation to pitch.

Such aspirated releases and sliding attacks and releases are tolerated as an example of artistic license or accepted as symptomatic of personal feeling or expression, a variable practice for which no symbols have been developed.

The peccadillos of the system discussed thus far should not obscure the fact that Western notation supports the tradition of European art music quite well.

84

It reflects the principal requirements of the music it serves. We might also call attention to the fact that Japanese notation serves the Japanese quite well and Chinese notation the Chinese. At this point I sound like George Bernard Shaw's Saint Joan: "England for the English, France for the French—long live the Bastard of Orleans!" It requires no special powers of precognition to guess that some readers, conceding Japanese notation to be all right for the Japanese, will insist we are considering notation as a tool of scientific method. And surely no other system can compare with the elaborate developments in Western notation! But then what happens when the transcriber attempts a cross-cultural transfer from Japanese musical sounds to Western notation?

THE CHRONIC PROBLEM OF 1893

In 1893, Francis Taylor Piggott made the following remarks about Japanese music:

> To the many beauties, and to the great merits, of the structure which has been raised upon [the rudiments of this music], only my own ears can bear witness.
>
> The difficulties which stand in the way of reducing the music into Western written forms are so great, that, unless Japanese musicians will come and play to us here in England [for the English], accurate knowledge of their art, due appreciation of their craft, can only come into being in the West very gradually…Much of the charm of the music, all its individuality, nearly, depend upon its graceful and delicate phrasing: and although I think that Western notation is capable of expressing these phrases to one who has already heard them, I feel a little uncertain whether their more complicated forms could be set down in it with sufficient accuracy to enable a stranger to interpret them satisfactorily.[8]

As an essayist, I am not sure whether it is reassuring or discouraging to point out that almost a century later we are still concerned with the same chronic problem. Let us be critical of the chronic solution, something that was referred to earlier as doctored Western notation.

Broadening our horizons somewhat, we can make the assertion that not only Japanese music but also most other kinds of non-Western music have been subjected to the process of fitting square pegs into the round holes of Western notation. It was indicated in our discussion of music dictation that various levels of phonemic-phonetic transcription (the G-S line again) are useful in different contexts of research. Accordingly, at the G end of the G-S line, the most general objectives can be met with a relatively crude accommodation; as we approach

[8] Sir Francis Taylor Piggott, *The Music and Musical Instruments of Japan*, 1st ed., B. T. Batsford, London, 1893, p. 5.

85

the specific end of the line, Western notation must be fitted out with a variety of elaborate devices, all aimed at showing that the notation does not look like the musical sounds it is meant to represent. Rather than review the strenuous efforts of numerous transcribers, displayed in all the current literature, by evaluating the relative effectiveness of sundry diacritical markings and other emendations to Western notation, let us evaluate different aspects of the system itself in terms of the most basic requirements of cross-cultural transcription.

Perhaps the most fundamental deficiency of Western notation for purposes of transcription of non-Western music is the limitation of twelve fixed pitches within the octave.[9] No musical culture outside the sphere of influence of the European art tradition employs this system of tuning. The intervals between the principal pitches that make up a given non-Western tuning system will not coincide with the intervals of the Western tempered system as represented in notation, which are always multiples of the smallest interval—the so-called half step of 100 cents between a white and a black key on the piano. A non-Western system, for example, might include intervals of 86 cents, 171 cents, 232 cents, and so on. No amount of pluses or minuses or similar diacritical markings added to Western notation can compensate for the inherent rigidity of the Western staff.

A theoretical solution to the problem of representing the pitches of non-Western tuning systems might be a lined staff with variable spacings (see Illustration 2-29). But the difficulty with such a solution applied, for example, to Javanese music lies in the fact that no two gamelan are tuned exactly alike; and, further, it appears that within a given gamelan each octave of the more than six-octave range has its own intervallic structure.[10] Even the term "octave" is not quite right, since a basic principle of Javanese tuning appears to include stretched and compressed octaves, that is, an interval that is predictably more or less than a difference of twice the number of cycles per second indicated by the Western conception of octave. Each gamelan, therefore, would require a unique set of seven staves in order to represent graphically the basic five or seven pitches of the sléndro or pélog tuning systems, respectively.

Many musical cultures have evolved an aesthetic that includes the conscious and studied usage of microtonal intervals, smaller than the Western half step, not only in the basic tuning system but also in melodic ornamentation in the course of attack, duration, and release of a pitch. In connection with the attack of a tone, Western symbols can indicate only modifications in stress or accent,

[9] Twelve successive white and black keys on the piano. The thirteenth key is the so-called octave of the first key and has twice the number of cycles per second in pitch. Literally the word "octave" refers to the eighth successive "diatonic" step, obtained by counting only the white keys.
[10] See further Mantle Hood, "Sléndro and Pélog Redefined," *Selected Reports*, vol. 1, no. 1, Institute of Ethnomusicology, UCLA, 1966, pp. 28–48.

and these in only a relative sense. In some cultures, the musical attack may begin with a rising or descending microtonal slide up or down to the sustained pitch. It may begin with a simple or elaborate microtonal ornament. It may start with a special tone quality. Duration is often more than a matter of how long the pitch continues, because it may include inflected changes of timbre. It may involve control in the intermittent absence, presence, speed, evenness, unevenness, and intervallic size of vibrato. It may be comprised of glottal stops, momentary deflections in pitch, and other stylistic modifications of sound. The release of pitch is also subject to such a variety of effects.

Not so many years ago, the tuning systems, scales, and ornamentation of musical cultures outside the European art tradition were simply considered out of tune. This ethnocentric prejudice, fortunately, has almost—but not quite—disappeared. A few years ago at an international congress in South America, I

Pitch	Cents
1	
	246
7	
	155
6	
	126
5	
	117
4	
	297
3	
	144
2	
	120
1	

Illustration 2-29
A staff with lines spaced proportionately to show the relative size of each interval as indicated under the heading "Cents." (The data is from Mantle Hood, "Sléndro and Pélog Redefined," Selected Reports, vol. 1, no. 1, p. 45.)

heard an excellent descriptive paper read on the subject of an Amerindian flutist. The recordings used for illustration were clear and did justice to the unmistakable artistry of the musician. At the end of the paper I could scarcely believe my ears when the young man who had read it apologized for the out-of-tuneness of the performance. I waited for some kind of explosion of protest from the floor. None came. The emperor was riding naked through the streets! After some polite discussion about other matters, it appeared we were about to proceed with the next paper. I asked for the floor and as tactfully as possible pointed out that the emperor was nude. The observation generated a very heated discussion that clearly separated a few supporters of an older generation's point of view from the large majority of younger scholars who had no difficulty in accepting the Indian flute as being in tune with its tradition.

If Western notation cannot represent the rhythmic refinements of its own oral tradition, as in the triplet, it requires little illustration to show its deficiencies in capturing the rhythmic subtleties of non-Western music. Two simple examples come to mind in relation to Japanese gagaku, the "elegant music" of the imperial household and the shrines.[11] First: in the opening of a movement of the orchestral piece the ensemble is guided by a quadratic meter that includes a momentary pause or "breath" after every phrase, a kind of elongation-by-consensus of the phrase. Second: the instrument leading the overall movement of the group, the kakko, is a double-headed drum played with two sticks in a variety of rhythmic patterns based on a gradual acceleration of strokes (hear LP Side I, Band 3) that

far exceeds the simple requirements given in our earlier example of ♩♩♩♩♩ .

Even in the matter of tempo markings—given all the gradations from grave (very slow) to prestississimo (very, very fast)—we have a problem. What kind of tempo (and meter) do we assign to music that has an elongated phrase? Probably the most cogent observation we can make in these terms about Japanese gagaku is that it ranges from very slow to slow to not-quite-so-slow. But again this is all quite relative. After the student has become saturated with the tradition of gagaku through performing it for many months or several years, he will probably come to regard the final movement of "Chogeshi" as having a rather bright and vigorous tempo—which, in the context of the tradition, indeed it has![12]

The assignment of a Western tempo marking to a Javanese orchestral piece introduces a different kind of problem. Considering the thirty to forty different rhythmic-melodic layers that make up this tradition of polyphonic stratification, to which level of density shall we assign *the* indication of tempo? The Javanese recognize three basic tempos: irama I, II, and III. In the "slowest" tempo, irama III, strokes, on the large gong, depending on the form of the piece, might occur anywhere from two to four or more minutes apart; the density of one of the improvising instruments might be close to 350 pulses per minute. Somewhere between these two extremes is the density of the so-called fixed melody, the actual tune that establishes the individuality of the piece and provides the foundation for improvisation. However, before we assign this stratum the place of honor with a tempo marking, we must be aware that as the piece moves through three levels of tempo—fast, moderate, slow—the relative density of the fixed melody sometimes doubles or quadruples and then doubles again through appropriate stylistic techniques. Or, we might explain the matter by saying, "The music gets slower by going faster."

[11] See further Robert Garfias, "The Togaku Style of Japanese Court Music," doctoral dissertation, UCLA, University Microfilms, Ann Arbor, Mich., 1965.

[12] Hear further Gagaku (Court Music): "Etenraku," "Bairo," "Chogeshi," performed by the Music Department of the Imperial Household, LP record, Columbia (Japan) CL 34.

88

As a medium of transcription for non-Western music, the standard symbols used in the notation of Western music pose problems in terms of pitch, rhythm, and tempo. What about loudness? We would seem to be on safe ground at last. No other musical culture has developed such a great range of dynamic change. Whatever the minuscule shortcomings within its own tradition, the notation for European art music would seem to be capable of registering relatively accurate dynamic markings for any other type of music.

But what level of dynamics do we select for a solo instrument like the Chinese chin? This seven-stringed zither, honored since the time of Confucius as a contemplative instrument played by the philosopher, the intellectual, has a sound that barely carries across the dimensions of a modest-sized room. Are we to register its dynamic range, which is extremely narrow, as pianissimo (*ppp*) to piano (*p*)? I am in doubt whether the finest gradation of Western dynamic markings could register the almost imperceptible sounds made when the left hand of the chin player shifts position several times along the stopped string, still vibrating from the initial attack by the right hand.

Many solo instruments as well as ensembles in the non-Western world perform within a very limited dynamic range. Some African ensembles appear to have no conscious change in dynamics at all. Even large orchestral groups like the Balinese or Javanese gamelan distinguish only between soft and loud styles of playing. Beyond this, the actual change in decibels produced by an ensemble depends on how many instruments are playing at a given time. In the Balinese tradition, sudden shifts of both tempo and dynamics by the whole ensemble and occasional passages by a solo instrument create an effect that has been compared to the dynamic contrast characteristic of the nineteenth-century music literature for the Western orchestra. The comparison may be valid and aesthetically comparable in relation to the abruptness of change, but the Balinese preference for loud, soft, and solo passages can hardly be compared to the wide gradation in dynamic range of the Western orchestra. The Javanese gamelan, on the other hand, tends to establish long plateaus of tempo and loud or soft dynamics. In both of these Indonesian ensembles, the conception of loudness bears no relationship to the Western gradation from *ppp* to *fff*.

Every aspect of Western notation represents a corresponding chronic problem in cross-cultural transcription. Existing publications in the field of ethnomusicology attest to the variety of chronic solutions that have been attempted. All these problems center on the disparity between a culturally determined system of notation and the musical sounds of some other culture it was never intended to represent. If it is true that a trained musician is expected to "hear" what he reads in notation, then most all these chronic solutions are no solution at all.

Mr. Piggott's projected speculations in 1893 were well founded.

We have explained the problem and criticized the solution. Is a better solution available now? Soon? In the distant future? I believe the answer is "yes!" to all three questions. For the sake of simplicity I shall assign a man's name to each stage of this composite solution to the problems of notation: The one available now we shall call the (Alfred James) Hipkins Solution; available soon, the (Charles) Seeger Solution; available in the distant future, the (Rudolph) Laban Solution. The three solutions have been referred to three stages of timing or availability (now, soon, future) in the development of a Composite Solution. But we should keep in mind that each of them in itself is a valid solution for particular aspects of the notation problem and that ultimately all three are necessary as a composite.

There is little doubt in my mind that Western notation in various guises of modification will continue to appear in the literature for some years to come. The fact that some of us are determined to conquer the problems of 1893, I am equally confident, will one day result in the abandonment of this ethnocentric crutch. By the time we have reached the Laban Solution, the last traces of doctored Western notation should fade away.

THE HIPKINS SOLUTION   As background for an explanation of the Hipkins Solution, we can do no better than refer to the introduction written by Alfred James Hipkins for the remarkable book on Indian music by Charles Russell Day, published in 1891:

> He shows us the existence of a really intimate, expressive melodic music, capable of the greatest refinement of treatment, and altogether outside the experience of the Western musician. What we learn from such inquiries is that the debated opinions of musical theorists, the cherished beliefs of those who devote themselves to the practice of the art, the deductions we evolve from historic studies— all have to be submitted to larger conceptions, based upon a recognition of humanity as evolved from the teachings of ethnology. We must forget what is merely European, national, or conventional, and submit the whole of the phenomena to a philosophical as well as a sympathetic consideration, such as, in this century, is conceded to language, but has not yet found its way to music.[13]

If I were to nominate someone as the Father of Modern Ethnomusicology, it would be Alfred James Hipkins. His gentlemanly admonition cited above should be memorized by every student of ethnomusicology. It challenges the theorist, the performer, the historian; it chides the musical provincial; it pricks the humanist's conscience. Above all, it is a reminder that the music of each culture must

---

[13] A. J. Hipkins, Introduction to Charles Russell Day, *The Music and Musical Instruments of Southern India and the Deccan*, Novello, Ewer and Co., London and New York, 1891, p. xii.

be known and understood in its own terms and in its own milieu. It should be adopted as the Hippocratic oath of the practicing ethnomusicologist.

Guided by the ethical code of the Hipkinatic oath, we are ready to evaluate an assertion made at the beginning of our discussion of notation: "All established systems of music notation have developed in response to the particular requirements of the tradition they serve...each one of them is sufficient unto its purpose or, when it ceases to be, is modified or discarded in favor of an improved system."

In his practical studies of non-Western music, the graduate student who is learning to play the Chinese chin or the Japanese koto will soon discover that Chinese or Japanese notation is sufficient unto its purpose. It requires a very short time to become familiar with the symbols of either system; and, once learned, they provide a more efficient guide to performance than any kind of transcription that could be devised. Imagine the cluttered modification of Western notation that would be required to represent the information contained in the composite Chinese symbol explained in my conversation with Pete Seeger!

I am not suggesting that every student of ethnomusicology learn to play the chin and the koto, however valuable such a requirement might be, but I am proposing that every professional ethnomusicologist should expand the literacy of his international musicianship to include the written ABCs of major musical cultures that have established systems of notation. The Hipkins Solution, a reading knowledge of the principal non-Western systems of music notation, is a feasible objective within reach of the serious student now. This is a first and minimal step in getting to know a given music in its own terms of reference.

How can such a program of study be undertaken in a practical sense? It can be argued that the musical cultures of China and Japan, for example, have many systems of notation, depending on the genre of music and the historical style period in question. The same observation, of course, can be made with regard to the tradition of European art music. I think I am not betraying a trade secret when I say that not all Western musicians or even all musicologists can read all genres and style periods of Western notation. To anticipate slightly, perhaps by the time we have attained the Laban Solution this state of affairs may change. But to continue, I am not suggesting that familiarity with the notation of all genres of all style periods of all musical cultures in the world is requisite to the successful implementation of the Hipkins Solution.

It was indicated earlier that there are both living and dead systems of notation. If our objective of international musical literacy is limited to living systems still in use and if among these only principal genres are included, the size of the undertaking shrinks to a manageable proportion. Given this delimitation,

91

how do we get on with the task? It is probably safe to conjecture that few if any ethnomusicologists at present have such a command of musical literacy. This is illustrative of the kind of objectives characteristic of this field that makes the professional an eternal student.

The reader may recall that in the Introduction one of the nine books outlined, considered, and subsequently rejected in favor of the present commission dealt with the subject of notation and transcription. Such a book should be accompanied by an album of recorded illustrations. Perhaps one day the concerted efforts of a number of scholars will make this important reference a reality.

Meanwhile, other approaches for acquiring such knowledge are possible. The most direct approach in learning a system of notation, of course, is through performance. Whatever the ultimate attainments of the student as a performer of non-Western music, he will have gained a fluency in reading and understanding the different systems of notation represented by his studies. His resources are probably twofold: practical courses of this type offered by the institution in which he is enrolled, and the surprisingly large number of ethnic enclaves found in most metropolitan centers. This is certainly the most thorough and most pleasant route of travel toward international literacy.

A second approach requires some digging in the archives. There are a number of scholarly publications that explain and evaluate systems of notation used in one or another part of the non-Western world. Such sources can be gleaned from the extensive bibliography in Kunst's *Ethnomusicology*.

A third approach requires a stiffening of the spine on the part of my professional colleagues. Even those who are willing to subscribe to the Hipkinatic oath—and I cannot think of an exception—may balk at my proposal of their responsibility in implementing the Hipkins Solution. I trust, at least, I can count on them to lend a sympathetic ear.

The usage of some form of modified Western notation for transcription purposes, in spite of the fact that its limitations are generally understood, tends to be self-perpetuating. Most scholars are critical of the problem. But when the chips are down and that postponed deadline for the press can be postponed no longer, Western notation, with all its faults for the purpose at hand, is usually selected as the medium of representation for musical examples and illustrations. It isn't perfect, it isn't accurate, it isn't even appropriate—so the argument goes—but there is more than a century of precedence that says it is acceptable. Besides, it is quite a chore to present a clear and simple explanation of a foreign system of notation. And who can be sure that the reader will have the patience and interest required to understand it? The safe solution is the chronic solution.

Sometimes as a salve to the sensitive conscience, various mitigative explanations may be offered to compensate for the sellout. In the meantime, there

92

is one more scholarly publication on record in the process of self-perpetuation.

I appeal to my colleague who specializes in one or another of the musical cultures of the Greater Orient which employ an established system of notation. If the next time (and the next and the next) in preparing a typescript for publication he remembers his Hipkinatic oath, we shall be well on the way to implementing the Hipkins Solution. He can assume that his reader audience is different from the reader of comic books and paperback sex novels. The time has come for the author of research publications to exhibit confidence in the intelligence and acquisitive interest of his reader. The scholar must kick the habit of his addiction to the Western staff.

Before I am thrown to the wolves, let me acknowledge my awareness that some research problems, especially those found near the S end of the G-S line, may well require graphic representations that exceed the symbolic vocabulary of the music under study. This is likely to be true of those aspects of musical performance that are dependent on the oral tradition supporting the indigenous notation. I might add that an accurate transcription of Western music as it is actually performed also exceeds the symbolic vocabulary of Western notation. Let us think the process through before joining the perpetuators.

If given research problems occupy a place near the G end of the G-S line, it is likely that the indigenous notation will accommodate them quite easily. Problems located farther down the G-S line may require emendations, diacritical markings, schematic representations, and so forth. But modification of Chinese notation to represent Chinese musical practice is a most direct and appropriate extension of scientific method compared to the diffuse hybridization of Western notation applied to the same problems. The writer need explain only those aspects of the notation required by his examples and illustrations. And his capability of offering the nonspecialist a clear explanation is a nice test of his own comprehension and mastery of the subject.

The man with this brand of courage will understand that the Hipkins Solution provides an opportunity to demonstrate his own sense of responsibility in the dissemination of international literacy in music. After a few such publications, he will have established a mode of communication that not only supports an honest presentation but also gives his readers the intellectual satisfaction of being at ease in the habit of reading non-Western notation.

The Hipkins Solution, the "now" stage of the Composite Solution, fulfills an important part, but only part, of our objective. It leaves dangling a number of problems. How do we handle the many musical details found near the S end of the G-S line, details that resist representation in any form of known notation? What do we use to transcribe the kind of music that has only an oral tradition, music for which no system of notation has ever been developed by its society?

THE SEEGER SOLUTION   These questions are closely related and introduce the need for the "soon" stage of the Composite Solution, namely, the Seeger Solution. There is excellent background material in print, and it deserves close scrutiny by the reader.[14] Rather than review or summarize available literature, I shall illustrate the problem by selecting an example that at first glance would seem to justify, most logically, transcription in Western notation: traditional songs of the American Negro. Granted that the African origins which contributed to the tradition carried no system of notation, the specific songs that were developed in the southern part of the United States had a greater or lesser infusion from white spirituals. It would seem reasonable to select Western notation for transcribing the music of this tradition.

And yet it was precisely this music that Milton Metfessel used in his publication in 1928 to demonstrate "that notating songs by ear [in Western notation] is insufficient to indicate many allusive facts of folk music. Much of the charm and distinctiveness of the singing Negroes lies in queer pranks of their voices, but these twists and turns occur too quickly…valuable detail and necessary accuracy have been lacking in studies of folk music."[15]

He stressed the fact that the perception of the transcriber is subject to his own conditioning, that, in effect, different persons "hear" differently. "Only when musicians are confronted by an objective analysis of the sound waves in music will differences of opinion cease to exist as far as the factual problems are concerned."[16] And in order to illustrate his contention, he developed a special motion-picture camera to capture a photographic record of sound waves. In this pioneering study, he reached the following conclusion:

> Phonophotography, by laying the foundation for definition of what a music is, by defining the terms used in music, by substituting objective experiments for opin-

[14] Milton Franklin Metfessel, *Phonophotography in Folk Music: American Negro Songs in New Notation*, with an Introduction by C. E. Seashore, The University of North Carolina Press, Chapel Hill, 1928, p. 20; Charles Seeger, "An Instantaneous Music Notator," *Journal of the International Folk Music Council*, vol. 3 (1951), pp. 103–107; Charles Seeger, "Toward a Universal Sound-Writing for Musicology," *ibid.*, vol. 9 (1957), pp. 63–66; O. Gurvin, "Photography as an Aid in Folk Music Research," *Norveg*, vol. 3 (1955), pp. 181–196; A. Krokstad, "Signal Analysator for Musik," *SINTEF's årsmelcling*, Trondheim (1963) pp. 57–60; P. A. Tove, B. Norman, L. Isaakson, and T. Czekajewski, "Direct-Recording Frequency and Amplitude Meter for Analysis of Musical and Other Sonic Waveforms," *Journal of the Acoustical Society of America*, vol. 39, no. 2 (Feb., 1966), pp. 362–371; Juichi Obata and Ryuji Kobayashi, "An Apparatus for Direct-Recording the Pitch and Intensity of Sound," *Journal of the Acoustical Society of America*, vol. 10, no. 2 (Oct., 1938), pp. 147–149; Miroslav Filip, "Spósoby Objektívneho Grafického, Zaznamu Melódie," *Hudobnovedné Studie*, vol. 7, Vydavatelstvo Slovenskej Akadémie Vied, Bratislava, 1966, pp. 176–191.

[15] Metfessel, *loc. cit.*

[16] *Ibid.*, p. 177.

94

ions, and by the utilizing of graphic and statistical methods, will assist in removing the uncertainties and prejudices that have pervaded the study of folk music.[17]

In time, others followed his lead in the search for some mechanical means of representing musical sounds in one or another form of graphic display. One of the most outstanding contributions among the several approaches to the problem was the automatic music writer, called the Melograph, which was developed by Charles Seeger. After more than fifteen years of painstaking effort, the third model of this instrument, Melograph Model C, holds great promise in meeting the objectives laid down by Metfessel. At this writing, Model C is still in the first year of testing.

This instrument is an electronic analyzer of musical sounds that includes computer logic circuitry to produce a three part continuous photographic display consisting of pitch, loudness, and timbre. It has a pitch range of seven octaves, an amplitude range of 40 decibels, and a spectral range of 15,000 Hertz. Designed expressly for the varied needs of ethnomusicological research, it can accommodate the widest range of flexibility in display format.

Those of us who have watched this development at close hand believe we have traded in our musical magnifying glass (Melograph Models A and B) for an electron microscope. Probably several years of usage and experimentation will be required before an adequate number of displays can be amassed for the purpose of supporting Metfessel's declared objective.

But "soon," among its potentials, the Seeger Solution should yield insight relative to such questions as the following: To what extent are the "queer pranks...twists and turns" of melody unique to the individual performer within a given tradition? To a given genre and/or style within the tradition? To the tradition as a whole? Can the graphic display of these pranks, twists, and turns be abstracted in such a way, at each of these levels of information, that it can become part of the symbolic language of a system of classification? To what extent can "envelope" and partial spectrum provide unique symbols for comparative purposes? Considering the element of time as a basic factor in music making, are there significant differences from one culture to another in the musical niceties that regulate tempo and rhythm? If such differences appear to exist from genre to genre or from style to style within a culture, are there more fundamental regulative principles to be identified? If identified, are they significant in cross-cultural comparisons? In a tradition that includes no tuning system of fixed pitches, that is, one limited to voice, strings, flutes, and so forth, can a reasonably stable intervallic system be identified?

[17] *Ibid.*, p. 178.

Can one or more aspects of the Melograph, the digital or the photographic display, contribute to a "future" symbolic language needed to establish whether various orders of stylistic features have a geographic distribution relating to, for example, language, language groups, root languages; religious literature (considered apart from language per se); degrees of literacy; systems of notation; social structure, relative freedom and/or independence of individuals in society; relative importance and interdependence of other performing arts such as dance and theater, other arts such as painting, sculpture, poetry; technology, economics, manufacture, agriculture, trade, hunting, gathering, or other developments relating to modes of livelihood; geography, climate, rainfall, flora, fauna, and other natural attributes of environment; intercultural commerce, communication, and peaceful or forceful conquest; and so forth?

Can patterns of geographic distribution be established in purely musical terms, such as ornamental devices, vocal techniques, instrumental practice, tuning practices, rhythmic organization, musical form, vocal quality, instrumental quality, the relationship between these two, the organization of pitch into hierarchies, multiplicity of pitches in the octave, total range of pitch, range of loudness, and so forth?

To be sure, these and related questions will occupy ethnomusicologists for some time to come. But Model C has been constructed in such a way that a large quantity of data basic to such research can be furnished at the same time the initial display of a given example is being recorded. The availability of information in a digital form permits a schedule of programming that can be routed through the computing center at UCLA during the initial run of the material. To the extent that these pre-programs can be developed, it will be possible to apply descriptive, analytical, and comparative methods simultaneously. Currently, cooperative projects involving the Institute of Ethnomusicology, the Linguistic Laboratory, and the Department of Psychology at UCLA are being initiated.

Precisely how "soon" the Seeger Solution can have wide application is difficult to say. But the fact that this costly precision instrument has already been constructed and is being tested justifies a certain optimism. As soon as routine procedures can be developed, the Institute at UCLA will offer the services of Model C for the cost of time and materials. Soon the ethnomusicologist should have available to him a precise graphic display of the musical details that have been alluding his most conscientious efforts in the past.

What are some of the immediate implications of the Seeger Solution applied to the problems of notation? Assuming that on a trial basis we may have won our arguments in support of the Hipkins Solution, the ethnomusicologist will be able to supplement the symbolic language of the indigenous notation with graphic displays of pertinent musical practice known only in the oral tradition.

96

The Seeger Solution will enable him to compare whatever indigenous or extra-cultural theories have developed in relation to the tradition with the precise musical happenings that actually occur in performance practice. Such an application, need I add, is also pertinent in the study of Western music.

But what about those musical cultures that lack an indigenous notation altogether? Is a system of highly detailed graphic displays, available in the Seeger Solution, the only way to represent African music, for example? Perhaps not. The transcriber has several possibilities open to him.

African songs are usually transcribed in Western notation. Forgetting for the moment the queer pranks, twists, and turns that cannot be represented in such notation (but can in the Melogram), how well do the five lines and four spaces or the twelve pitches of the Western staff correspond to the principal pitches of an African song? The following vignette, which actually applies to an even more severe question, may give us the answer.

During two field trips to Ghana in 1962 and in 1963–1964, I was interested, among other things, in testing certain recording techniques applied to African ensembles. Anxious to manage the widest range of sampling, I not only recorded a variety of traditional groups but also included a number of Hi-Life dance bands, a very popular tradition that had begun around 1900 as a mixture of European and African elements. After I had gathered half a dozen or more of the best examples of Hi-Life in the night clubs of Accra and Kumasi, I was engaged in a discussion with some of my African colleagues about this genre of music. The Hi-Life dance band consists of traditional Western instruments like the saxophone, trumpet, guitar, double bass, as well as some Latin American percussion instruments like bongos and a Congo drum. Vocal solos and chorus are an important part of the idiom. We had been considering some of the recent innovations in the style of dance also known as Hi-Life with the observation that this form of social dancing in the night clubs was being influenced increasingly by movements borrowed from various tribal dance traditions. The conversation led to an evaluation of a similar trend in relation to the musical style of the dance band. Some ensembles were beginning to include traditional Ewe and Ashanti instruments and style of drumming. One of the best-known bands sometimes incorporated a complete Ashanti ensemble known as adowa, consisting of a pair of master drums called atumpan, several types of stick and hand drums, rattles, and double bells.[18] The ease with which African instruments were combined with the original ensemble of Western instruments suggests the strength of African ingredients already present in the tradition of Hi-Life.

[18] A short scene is devoted to this ensemble in the documentary-narrative motion picture *Atumpan* available from the Institute of Ethnomusicology at UCLA. For an illustration of typical Hi-Life intonation discussed on page 98 hear Side III, Band 1 of the accompanying LPs.

97

At some point, I made the comment that even without the inclusion of African instruments, the Hi-Life band was unmistakably African. Was I referring to characteristic rhythm, melodies, and lyrics? I was asked. Yes, of course, but more especially to the intonation of the instruments and voices. I remarked that it was strange and at the same time musically very refreshing to hear saxophones and trumpets playing in one or another tribal intonation, pitches that fell somewhere between the cracks on the piano keyboard. My African colleagues looked at me in surprise. Did I really mean what I said, that melodies played by Hi-Life bands on Western instruments were actually built on African scales? I assured them that was exactly what I meant, and added that perhaps as a newcomer to these sounds, the difference was more apparent to my ears than to someone already conditioned to the tradition.

A few days later, I spliced together two different tape recordings: one was a recording of a Hi-Life band, which I cut off in the middle of a musical phrase, and the other, butted to the first, was a dubbing of an American jazz band which my wife had been using to teach the rudiments of modern jazz to dance classes at the University of Ghana. When it was played back for my friends, the abrupt change from African to American intonation at the point of the splice produced a perceptible physical shock in the listeners. The wind family of modern Western instruments, even with their valves or keys, pads, and springs, permit considerable latitude in intonation; the double bass, of course, can play any series of pitches; ensembles that include the guitar, with its fixed Western frets, simply have one instrument out of tune with the rest of the group.

One way of approaching the problem of tribal intonation would be to apply the Seeger Solution in determining the precise intervallic structure involved. From these data a staff with variable spacing, mentioned earlier in connection with Javanese gamelan (Illustration 2-29), could be established for each species encountered. Since there are no "standard pitch" and no "standard intonation" presently known in one or another region of Africa, such a process might lead to a great variety of unique staves. While for comparative purposes this result has important consequences, it would pose practical problems for purposes of notation, since it is possible that a different staff might be required for every tribe. What about sticking to the Western staff? It is not accurate for any one tradition, but it might give a sufficient impression of all of them. Perhaps for musical cultures without a system of notation, the Western staff, together with appropriate reliance on the Seeger Solution, might make the best solution after all.

But before we relax into the chronic habit of the times, let us consider in more detail what the Western staff represents. The treble clef added to the five lines and four spaces indicates that the second space from the bottom of the

staff is the pitch A vibrating at the rate of 440 cps (cycles per second) ♭𝄞 o .
In the United States, this pitch is sometimes referred to as concert pitch, something
the orchestra uses as a reference for tuning (actually it tunes to the A of the óboe).
Some piano tuners prefer 441 or 442 cps or even more for this pitch, with the
claim that an instrument so tuned gives a "brighter" sound. The so-called international pitch of Europe is slightly lower, 435 cps. Be that as it may, it is understood
that all instruments and voices in an ensemble, and all ensembles in the United
States or in Europe refer to one or the other of these standards. It is also understood, whichever standard of pitch reference is used, that all the other lines and
spaces indicate pitches and intervals that are always intended to be performed
the same, either in the nontempered intonation of the orchestra or in the tempered
intonation of keyboard instruments.[19] In other words, when a musician sees a note
on a Western staff he hears it in reference to an accepted aural standard. The
lines and spaces of the staff refer to a specific standard of pitch and interval. This
standard is the basic stuff of which Western music is made.

In African music, there is no standard of pitch or interval. The same may
be said of other parts of the non-Western world, and, where systems of notation
have been developed, they reflect the lack of such standards. Said another way,
various forms of notation in non-Western systems take into account the variability
of pitch and interval in the tradition. It has already been pointed out that with
the five- and seven-tone tuning systems of Java, sléndro and pélog respectively,
no two gamelan are tuned exactly alike. Both cipher notation and kraton script
(Illustration 2-12 and 2-13) accommodate this condition. In the kraton script for
sléndro, the six vertical lines refer to a closed octave of the five pitches: barang,
djangga, ḍaḍa, lima, nem, barang alit; or, in cipher notation, pitches 1, 2, 3, 5,
6, i̇. The pitch of lima (5), for example, could be 440 cps.[20] But it can also vary
from 395 cps to 455 cps.[21] The size of the interval from lima to nem (5 to 6)
may vary from 208 cents to 281 cents.[22] Both the lines of the kraton script and
the numbers of the cipher notation accommodate either extreme and every
possibility between. The notation provides a *graphic reminder* that pitch and
interval are variables in the tradition of Javanese gamelan. If the transcriber were

[19] Stringed instruments tend to perform in "Pythogorean" intonation and wind instruments
in "just" intonation; when combined with a keyboard instrument they are required to make constant
adjustments in order to approach equal temperament.

[20] Jaap Kunst, *Music in Java: Its History, Its Theory and Its Technique*, 2 vols., 2d ed.,
Martinus Nijhoff, The Hague, 1949, p. 574, Ex. 3.

[21] *Ibid.*, Exs. 32 and 19, respectively.

[22] *Ibid.*, Exs. 34 and 39, respectively (based on the demung octave only); 100 cents = the
European tempered half step.

using Western notation, he would have to decide arbitrarily whether to represent the pitch lima by G, G♯ or A (+). None of these three choices could indicate the important fact that the pitch of lima varies as much as 60 cps (about 228 cents in this register) from one gamelan to another.

The European idea of standardization in pitch and interval is alien to the musical cultures of the non-Western world. As an extension of the Hipkins Solution, those cultures lacking a system of notation might better turn to other musical cultures of the non-Western world for an answer to the problem. Since, in any event, we are speaking of borrowing a system of notation outside the culture of the music being transcribed, is it not logical to seek out the most kindred musical culture for the purpose?

Some of my African colleagues who have had a long conditioning to the usage of Western notation will not readily endorse this suggestion. But if they intend to reach a reader audience both within and outside the European tradition, I might remind them that some form of cipher notation is in common usage in both the Western and non-Western worlds. As one of several possibilities that could provide a graphic reminder of variable pitch and interval, cipher notation has the practical advantage of requiring no special form of score paper—it even lends itself to the typewriter. The beginning phrase of "Mary Had a Little Lamb": 3 2 1 2 3 3 3 . 2 2 2 . 3 5 5 ., and so forth. Or the beginning of the first theme of Mozart's *Sonata in F Major:* 1 . 3 5 . 3 4 . $\dot{2}$ $\overline{17}$ 7 0 $\dot{1}$ 3 6 2 5 .3 1 . . . , and so forth. Played on the piano, these little tunes will be in a tempered intonation, on the violin, in a Pythagorean intonation; the reader may sing them in either intonation (probably the latter) in any comfortable key. As a Western musician, the most serious problem I have encountered in the use of cipher notation is a certain conflict of interest when I consult a telephone directory.

It is also possible to borrow from the Javanese kraton script by employing a vertical or horizontal lined staff in which the spaces between the lines carry no reference to pitch or specific intervallic size. If it were important for the particular purposes of the transcriber, a schematic representation showing the details of pitch and interval could be included at the beginning of a cipher transcription, a lined staff or some other form that did not suggest pitch standardization. Such a scheme could show, for example, the range of intervallic variation encountered in sampling, let us say, sixteen different Ashanti singers in one village or *x* number of singers from several Ashanti villages or from all the Akan tribes of Ghana or from all tribes of Ghana or from selected tribes in West Africa, and so forth (see Illustration 2-30). If, at the other extreme, the transcription is meant to represent a specific performance of a piece, the scheme could indicate precise pitches in cycles per second and intervallic structure in cents (see Illustration 2-31).

100

This extension of the Hipkins Solution together with the Seeger Solution permits far more accurate transcription of oral traditions of music than is possible in the current practice of using Western notation. Such an approach to notation avoids any reference to Western standards of pitch, thereby providing a reminder

Pitch		Cents
1		
		115–210
7		
		118–206
6		
		188–225
5		
		108–220
4		
		110–205
3		
		185–210
2		
		190–208
1		

Illustration 2-30
A staff with equidistant horizontal lines showing a composite of the range of intervallic variation of sixteen hypothetical Ashanti singers in one village. (The data is based on J. H. Nketia's comments in African Music in Ghana, Longmans, Green, and Company, Ltd., Accra, 1962, p. 35.)

Pitch	Hz (cps)	Cents
1	930	
		283
5	790	
		137
4	730	
		255
3	630	
		350
2	515	
		311
1	430	

Illustration 2-31
A staff with equidistant horizontal lines showing the precise pitches in cycles per second and the intervallic structure in cents. (Hz figures for pandingbwa free-key xylophone of the Azande tribe, from Olga Boone, Les xylophones du Musée du Congo belge, Ethnographie Ser. III, Tome III, fasc. 2, Tervuren, 1936, p. 79.)

that non-Western pitch and interval are not standardized and relieving the reader of the ambivalence required in looking at a Western staff and trying not to hear Western pitches.

THE LABAN SOLUTION The "now" Hipkins and the "soon" Seeger segments of the Composite Solution should be continually applied both independently and interdependently to particular problems in transcription. They are also important to the "future" Laban Solution—the Hipkins because of its international orientation and the Seeger because of its descriptive accuracy.

For many years in the field of dance, only primitive forms of notation were known. In creating a dance or in trying to remember a dance from the time of its original performance until its sometime revival or for purposes of analysis, choreographers and dancers resorted to such forms of manual notation as stick figures, footprints, patterns of Xs, and so forth. At this stage of development, dance notation could represent only the gross aspects of dance. Compared with Western music notation, the results were truly primitive. More sophisticated forms of dance notation never gained wide acceptance. Then, in 1905, Rudolph Laban developed an elaborate manual system known as Labanotation; it has been widely disseminated through publication of the system by one of his students, Ann Hutchinson.[23] Today the comparison must be reversed: Compared to Labanotation, which approaches universal efficiency, all established manual systems of music notation are truly primitive. Labanotation is being used to transcribe not only all kinds of Western dance—classical ballet, modern jazz, ballroom, the latest teen-age innovations, modern dance—but also any dance tradition from any part of the non-Western world.

The system is a complex "phonetic" one made of many monomial symbols which, in various combinations, can represent detailed movements of virtually all parts of the body. Labanotation is a scientific tool for descriptive, analytical, and comparative methods; for the dance historian, it furnishes a reliable representation for reconstruction; it has many possibilities for the application of synthetic method. From a transcription of choreography in this "phonetic" notation, a dancer can recreate movements that may have been originally performed years before or thousands of miles away—provided he is sufficiently trained in the movements of the tradition; "phonemic" supplementation by the documentary film, photographs, and some notation like stick figures is, of course, desirable.

I cannot go so far as some of the champions of Labanotation who mistakenly believe it provides a complete record of dance. No two-dimensional representation of this lively art—including the motion-picture film—can capture a complete record. Dramatic and lyrical quality, personality, mood, verve, élan, spiritual dedication, semihypnotic states of trance—certain personal as well as socially prescribed attributes and attitudes of the dancer exceed the requirements of kinesthesia for which Labanotation was developed.

These attributes and attitudes are a significant aspect of the dance tradition. We might consider one illustration. Moments before the traditional Javanese

---

[23] Ann Hutchinson, *Labanotation*, illustrated by Doug Anderson, New Directions Books, New York, 1961.

male dancer makes his entrance along one side of the polished marble floor of the dance pavilion, he has already entered into a mental state of introspection. His thoughts are turned inward in a kind of spiritual detachment inspired by the responsibility he has undertaken in entering the role of one of the heroes or gods—evil or good, coarse or refined—who people the religious stories of the *Mahabharata*. He is already partly in character as he walks along in a somewhat stylized manner to the spot in the pavilion where he will sit cross-legged for a moment and then execute the sembah, a formal supplication to the gods, to the ancestors, to the audience. All these movements and the dance that follows can be represented by Labanotation. But in the two-dimensional plane of notation, this inspired performance will look no different from a routine rehearsal that might have taken place the day before. I might paraphrase Piggott's concern over the Western notation of Japanese music by questioning whether someone who had never seen Javanese dance could capture the intrinsic spirit of the tradition only by reading the admittedly superlative symbolic language of Labanotation.

Do not misunderstand. My intention is not to belittle a system of notation that far surpasses anything known in the field of music but rather to call attention to the realistic limits of any abstract system of notation. In Chapters Four and Five we shall consider a similar critique hinted at in my reference to the motion picture as a medium of dance transcription. For the time being, however, the reader may wish to review the remarks mentioned earlier about the limitations of professional recording (page 33), a reasonably parallel medium in the field of music.

The ultimate realization of a universal system of music notation must have some practical limits. Certain attributes and attitudes characteristic of musical performance, analogous to similar features in dance, are likely to be resistant to any form of graphic representation. However, if one day this final stage of the Composite Solution can provide a universal symbolic notation for music equal in the amount of information it contains to Labanotation in the field of dance, the last major obstacle will have been passed in the problems of transcription.

What order of information do we seek? What kinds of symbols are needed to represent it?

To the best of my knowledge no one has yet asked the interesting question "To what extent might various symbols and their juxtaposition in Labanotation itself provide a model for a universal system of music notation?" There are some striking parallels between the two arts in their descriptive terms of reference: movement, attack, accent, stress, duration, hold, release, quality, dynamics, time, tempo, rhythm. The different aspects of the two arts to which these terms refer also have much in common.

The notation of three-dimensional, curvilinear movements of the human

103

body and all its parts would seem to be at least as demanding as the notation of multiple melodic movements, including the variable pitch of melodic contour, attack, duration, and release. The registration of loudness in music should not be more difficult than the representation of tension and relaxation in dance defined through accent, hold, and release. Notational problems of time, tempo, and rhythm should be nearly equal in both fields. The only other principal problem mentioned in our discussion of music notation is timbre or—together with attack, decay, and release—what we referred to earlier as the quality of sound.

Perhaps the problem of notating quality of sound need not be so difficult. The human body is the "instrument" of expression in dance. In this sense, we might also refer to all types of musical instruments by the collective designation: "the instrument of sound." Following this line of reasoning a bit farther, we might think of the oboe as a particular aspect of "the instrument of sound." Relying on the Seeger Solution to provide Melograms of all the different kinds of oboes found in the world, we might learn, for the sake of illustration, that the oboe pattern of Melogram—as distinct from the trumpet pattern or the clarinet pattern—comprises a *species* in the *genus* of winds in the *family* of aerophones, or wind instruments. We might learn further that within the oboe pattern six distinct subspecies can be identified which, arranged in order of increasing complexity of partial structure, attack, decay, release, and loudness, might be exemplified by: (1) the Western oboe, (2) the north Indian shanai, (3) the Thai pi-nai, (4) the Korean piri, (5) the Japanese hichiriki, and (6) the Chinese so-na. (See Illustrations 2-32 through 2-37.) A comparison of all Melograms establishes the fact that all types of oboes (or shawms) can be classified according to one of the six subspecies.

Illustration 2-32
The Western (open-ring) oboe. This and the following Melograms (Illustrations 2-33 through 2-38) have been rated from simple to complex on the basis of eleven different parameters, the weighting of which is still being tested. In the lower portion of each Melogram, for example, a partial spectrum with characteristically stronger upper partials (indicated in the display by whiter bands) is considered more complex than one with only strong lower partials. Such other factors as rise time and fall time of the transient, as well as decay time, articulation time, and their corresponding loudnesses, are also taken into account.

104

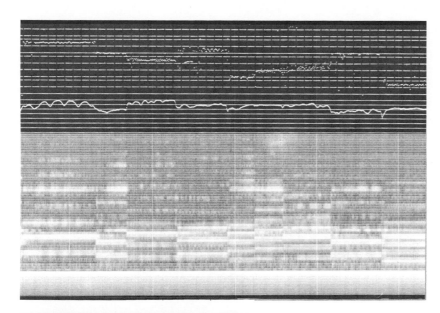

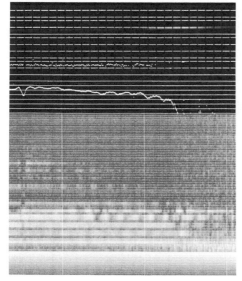

(*Melogram
continues
at left below.*)

105

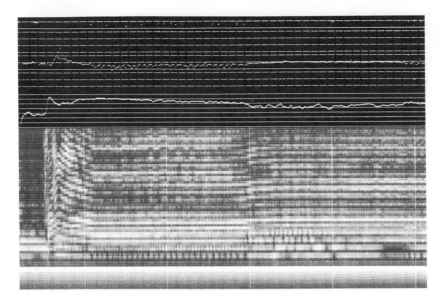

*(Melogram
continues
at left below.)*

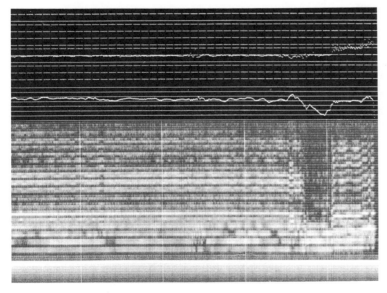

*Illustration 2-33
The North Indian shanai.*

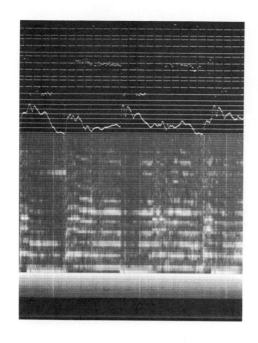

Illustration 2-34
The Thai pi-nai.

Illustration 2-35
The Korean piri.

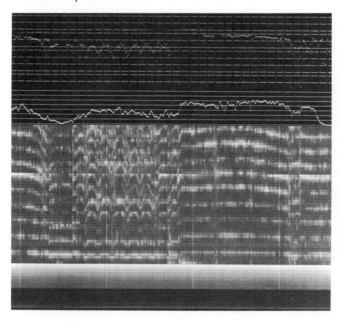

107

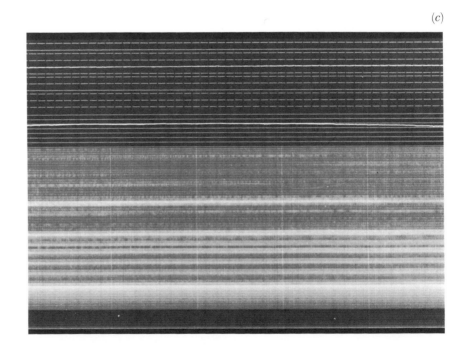

(a)

(c)

Illustration 2-36
The Japanese hichiriki.
(Letters in parentheses
indicate sequence of Melo-
gram, separated only for
convenience of reproduction.)

108

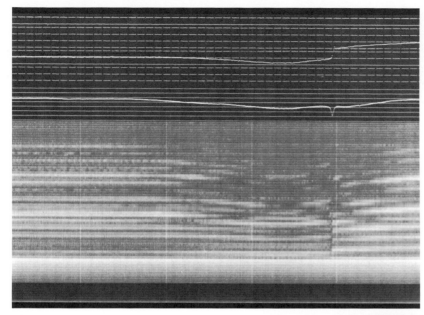

(b)

(d)

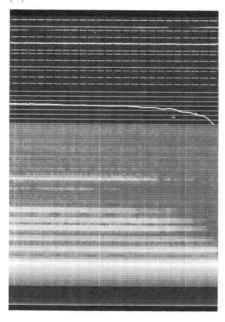

109

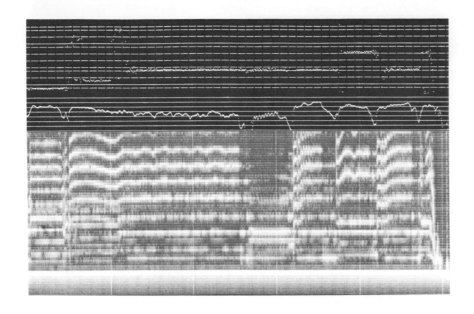

Illustration 2-37
The Chinese sona.

110

Now we are ready to attempt a symbolic representation, which might take the following forms: let a circle represent the *family* of aerophones: ○ ; let the left half represent the *genus* of reed-vibrated winds (e.g., oboes): ◖ ; the right half, the *genus* of edge-vibrated winds (e.g., flutes): ◗ ; the lower half of the symbol for reed-vibrated winds, the *species* of multiple-reed instruments: ◣; the upper half, the *species* of single-reed instruments: ◢ ; further, let the six *subspecies* of ◣ be represented by the following six modifications: (1)◣ , (2) ◣ , (3) ◣ , (4) ◤, (5) ◥ , (6) ◡ .

Such a symbol need be included only occasionally in the course of notating a specific instrument, as a reminder of the tonal quality of the melodic line being followed. If, for example, the instrument in question were the south Indian nagaswaram, the name alone, for someone who had never heard its characteristic sound, would furnish no clue to its particular quality. In fact, because its origin is southern India, an unenlightened reader of the notation might mistakenly infer that the sound of the nagaswaram is similar to subspecies (2), ◣ , exemplified by the northern Indian shanai, whereas its quality requires classification under (6), ◡, exemplified by the Chinese so-na (see comparative Illustration 2-38 and hear LP Side I, Band 4 in connection with Illustrations 2-32 through 2-38). Such a set of symbols, therefore, would permit a notation that is relatively accurate for descriptive purposes and, of course, invaluable for comparative studies.

Let me make it quite clear that this flight of fancy is based on limited laboratory sampling, that it was introduced simply as an illustration of one possibility of symbolic representation of one of the most complex and elusive aspects of music, namely, the quality of sound itself. The instrumental classification used for the family of aerophones was a figment of imagination that departs from the generally accepted Sachs-Hornbostel system. Specific problems encountered in instrumental classification will be considered presently.

Assuming that some symbolic system similar to Labanotation can be devised to serve universal music notation, we might ask in more detail what kind of information about music needs to be represented by such a set of symbols. Let us begin by reviewing the problems already cited in examining Western notation as a medium for transcribing non-Western music.

111

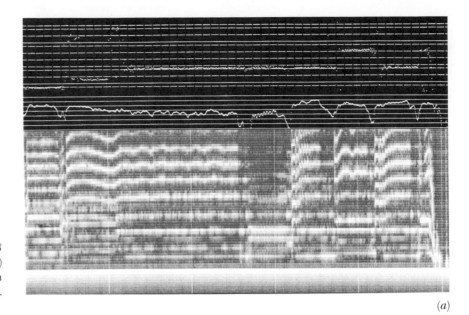

*Illustration 2-38
The Chinese sona (a)
and the South Indian
nagaswaram (b and c).*

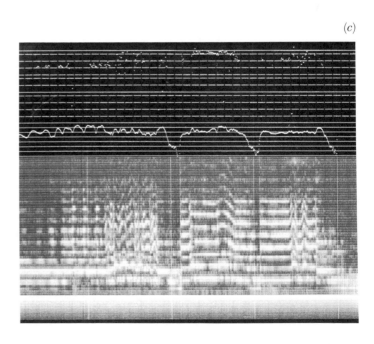

112

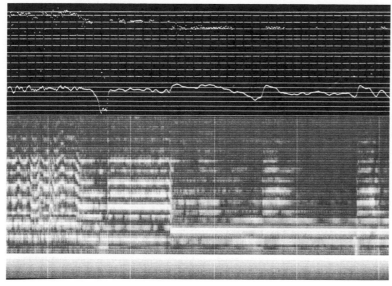

(*b*)

113

Density Referent. Time, tempo, and rhythm have variable emphases and development in different cultures: perfect time or relative time, a narrow or wide range of either relative or precise tempos, divisive rhythm or additive rhythm governed by one or the other modes of time and tempo. In the course of our studies of musical time in the Seminar at UCLA, we soon discovered the need for some kind of standard referent that could be applied to all the musical traditions being compared. If a student described a piece in one tradition as having a basic pulse of 60 per minute and a piece in another tradition a basic pulse of 120 per minute, was the tempo of the two pieces the same? A second student given the same assignment might identify the basic pulse of the first piece as being 120 per minute and that of the second piece as 30 per minute!—the moot point being, what *is* a basic pulse? It was agreed that it was a regular pulse, a beat to which you could tap your foot. But some feet are inclined to tap at a faster or slower rate than others, twice as fast or half as fast. Identification of the underlying beat or basic pulse tends to be subjective.

We decided to try the other end of the G-S line. What was the fastest pulse in the piece, discounting momentary doubling or tripling characteristic of rhythmic ornamentation? Although no one could say what the slowest pulse of a piece might be, everyone agreed that each piece has a fastest pulse. This measuring device was dubbed the Density Referent (DR). If the DR for the pieces in one tradition was around 600 ppm (pulses per minute) and the DR for representative pieces from another tradition was around 200 ppm, we knew something specific about each tradition in terms of the relative density of musical events and had in addition comparative information that the music of one tradition had a density of musical events three times that of the other.

So much for relative density. But what can this approach tell us about tempo? In tabulating changes of tempo it is at least as convenient as the foot-tapping method and is more reliable for comparative purposes. If the tempo accelerates to the point of actually doubling, the foot-tapping pulse is likely to be cut in half—an arbitrary decision by the foot-tapper, depending on the speed of his initial designation of basic pulse. By sticking to the S end of the line, there is no question as to whether the DR doubles with a doubling of tempo: it either does or does not. Approaching the point at which the tempo doubles, if the DR is cut in half, because continued acceleration is unplayable, it suggests that perhaps our very concept of tempo needs to be reexamined.

In the European tradition of music, one is inclined to think of tempo as the *governing* aspect of time, which regulates such specific divisions as meter, rhythm, and density. Whatever the metrical, rhythmical, and density divisions of a Western score, the musician's first question is always "What is the tempo?" It is possible that in some cultures such a question is either not of primary concern

114

or even that it is altogether inappropriate. We should bear in mind two points: (1) many cultures of the non-Western world, especially those using some form of stratification, recognize only a few basic tempos, and (2) in the European tradition by contrast, as we observed in connection with loudness, there is a wide range of recognized tempos. To anticipate momentarily, I am suggesting that the Western range of tempos, like the Western range of loudness, may have little or no application to African and Asian music. Our Density Referent, on the other hand, seems to accommodate the situation quite well.

By way of illustration, let us pursue further the earlier discussion of Javanese tempos: irama I, II, and III. When we say the music becomes slower by getting faster, what do we mean? Can "irama I, II, and III" really be translated as "tempos I, II, and III"? Such an explanation is quite common.[24] As someone guilty of this kind of cross-cultural oversimplification, I can attest to the fact that the habit of one-word or single-phrase translations tends to obscure significant differences in musical concepts from one culture to another. Although in Javanese music there are several uses of the word "irama,"[25] its basic implication appears to be not so much a matter of "speed" or pulses per minute as an indication of the relationship, in terms of relative density, among thirty to forty levels of stratification. Irama I, II, and III represent three different relationships between the fastest, regularly recurring pulse—the DR—and all other strata of lesser density. Within any one of the three plateaus of tempo, and even to some extent within transitional accelerations or ritards, the DR of Javanese gamelan remains fairly close to what I have termed "saturation density." That is, the fastest pulse of certain improvising instruments operates within the rather narrow limits of the fastest possible, but physically comfortable, density. In several places, I have mentioned the Javanese sense of perfect time. Saturation density, a filling up of all possible time units, is a hallmark of polyphonic stratification in Javanese gamelan and may be a principal factor in developing this acute sensitivity to perfect time.

Some musical ensembles in Ghana—for example, among the Ewe, the Ashanti, the Fanti, and other Akan peoples—also appear to be operating close to saturation density. But in these instances, the DR is established, not by a single stratum of individual instruments, as in the Javanese gamelan, but by the resultant of interlocking pulses supplied by the total ensemble. In other words, the individual parts played by various drums, bells, and rattles may not have a particularly high density, but the manner in which they are combined produces a resultant that approaches saturation density. It appears that these Ghanaian musicians have not

---

[24] Kunst, *op. cit.*, p. 333.
[25] See further *ibid.*, p. 639.

115

developed "perfect time" in the sense it is known among Javanese but instead have achieved a nearly absolute perception of saturation density. A master drummer perceives immediately even a fractional displacement of a stroke by any drum, bell, or rattle.

If Western and non-Western conceptions of time are different, as these preliminary studies seem to indicate, then a universal music notation must accommodate both the Western tradition of a wide range of tempos and the African and Asian traditions of DR and saturation density. Neither requirement is in conflict with the other, but each must be capable of representation in a symbolic configuration. This aspect of the notation system should also include a designation as to whether a tradition operates within perfect or relative time.

The recognition of basic requirements in the notation of Western tempo, non-Western DR, and perfect or relative time will afford the proper foundation for the intricacies of rhythmic notation. Melograph Model C gives promise of a solution to the problem of rhythmic subtleties. The representation of duration, which on this laboratory instrument can be refined through the graphic display of attack, decay, and release, might be based on a modification of the symbols employed for discreet or indeterminant pitch. With this refinement in display, different types of accent would require modification of the symbols to indicate variants in: (1) duration itself, (2) loudness, (3) metrical pulse, (4) timbre. Or, considering the gestalt of these requirements, it might be better to devise a unique symbolic configuration unrelated to that of pitch.

Pitch. Symbolic representation of pitch should take into account the following: (1) it should be coded for (a) standardized pitch and interval (e.g., Western music) or (b) the known range of variable pitch and interval (e.g., Javanese gamelan) or (c) specifications in cycles per second and cents for a specific example as a refinement of the coding for (b); (2) the total compass of pitch (e.g., in Javanese gamelan slightly less than seven octaves); (3) the principal pitches of the tradition (e.g., twelve in Western music; three, four, five, six, or seven in Balinese music); (4) an indication of recognized microtones used within a specific tuning system (e.g., twelve microtones in addition to the five-tone sléndro system of the Sundanese, five in addition to the five-tone sléndro system of the Javanese); (5) a differentiation that would show the hierarchy of pitches associated with mode, chant, "pillar tones," and so forth; (6) monomial symbols which in various composites represent all varieties of ornamentation; (7) the special requirements of attack and release.

The Quality of Sound. Symbols representing the quality of sound, as we have suggested before, should indicate timbre as it may be modified by attack, decay, and release. Timbre itself might be sufficiently represented by some approach similar to the one illustrated in our discussion of the world of oboes. Or

116

it could be further refined by taking into account characteristic differences of different registers of an instrument or voice. Or, if the tradition required it, symbolic modification might be required to indicate controlled change of timbre within a given register as an aspect of musical style. Sufficient sampling on the Melograph should establish a "library" of musical envelopes (attack, decay, release); classification of the materials in such a library would constitute an important foundation for comparative studies and indicate the magnitude of the symbolic configuration required.

In addition to the Melograph, two other approaches are being investigated at UCLA in relation to timbre. The first, less refined than the Melogram, is a digital comparison which we have termed Quality Index (timbre index would be a more accurate designation, but habit has sanctified the label "QI").[26] The QI machine, still in an early stage of development, establishes the fulcrum point at which the prominent and weak partials are in perfect balance. Different registers in the compass of one instrument or voice or the total compass of different instruments and voices can be compared on the basis of this fulcrum. Each side of the fulcrum can also be measured, thereby establishing two additional fulcrums, for more refined comparison.

The second approach to a comparative recognition of timbre we have called the Hardness Scale for Quality (HSQ). Thus far, it remains a purely subjective rating of musical instruments on a scale from 1 to 10, 1 indicating the simplest partial structure and 10 the most complex. When these subjective ratings have been revised on the basis of precise laboratory measurements, we shall arbitrarily select ten examples from the world of musical instruments against which the relative hardness of all others can be quickly, if somewhat grossly, measured. As a refinement of this approach, it might be desirable to establish a separate HSQ for each family of instruments. Both the QI machine and the HSQ offer less refined information than is available in a Melogram, but each may have important application in relation to the different levels of information that should be contained in a universal system of music notation.

Loudness. The registration of loudness is subject to several variables: the size of the ensemble, the nearness or farness of the perceiver, the acoustical relationship of both these to the environment, and to some degree the climate of relative humidity and temperature.[27] A Balinese gamelan orchestra of forty or more musicians heard, let us say, in a large, heated theater in New York City

[26] See further Leon Knopoff, "An Index for the Relative Quality among Musical Instruments," *Ethnomusicology*, vol. 7, no. 3 (Sept., 1963), pp. 229–233.

[27] Vern Knudsen, "The Effect of Humidity upon the Absorption of Sound, and a Determination of the Coefficients of Absorption of Sound in Air," *Journal of the Acoustical Society of America*, vol. 3, no. 1 (July, 1931), pp. 126–188.

117

in the month of November gives quite a different impression of loudness when compared to a performance by the same ensemble in the village of Pliatan playing outdoors on a warm humid night in South Bali. We have already indicated that the wide range and gradation of loudness characteristic of Western music offer a questionable measuring stick for non-Western musical cultures that operate within a limited gradation of loudness. Tape and disc recordings give no indication of the actual range of decibels involved relative to the variables mentioned above.

What order of information about loudness is appropriate for a universal system of music notation? Do all the variables render this aspect of music meaningless?—or so relative that from a universal point of view there is no way to measure loudness? Let us speculate on an approach that in time might accumulate considerable usefulness. Returning to our discussion of the Chinese chin in relation to loudness, we might suggest that there are two significant aspects of loudness that a notation ought to convey: (1) the fact that the chin has a very small sound and (2) within that range of small sound there are differences in loudness that are an important aspect of musical style. It should not be too difficult to invent a symbolic representation for these two kinds of information, once we have established some mode of reference that is valid in a universal application. To create a standard, we might begin by establishing a Hardness Scale for Loudness (HSL), for example, by dividing 120 decibels (db) into ten divisions: 1, 1–12 db; 2, 13–24 db; 3, 25–36 db; and so forth.

Let us assume that next we measure a performance on the chin in its traditional environment at a distance from the instrument where the listener would ideally be located. I have chosen an extreme example; traditionally the chin is played for one's own enjoyment. So our measurements will be taken in the approximate location of the performer's own ears. In decibel readings, we learn that the total dynamic range of the instrument lies in the 1–2 range of the HSL, that is, from 1 db to 24 db. Turning now to a consideration of musical style, we note that there are four levels of loudness characteristic of the instrument: (1) at the lowest level, the sound produced by changing the position of the left hand stopping the string *after* the initial plucking by the right hand, depressing the string to change pitch, and similar techniques; (2) the sound of harmonics;[28] (3) normal plucking by the right hand and scraping or rubbing the string by the left hand; (4) plucking two strings at one time. In summary: the chin produces four levels of loudness within the 1–2 range of the HSL. Similar measurements of a large Balinese gamelan might reveal that it has five levels of loudness within the 3–10 range of the HSL. A Western string quartet playing in a chamber salon might have eighteen levels within the 2–6 range of the HSL.

[28] An ethereal sound produced by lightly touching the string with the left hand at one of the nodes of the upper partials, the "harmonics" of the fundamental pitch.

Scale	1	2	3	4	5	6	7	8	9	10
Decibels	1-12	13-24	25-36	37-48	49-60	61-72	73-84	85-96	97-108	109-120
Chin										
Balinese gong kebyar										
String quartet										
Amplified hard rock group										

Illustration 2-39
A diagrammatic comparison, for the sake of illustration only, of four different traditions.

These projections, of course, are based on subjective guesswork for the sake of illustration in our speculations. If the ethnomusicologist added to his field equipment a decibel meter, it would not take too long to establish the number of levels of loudness for different traditions and their place within the range of the Hardness Scale for Loudness. Giving free reign to the imagination for a moment, someday we might be able to produce a number of comparative charts like the one invented for Illustration 2-39. Symbolic representation of these particulars would be a simple matter.

More to Come. The basic guidelines suggested here in relation to the kind of information needed for implementing the Laban Solution are by no means exhaustive. They do, however, indicate the order of information required and furnish illustration of some of the laboratory developments that will replace subjective differences of opinion with objective measurements. No one scholar, no one center or institution, in my judgment, can achieve this final stage of the Composite Solution in isolation. If students and professionals alike in the field of ethnomusicology can arrive at a reasonable consensus in approaching the problem, then we can safely assume that a major hurdle in our race against the threats of our technological time has been cleared.

Ignoring the question posed earlier as to whether specific symbols in Labanotation might withstand transfer to our universal music notation, let us emphasize one significant feature of this symbolic language for dance. Some of the basic symbols give a visual suggestion of the parts of the body they represent. This is an important visual aid in learning, memorizing, and acquiring fluency in reading a complex system of notation. The staff (see Illustration 2-40) is oriented to a center line and reads up the page with horizontal divisions marking off time units. The symbol for the head, C , for the pelvic girdle, ▣ , for the torso, (torso symbol), for the foot, ≣ , are simple visual abstractions of the body parts represented.

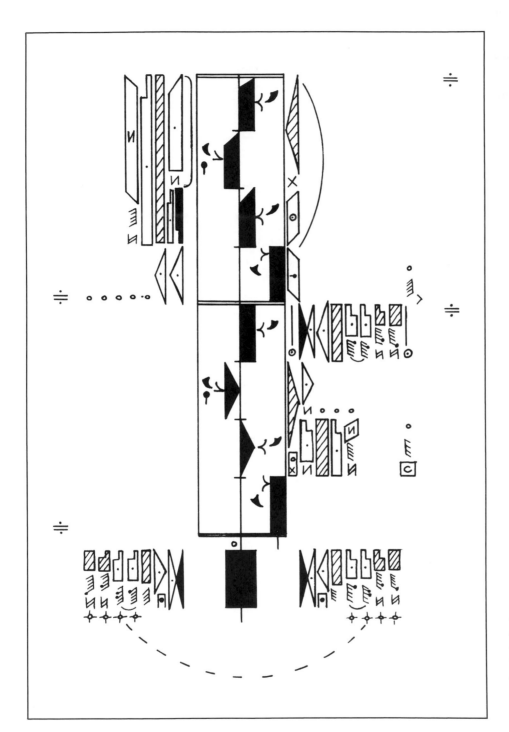

Illustration 2-40
An example of Labanotation
of Bharata Natyam adavu,
notated by Judy Miner,
August, 1970.

The location of these symbols, right or left, in relation to the center line and the addition of various monomial symbols indicate change and direction of movement, accent, tension, and so forth.

Further details of this system of notation can and should be learned from Ann Hutchinson's publication. If I were running a dormitory for ethnomusicologists, I would insist that each inmate sleep with a copy of the *Harvard Dictionary of Music* under his pillow and a copy of *Labanotation* under his feet. Emanations from both sources would supply subliminal regeneration for the heart of the ethnomusicologist all night long.

The basic format of Labanotation is worth considering as a model for a universal music notation. The vertical staff reading up the page offers no resistance to reading habits of left to right or right-to-left. Its orientation to a center line could represent the center of the musical compass being notated. Basic symbols used to represent different aspects of the musical fabric might give some visual suggestion of the thing symbolized. Who knows, perhaps the wavy lines of the veteran of the Korean War, the would-be composer, are a reasonable abstraction of melodic contour—if we were to add a reference grid representing whatever particulars were entered in the coding of pitch (see Illustrations 2-30 and 2-31). A similar representation, but in a unique location on the staff, could accommodate loudness: the grid coded according to the Hardness Scale at the beginning of the score and fluctuations in loudness represented by a wavy line. Both pitch and loudness take this form of graphic display on the Melogram. Abstracting them in a vertical arrangement would be quite easy. The family, genus, species, and subspecies of quality that are displayed on the Melogram might also be abstracted in characteristic shapes that with a little practice could be read as easily as the changing clefs of Western notation—with the notable difference that the abstraction of the Melogram would constitute a composite symbol containing much more information.

And so forth, and so forth, until through trial and error, rejection and acceptance, we finally realize the Laban Solution to the problem of notation and transcription. Surely no self-respecting musician—notwithstanding his essentially conservative bent and lifelong conditioning to primitive forms of notation—is willing to concede that the field of dance has forevermore a symbolic language superior to anything known in the field of music.

If by now our beginning graduate student is feeling a bit giddy after the tortuous maze he has been following in pursuit of the problems of notation and transcription, it might help him regain his balance and resolve by pointing out that probably no other field in the humanities demands such a degree of pioneering spirit. In this supersophisticated age, when the obvious frontiers are thought to

121

be limited to outer space and the ocean floor, isn't it exciting to know that the stone adze or the machete of our ancestors must be picked up again in a different kind of attack on the wilderness?

If that touch of poetic license has the heart pounding, strong and steady, we can face together another kind of problem in the next chapter, which, in spite of its title, comprises a logical extension of our discussion of notation.

Chapter Three

ORGANOLOGY

MUSICAL INSTRUMENTS can provide information vital to the work of the ethnomusicologist. Let us consider one fundamental question and its consequent: "What unique information is represented by a musical instrument?" "What is the most practicable form in which such information can be made available?"

MUSICAL INSTRUMENTS AS A UNIQUE SOURCE OF INFORMATION

Even though it is not found in the *Harvard Dictionary of Music*, the term "organology" has gained wide acceptance in the oral tradition among musicologists. As it is commonly applied to music, the term tends to be limited to description of the physical features, acoustical properties, and history of musical instruments. I suggest the revival of a more accurate term for the descriptive concentration, namely, "organography," defined in the second edition of Webster's unabridged dictionary as "1. A description of instruments. *Obs.*"

Organology—the science of musical instruments—should include not only the history and description of instruments but also equally important but neglected aspects of "the science" of musical instruments, such as particular techniques of performance, musical function, decoration (as distinct from construction), and a variety of socio-cultural considerations.

ORGANOGRAPHY

Principal Systems of Classification. Only the musical cultures of China, India, and Western Europe have developed a taxonomy for musical instruments. The ancient Chinese classification is based on eight materials: metal, stone, earth, skin, silk, gourd, bamboo, and wood.[1] The Indian system, described in the *Natyashastra*, dating from about the first century B.C., consists of four groups: (1) cymbals, gongs, bells, and the like, (2) drums, (3) strings, (4) winds. In 1880, Victor Mahillon, curator of the instrumental collection of the Brussels Conservatory, developed a system of classification, which was revised and expanded in 1914 by Curt Sachs and Erich von Hornbostel.[2] The four basic groups of the European system are like those of the Indian classification:

Idiophones	Characteristic vibration determined by the nature of the material, free of any kind of applied tension (e.g., cymbals, gongs, bells, wood blocks, rattles)
Membranophones	Characteristic vibration of stretched skin or other membrane (e.g., drums)
Chordophones	Characteristic vibration of stretched strings (e.g., lutes, lyres, zithers, harps)
Aerophones	Characteristic vibration of an air column (e.g., flutes, trumpets, clarinets, oboes)

Among some Western performing musicians, reference is still made to a three-part division: percussion, strings, and winds—the last sometimes subdivided into woodwinds and brass. The first, unlike the other two, refers to a method of

[1] See further Georges Soulié, *La Musique en Chine*, E. Leroux, Paris, 1911, p. 25; and Maurice Courant, "Essai historique sur la musique classique des Chinois, avec un appendice relatif á la musique coréenne," in Albert Lavignac, *Encyclopédie de la musique et dictionnaire du Conservatoire*, Part I, vol. I, Librarie Delagrave, Paris, 1922, p. 80.

[2] Erich M. von Hornbostel and Curt Sachs, "Systematik der Musikinstrumente," *Zeitschrift für Ethnologie*, vol. 46, nos. 4–5 (1914), pp. 553–590; also see English translation by Anthony Baines and Klaus P. Wachsmann, "Classification of Musical Instruments," *Galpin Society Journal*, vol. 14 (1961), pp. 4–29.

playing and includes such diverse instruments as gongs, drums, and the piano, a mixture of types that spreads across the first three groups of the Sachs-Hornbostel system. Very few scholars, however, cling to this outmoded terminology.

The Sachs-Hornbostel classification has achieved wide endorsement, but there has been some valid criticism of the system. Kunst draws attention to the following weaknesses:

> Each of the...four main groups has naturally been subdivided. In this subdivision, however, there is not the same unity of criterion as seen in the main groups. The idiophones are classed and arranged according to the playing method; the membranophones, in the first instance, also according to the playing method, but further according to shape; the chordophones are first split into two groups, i.e., that of the simple, and that of the composite instruments, and they are further classified according to shape; in the case of the aerophones we first find a division into "free" aerophones and wind instruments proper, after which the latter group is again subdivided according to the manner in which they are blown. In this subdivision, therefore, homogeneity of criterion is again conspicuous by its absence. Von Hornbostel and Sachs, of course, intended this to be so; indeed, they say, in their Introduction:... "Since we purposely refrained from subjecting the various groups to some homogeneous principle, and, on the contrary, adapted the basis of our subdivisions in each case to the typical character of the group in question, certain subgroups of the same order of precedence are not always coordinated in our system."[3]

After reviewing other approaches to classification, largely inspired by similar criticism of the Sachs-Hornbostel system,[4] Kunst concludes: "I have thought best to adhere to Mahillon's system, as perfected by von Hornbostel and Sachs; my own experience being that only in extremely rare cases does it let the investigator down."[5]

If the student of ethnomusicology acquaints himself with the several approaches mentioned by Kunst in his survey,[6] he will begin to appreciate some of the difficulties peculiar to the task of creating a logical system of instrumental classification. Perhaps as Sachs and Hornbostel decided, it may not be too important that their subdivisions lack consistency in the criteria on which they are founded. On the other hand, it is likely that attempts to improve the system or to devise a different and better taxonomy will continue to provide a fascinating

---

[3] Jaap Kunst, *Ethnomusicology*, 3rd ed., Martinus Nijhoff, The Haque, 1959, p. 59.
[4] See further Kunst's overview of different approaches to instrumental classification, *ibid.*, pp. 55–63.
[5] *Ibid.*, p. 61.
[6] Especially those of André Schaeffner, "Projet d'une nouvelle classification méthodique des instruments de musique," *Revue musicale*, vol. 13, no. 129 (Sept.–Oct., 1932), pp. 215–231; and Hans Heinz Dräger, *Prinzip einer systematik der Musikinstrumente*, Bärenreiter-Verlag, Kassel, 1948.

challenge. Tackling the problems of instrumental classification constitutes a worthy exercise for the student's critical faculties.

Rather than criticize further the established system or the work of its critics, I want to introduce certain areas of consideration that take us beyond the usual requirements of descriptive taxonomy. I must admit at the outset that this line of thought further compounds the problem. But if better solutions are in the hands of succeeding generations of students, then these researchers of tomorrow should be armed with whatever pertinent experience may have emerged from the activities of the doers of today.

Let us repeat the questions with which this chapter began: "What unique information is represented by a musical instrument?" "What is the most practicable form in which such information can be made available?"

Physical Description. As an illustrative procedure we might examine the requirements of the first question by sampling the G-S line from one end to the other. Earlier, we illustrated some of the problems of the Laban Solution to notation by considering one type of multiple-reed aerophone; for the sake of variety we might now consider the family of membranophones. The family designation makes it clear that these musical instruments are characterized, through one or another medium of excitation, by the vibrations of a stretched membrane. Even this most general information may be of some value in comparative studies. The aborigines of Australia, for example, lack such an instrument. Their only "drum" is the ubar, a hollow log played with a stick and classified, therefore, as an idiophone (see Illustration 3-1). After the family designation, the

Illustration 3-1
Decorating the ubar of Australia; from Heinrich Besseler and Max Schneider (eds.), Musikgeschichte in Bildern, *vol. 1, part 1 ("Ozeanien," by Paul Collaer), VEB Deutscher Verlag für Musik, Leipzig, 1965, pl. 63, p. 109.*

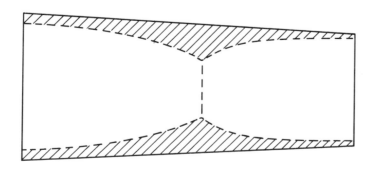

Illustration 3-2
Photograph of Balinese
kendang showing the external
conical shape.

description of a drum might indicate whether it has a stretched membrane on only one end of the shell or frame or on both ends. Perhaps next in the order of description we should know the basic shape of the shell: barrel-shaped, cylindrical, conical, bowl-shaped, hourglass-shaped, a frame, or some other form.

In any classification system, the basic shape of a drum is an order of information that is still quite general in terms of the G-S line of instrumental description. Even at this level, however, we encounter a serious oversight in the taxonomy of the established system. The external shape of a drum, its basic conformation, is an important and easily recognizable aspect of description. But the sound produced by the drum depends on the *internal* shape of the shell, a fundamental aspect of description that has not yet been accommodated. If, for example, we classify the Balinese kendang used in gamelan gong kebyar according

Illustration 3-3
Drawing showing the hour-
glass internal shape of the
Balinese kendang.

127

Illustration 3-4
Photograph of the Ashanti atumpan showing its external shape,
a bowl standing on a foot.

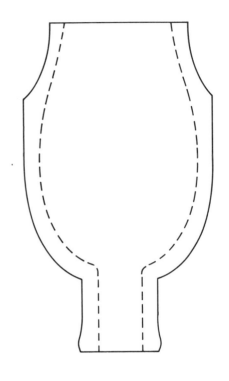

Illustration 3-5
Drawing showing the
internal shape of the
atumpan, showing the com-
pound structure of a bowl
opening into a cylinder.

to the Sachs-Hornbostel Dewey decimal system, it would be represented by the numbers 211.25. The fifth digit indicates that this particular drum has a conical shape—quite valid, as far as it goes. But the internal shape of the instrument, which determines its sound characteristics, is in the shape of an hourglass, 211.24 in the taxonomic symbols for external shape (see Illustrations 3-2 and 3-3). The Ashanti atumpan, judging from its external shape, is a bowl, like a timpani (211.1), standing on a foot. But the foot is hollow, so that the internal shape is compound,

128

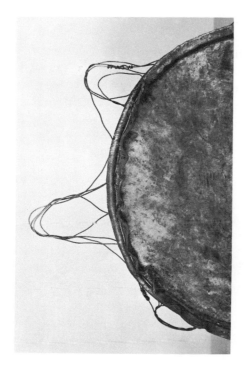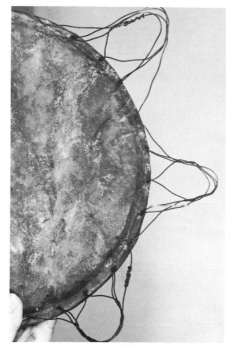

Illustration 3-6
The atumpan head is wired
onto a supporting hoop of
rattan.

a bowl (211.1) opening into a cylinder (211.21)[7] (compare Illustrations 3-4 and 3-5). If the foot were solid, the drum would have quite a different sound.

An efficient taxonomy must accommodate both principles of construction: external shape as a basic visual identification and internal shape as the determinant of characteristic sound. Both are important to descriptive, analytical, and comparative methods. Another principle of construction included near the G end of the line is the manner in which the head or heads are attached to the shell—for example, laced, nailed, pegged, glued, and so forth. The precise style of lacing, nailing, or pegging is another hallmark of descriptive information.[8] The particular manner in which a laced head is fixed by its supporting hoop may also be extremely important for comparative purposes, as the examples in Illustrations 3-6, 3-7, and 3-8 indicate. A drumhead may be single or compound; for example, the mridangam of southern India has three skins on the right head and three on the left. It is important to know whether the heads are tuned and if so by what manual or mechanical devices—for example, by pounding the rim or covered hoop with a

[7] 211.2 designates a tubular shape; 211.21, cylindrical; 211.22, barrel-shaped; and so forth.

[8] In the Sachs-Hornbostel system, the designation of these features is assigned to a suffix: -6, -61, and so forth.

129

stone or a metal or wooden hammer, by increasing the tension by sliding rings or moving tuning blocks on the lacing (see Illustrations 3-9 and 3-10), by tightening mechanical dogs (Illustration 3-11), by wetting the heads, by heating the heads, by applying tuning paste. We should also know whether the heads are tuned to precise or to relative pitches and to what they relate. For example, the tabla and bayam of northern India are usually tuned to the sa (tonic) of the raga, while the two ntumpan of the atumpan (the pair) are tuned, by wetting the heads and pounding in the pegs which support the wire or rattan lacing, to a high-low relationship that may vary from one pair of instruments to another from about 300 cents (a minor third) to 1,000 cents (a minor seventh).

Illustration 3-7
The three skins on each head of the South Indian mridan-gam are sewn together with strips of buffalo hide wound around a supporting hoop of one or two strands of buffalo hide.

130

Illustration 3-8
The two heads of the Java-
nese keṭipung are lapped
under their supporting rattan
hoops when wet in such a
way that they bind them-
selves when dry.

Illustration 3-9
Braided rattan or, sometimes,
leather rings are used to
tighten the lacings of the
Javanese kenḍang. Additional
tightening may be accom-
plished by pounding the rim
of the drum head so that the
covered hoop is forced
farther onto the tapered
shell of the drum.

Illustration 3-10
The North Indian tabla is
tuned by pounding the rim
of the head and by adjusting
the tuning blocks.

Illustration 3-11
The head of this type of
Persian dumbak is tuned by
tightening mechanical dogs.

This approach to the physical description of instruments exceeds the order of information included in present systems of classification. It represents unique information fundamental to efficient taxonomy and should be included as a standard procedure in organography.

Now let us move from organography to a broader consideration of organology.

TECHNIQUES OF PERFORMANCE   We should have precise information about the means of excitation. If the drum is played with the hand or a stick or the heel of the foot, we should know which hand and which heel does what. (See Illustrations 3-12, 3-13, and 3-14.) We should also know whether the *shell* of the drum is struck, as, for example, in the style of the master drum of the Ewe (Illustration 3-15), in which the stick held in the right hand plays both drumhead and shell. We need not debate whether this instrument is, therefore, both a membranophone and an idiophone—any more than we need ask whether striking the body of a guitar makes it a chordophone-idiophone; or whether the technique in playing Japanese shamisen, in which the plectrum (bachi) strikes both the string and the stretched membrane of the sound box, makes it a chordophone-membranophone. The family of each is clear in terms of its source of "characteristic vibration."

The method of playing should include information about the relationship between performer and instrument. Is it held in a stand, vertically, horizontally,

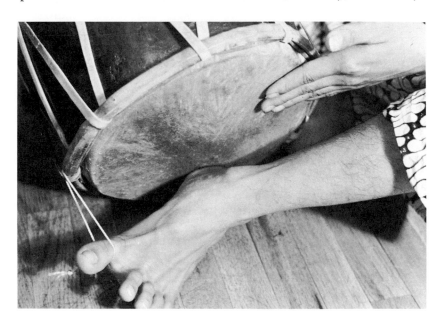

Illustration 3-12
The Sundanese drummer of West Java applies tension with his heel to obtain a wide range of pitch.

133

Illustration 3-13
The Ga musician of Ghana uses his heel to effect changes of pitch in playing
the frame drum.

134

Illustration 3-14
In one style of drumming, the Balinese musician uses a stick on the large head of the kendang and his hand on the small head.

135

*Illustration 3-15
Both the head and the shell
of the Ewe master drum of
Ghana are struck by the
stick.*

at an angle, between the player's legs, across his lap, under his arm, over his shoulder, slung at his side, in one hand, surrounding him in a circle, mounted on horseback, hanging in a tree, carried by someone else?

MUSICAL FUNCTION   We should also know something about the musical function of the drum (or any other musical instrument). A picture of a drum, a detailed description of its physical and acoustical features, its construction, the materials of which it is made, the manner in which it is played, its location in relation to the player—all these remain mute evidence in terms of its musical role. It might be argued that this is more properly the concern of analysis, that organology could hardly be expected to include *musical* information per se, that our requirements thus far have already exceeded the normal expectations of a system of instrumental classification. But our original question was "What unique information is represented by a musical instrument?" We are not classifying flora or fauna or languages, for which, incidentally, phonology is a correlative concern.

A musical instrument, above all else, is an instrument of music. Certain

Illustration 3-16
The Javanese tjiblon, the
dance drum of Surakarta.

137

basic facts about its musical function comprise an invaluable part of the unique information represented by a musical instrument.

What kind of musical facts might be significant and at the same time practicable within a system of classification? As a start, let us determine where our drum lies on the Hardness Scale for Loudness; assuming it is a Javanese tjiblon, the dance drum of Central Java (Illustration 3-16), let us assign it, for the sake of example, an HSL of 3–8 (25–96 db). The Hardness Scale for Pitch (HSP), arbitrarily spanning a range of ten octaves from 16 cps to 16,384 cps, tells us that the tjiblon has an HSP of 4–5 (129–512 cps). The Melogram for the tjiblon, when matched against the Hardness Scale for Quality, indicates an HSQ of 6. While we are at it, we had better also devise a Hardness Scale for Density (HSD). Given the range of less than 1 pulse per minute ($<$1 ppm) to more than 600 pulses per minute ($>$600 ppm), our HSD would be: 1, $<$1–60 ppm; 2, 61–120 ppm; 3, 121–180 ppm; and so forth. Let us assume that the versatile tjiblon has an HSD of 2–9 (61–540 ppm). A few more examples with the imagination supplying the HSD: the master drum known as the keti used by the Ashanti (Illustration 3-17) might be HSD 3–10 (121–$>$600 ppm); the Javanese beḍug (Illustration 3-18) might be HSD 1 ($<$1–60 ppm); the Japanese taiko used in gagaku (Illustration 3-19) might be HSD 2 (61–120 ppm); and so forth.

A summary of musical information about the batangan can be presented in the following form:

HSL: 3–8
HSP: 4–5
HSQ: 6
HSD: 2–9

This order of information in no way preempts the need for musical analysis; but it provides musical facts that not only are invaluable for comparative purposes but also offer no particular problem for incorporation within a system of instrumental classification.

DECORATION Keeping in mind our guiding question, let us move nearer the S end of the G-S line. Kunst and others have called attention to the fact that in comparative studies it is often the nonessential details of construction that offer the most convincing evidence of some kind of contact and influence between two different cultures.[9] To be more specific, if cultures A and B both use a drum with a stretched membrane on each end of a barrel-shaped shell, a cylindrical inner shape, and heads that are fastened by a so-called Y form of lacing, and the drum

[9] Jaap Kunst, *Cultural Relations between the Balkans and Indonesia*, Publication 107 of the Royal Tropical Institute, Amsterdam, 1954.

138

Illustration 3-17
The Ashanti keti.

139

Illustration 3-18
The Javanese beḍug.

is held across the lap and played with two bare hands, we still cannot say that there is necessarily evidence in these facts of intercultural influence. If, however, we find the same decorative motif incised about two inches from each end of the shell or a flying crane carved on the center of the shell or two slight protuberances raised above the surface of the shell on either side of one end, like two nonfunctional ears or handles or residual stumps that once may have been pegs to which a carrying strap was attached, these nonessential details of construction carry some weight in the accumulation of evidence of cultural contact.

A systematic consideration of decorative details in organology, if Kunst is right, is indispensable to comparative method. Therefore, organography, the physical description of musical instruments, must come to include such information. Perhaps with the help of the art historian acquainted with the details of iconography, we could devise various Hardness Scales for (1) *Techniques,* such as incising, embossing, carving, relief, inlay; (2) *Finishes,* such as paints, oils, lacquers, gold leaf, tempera; and (3) a catalogue of *Motifs,* such as herringbone; cross-hatch; meanders; swastikas; animal, plant, and anthropomorphic design. Such a concern

140

Illustration 3-19
The Japanese taiko used in gagaku. Photograph by Don Chipperfield.

141

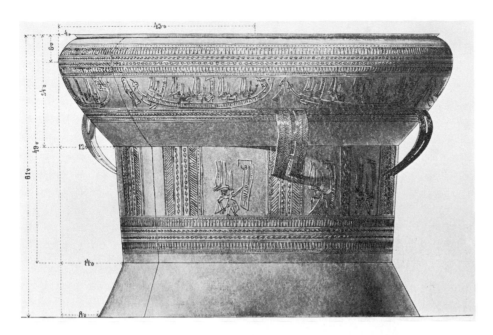

Illustration 3-20
On this bronze drum such designs as the soul ship or ship of the dead, the crane, and characteristic costume and headdress of the warrior are significant decorations. Illustrations 3-20, 3-21, and 3-22 are from Franz Heger, Alte Metalltrommeln aus Südost-Asien, Kommisions-Verlag von Karl W. Hiersemann, Leipzig, 1902, vol. 2 (Tafelband), pls. I, VII, and VIII, respectively.

Illustration 3-21
On this bronze drum abstract designs, including a styliza-tion of the soul ship, as well as the sculptured figures on the top, are significant decorations.

142

has been extremely important among the numerous studies devoted to an instrument like the bronze drums of Southeast Asia and the Far East.[10] (See Illustrations 3-20, 3-21, and 3-22.) Perhaps it should be noted in the context of our present discussion that the so-called bronze drums are actually idiophones.

SOCIO-CULTURAL CONSIDERATIONS   With some help from the ethnologist as well as from indigenous musicians of cultures under study, we might be able to establish Hardness Scales for another kind of unique information associated with musical instruments. Aside from anthropomorphic clues in decoration or shape, we should know whether a drum is regarded as male or female and whether these

[10] For an excellent summary of the literature, see Van Heerkeren, "The Bronze-Iron Age of Indonesia," *Verhandelingen van het Koninklijk Instituut voor Taal-, Land- en Volkenkunde*, vol. 22, Martinus Nijhoff, The Hague, 1958.

Illustration 3-22
The top of the bronze drum shown in Illustration 3-21 includes a central star with twelve rays and stylization of the flying cranes.

143

designations are associated respectively with high and low pitches or vice versa. Is the drum reserved for players of one or the other sex? Is it or the ensemble to which it belongs the exclusive property of a special group in society? Has it special associations with persons of high social status or low social status? How is it regarded in the Hardness Scale of Values by the whole society? By a special group in the society? By the performer? What is its monetary value compared to other instruments in the society? Does it carry a proper name of its own? Does it represent the souls of the ancestors or the soul of the tree from which it was made? Are offerings made or libations poured in recognition of this connection with the ancestors? Is it believed to have some magic power? Is there ritual connected with its manufacture? Is the instrument maker accorded a special status in his society? Is the player also the maker of the instrument? Does the drum have an indispensable role in the life cycle of man?

These considerations of our basic question have not been exhaustive but are illustrative of the kinds of information the ethnomusicologist finds significant in his study of musical instruments. I hope that tomorrow's researchers will be inspired to a more systematic and more exhaustive pursuit of the problem than I can include within the scope of this essay.

Now we are ready for the consequent of our first question, namely, "What is the most practicable form in which such information can be made available?" Once again our procedure will be illustrative rather than exhaustive.

SYMBOLIC TAXONOMY: ORDERLY PHYLA

Inspired by the symbolic language of Labanotation, suppose we consider the possibility of a symbolic taxonomy for musical instruments. The Dewey decimal system of the Sachs-Hornbostel classification has a strong advantage in that one can extend the decimals to infinity to accommodate any degree of detail. On the other side of the coin, however, it is difficult to carry around in one's head long chains of variable numbers. For the sake of speculation, let us try out a set of basic symbols and follow through with a consideration of possible genera and species. We shall include *five* basic families, as shown in the margin, in recognition of developments in the latter half of the twentieth century.

Perhaps we are stretching the importance of an abstract resemblance between symbol and object represented, but it may serve as a starting point to let a square represent the myriad forms of the idiophone by rationalizing that it could remind us of a wooden box (or wood block). The horizontal rectangle might suggest a drum, even through membranophones take all kinds of shape. The vertical rectangle might suggest the cello, the rebab, a koto propped against the wall waiting for its player, or any other mnemonic association we care to

Idiophones

Membranophones

Chordophones

Aerophones

Electronophones

devise. The circle is not too farfetched to suggest the large family of aerophones related by a vibrating column of air. So far as I know, the diamond has nothing to do with electronics; but at least it provides a form that is distinct from the other four.

To accommodate genus, species, and subspecies, these five basic shapes might be segmented as shown in the margin, so that each resulting symbol retains a unique identity. Perhaps not all or perhaps even more segments would be needed in each family if the details of the system were worked out.

A similar approach was considered for the sake of illustration in representing various qualities in one species of the family of aerophones in our discussion of the Laban Solution to notation. We divided the aerophone circle into two genera: reed-vibrated aerophones represented by ⟨ and edge-vibrated instruments represented by ⟩. The former was subdivided into two species: single-reed, ◁, and multiple-reed, ⊔. The latter also might be subdivided into two species: one in which the player's lips direct air to excite vibrations in the air column, ◻, for example, the Western flute, the Japanese shakuhachi (Illustration 3-23); and the other in which some intermediary device directs the flow of air, ▱, for example, the Sundanese ring-stop flute (Illustration 3-24), the recorder or fipple flute.

Some organologists might recommend that more than four species are required. So, the family symbol for aerophones given above has been divided into eight parts. Now we can split the species for instruments with air supplied directly by the player, △, into two species: one representing instruments *without* keys, valves, springs, and pads, ▷, for example, the shakuhachi; and the other representing instruments *with* mechanical additions, ◁, for example, the Western flute. A similar division can be made in all the other quadrants of the circle. Any number of species, however defined, can be accommodated through this process, as long as each resulting segment of the aerophone circle retains a unique shape when positioned in relation to a perpendicular and a horizontal line dividing the circle, ⊕. More and/or different genera also can be symbolized in this way if desirable.

Let us return to the membranophones for a moment. Arbitrarily we might create four genera based on the following general shapes:

Membranophones

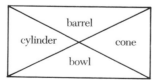

Idiophones

Membranophones

Chordophones

Aerophones

Electronophones

145

Species within the genera might be represented by the following segmentation:

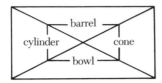

This would permit, for example, two species within the genus of cylinder, ▷, that could represent a double-headed cylindrical drum, ▯, and a single-headed drum, ▷. We might represent an hourglass shape by introducing a symbol for "deformation" of the cylinder indicating that it is squeezed in at the middle, for example, ▷ and ▷. Similar species divisions would also be appropriate for the other quadrants of the rectangle. Additional deformation symbols could be designed for the round or square frame drum, the goblet shape, and so forth.

Suppose we move over to the other side of the chessboard and take a critical look at our last few moves. As far as we have gone with aerophones and membranophones, each symbol has retained its unique identity. But the motivation for this line of attack—producing orderly phyla of families, genera, species, and subspecies—has resulted in the loss of one important feature of symbolic notation; that is, a visual reminder of the object represented, like the Laban symbols for foot, ≑; torso, ▣; pelvic girdle, ◙; and so forth. It is true that ◁ reminds us of a cone; but ▽ looks like anything but a barrel!

SYMBOLIC NOTATION: THE ORGANOGRAM

Ignoring the scientific serenity that justifies the desire for orderly phyla, let us try a counterattack on the problem and begin again with the symbol for membranophones, letting practical considerations guide our moves.

Remembering the ideal requirements established in answer to our basic question concerning information unique to a musical instrument, I have invented a pair of drums by way of illustrating another approach to the symbolic notation of musical instruments. The final result will be a composite symbol, with apologies to the Chinese chin, a kind of ideogram that packs in a lot of unique information in a visual form that is not too difficult to assimilate. We might call it the "organogram."

146

Illustration 3-23
The Japanese shakuhachi.

147

Illustration 3-24
The Sundanese suling.

148

Beginning with the basic rectangle indicating membranophones

we add a line above it that tells us that the internal shape is a cylinder

and another line above that representing the external shape of a barrel

If we were representing the Balinese kendang mentioned earlier, which has the external shape of a cone and the internal shape of an hourglass, it would look like this:

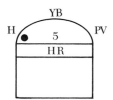

Returning to our pair of imaginary drums, let us add the following letters to the top part of the composite symbols:

Reading from left to right we learn that the drum is tuned with a H(ammer), has Y lacing and tuning B(locks), is tuned to a P(recise) pitch, rather than R(elative) pitch, that is V(ariable) through playing technique. HR tells us that the heads are lapped over the shell or body of the drum held in place by a H(oop) R(ing) rather than a C(ord) R(ing). The number 5 refers to a Hardness Scale for Materials based

149

on a modification of the Chinese system of classification and indicates the material from which the shell is made: 1, gourd; 2, earth; 3, skin; 4, plastic; 5, wood; 6, bamboo; 7, bone; 8, glass; 9, stone; 10, metal. In rating this list of different materials from 1 to 10, I am aware that the order is subjective; whether metal (10) can scratch stone (9) depends on whether we are talking about vanadium steel and sandstone or lead and granite. But a standard of hardness per se is, of course, not intended, but merely offers a convenient expression of scale.

The next portion of the composite

indicates at the top of the rectangle that the drum has two heads, rather than one

and at the bottom of the symbol shows that the left head (player's left) is a composite of two skins and the right three skins.

In the next representation, we learn that the double-headed drum

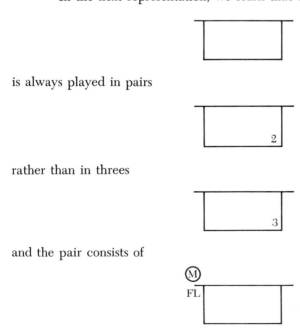

is always played in pairs

rather than in threes

and the pair consists of

150

M(ale) and F(emale) with the latter being the L(ower) in pitch; the circle around the M, Ⓜ, indicates that the drums can be played only by males rather than by females, Ⓕ.

From the following portion of the composite

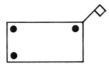

we learn that the drums are played with both left and right hands and the heel of the left foot, which affects variable pitch

We see that the right hand also wields a stick, ╱ , which sometimes strikes the shell, ⟋◇. The square on the end of the stick is a reminder of the idiophone group, ▢. If only the M(ale) drum had this function, it could be represented by ⟋◈. The stick might be crooked, ⟋ˡ, or be a padded beater, ⟋• , or be mechanically actuated, as in the bass drum of the dance band, ◿• . The next details show that the drum is played in a horizontal position

rather than vertical

or at an angle

and that it is held across the player's lap

instead of being held by a stand

or between his legs

or under his right arm

or left arm

or on his right shoulder

or left shoulder

152

or against his right side

or left side

or by his hand

or surrounding him in a circle

or some O(ther) support from someone else, an animal, or a tree.

The numbers in the following portions

3-8	4-5
6	3-9

represent the Hardness Scale ratings for

Loudness	Pitch
Quality	Density

153

Key letters for these references to Hardness Scales can be omitted by always maintaining the same order

with a possible memory mnemonic: Loud Pitches are Quite Deafening.

The following symbols on the left side of the rectangle

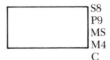

indicate that the pair of drums is associated with a special G(roup) of H(igh), rather than L(ow), social status and the Group's rating for the drums on the Hardness Scale of Value is 9. The two instruments S(ymbolize) the soul of a person, animal, or tree and are honored by O(fferings), rather than L(ibations). The drums have personal N(ames) and are believed to possess magic P(ower). There is R(itual) involved in their manufacture and/or usage. A possible mnemonic: Group (high or low) Symbolizes (with offering or libations) Name (with or without magic power) of Ritual.

On the right side of the rectangle

S(ociety) values the drums at 8, the P(erformer) values them at 9, the M(aker) of the drums enjoys a special S(tatus) (MP if made by the performer), their relative M(onetary) value compared to other instruments in the culture is 4, and the drums are indispensable in the life C(ycle) of man. A possible mnemonic: Some Players Make Money, some Culture.

The figures at the bottom of the rectangle

tell us that on the Hardness Scale for Techniques of decoration the drums rate 6–9; on the Hardness Scale for Finishes they rate 4; and for the catalogue of Motifs the rating is 5. A possible mnemonic for remembering the order: Technique Finishes the Motif.

154

The total composite symbol for this pair of fictitious drums looks like this:

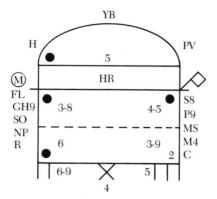

For the sake of comparison let us examine the composite symbol for the atumpan, the pair of master drums that plays such an important role in the life of the Ashanti and other Akan peoples of Ghana:

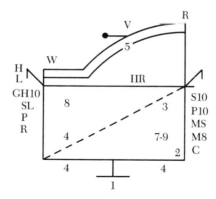

The notation indicates that the ntumpan has the external and internal shape of a bowl opening into a cylinder made of (5) wood, has a single head fastened by a H(oop) R(ing) and is played with two crooked sticks, is used in pairs (the pair is called atumpan), is tuned by W(etting) the heads and by means of tuning pegs, ●——, supporting V lacing, to a R(elative) pitch of H(igh) and L(ow). The drums are held in a slanting position by a stand. The pair has the following Hardness Scale ratings: Loudness, 8; Pitch, 3; Quality, 4; Density, 7–9; Technique, 4; Finish, 1; Motif, 4. They are associated with a G(roup) of H(igh) social status that values them at 10, they S(ymbolize) the soul of ancestor drummers and a tree, are honored with L(ibations), have magic P(ower), and R(itual) is involved in their manufacture

155

and when they are played. S(ociety) values them at 10, the P(layer) values them at 10, the M(aker) of the drums is accorded a special S(tatus), their M(onetary) value is 8, they are indispensable in the life C(ycle) of man.

Two more illustrations for comparison:

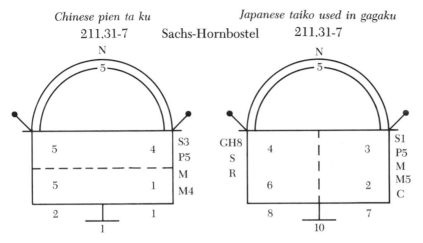

These two instruments are both circular frame drums with two N(ailed) heads and are played with two padded beaters. The Chinese pien ta ku, supported horizontally in a stand, is part of a modern orchestra of mixed instruments used for entertainment and has no association with a special group, symbolizes nothing, has no magic power, has no ritual associated with its usage or manufacture. It is given a fairly low value by society, not too high by the player, does not cost very much, is made by someone other than the player but the maker is accorded no special status. The reader may wish to compare these details with those of the Japanese taiko used in gagaku. Note the difference in value rating for the taiko by the special group (the members of imperial household and the temples) and by society. The difference between these two closely related drums in technique, finish, and motif may be seen in Illustration 3-25.

If our opponent at chess has been following all these moves closely, he may at this point come up with a fork play by asking, "What good is this complicated strategy if you don't have enough pieces on the board to complete the play?" In other words, what good is our elaborate symbolic notation if we lack some of the information it will accommodate? Good question.

It is true that our Hardness Scales, at the present writing, are based on subjective imagination. Although I for one shall continue to work toward achieving a consensus among my colleagues that will result in the objective formulation of these useful standards, let us admit they are not yet realized. Much of the ethno-

Illustration 3-25
The Japanese taiko used in gagaku (left) and the Chinese pien ta ku (right).

logical information symbolized on the left and right sides of the composite symbol, on the other hand, is presently available from the specialist in a given musical culture. And the Hardness Scales for Value among special Groups, Society, and the Player and the Monetary value need not wait on a consensus of ethnomusicologists—they can be supplied by members of the culture under study. But, for the sake of rebuttal to our friend who has engineered a fork play, let us also dispense with this area of information.

As a test of usefulness, let us take several of the entries from the Sachs-Hornbostel system and translate them into symbolic notation. We might start with a simple instrument like the tambourine: 2, membranophones; 21, struck drums; 211, drums struck directly;[11] 211.3, frame drums; 211.31, frame drums without handle; 211.311, single-skin frame drums;[12] 211.311-6, with membrane glued to drum.[13]

[11] "The player himself executes the movement of striking; this includes striking by any intermediate devices, such as beaters, keyboards, etc.; drums that are shaken are excluded." Hornbostel and Sachs (English trans.), *op. cit.*, p. 14.

[12] Actually "single-headed" drums is the intention; there is no designation in the Sachs-Hornbostel system for simple or compound heads, that is, two or more skins put together to form one head.

[13] Compare Hornbostel and Sachs (English trans.), *op. cit.*, p. 18.

157

The same information in symbolic notation would look like this:

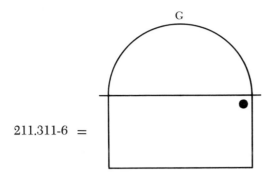

$$211.311\text{-}6 \;=$$

Our notation even in this minimal form includes the additional information that the drum has a simple rather than compound head, indicated by the omission of double or triple lines at the bottom of the rectangle, and that it is played with the right hand. It is tempting to add a little more information that will help us distinguish the tambourine from the Chinese pangku:

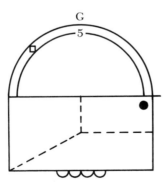

Now we see the internal shape and are aware that the frame of the tambourine is made of wood (5), that it has idiophonic attachments, ☐ , and that it is held in the hand in variable positions when played. Accepting Sachs-Hornbostel's definition of a frame drum, "The depth of the body does not exceed the radius of the membrane,"[14] we might represent the Chinese pangku (see Illustration 3-26) as follows:

[14] *Ibid.*

158

Pangku 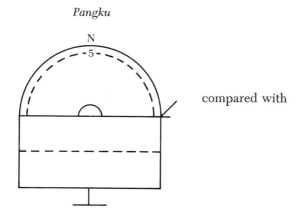 compared with *Tambourine*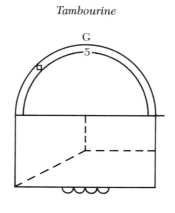

as opposed to:

211.311-7   compared with   211.311-6

Illustration 3-26
The Chinese pangku.

In the Sachs-Hornbostel system, closed cylindrical drums—that is, the end opposite from the membrane is closed—are represented by 211.211.2. In our notation:

$$211.211.2 \;=\;$$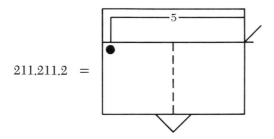

with the added information that the drum has a simple head, a wooden shell, is played in a vertical position with the left hand and a stick in the right hand, and is supported between the legs of the player.

The Sachs-Hornbostel system distinguishes several other modes of excitation among the membranophones: rattle drums, 212; plucked drums, 22; friction drums, 23; singing membrane,[15] for example, the kazoo or paper-and-comb, 24. Our symbolic notation for these might be:

| *Rattle drums* | *Plucked* | *Friction* | *Singing* |

I believe we have established several diversionary tactics that foil our adversary's fork play in this chess game of symbolic notation. In my judgment and experience, the organogram can provide a practical supplement, not necessarily a replacement, for one or another system of instrumental classification. The decimal system is very handy for entries on IBM cards; but I have also been assured that the present sophistication of programmers for the computer could easily translate all of the additive symbols of our proposed notation into the language of the computer. With a little imaginative application of existing techniques, I am told, we could be furnished with printouts of our original symbols.

The use of the composite symbol to represent musical instruments has a number of advantages. The composite can show only the information germane to a given purpose. For example, perhaps we are making a comparative study of

[15] For a recording of an African instrument of this type, hear "Bantu Music from British East Africa," ed. by Hugh Tracey, *The Columbia World Library of Folk and Primitive Music*, vol. 10, LP record, Columbia SL 213, "Singing Horns," Side 2, Band 1, Selection 17.

all the drum shapes (internal and external) found in West Africa. Only the top part of the composite need be used. Or perhaps we are solely interested in ethnological information: the basic horizontal rectangle, key letters on the left and right sides together with value ratings and, if available, the Hardness Scales for Finish, Technique, and Motif are sufficient unto the purpose. If our interest centers on a comparison of playing techniques, other information need not be represented in the composite. And so forth.

However complete or incomplete the composite symbol, it suggests in no way the arbitrary decisions that must be made in arranging orderly phyla as to whether internal or external shape or number of heads, or method of attachment or method of playing, and so forth, should be given priority as to genera, species, or subspecies. Indeed, the relative importance of different aspects of a musical instrument shifts with the research objective guiding the investigator. The absence of any notion of hierarchy also obviates any inconsistencies from one instrumental family to another in terms of the criteria used for their subdivisions.

Compelling support for using composite symbolic notation in organology is the simplicity with which the visual representation corresponds to the object being represented. Symbolic notation for the Chinese pangku and the tambourine given above bears a reasonable resemblance to the instruments in question and contains considerably more specific information than is found in 211.311-7 and 211.311-6.

The various symbols that combine to make up an organogram can be quickly memorized and conveniently used for purposes of publication, the archive, and computer programs for analysis and comparison, which involve organography (physical and acoustical description), any system of classification, techniques of performance, musical function, decoration, and an endless variety of socio-cultural information. On the following pages are given suggested symbols based, for the sake of illustration, on the requirements of the four instrumental families of the Sachs-Hornbostel classification as well as a summary of certain detailed symbols that might apply to more than a single family. The letter symbols and their respective Hardness Scales for Value used on the left and right sides of the basic organogram in the foregoing examples can be altered to suit the unique require-ments of a given subject, as long as the transcriber of the information provides a clear explanation of his intention. Other Hardness Scales created for the purpose of illustration out of imagination in the examples given above may, in fact, not be long in becoming a reality with such laboratory tools as the Seeger Melograph Model C now in operation. For the sake of convenient reference, these Hardness Scales are also given in summary.

I hope that students of ethnomusicology and my professional colleagues, using this material as a guide, will have as much fun as I have had by notating

161

organological information within their sphere of expertise. With the benefit of their constructive criticism and some trial and error, we can reach a consensus through usage of the organogram and establish a standard set of symbols that will fill a critical lacuna.

HARDNESS SCALES

HSL(oudness) (1 db–>120 db)		HSP(itch) (16 cps–16,384 cps)		HSQ(uality) (globular flute–cymbal)		HSD(ensity) (1 ppm–>600 ppm)		HSM(aterials) (gourd–metal)	
1	1–12 db	1	16–32 cps	1	globular flute	1	<1–60 ppm	1	gourd
2	13–24 db	2	33–64 cps	2		2	61–120 ppm	2	earth
3	25–36 db	3	65–128 cps	3	Melograms of	3	121–180 ppm	3	skin
4	37–48 db	4	129–256 cps	4	instruments	4	181–240 ppm	4	plastic
5	49–60 db	5	257–512 cps	5	now under	5	241–300 ppm	5	wood
6	61–72 db	6	513–1024 cps	6	comparative	6	301–360 ppm	6	bamboo
7	73–84 db	7	1025–2048 cps	7	study	7	361–420 ppm	7	bone
8	85–96 db	8	2049–4096 cps	8		8	421–480 ppm	8	glass
9	97–108 db	9	4097–8192 cps	9		9	481–540 ppm	9	stone
10	109–>120 db	10	8193–16,384 cps	10	cymbal	10	541–>600 ppm	10	metal

Four of the five Hardness Scales given above have an immediate practical application. Ratings on the Hardness Scale for Loudness should be determined with a decibel meter placed in the normal proximity and environment of the listener, as suggested in Chapter 2. A rating should express the range from the softest to the loudest sounds in characteristic, idiomatic performance (e.g., 41–69 db = HSL 4–7). A Stroboconn or similar device can be used to determine the lowest and highest pitch of an instrument with a rating expressed on the Hardness Scale for Pitch in terms of total range (e.g., 148–3012 cps = HSP 4–8). At this writing, the Hardness Scale for Quality has been tentatively determined through a comparative study of Melograms of a variety of instruments. However, until it has been tested by a wider sampling, only the absolute extremes represented by number 1, the globular flute (e.g., the Chinese hsün), and number 10, the cymbal, can be offered with certainty. The range of ratings on the Hardness Scale for Density, running from less than 1 ppm to more than 600 ppm, can be determined by a stop watch (e.g., 65–289 ppm = HSD 2–5). As indicated earlier, the Hardness Scale for Materials is admittedly subjective; but, if this is tolerated, it can serve a practical purpose in indicating the principal materials of an instrument symbolized in the organogram.

As yet, we can only aspire to the eventual establishment of Hardness Scales for Techniques, Finishes, and Motifs. Perhaps with sufficient clamor we shall be

162

able to evoke the curiosity and cooperation of the art historian and iconographer. As suggested above, pertinent Hardness Scales for social and cultural Values will vary somewhat from one subject to another. The examples of organograms already given in connection with different membranophones were quite real and were meant to be suggestive of the type of socio-cultural information that deserves attention; using these illustrations as a guide, the researcher will have to determine what information is appropriate to his subject and also, in collaboration with carriers of the tradition, establish pertinent Hardness Scales for Value.

INSTRUMENT POSITION   The following basic symbols indicate the playing position of an instrument in its relationship to the performer for each of the four families.

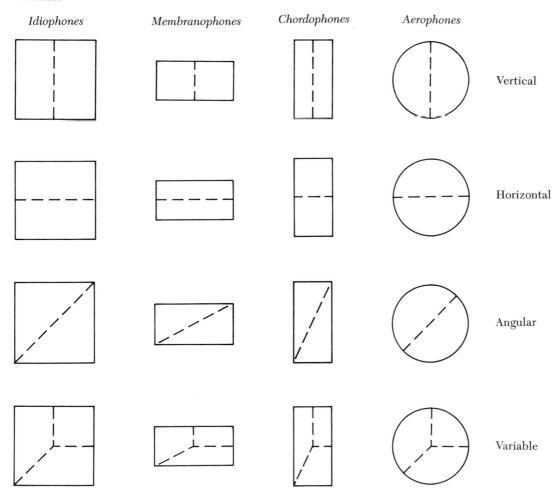

Idiophones	Membranophones	Chordophones	Aerophones	
				Vertical
				Horizontal
				Angular
				Variable

PERFORMER'S POSITION   The position of the performer can be indicated by the placement of a small circle (to suggest the height of his head) as indicated below, using the family of idiophones for the sake of illustration ("high" is reckoned from either the top or right side of the organogram).

High (e.g., standing)	Middle (e.g., seated on a chair)	Low (e.g., cross-legged on floor)

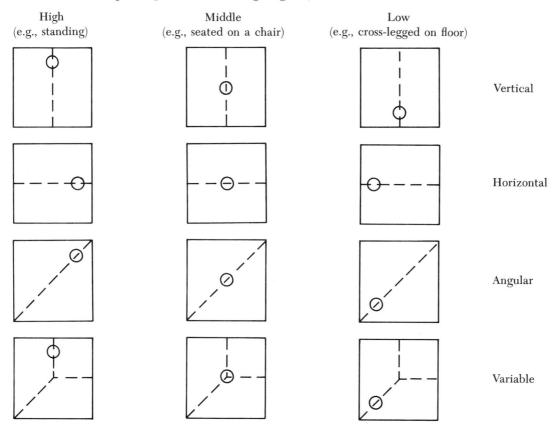

Vertical

Horizontal

Angular

Variable

INSTRUMENT SUPPORT   The symbols that follow are appended to the bottom of the basic family symbol to indicate the manner in which the instrument is supported.

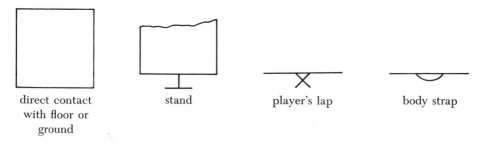

direct contact
with floor or
ground

stand

player's lap

body strap

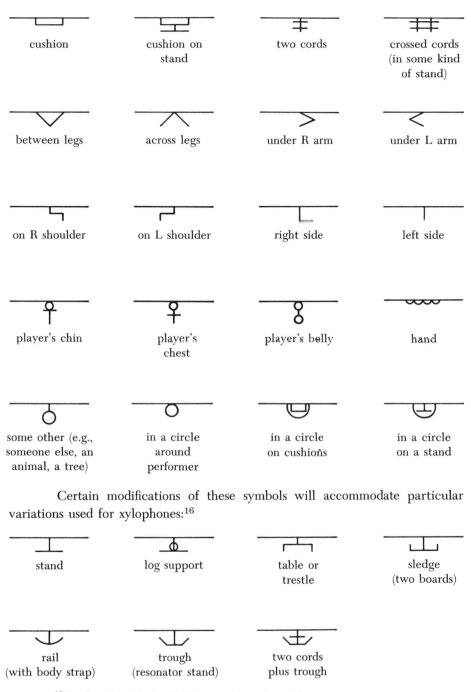

cushion	cushion on stand	two cords	crossed cords (in some kind of stand)
between legs	across legs	under R arm	under L arm
on R shoulder	on L shoulder	right side	left side
player's chin	player's chest	player's belly	hand
some other (e.g., someone else, an animal, a tree)	in a circle around performer	in a circle on cushions	in a circle on a stand

Certain modifications of these symbols will accommodate particular variations used for xylophones:[16]

| stand | log support | table or trestle | sledge (two boards) |
| rail (with body strap) | trough (resonator stand) | two cords plus trough | |

[16] Hornbostel and Sachs (English trans.), *op. cit.*, p. 13.

165

A number of auxiliary symbols can be useful for more than one family of instruments:

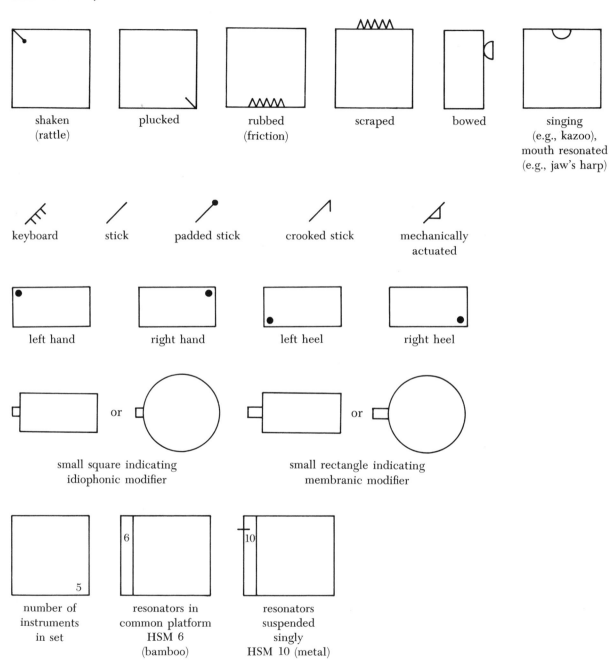

shaken
(rattle)

plucked

rubbed
(friction)

scraped

bowed

singing
(e.g., kazoo),
mouth resonated
(e.g., jaw's harp)

keyboard

stick

padded stick

crooked stick

mechanically
actuated

left hand

right hand

left heel

right heel

or

small square indicating
idiophonic modifier

or

small rectangle indicating
membranic modifier

number of
instruments
in set

resonators in
common platform
HSM 6
(bamboo)

resonators
suspended
singly
HSM 10 (metal)

Following are illustrative examples of instruments using membranic or idiophonic modifiers:

Resonator modified by membrane attachment (e.g., spider egg case in African xylophone gourd resonator producing buzz)—description: player standing or seated on ground; instrument in horizontal position and supported by rail with body strap; 12 (#12) wooden (HSM 5) keys played with two padded sticks; gourd (HSM 1) resonators suspended singly and modified by attached membranes

African xylophone

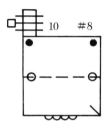

Instrument modified by idiophonic attachment producing buzz (e.g., African mbira)—description: player standing or seated on ground; instrument in horizontal position supported by player's hands; 8 (#8) metal (HSM 10) lamellae plucked by left and right hands and modified by idiophonic attachments

African mbira

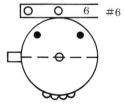

Membranic modifier (e.g., Chinese ti tse)—description: player seated on chair; instrument in horizontal position (side blown); made of bamboo (HSM 6) and has six (#6) finger holes; supported and fingered by right and left hands; membranic modifier covering additional hole

Chinese ti tse

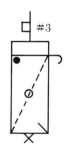

Idiophonic modifier (e.g., in neck of some Chinese san hsien)—description: player seated on chair; instrument in angular position and held in player's lap; 3 (#3) strings plucked by plectrum (⌐) in right hand, fingered with left hand; idiophonic modifier in neck

Chinese san hsien

167

BASIC ORGANOGRAMS   Following is a set of basic organograms for each of the four instrumental families of the Sachs-Hornbostel classification together with the Dewey decimal equivalents, explained by a few key words. For a more detailed explanation of these decimals the original source should be consulted. In some instances a single organogram will accommodate a number of successively smaller decimal subdivisions without omission of any detail. In a few instances, organogram notation has been given for certain essential details not found in the Sachs-Hornbostel classification.

Principal subdivisions as organized by Sachs-Hornbostel are given in summary at the beginning of each family of instruments.

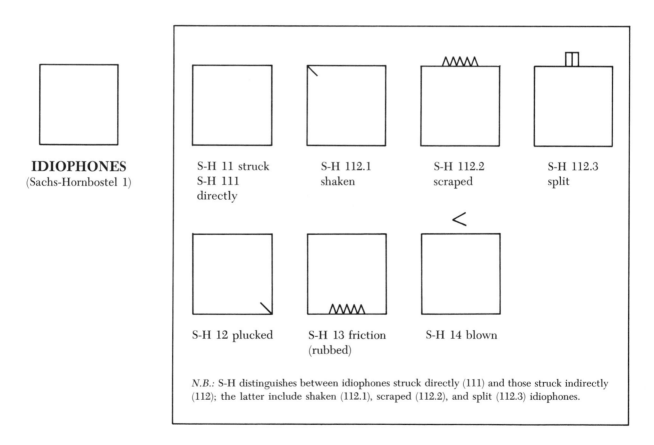

IDIOPHONES
(Sachs-Hornbostel 1)

S-H 11 struck
S-H 111
directly

S-H 112.1
shaken

S-H 112.2
scraped

S-H 112.3
split

S-H 12 plucked

S-H 13 friction
(rubbed)

S-H 14 blown

N.B.: S-H distinguishes between idiophones struck directly (111) and those struck indirectly (112); the latter include shaken (112.1), scraped (112.2), and split (112.3) idiophones.

S-H 11 struck
S-H 111
directly

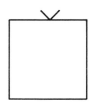

111.1 concus-
sion (two or
more sonorous
objects struck
together)
111.11 sticks or
stick clappers

111.12 plaques

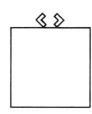

111.13 troughs

111.14 vessels
111.141
castanets

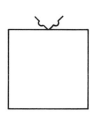

111.142
cymbals

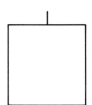

111.2 percus-
sion (struck
with or against
nonsonorous
object)
111.21 sticks
111.211 indi-
vidual sticks

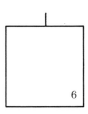

111.212 sets of
sticks

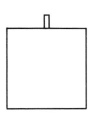

111.22 plaques
111.221
individual

111.222 sets

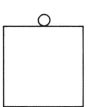

111.23 tubes
111.231
individual

169

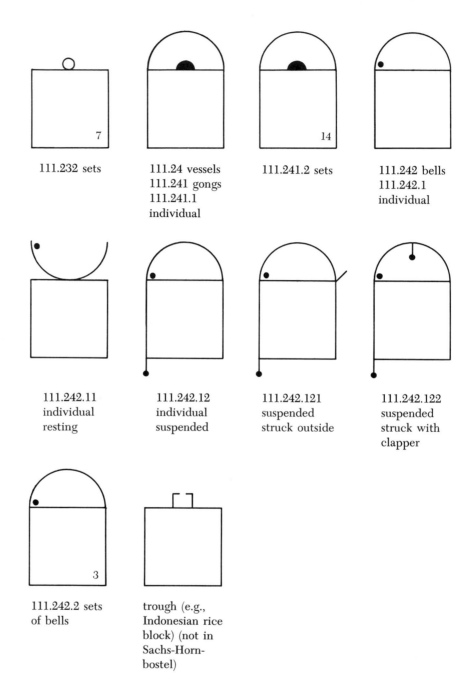

111.232 sets

111.24 vessels
111.241 gongs
111.241.1
individual

111.241.2 sets

111.242 bells
111.242.1
individual

111.242.11
individual
resting

111.242.12
individual
suspended

111.242.121
suspended
struck outside

111.242.122
suspended
struck with
clapper

111.242.2 sets
of bells

trough (e.g.,
Indonesian rice
block) (not in
Sachs-Horn-
bostel)

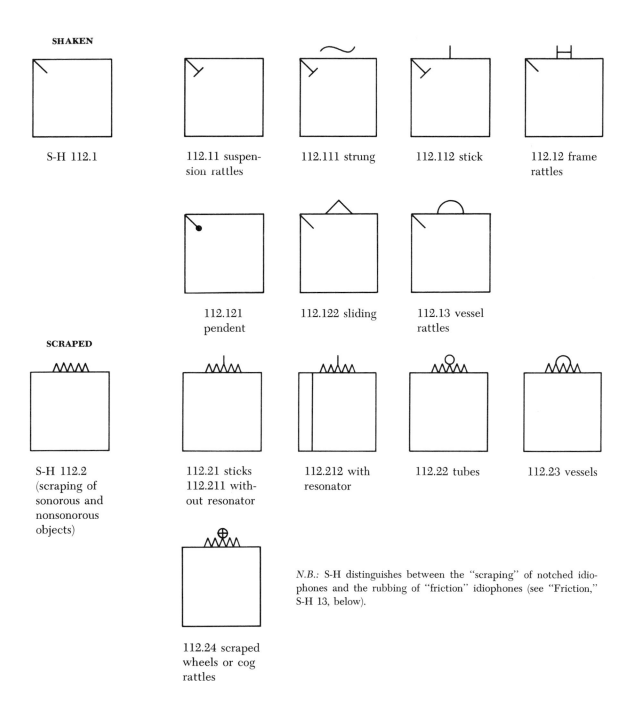

SHAKEN

S-H 112.1

112.11 suspension rattles

112.111 strung

112.112 stick

112.12 frame rattles

112.121 pendent

112.122 sliding

112.13 vessel rattles

SCRAPED

S-H 112.2 (scraping of sonorous and nonsonorous objects)

112.21 sticks
112.211 without resonator

112.212 with resonator

112.22 tubes

112.23 vessels

112.24 scraped wheels or cog rattles

N.B.: S-H distinguishes between the "scraping" of notched idiophones and the rubbing of "friction" idiophones (see "Friction," S-H 13, below).

SPLIT

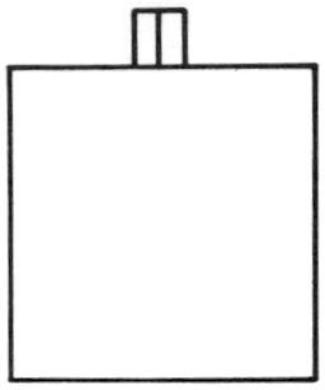

S-H 112.3

"Instruments in the shape of two springy arms connected at one end and touch at the other: the arms are forced apart by a little stick, to jingle or vibrate on recoil" (Hornbostel and Sachs, p. 16; cited in Note 2).

PLUCKED

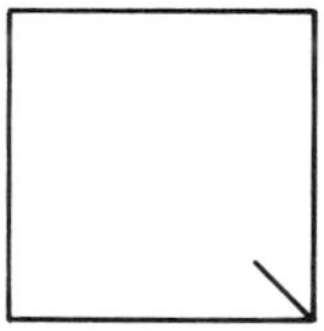

S-H 12 vibrat-
ing lamellae

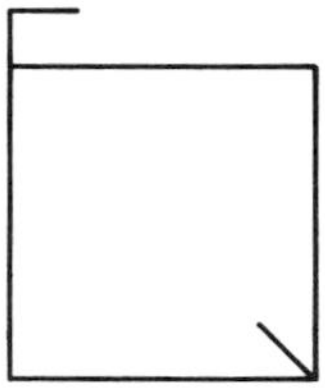

121 lamellae
in a frame

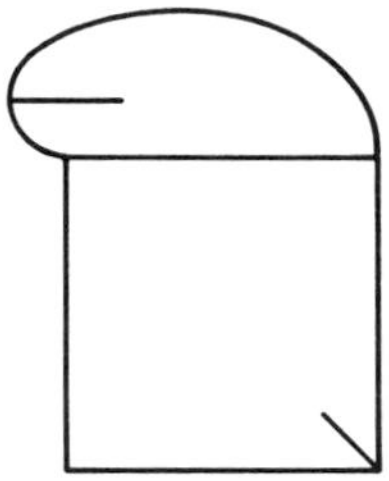

121.1 lamellae
carved in fruit
shell resonator

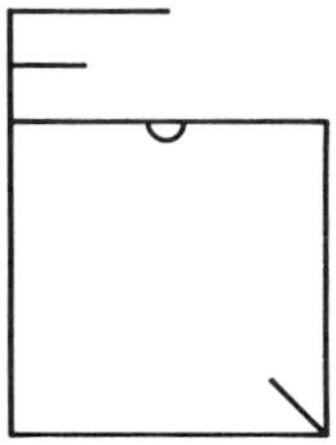

121.2 jaw's
harp mouth
resonator
121.21 lamella
carved in frame

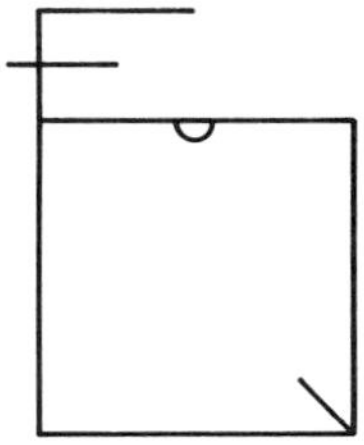

121.22 lamella
attached to
frame
121.221 single

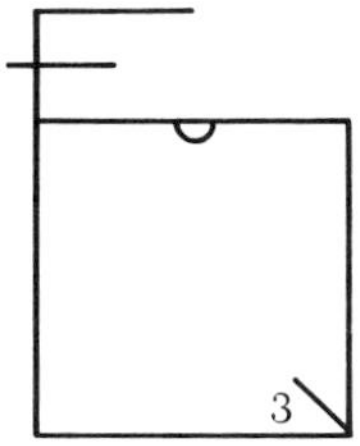

121.222 sets

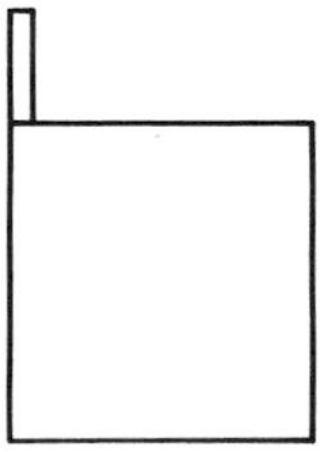

122 board or
comb form

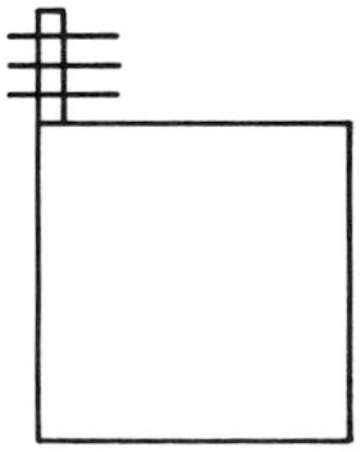

122.1 lamellae tied
on (e.g., mbira)
122.11 without
resonator

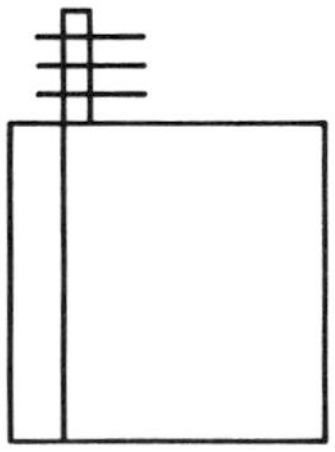

122.12 with
resonator

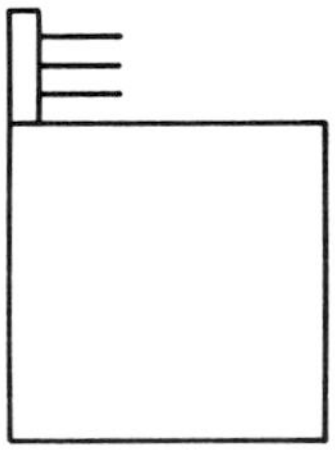

122.2 cut-out
lamellae

172

FRICTION

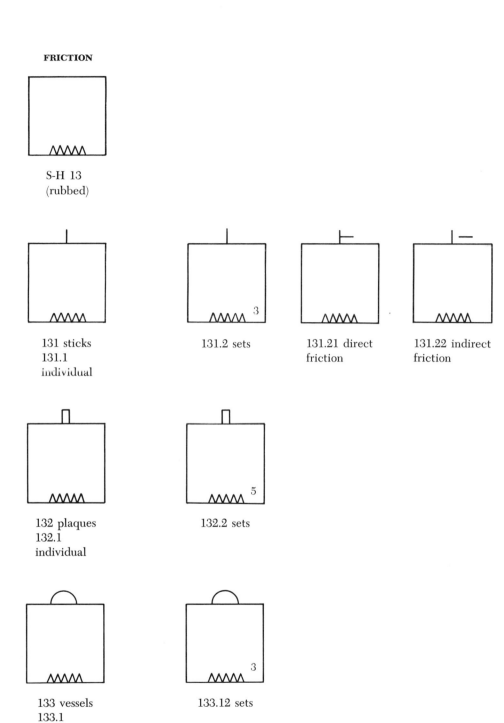

S-H 13
(rubbed)

131 sticks
131.1
individual

131.2 sets

131.21 direct
friction

131.22 indirect
friction

132 plaques
132.1
individual

132.2 sets

133 vessels
133.1
individual

133.12 sets

173

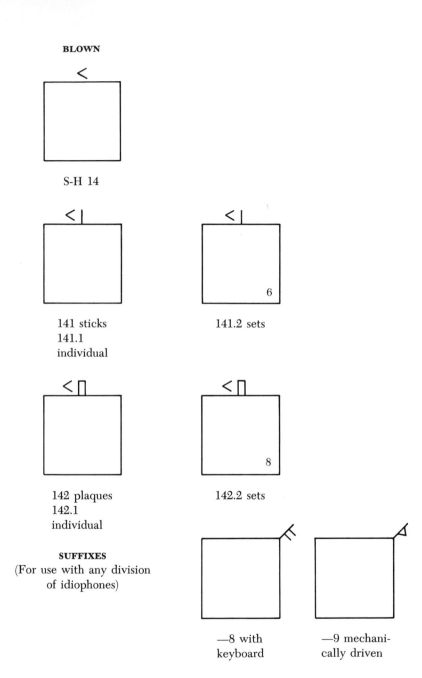

S-H 14

141 sticks
141.1
individual

141.2 sets

142 plaques
142.1
individual

142.2 sets

—8 with
keyboard

—9 mechani-
cally driven

MEMBRANOPHONES
(Sachs-Hornbostel 2)

S-H 21 struck
S-H 211
directly

S-H 212 shaken
(struck
indirectly)

S-H 22
plucked

S-H 23
friction
(rubbed)

S-H 24
blown

N.B.: S-H distinguishes between membranophones struck directly
(211) and those struck indirectly, or shaken (212).

STRUCK DIRECTLY

S-H 21 struck
S-H 211
directly

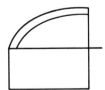

211.1 kettle
drums
211.11
individual

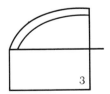

211.12 sets

175

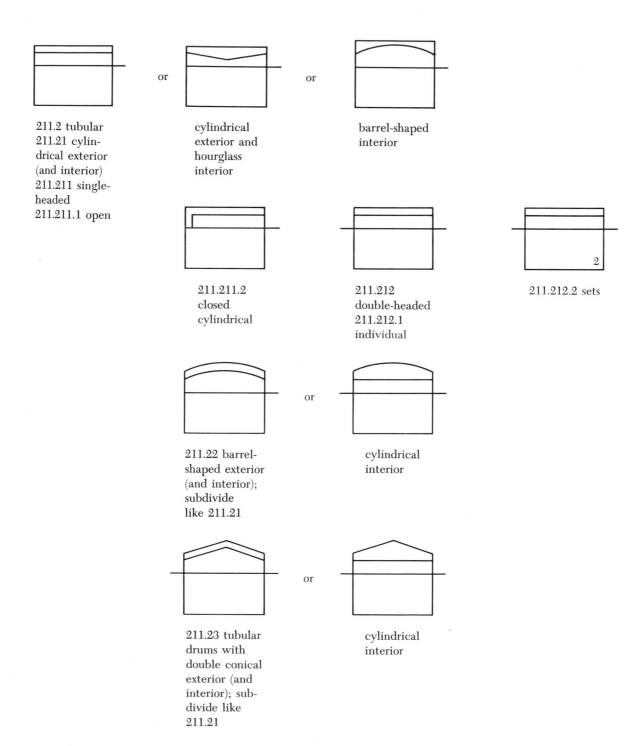

211.2 tubular
211.21 cylin-
drical exterior
(and interior)
211.211 single-
headed
211.211.1 open

or

cylindrical
exterior and
hourglass
interior

or

barrel-shaped
interior

211.211.2
closed
cylindrical

211.212
double-headed
211.212.1
individual

211.212.2 sets

211.22 barrel-
shaped exterior
(and interior);
subdivide
like 211.21

or

cylindrical
interior

211.23 tubular
drums with
double conical
exterior (and
interior); sub-
divide like
211.21

or

cylindrical
interior

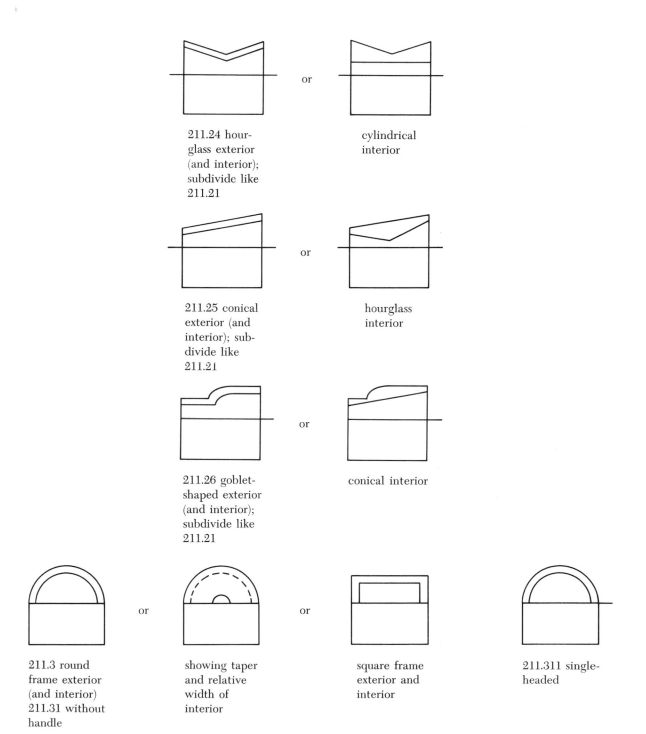

211.24 hour-glass exterior (and interior); subdivide like 211.21

cylindrical interior

211.25 conical exterior (and interior); sub-divide like 211.21

hourglass interior

211.26 goblet-shaped exterior (and interior); subdivide like 211.21

conical interior

211.3 round frame exterior (and interior) 211.31 without handle

showing taper and relative width of interior

square frame exterior and interior

211.311 single-headed

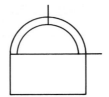

211.312
double-headed

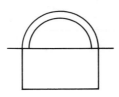

211.32 with
handle
211.321 single-
headed

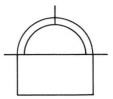

211.322
double-
headed

SHAKEN
(STRUCK INDIRECTLY)

S-H 212
impact of
pendent or
enclosed
pellets

PLUCKED

S-H 22 string
knotted under
membrane and
plucked to
transmit vibra-
tions to
membrane

FRICTION

S-H 23 friction
(rubbed)

178

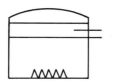
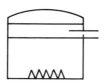
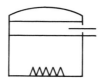
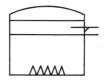

231 rubbed
stick
231.1 inserted
through
membrane
231.11 fixed

231.12 semi-
fixed

231.13 free

231.2 tied to
membrane

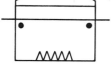

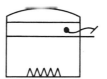

232 rubbed
cord attached
to membrane
232.1
stationary
232.11
single-
headed

232.12
double-headed

232.2 cord
rubs holding
stick

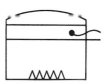

233 hand
friction

"SINGING MEMBRANES"

S-H 24

241 free kazoos
(paper and
comb)

242 tube or
vessel kazoos

179

—6	G	(glued membrane)
—7	N	(nailed membrane)
—8 —81 —811	L	(lacing cord without special devices for stretching)
—812	H	(H-shaped lacing)
—813	Y	(Y-shaped lacing)
—814	B	(tuning blocks or wedges)
—82	ɣ	(cord laced to nonsonorous hide)
—83	V	(laced to auxiliary board)
—84	V or ‿Y	(laced to flange of drum shell)
—85	ɣ	(laced to belt of different material)
—86	.Y or V.	(laced to pegs stuck in drum shell)
—9 —91	CR	(membrane lapped on by cord ring)
—92 —921	HR	(membrane lapped on by a hoop without mechanism)
—922 —9221	HR ▷	(with mechanism but without pedal)
—9222	HR ▷	(with pedal)

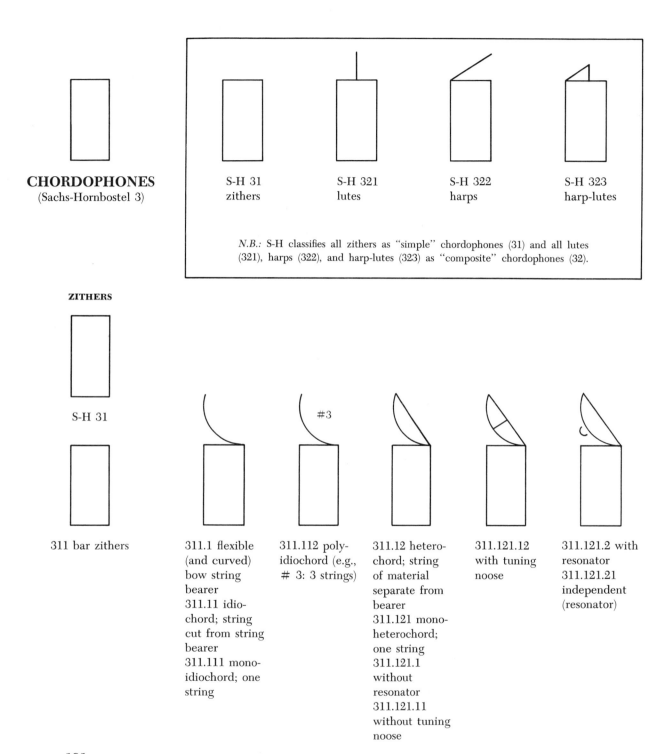

CHORDOPHONES
(Sachs-Hornbostel 3)

S-H 31
zithers

S-H 321
lutes

S-H 322
harps

S-H 323
harp-lutes

N.B.: S-H classifies all zithers as "simple" chordophones (31) and all lutes (321), harps (322), and harp-lutes (323) as "composite" chordophones (32).

ZITHERS

S-H 31

311 bar zithers

311.1 flexible (and curved) bow string bearer
311.11 idiochord; string cut from string bearer
311.111 mono-idiochord; one string

311.112 poly-idiochord (e.g., # 3: 3 strings)

311.12 hetero-chord; string of material separate from bearer
311.121 mono-heterochord; one string
311.121.1 without resonator
311.121.11 without tuning noose

311.121.12 with tuning noose

311.121.2 with resonator
311.121.21 independent (resonator)

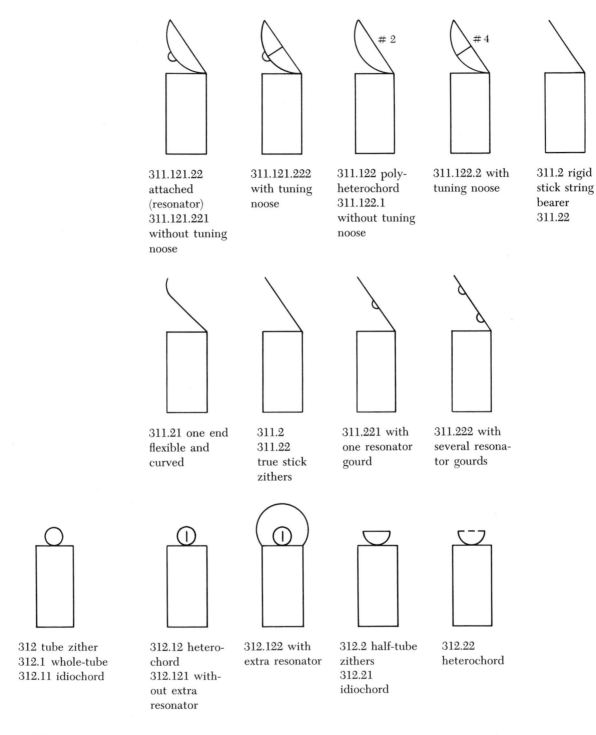

311.121.22
attached
(resonator)
311.121.221
without tuning
noose

311.121.222
with tuning
noose

311.122 poly-
heterochord
311.122.1
without tuning
noose

311.122.2 with
tuning noose

311.2 rigid
stick string
bearer
311.22

311.21 one end
flexible and
curved

311.2
311.22
true stick
zithers

311.221 with
one resonator
gourd

311.222 with
several resona-
tor gourds

312 tube zither
312.1 whole-tube
312.11 idiochord

312.12 hetero-
chord
312.121 with-
out extra
resonator

312.122 with
extra resonator

312.2 half-tube
zithers
312.21
idiochord

312.22
heterochord

182

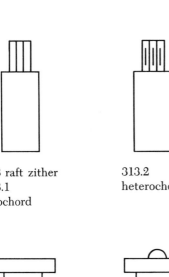

313 raft zither
313.1
idiochord

313.2
heterochord

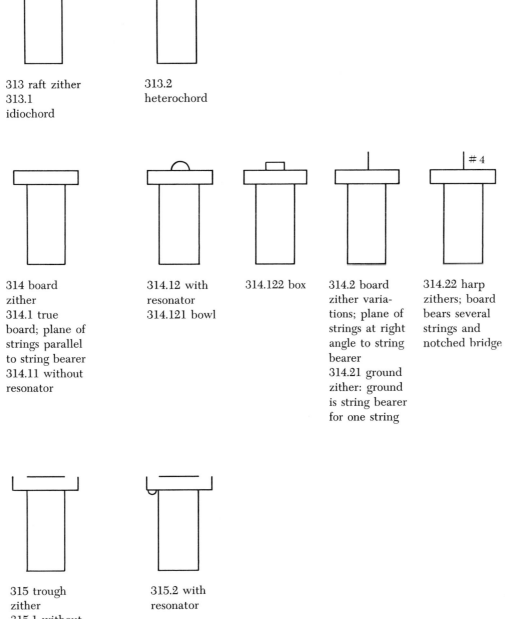

314 board
zither
314.1 true
board; plane of
strings parallel
to string bearer
314.11 without
resonator

314.12 with
resonator
314.121 bowl

314.122 box

314.2 board
zither varia-
tions; plane of
strings at right
angle to string
bearer
314.21 ground
zither: ground
is string bearer
for one string

314.22 harp
zithers; board
bears several
strings and
notched bridge

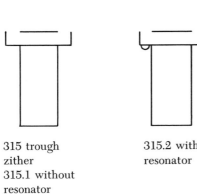

315 trough
zither
315.1 without
resonator

315.2 with
resonator

183

316 frame
zither
316.1 without
resonator

316.2 with
resonator

LUTES

S-H 321

321.1 bow
lutes; each
string has its
own flexible
carrier

184

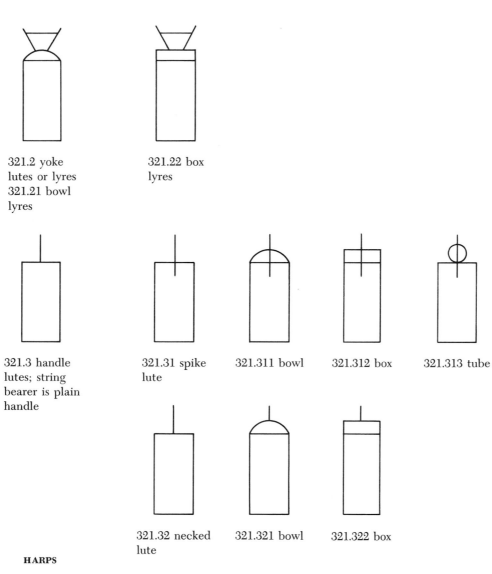

321.2 yoke
lutes or lyres
321.21 bowl
lyres

321.22 box
lyres

321.3 handle
lutes; string
bearer is plain
handle

321.31 spike
lute

321.311 bowl

321.312 box

321.313 tube

321.32 necked
lute

321.321 bowl

321.322 box

HARPS

S-H 322

185

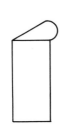

322.1 open (no
pillar)
322.11 arched
or bow

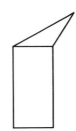

322.12 angular

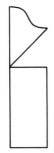

322.2 frame
harps (with
pillar)
322.21 without
tuning action
322.211
diatonic

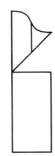

321.212
chromatic
321.212.1
strings in one
plane

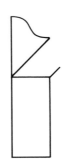

321.212.2
strings in two
crossing planes

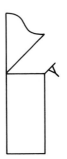

322.22 with
tuning action
322.221
manual

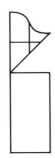

322.222
pedal

HARP LUTES

S-H 323

186

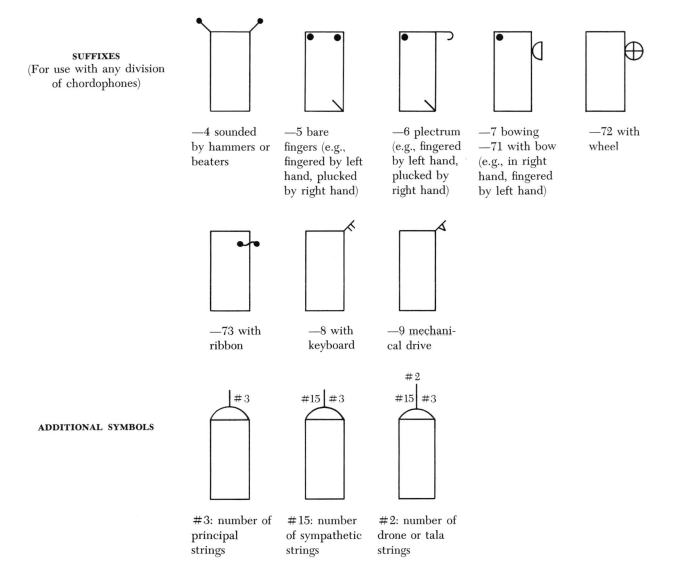

SUFFIXES
(For use with any division
of chordophones)

—4 sounded
by hammers or
beaters

—5 bare
fingers (e.g.,
fingered by left
hand, plucked
by right hand)

—6 plectrum
(e.g., fingered
by left hand,
plucked by
right hand)

—7 bowing
—71 with bow
(e.g., in right
hand, fingered
by left hand)

—72 with
wheel

—73 with
ribbon

—8 with
keyboard

—9 mechani-
cal drive

ADDITIONAL SYMBOLS

#3

#15 #3

#2

#15   #3

#3: number of
principal
strings

#15: number
of sympathetic
strings

#2: number of
drone or tala
strings

187

AEROPHONES
(Sachs-Hornbostel 4)

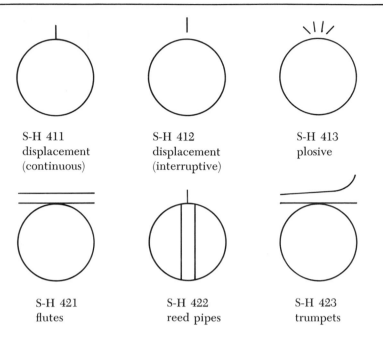

S-H 411
displacement
(continuous)

S-H 412
displacement
(interruptive)

S-H 413
plosive

S-H 421
flutes

S-H 422
reed pipes

S-H 423
trumpets

N.B.: S-H classifies aerophones in which the vibrating air is not confined by the instrument (411, 412, 413) as "free aerophones" (41) and aerophones in which the vibrating air is confined by the instrument (421, 422, 423) as "wind instrument proper" (42).

DISPLACEMENT
(**CONTINUOUS**)

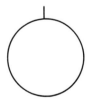

S-H 411 whip,
sword blade

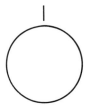

S-H 412

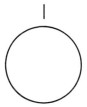

412.1 idio-
phonic (e.g.,
organ reed
stop)

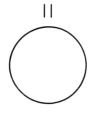

412.11 concus-
sion (e.g., split
grass-blade)

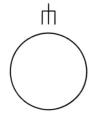

412.12 percus-
sion roods
412.121
individual

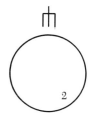

412.122 sets

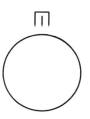

412.13 free
reeds
412.131
individual

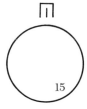

412.132 sets
(e.g., Japanese
sho)

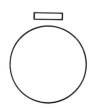

412.14 ribbon
reeds

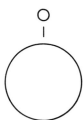

412.2 non-
idiophonic
interruptive

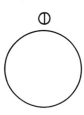

412.21 rotating
(e.g., siren)

412.22 whirling
(e.g., bull-roarer)

413 plosive (pop guns; also "water jug" master drum of Idja in Nigeria)

FLUTES

S-H 421

421.1 without duct

421.11 end-blown
421.111 single
421.111.1 open
421.111.11 without fingerholes

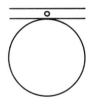

421.111.12 with finger-holes

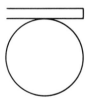

421.111.2 stopped, single end-blown flutes
421.111.21 without fingerholes

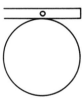

421.111.22 with finger-holes

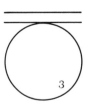

421.112 sets of panpipes
421.112.1 open

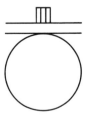

421.112.11 bound in raft

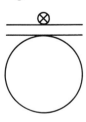

421.112.12 in round bundle

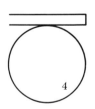

421.112.2 stopped panpipes

190

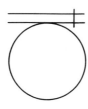

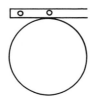

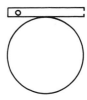

421.112.3
mixed open
and stopped

421.12 side-
blown flutes
421.121 single
421.121.1 open
421.121.11
without
fingerholes

421.121.12
with finger-
holes

421.121.2
partly stopped

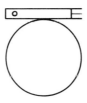

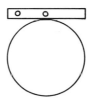

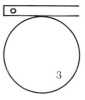

421.121.3
stopped
421.121.31
without
fingerholes
(nonexistent?)
421.121.311
fixed lower end

421.121.312
adjustable
lower end;
piston flutes

421.121.32
stopped with
fingerholes

421.122 sets of
side-blown
flutes
421.122.1 open

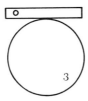

421.122.2
stopped

421.13 vessel
flutes; without
distinct beak

421.2 flutes
with duct

421.21 external
duct
421.211 single
421.211.1 open
421.211.11
without
fingerholes

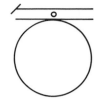

421.211.12
with finger-
holes

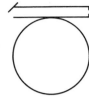

421.211.2
partly stopped

421.211.3
stopped

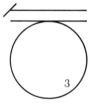

421.212 sets
with external
duct

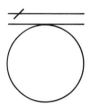

421.22 internal
duct
421.221 single
421.221.1 open
421.221.11
without
fingerholes

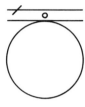

421.221.12
with finger-
hole; e.g.
recorder

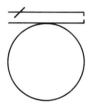

421.221.2
partly stopped

421.221.3
stopped
421.221.31
without
fingerholes
421.221.311
fixed lower end

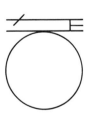

421.221.312
adjustable
lower end

421.221.4
vessel flute
421.221.41
without
fingerholes

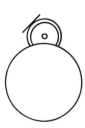

421.221.42
with finger-
holes

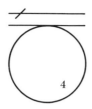

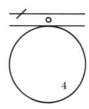

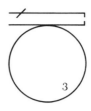

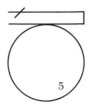

421.222 sets
with internal
ducts
421.222.1 open
421.222.11
without
fingerholes

421.222.12
with finger-
holes

421.222.2
partly stopped

421.222.3
stopped

REED PIPES

S-H 422

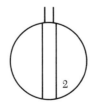

422.1 oboes
422.11 single
422.111 cylin-
drical bore
422.111.1
without
fingerholes

422.111.2 with
fingerholes

422.112 conical
bore

422.12 sets of
oboes
422.121 cylin-
drical bore

422.122 conical
bore

 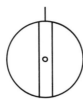  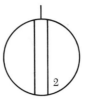

422.2 clarinets
422.21 single
422.211 cylin-
drical bore
422.211.1
without
fingerholes

422.211.2 with
fingerholes

422.212 conical
bore

422.22 sets of
clarinets

 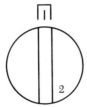

422.3 reed
pipes with free
reeds
422.31 single

422.32 double

TRUMPETS

S-H 423

N.B.: S-H distinguishes between "natural" trumpets (423.1)
and "chromatic" trumpets (423.2).

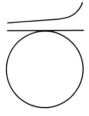

423.1 natural
trumpets

423.11 conches
423.111 end-
blown
423.111.1
without
mouthpiece

423.111.2 with
mouthpiece

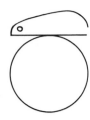

423.112 side-
blown conches

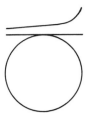

423.12 tubular
423.121 end-
blown
423.121.1
straight
423.121.11
without
mouthpiece

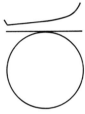

423.121.12
with
mouthpiece

423.121.2
natural horns;
curved or
folded
423.121.21
without
mouthpiece

423.121.22
with
mouthpiece

423.122 side-
blown natural
trumpets
423.122.1
straight

423.122.2 horns

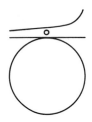

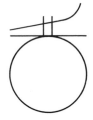

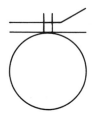

423.2 chro-
matic trumpets
423.21 with
fingerholes

423.22 with
slide

423.23 with
valves
423.231 conical
throughout

423.232 pre-
dominantly
conical

423.233 pre-
dominantly
cylindrical

SUFFIXES
(For use with any division
of aerophones)

—6 with air
reservoir
—61 air
reservoir rigid

—62 flexible

—7 fingerhole
stopping
—71 with keys

—72 with
Bandmechanic;
presumably
perforated roll
or ribbon

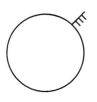

—8 with
keyboard

—9 with
mechanical
drive

196

Chapter Four

FIELD METHODS
and the HUMAN EQUATION

ABOUT TEN O'CLOCK in the morning my wife and I reached the village of Akumudan to find the area of the drum maker's workshop deserted except for one of his wives. It was the third day of shooting a documentary-narrative film about the atumpan, the talking master drums of the Ashanti and other Akan peoples of Ghana. We had expected to find five or six of the principals in our cast ready to continue with the filming. One of the Ashanti graduate students accompanying us questioned the drum carver's wife. She said we were "expected" down at the court-house—immediately.

For nearly a week, we had got up around six o'clock each morning in the city of Kumasi, capital of the Ashanti country, eaten a hasty breakfast, packed our gear, and driven over nearly impassable bush roads for three hours to reach the village some sixty miles away. During the first few days of negotiations with the council of elders and the chief, we had discovered that we could stay overnight in the village only occasionally because there was no electricity for recharging camera batteries. Therefore, we had established a daily shooting schedule from 10:00 A.M. until about 4:00 P.M. which, with the required driving and sundry amenities that arose after working hours, represented a workday from 6:00 A.M. until midnight.

As I heard the news, I was concerned about the prospect of losing valuable daylight hours—and more than a little apprehensive about this unscheduled meeting in the courthouse. We got back into the car and drove a short distance outside the village proper to the small white building designated as the courthouse. We left everything in the car except for a slim folder of papers, which I tucked under one arm as we approached the door.

The folder contained about two weeks' preliminary work with the eight African students I was guiding in a seminar in field and laboratory methods at the University of Ghana. Together we had researched the subject of the atumpan: its method of manufacture; the materials used; rituals connected with it; its traditional function in three modes of drumming (signaling, speech, and dance); its association with special groups, with a chief, with a paramount chief; its role in two kinds of ensembles, adowa and fontonfrom; its importance in opening the House of Parliament each year; its usage in radio broadcasts; its role in the modern Hi-Life dance bands, in the public schools, in honoring the boxing champion, in Christian church services, in memorial funeral ritual; its value to society, to the chief, to the paramount chief, to the warriors' association, to the master drummer; its monetary value; the status of the drum maker. In addition, because we wanted to show its actual manufacture, we had sought out the most auspicious and appropriate reason for ordering a new atumpan, the pair of drums, to be made. The best occasion for our purpose seemed to be the elevation of a chief to the status of paramount chief, which required larger and more beautiful drums, befitting the higher office.

All this information we had woven into a shooting script that included a slight thread of story line centered on a young boy who dreamed of becoming a master drummer himself one day.

Learning that the best drum carver was located in the village of Aku-mudan, we visited him in his workshop and explained that through this film we hoped to make widely known, not only in other parts of Africa but also in other parts of the world, the unique significance of the atumpan in the lives of the Akan peoples. The drum carver, who himself was in the lineage of Ashanti chiefs, grasped the broad implications of our project and agreed to go with us to petition the council of elders for permission to engage their chief to enact the role of elevation to paramount chief. After a couple of days of deliberation with the council and the chief, we were allowed to begin. In recompense, we established token stipends for the principals in the cast, a monetary gift to the council of elders for the benefit of the villagers of Akumudan; and we agreed to purchase the new set of drums we had ordered.

During the first two days of shooting, things had gone extremely well. Now, as we walked into the courtroom and faced the chief of police from Kumasi, two unknown plaintiffs, and the principals in our cast, I wondered what had gone wrong and how our hard work of the past few weeks might have been put in jeopardy.

Our real test had come the first day of shooting. At that time, I was the rawest of amateurs at film making. I had been given rather vague verbal instructions, for example, on how to load a 400-foot external magazine for a Bell and Howell camera. Not wanting to trust this inadequate instruction on the first day of shooting, I had gone to the Ghanaian Film Board several days earlier and asked for assistance in loading the magazine. They had been extremely helpful, but I was slightly perturbed to learn that all of the equipment with which they were familiar in making news coverage was 35 mm; we were using 16 mm. Nonetheless, the magazines were loaded with only a minimum of hesitation, and I had set off for the village quite confident. My eight graduate students, I believe, were rather puzzled over the whole venture. It was understandably difficult for them to equate our modest camera and sound equipment, not to mention my honestly declared inexperience, with their image of the motion-picture business as represented by Hollywood productions.

For several reasons, I had decided to tackle first what promised to be physically the most difficult day of shooting. These scenes were laid in the bush, in the rain forests of central Ghana, where more than a year before the drum maker had felled large logs, with traditional ceremony, and left them to season. From the description of the location, I knew we would have to carve our way through dense tropical undergrowth that would probably pose some problems for the cameraman. It was only weeks later that I learned about the more dramatic reality of the green mambo, a snake that lives in the trees and whose bite is lethal within twenty or thirty seconds.

For some time, first by car and then by foot, we had followed a worn path through the forest of giant trees. As we neared the actual location, I saw several women coming down the path toward us bearing loads of cassavas on their heads. It struck me as potentially useful footage in establishing the scene, so we asked whether they would consent to being filmed. After some giggling, they agreed; and we set up a camera to record an accidental meeting between our party—made up of the drum carver, his wife, his assistant, the master drummer, the boy—and the party of young women bearing cassavas. It was a beautiful scene

199

that will remain etched on my memory for many years to come. Unfortunately, that is the only way it was preserved. After running for about 150 feet of film, making a strange and laborious sound, the Bell and Howell ground to a stop. The magazine had not been properly loaded.

A quick decision had to be made. We were carrying two other cameras, one that took a 100-foot reel and the other, a 50-foot cassette. Should I admit the problem and reshoot the scene? Everyone was waiting for me to say something after the Bell and Howell stopped. I walked up to the women and thanked them as profusely as my few words of the Twi language allowed, turned to the drum carver and his party with a warm handshake telling them that it was a beautiful scene. I nodded toward the solid wall of bush within which lay the subject of the day's shooting, indicating that we had better get started with the machetes. I explained to the students that for the next few scenes we would dispense with the heavy tripod and the Bell and Howell and rely on a hand-held camera and a light tripod. As we worked our way deep into the bush, I reflected on the decision that had been made without perceptible hesitation, wondering whether my intuitive reaction had guided me properly. For the same reason that I had chosen the most difficult location for the first day's shooting, it seemed wise now to brush by the dismal failure of my attempt to film the first scene. There was little doubt in my mind that I was on trial; if in the eyes of the Ashanti I could win my spurs on the first day of shooting, then we could probably count on the cooperation needed to finish the film.

The rest of the day had gone along very well indeed. It was something of a nuisance to have to stop to change film every 100 feet; but to my great relief we finished shooting all the scenes that had been scheduled for the bush.

Hot, dirty, and tired, we had returned to the village around 6:00 P.M. to be greeted by the linguist of the tribe, who carried an invitation for us to visit the chief and the council of elders in the palace. It was a large gathering in celebration of our first day of filming. Bottles of gin were passed around, and soon it became apparent that my wife and I and the University students, who were not recently accustomed to fighting the bush, were being honored for the display of physical endurance that had carried us through the day. Everyone was enjoying the gin; and the master drummer, with a few drinks to encourage him, was playing the atumpan of the royal court. One of the Ashanti students approached me and said, "I think you should know what the master drummer is saying on the atumpan. He says, you have the heart of the lion, you are strong like the elephant." And this line of drum declamations went on for some time. I tried to push the 400-foot external magazine out of my mind and concentrate on the drummer's comforting poetic imagery.

Now, three days later, as I stood before the chief of police from Kumasi in the little white courthouse, I kept reminding myself that I had the heart of the lion and the strength of the elephant. He asked us to sit down.

This was November, 1963. There was a great deal of political unrest in Ghana, particularly among the Ashanti, who felt that the regime in power had betrayed fundamental assurances and abrogated traditional guarantees of personal freedom. It was also a time when Americans were not too popular.

I shook hands with the chief of police and introduced him to my wife and the graduate students. He spoke English quite well.

His manner was grave as he mentioned the names of the two plaintiffs, and I noticed with some discomfort that he had not returned my smile. He explained stiffly that the men were emissaries from the courts of two different paramount chiefs in villages located some distance from Akumudan. The day before they had lodged complaints with police headquarters in Kumasi of such a serious nature that the chief of police had decided to hold this hearing himself.

When I learned the nature of the complaint, it was only the minacious eyes of the plaintiffs that kept me from laughing out loud. Police headquarters had been informed by two paramount chiefs that an American had come to the village of Akumudan for the express purpose of elevating the local chief to the exalted status of paramount chief. In these times of political maneuvering, every additional elevation weakened to some extent the power of existing paramount chiefs. Moreover, they knew the precise day on which the ceremony was scheduled to take place. It would happen at the next Odai Festival the following month. And of course superficially their information was quite correct. We had timed our staged elevation to occur in conjunction with the next Odai, a festival held every forty days, because we had been informed that several thousand persons would be in attendance with all of their finery. It made the perfect setting for the important event we were portraying in our story.

I laid out the shooting script before the chief of police and began by explaining that I was a visiting professor at the University of Ghana. Briefly, I outlined our simple story, stressing the importance of making known to other societies the singular role of the atumpan among the Ashanti. Of course, the chief of police was himself an Ashanti. The more I explained the wider he grinned. When I had finished, he turned to the two plaintiffs and summarized the facts. Then they, too, began to smile; and within a few minutes we shook hands all around and went our separate ways. A half hour later we were back on our shooting schedule.

The next day when we reached the drum carver's workshop, we found the two emissaries waiting for us. My first thought was that they had not been satisfied with the chief of police's hearing and had returned on their own initiative. Each of them handed me a rather formal-looking letter written in Twi. I asked

201

one of the graduate students to translate and learned with relief that we now had invitations to come and make films in the villages of the two neighboring paramount chiefs. I asked the student to offer my thanks through the emissaries to the paramount chiefs, adding that I sincerely hoped some day to return to Ghana and accept their invitations.

I chose this little vignette (see Illustrations 4-1, 4-2, and 4-3) as a pertinent opening for a chapter devoted to field methods because I believe very little of his preliminary training would give the graduate student in ethnomusicology adequate preparation for such a chain of events—perhaps with the exception of learning how to load an external magazine.

Success in field work depends on the combination of three things: technical know-how, substantive knowledge of subject, and a great sensitivity to the values and feelings of other human beings—these listed in inverse order of importance. Good tape recordings, selective still photography, significant film footage, and thorough documentation of such materials require the constant interplay of technical, substantive, and sensitive forces.

Field work is hard work; but, properly approached, it can be one of the most rewarding activities of the ethnomusicologist. Success cannot be measured by the quantity of material collected. To be sure, each subject requires its own optimum number of examples to ensure representative sampling. In my experience, however, a modest collection of well-recorded, selectively filmed, and thoroughly documented materials has far more significance than a larger indiscriminate stockpile of random samples. It is not too surprising that in a field of study like ethnomusicology, which has not yet come of age, there is much material already collected that is sparsely documented, poorly recorded, and not truly representative of the musical cultures sampled.[1] The reasons are quite tangible: inadequate training and technical knowledge, inferior equipment, and too often a vague, ill-defined purpose or objective.

But the rewards of field work include more than the quality and quantity of materials assembled. Sometimes I think recordings and films, separated as they are from the cultural context of the subject, are likely to deceive as much as enlighten, to misdirect as much as guide the listener-viewer unfamiliar with their origin. In the same way that a recording, for the variable reasons mentioned earlier, is a selective transcription that attempts to simulate the reality of musical performance, so the motion picture—to an even greater extent—is a selective attempt to simulate reality. The variables, the choices, the techniques, the equipment in film making are almost infinite. The motion picture filmed in color with synchro-

---

[1] See further Mantle Hood, "Musical Significance," *Ethnomusicology*, vol. 7, no. 3 (Sept., 1963), pp. 187–192.

nized sound is the most powerful medium of documentation available to the ethnomusicologist—and one that is subject to the grossest misuse. We shall take a hard look at some of these problems presently.

The greatest reward in field work, in my judgment, is the intimate knowledge of subject, both in breadth and depth, it affords the researcher. The products of recording and photography, "the bare facts" to which Fox Strangways referred, "are not of much use without the ideas on which to string them." Yes, we have turned a corner since that pregnant comment was written. Today, the field worker and the home worker must be the same man.

In most non-Western societies, and in some traditions of the Western world, the subject of our concern is quite fragile. Music, dance, drama, and the allied arts with which they are often inseparably integrated bespeak some of man's highest values. To watch the eyes of a master drummer as he tunes the atumpan, as he proudly demonstrates its technical requirements in playing, points out the symbolism in its shape or carving, tells you about its magic power, its connection with his ancestors, with the spirit of the tree that lives on in the drums, pours libations before each performance thereby honoring these spirits—to watch his eyes is a privileged reward of field work that no form of documentation can capture. The moment the impersonal eye of the camera is turned on, the delicate bond of confidence and enthusiasm between you and the musician is likely to snap. Some kinds of confidences are best recorded only by memory.

Sometimes the most informative and convincing scenes in making a film like *Atumpan* occur when the cameras are not running. During that first day of shooting in the bush, we had scheduled a sequence of scenes in flashback to show the actual tree-felling ceremony that had occurred a year before the time of our story line. After we had hacked our way through the bush to the location where the seasoned logs had been stored, the drum carver selected a magnificent tree that towered some 70 or 80 feet above the floor of the forest. We filmed the several stages of the ceremony right up to the moment when the large axes began chopping into the base of the trunk. After half a dozen blows that sent large chips flying, the point of felling had been made, and I signaled that we were through with the scene. But the two men wielding axes went right on with their task. I ran up quickly to the master carver, gesturing to him that the scene was finished and that he should stop the cutting before the giant tree was permanently damaged. Through one of the students who translated for me, I explained that there was no need to fell the tree. I could see there were already on hand a number of seasoned logs waiting for future orders for new drums. The atumpan is made from the ofema tree, a relative of the cedar that is very valuable. The drum carver halted the axmen. I looked at the deep cut that had been made and shook my head with genuine concern. The drum carver came over to me, put a hand on

203

*Illustration 4-1
(Opposite page, top)
Principals of the cast in
Atumpan during the filming
and recording of an
important scene. Photograph
by Joe Franklin.*

*Illustration 4-2
(Opposite page, bottom)
Filming details of construction of the atumpan. Photograph by Joe Franklin.*

*Illustration 4-3
Ashanti children's advice on
loading a camera. Photograph
by Joe Franklin.*

my shoulder, and spoke in Twi. His eyes had a wonderful, mischievous light and little wrinkles appeared at the corners; I was impatient to hear the translation of his words. He was telling me with deep satisfaction that the tree they had begun to fell was *not* an ofema, even though it resembled one. He explained that they could not fell the ofema and risk offending the spirit of the tree without the justification of real need. To watch his eyes as he explained this simple fact in the Ashanti scale of values was a privileged reward of field work, an indelible underscore of a fact I had long since read about that suddenly came to life with meaning.

Such are the indispensable ideas on which the bare facts must be strung.

The researcher working in the laboratory, at his desk, communicating through lectures and publications, is not an ethnomusicologist in the best sense of the term unless the generating force of his activities arises from the kind of spirit and enthusiasm, insight and intimate knowledge that can be won only from the experience of doing his own field work.

Is his mode of operation in the field different from that of a linguist? An ethnologist? A folklorist? I believe it is. The very nature of his subject is different, and so are its requirements. What kind of preparation should he have? Assuming that the best place to learn field methods is in the field, how can he learn to swim before venturing into the water?

The answer lies in a more basic question: "Where is the field?"

PREPARATION AND THE SLOW BEGINNING

The beginning graduate student is likely to have a rather romantic notion that "the field" is synonymous with an African safari or a battle with malaria in the swamps of Borneo (Kalimantan) or a team of Eskimo huskies pulling a sled in Alaska or grass-skirted dancers on a lush tropical island in the South Pacific. And indeed it might be any of these. It might also be an enclave of Yugoslavs living in the San Pedro area of greater Los Angeles. Or the Chinese community of San Francisco or New York City. Or a shabby night club in any metropolitan area where musicians are way out with the rock beat nightly.

The field is wherever you find the subject in its natural environment. Music and dance of the Yugoslavs in San Pedro is a different subject from the music and dance of Yugoslavs in Yugoslavia. Each offers its own attractions to the field worker, and each is important to the other for comparative purposes. The "field" is *not* a group of musicians and dancers from India on a tour of the United States. But for the scholar who already knows India, contact with such a group may be valuable for filling in those inescapable lacunae that mark the aftermath of field work.

206

Preliminary training in field work should occur in the course of a graduate seminar in field and laboratory methods, a combination of theory and practice. Each student can choose his own subject, within whatever range of possibilities local conditions permit, and let it define the location of his training in the field. He may wish to tackle local field work by himself; or there is something to be said for the experience of working in two-man teams, but usually not more than two. In the latter approach, one student has the role of the principal investigator and the other is his more or less silent assistant in recording and filming. The same pair can switch roles when the assistant becomes director of his own project.

Such a seminar is normally given in the span of one semester or one or two quarters, a very concentrated period of study considering the variety of requirements. Nonetheless, even this brief, compact exposure to the problems of field work affords invaluable experience that may save the researcher on many occasions when he actually reaches the field of his ultimate choice. Training on the local scene, however remote the subject may appear to be from the student's eventual area of concentration, must be undertaken with the same serious intent and sense of devotion that one day will guide him in Africa, Asia, Alaska, or the bistros of Paris.

Before I am accused of not practicing what I preach—an occupational hazard of the teaching profession—I might sketch in the background of circumstances that found me in Africa with a commitment to make a documentary film but with far too little experience for the assignment. On my first trip to Africa, the year before, I had been so impressed by the program of music and dance in the Institute of African Studies at the University of Ghana that I suggested to the director, Professor J. H. Nketia, that we might interest an American foundation in backing a three-year program of training, research, and documentation. Eight months later the proposal was accepted with enthusiasm by a major foundation; and I was given authority to hire a cameraman, order equipment and supplies, and set in motion all the organizational details necessary to a sizable expedition. At the suggestion of the foundation our original budget request was even increased!

A few weeks before we were to leave for Africa, the whole house of cards collapsed. A basic shift of policy in the foundation left us without one cent of support. Fortunately, in spite of constant reassurance from the New York office, I had only put a reservation on equipment and supplies, being reluctant to spend money I did not yet have in hand. The foundation was relieved to hear this. Meanwhile, my wife and I had accepted visiting appointments at the University of Ghana as well as a travel grant. Moreover, by this time we felt a moral commitment to the faculty and students in Ghana to make a documentary film, which was to have been one of several major projects undertaken. So we borrowed equipment, scraped together a modest budget for supplies, apologized to the cameraman for leaving him behind, and then left for Ghana with more courage than wisdom.

Apparently all the Ashanti gods smiled on the project because subsequently the finished film received wide endorsement, not only in Ghana, where former President Nkrumah described it as "the first truly African film" he had ever seen, but also in Europe, Asia, and the United States. If in the beginning we had realized how little we knew and how much there was to know, we might never have made the attempt. But there were two compelling reasons for attempting the nearly impossible: a moral commitment to colleagues in Ghana and a very stubborn resolve that had been forming for a number of years. The latter deserves some explanation.

NINE VIOLATIONS OF THE MUSES At the time we established our archive in the Institute at UCLA, the librarian was given the continuing responsibility of seeking out documentary films on the subject of music and dance from any part of the world in which they might be located. Systematically, through the years, we have viewed these to determine which of them to put on a purchase list and which to rent as occasion demanded. During the first couple of years, we were appalled by the material previewed. One or two films were put on our to-be-rented list; we found none that in our estimation was worthy of purchase.

In this important medium of documentation, most of the films we have seen suffer from one or a combination of nine problems.

1. The majority are made by technicians who have little or no familiarity with the subject. The result is very frustrating. When the camera should be trained on the upper portion of the dancer's body, it may instead be focused in a tight close-up of the feet. At the very moment that the expressive detail of eye movements or gestures with the hands should be given prominence, the camera cuts to a long shot in which all of the details are lost. Intercuts to supporting musicians are likely to be taken from angles that hide the articulation of the performer's hands or to be so fleeting they do not read. Essential movements of both musicians and dancers may be "cut off" by bad framing; that is, either the frame was not large enough to accommodate the full range of movement or the cameraman, in ignorance of the choreography, was unable to pan with the movement of the subject. This type of so-called documentary film, concentrating exclusively on the subject, at the wrong time and place, makes no attempt at contextual documentation; and it fails as a technical film because the cameraman and the editor are ignorant of the requirements of the subject.

2. The subject has been lifted out of its social context and placed on a stage with a frontal orientation. In addition to suffering from the faults mentioned above under 1, this type of film creates an artificial environment that produces

208

a visual conflict between native dress and theatrical draperies and lighting. As if to compensate, sometimes the costumes are jazzed up, à la Sol Hurok. In natural surroundings, the orientation of the performers may have been circular, a ring of spectator-participants who form a circle around the music-dance area; or it may have been three sides of a square if the place of performance was an open pavilion. On stage, the subject has been reoriented to face the front.

3. Theatrical license in choreography and even "plot" are introduced to give the traditional subject more sex appeal.

4. The film has an ethnological point of view with some arbitrary intercuts of music and dance, often with an unrelated sound track dubbed in.

5. The camera or cameras have been turned on and allowed to "bake" while the subject goes through its paces. This static technique can turn a vital and exciting music-dance performance into a dull and monotonous routine.

6. The sound track is so filled with redundant narration that the music is multilated and the viewer is insulted by superficial description of the thing he is seeing.

7. The versatility of the motion picture has not been utilized. Film footage of a folk singer standing before a microphone does very little more than could be accomplished by a good recording and some sensitive still photography. In one sense, it does considerably less by forcing the viewer to watch a subject whose primary interest is aural. Even a telecast of the New York Philharmonic playing a Haydn symphony is pretty dull; the same group, wrestling with the acrobatic showmanship of an avant-garde work, provides a subject with considerably more visual interest.

8. The subject filmed is not representative of the tradition. Sometimes a student from abroad, who may be majoring in political science or agriculture, is asked to perform the music or dance of his culture. It is likely that such a performer, with the best of intentions, will grossly misrepresent the very traditions he respects. The same problem can also arise if the uninformed collector in the field makes no effort to locate performers who represent the best quality of the tradition.

9. The motion picture is filmed and edited by a "film maker" who believes his first obligation is to "express himself." The subject of the film is likely to be smothered in tricky camera and editing techniques, which may lend themselves to artistry but not to documentation.

By 1962, I had seen many dull films of subjects which, had they been properly approached, might have been vital, exciting, dramatic, and informative. In the process of the survey, I became convinced that such a state of affairs need not be. If an ethnomusicologist were to work closely with a professional camera-man and an editor, the final product ought to be a marked improvement over the films previewed. I was determined to demonstrate the validity of such collaboration. It was with great misgivings and disappointment, therefore, that we set out for Africa leaving the cameraman behind.

But the hardship proved to be a blessing in disguise. Before that venture, had anyone asked me, I would have said that the training and field methods of the ethnomusicologist were already too demanding to expect him also to cope with the problems of the documentary film. His only recourse, it seemed to me, was collaboration with professional film makers whenever that ideal circumstance was possible. I no longer believe this to be true. In fact, recent work with graduate students in ethnomusicology has proved it not to be true. It is far easier to train the advanced graduate student in ethnomusicology in the basic techniques of filming and editing than to acquaint the professional film maker with the manifold requirements of ethnomusicology. If the student is sensitive to the demands of working with other human beings and has a solid preparation in his subject, he needs only minimal technical knowledge and practical experience to capture truly significant documentation on film. Once back from the field, he should seek the help of a professional film maker in editing his footage. But again, it is his personal experience with musicians and dancers in the field and his knowledge of subject that must provide the appropriate point of view in editing. These matters will be discussed in more detail presently.

SLOW AND STEADY   The assurance of successful field work is a successful beginning. And the beginning starts at home. The more thorough the preparation, the more likely there will be good results in the field. Preliminary contacts and introductions are very important. Whether the location of the field work is San Pedro or Ghana, the researcher should consult someone who knows the community under study, someone likely to appreciate the purposes and objectives of the project. He might be a member of the community itself, a member of a university faculty, or someone in the community at large involved in local or international affairs. He may have immediate suggestions as to the best musicians and dancers in the community or at least know whom to consult. He will probably volunteer introductions through a letter or, on the local scene, by telephone or even offer to go along on the initial visit. Entrée through a disinterested third party constitutes an endorsement by someone known to the community and bespeaks a sincerity of purpose on the part of the researcher. Simply knocking at the door like a Fuller Brush man is likely to close it quickly on the whole venture.

At this point, the reader may be testing such an approach applied to a remote tribe of Amerindians along the Amazon or a tribe in the interior of New Guinea that has only been glimpsed from the air. Considering even these extreme examples, it is remarkable what a little research may uncover. There are few if

210

any communities that do not have some kind of contact with the outside world. Entrée to a village three tribes removed from the objective can be transmitted from tribe to tribe if that is the only solution. But let us assume that our researcher drops down out of the skies in the middle of his subject community. The situation will serve to illustrate a second important point in preliminary contacts.

In the remote village, with or without benefit of previously obtained introductions, the first interview must be with the village headman or mayor or council of elders or whatever appropriate body represents local authority. Without this level of approval and goodwill, little can be accomplished. This seat of authority, of course, can provide direct entrée to the performer. A guide may be assigned to lead the researcher to the home of the musician or dancer. Up to this point the tape recorder, still cameras, and motion-picture cameras have been kept out of sight. Are we ready to haul them out and get on with the action? Not quite yet.

A slow, very slow, beginning is the best beginning. The delay in starting actual documentation, of course, must be proportionate to the amount of time available. Are we in the field for three months? Six months? Two years? In my judgment the minimal time for the ethnomusicologist making an initial exploration in the field is one year. If the "field" is a local situation for the purpose of training, this may have to be scaled down to one semester or one or two quarters. But let us assume that we have reached the location of our professional objective and have settled in for one or possibly two years. Such a commitment is necessary if our objective centers on knowing and researching the subject in depth. Comparative studies requiring sampling in different locales or regions of an area have about the same requirements of timing even though the researcher's project involves several locations.

The first five or six months of the ethnomusicologist's first trip to the field will be spent in getting established in the community, winning acceptance to the point of not attracting undue attention, and gaining the confidence of the performers with whom he is working. During that same period, he will be acquiring some confidence in himself, discovering those areas in which his preparatory training has been adequate and those in which he must perforce rely on the rigorous school of on-the-job, or rather in-the-field, training. That first six months is a period of trial and error, loss and recovery. It is a stimulating experience filled with encouragement and despair, lucky breaks and frustration, minor victories and defeat. It is a time of testing that makes or breaks the field worker.

In the second six months, his initial labors will begin to show results. And in the course of the second year, he may look back at the period of the first six months with a truly comfortable shudder at the wonder of his initial naiveté.

In most circumstances, the ethnomusicologist will gain time in the long

211

run if during the first month or six weeks he restricts his association with performers to a lot of listening and watching, with some general discussions but no direct or vital questions, and postpones recording and filming. In that first month, he might take some pictures of local monuments or flora and fauna, but he should avoid aiming the camera at people or at military and strategic installations or certain sacred subjects. Perhaps with permission he might take a few pictures of musical instruments—but no players, unless invited to do so. After a few weeks, it will be widely known that he takes pictures, and the novelty of the equipment will have worn off somewhat. If the village has been occasionally or, worse still, frequently touched by the sprawling tentacles of tourism, this casual approach to photography will not be associated with the insatiable appetite of the camera-clicking tourist.

If electricity is available, he will keep batteries on charge for tape recorder and cameras. Occasionally, he might play back any kind of recording just loud enough so that it can be heard a moderate distance from his quarters. He might record his own voice a few times, singing or practicing the language, especially if there are some casual observers looking on from a distance. Aside from this, his equipment should repose quietly and unobtrusively for about six weeks, sitting out the slow, very slow, beginning.

Meanwhile, he is quite busy at two other important activities. In the first few interviews with performers, he will have made inquiry about two kinds of teachers: one for instrumental, vocal, and possibly dance lessons; the other for lessons in the regional language. In this quiescent period of the first six weeks, he should work long and hard hours to gain a foothold in these two kinds of study. Depending on his previous preparation, lessons in language should probably continue systematically for the first six months. Lessons in music and dance, depending on the different genres involved, should probably continue throughout the length of his stay in the field. These two modes of discourse, speech and music, are the foundation on which the success of his field work depends. They require prime attention, energy, and time. Never mind the musical performances not recorded or the dance or ritual not filmed during the first couple of months.

To a great extent, it is the challenge of learning to perform in a strange musical language that requires a minimum of one year's duration for the first field trip. Technical skill in instrumental and vocal music and the techniques of dance simply cannot be learned in a few months. Daily practice over a long period is necessary to train nerve endings and muscular coordination essential to performance skills. There is no shortcut to this aspect of international musicianship. We shall discuss the importance of such studies as a tool of field work presently.

In the course of his practical studies, the ethnomusicologist also gains a much better idea of what and when to record and film, not to mention the ground

212

gained among the performers with whom he is working. This kind of beginning is slow only in relation to mechanical documentation. His schedule of daily lessons, listening and watching, learning the ropes of daily living, becoming accustomed to the habits of a strange society will leave him little time to fret over the postponement of the first recording session.

In this initial period, he may discover, especially among certain cultures in the Orient, that within the field of the performing arts there are differing factions or centers. Traditionally, identification with one may automatically mean rejection by another. It will require the greatest finesse if he is able to begin his studies in one center and at the same time establish and maintain an open possibility of eventually joining a rival center. Perhaps studies with the rival faction may have to wait until his second trip to the field. But if he can establish the fact that he has a pure disinterest in the subject, clearly above the differences of local rivalry, it is possible to keep the door open. And, of course, in the long range, the demonstration of such an attitude is essential if comparative studies are part of the objective. The required exercise in diplomacy will add a certain challenge to the working schedule of the first few months. It is during this busy period of a slow start that all important avenues of acceptance and cooperation must be opened.

Within the first month, the ethnomusicologist will also be occupied with the search for an assistant, someone who can help with the practical chores in recording and filming that require more than two hands. The same person will serve as a guide and sometimes as a translator when discussions go beyond the researcher's knowledge of the language. Selection of an assistant should not be precipitous; he forms a very important part of the team. Some cautious inquiry, without commitment, and a few weeks of careful observation are worth the time invested. The village headman and one or two others responsible for the welfare of the village should be consulted about appropriate fees for the assistant, for teachers of music, dance, and language, for performers.

The day is about gone when services of this kind can be rewarded by glass beads and trinkets.[2] On the other hand, whatever the financial resources of the ethnomusicologist (and they are usually very limited), it is extremely important that such fees not be out of proportion to recompense normal to the local economy. Overpayment will be criticized more severely by the community than underpayment. A third party's judgment as to the proper amount will usually be accepted or at least can serve as a basis for negotiation. At any rate, the matter should be settled in advance.

It is important, of course, that the right "third party" be consulted. I recall

[2] Compare Jaap Kunst, *Ethnomusicology*, 3rd ed., Martinus Nijhoff, The Hague, pp. 14–15.

213

one incident when this procedure backfired. An instrumental teacher with whom I was planning to study indicated he had no idea of the amount to charge me for lessons and suggested a third party himself to set the fee. I was to take three lessons a week. The young man he designated had had some training in a university. When the fee was announced a few days later, it amounted to a monthly charge that was nearly equal to the monthly salary of an American professor paid in dollars! I explained that I was in the field on a modest grant, on leave from the university without salary, and that the fee asked for three lessons a week was about four times my total monthly stipend. I turned to the third party and asked him to explain how he had reached the figure. He said that a professor in the university only taught three classes a week, and that in America they were paid a large sum for their services. I laughed and assured him that professors worked many more hours than their class schedule might suggest. The teacher was embarrassed when the matter was fully explained. Then he asked me how much I could pay. I had been in the community for some months and already had a reasonable idea of an appropriate fee. Putting caution to the wind I told him I would pay him an amount that was double what it really should have been. He shook his head, reached for his instrument and said, "I will charge you nothing. But you must be willing to take four lessons a week instead of three. Then you will learn to play well, and that will be my payment." No amount of persuasion would change his mind, and there the matter stood. I began taking four lessons every week and periodically brought gifts for him and his family. At the end of my studies, yielding to pressures from his creditors, he finally accepted a substantial payment in cash.

The relatively expensive field equipment carried by the ethnomusicologist is often interpreted as evidence that he is wealthy. And in a relative sense, compared to the economic status of the society in which he might be working, he is. The equipment may be the property of his home university. His supplies have probably been purchased from the limited funds of a grant which also provides for reasonable living costs and miscellaneous field expenses. With dollar commitments continuing at home, he is likely to be following a tight budget. Still, his accoutrements give the impression of opulence. If the habits of his daily living are simple and within the range of local standards, he may gradually be accepted as a person of moderate means, more or less separated in the minds of the observer from the monetary status accorded his equipment. Nonetheless, he should be prepared to encounter two extreme attitudes in connection with payment for services: the person out to exploit him at every turn and the one who gives unstintingly of time, energy, and talents but refuses any payment.

Some years ago in Indonesia, I wanted to record a very popular radio singer for purposes of comparison with other singers, who by some standards were considered better but were not nearly so popular. My request was forwarded to the singer's manager. The next day I received word that a two-hour recording session would cost me 2,000 American dollars for the singer and 400 for the accompanying musicians. I meekly declined the proposal. Most often I have met the opposite extreme; and when a performer refuses to accept any payment, it is incumbent on the ethnomusicologist to find other means of compensation. I have often wondered, as a point of comparison, what kind of reception the Indonesian or African ethnomusicologist would get if he were to show up with his tape recorder at the Los Angeles studios of NBC or CBS with the explanation that he wanted to record representative broadcasts of their daily schedule as part of a large study devoted to the ethnomusicology of Los Angeles. By comparison, the Indonesian singer's fee might look quite modest.

Keeping in mind the importance of a slow beginning, let us consider in proper order the three requirements mentioned earlier: sensitivity to the human beings with whom the field worker is involved, thorough knowledge of subject, and technical know-how. Success in the field depends on the constant interplay of these forces.

THE HUMAN EQUATION

Part of the citation quoted earlier from Fox Strangways is worth repeating: "Without the willing co-operation of the singers and dancers they will do little, and that willingness is only to be bought with unfeigned sympathy, inexhaustible curiosity, lively gratitude, untiring patience and a scrupulous conscience."

In these times of rapid assimilation and the cultivation of speed-reading, I wonder how often the carefully weighed words of the writer are passed over too quickly to get at the point. Anyone who has spent some months or years in the field will appreciate the qualifying adjectives and pertinent nouns selected by Fox Strangways.

I have observed the collector at work feign sympathy or show no concern at all for the generous performer who had consented to the tiring ordeal of a perfect "take," not for money but out of pride for his achievement in an artistic form of cultural expression. The damage done by such disregard of other human beings may ruin an important field of study for others who follow. In this circumstance, sympathy is established or it is not. It cannot be feigned.

I have also watched the collector, anxious to get on with his recording, make it overtly clear that he was not interested in hearing about the details of playing techniques or construction of a musical instrument or the intrinsic value it held for the performer as an inheritance of several generations. And I watched the musician withdraw into himself and deliver a perfunctory performance. It could have been an inspired one, if the collector had had some of Fox Strangway's inexhaustible curiosity.

215

Lively gratitude at the end of a hard day's work may amount to no more than a warm smile and some genuine concern over the performer's fatigue. If the collector is truly enthusiastic about his subject, he will probably not realize that he, too, is exhausted until after he has reached his base camp, unloaded his gear, put batteries on recharge, and sat down to summarize the events of the day.

Untiring patience is a very special quality. In most instances, the performer being recorded or filmed will never before have had to face a microphone or a camera. He is probably unaccustomed to the variety of attention that is being paid to the details of music and dance that to him are commonplace. During the entire process of documentation, he will be facing one new experience after another. Mistakes, confusion, and a series of retakes are almost inevitable. Field work requires a kind of patience for which the collector, living in an age of automation, has had little or no experience.

On my initial trip to Ghana, I was granted the privilege of making the first special recordings of the royal drummers of the Asantehene, the head of all paramount chiefs of the Ashanti. The appointment was set for eight o'clock in the morning. I arrived at seven-thirty and was all set up by the appointed hour. The first drummer appeared about ten o'clock. After a frantic day of phone calls, messengers, a chartered taxi—and large quantities of untiring patience—we began our three-hour recording session about five o'clock in the afternoon. Such a situation, and it is not uncommon, requires a special kind of patience, without the slightest show of frustration or weariness or anxious glances at a wristwatch: untiring patience.

The rigors of a scrupulous conscience must be applied to every factor of field work. Never eavesdrop with a microphone; ask permission to record. If it is denied, respect the opportunity of at least being allowed to listen with your own ears. If a performer has indicated that all or a portion of the recording or filming you are making is restricted to your own usage, honor the agreement. I have been sitting on about 180 tape recordings of Javanese and Sundanese gamelan for more than a dozen years. A lingering distrust after years of colonial exploitation and political conditions at the time of recording were probably justification in the mind of the director general of Radio Republik Indonesia who restricted my materials to my own research—with an added directive that when I had finished researching the tapes they must be erased! Needless to say, I shall continue my study for many years to come. Meanwhile, times have changed, and the political climate of today is far different. Casual collectors have recorded in Java since then with no restriction in the release of recordings. For a number of years, UNESCO has been requesting that I make up an album from my collection for their series. High-ranking Indonesian officials have been consulted and none sees any objection to the proposal. But neither has anyone offered to supply a letter of authority that would release the restriction. It has been suggested that since the climate of the times has changed I should go ahead and make some of the material available. This I could easily do, if I were not plagued by the kind of scrupulous conscience referred to by Fox Strangways.

One could cite innumerable examples of situations in the field that demand a scrupulous conscience. Sometimes they have nothing to do with music. Often they are involved with some of the deepest of human values.

Perhaps it is the very nature of his subject and the consequent manner of his approach to it that on occasion tend to land the ethnomusicologist in rather delicate circumstances, not of his making and probably not of his own volition. In one of the several countries abroad in which I have done a greater or lesser amount of field work, I became acquainted with a young man in the course of several recording sessions who aspired to be a writer for an English-language newspaper published in that country. He asked me one day whether I would look over some things he had written and correct the English. I agreed to do so. After that, whenever a busy schedule permitted, I would make an appointment to see him at the house in which I was staying. The sessions on writing usually lasted an hour or so.

One afternoon, after we had finished working over a short article, he picked up the typescript, folded it and laid it on his lap. Half out of my chair at this point, I sat down again puzzled. He had always been considerate of the busy program I maintained and quick to leave the moment our session was finished. At first, I thought perhaps he wanted to discuss another idea for an article. So I offered him a cigarette, and for some minutes we made small talk. Suddenly, with a slight movement, as though he were adjusting his tunic, he pulled out a gun and sat with it lying in his open palm across his lap. I glanced at the weapon and then at him, trying to appear as calm as though I had just been shown a new ballpoint pen. He stared at the gun with a strong mixture of emotions showing in his face. "There are many of us with guns," he said, "waiting for the right time." I could not think of an appropriate comment, so I simply nodded. Then as though the dam had broken, out poured the beginning story of a large underground movement dedicated to insurrection, assassination, and civil war. I stopped him in mid-sentence by saying, "I value your trust in me. But please tell me no more. What I do not know, no one can force me to tell." He looked at me for a moment, then his face relaxed into a smile and he put the gun back in his tunic. Our English lessons continued from time to time, and the episode was not mentioned again. It is only because recent history has borne out his words that I feel free to mention it now.

There have been other similar instances of having deep confidences thrust forward without warning. And from them comes an interesting residue of an ethical nature, which the student of ethnomusicology may wish to ponder. If unwittingly he is entrusted with such confidences and thereby has a knowledge of facts that might be of critical importance to his own government, to which loyalty does he apply a scrupulous conscience?

What inspires such confidences? Ultimately, I suppose, it depends on the degree of rapport that can be established between two human beings. But I believe there are other considerations to be taken into account. Similar incidents have been reported to me by colleagues and students in ethnomusicology. I am convinced that the frequency of occurrence of this personal level of communication and trust has something to do with the nature of the subject and the manner in which it is approached.

AVOIDING THE QUESTION   In disciplines other than music and dance,[3] field work is carried on largely through questioning informants. Whether the researcher is speaking the language native to the informant or working through an interpreter, he is regarded as someone who asks a lot of questions. And ask questions he must; it is his principal mode of operation. I suppose it is only human nature, whatever assurances are offered, to be slightly on guard in the process of continual questioning. This is not to suggest any lack of sensitivity on the part of the questioner or any exaggerated notion that the informant may feel he is on the witness stand. Still, the questioning process itself is likely to discourage rather than to inspire personal confidences.

The ethnomusicologist must ask questions, too. But the subject of study, by its very nature, requires a different approach. And the subject refers to a different mode of communication. In the course of his practical studies, his lessons in music and dance, the ethnomusicologist is involved in this mode of communication. It is probably impossible to convey to someone who has never been a performer the extent to which making music together or moving together in dance is a mode of discourse, a mode of communication. It is different from "talking together"—as opposed to questioning and answering—probably because music and dance are more abstract modes of discourse than is a spoken language and at the same time are more responsive to concrete and precise communication. A beat in music or a movement in dance either is in time or it is not; a pitch is correct, a quality of movement right, or they are not. For the participants such facts are readily discernible. Two or more musicians or dancers can communicate at this level of expectation, without ever uttering a word, for hours on end. The level of communication established in the process has no equivalent in the spoken

[3] My frequent mention of "music and dance" is intended as a reminder that in many cultures the two subjects are inseparable; a true knowledge of either one requires the study of both.

218

language. And making music well together, or even aspiring to do so, creates a bond between the participants that is of a different order from that of the questioner and respondent. In fact, this mode of communication is unique among the various modi operandi of field workers. If the reader is a performer, he will have experienced what I am trying to describe; if he is not, I can only hope he may be able to imagine it.

The manner of approach in asking questions about music and dance is also different from that required in other disciplines. In the first place, admitting personal whimsy, I find it difficult to think of musicians and dancers as "informants," which, I suppose, in one sense they may be. But in the usual application of the term, an informant gives information through the spoken language or, even more specifically, according to Webster, is "a native speaker who repeats the forms, correct sounds, etc., of his language for the benefit of linguists, teachers, translators, etc." If we concede that the language in question is music or dance, then, of course, the musician's or dancer's mode of informing is by making music or dancing. A minute point, perhaps, but one that has a direct bearing on the manner of approach used in asking questions.

In the second place, in most cultures of the non-Western world, musicians are not accustomed to talking about music. They perform it, they compose it, they alter and change it, they improvise within the standards of its tradition. But they spend very little time talking about it. Speaking and writing about music are cultivations of the Western world. The ethnomusicologist, whatever his national origin, is a product of, or, let us say, an extension of, that cultivation. He must be careful not to allow his training in scientific methods, his intellectual curiosity, and, above all, his habit of talking about music get in the way of information that potentially music and musician can provide.

Therein lies the key to the manner of approach in questioning—music and musician. It is difficult to assess the quantity of misinformation that has accumulated in ethnomusicology as a result of a failure to understand the total interdependence of this duality. In many societies, if someone is asked a question, he is obliged to answer. Not to do so would be considered rude and might indicate ignorance on the part of the respondent, a loss of face. Whether he knows the answer to the question or whether he understands the question or even whether the question is germane to the subject—in the accepted behavior of his society these considerations may not even concern him. They are of vital concern to the questioner.

Let us imagine such an interview.

QUESTION: Is this pitch in your song [*the questioner sings "do"*] more important than the other four pitches?

219

ANSWER: [*The respondent hesitates, trying to decide whether to say "yes" or "no."*]

Q: Do most of your songs end with this pitch, or some other pitch?

A: Yes.

Q: They end with this pitch?

A: Yes...sometimes.

Q: Sometimes they end with other pitches; but most of the time with this pitch? [*He sings "do" again.*]

A: Yes.

Q: You always sing this song the same way? You change it sometimes?

A: Yes...[*some confusion appearing in the eyes*]...no.

Q: [*frowning*] Can you change it like this? [*He sings "do mi do" instead of "do fa do."*]

A: [*with appreciation for the attempt at singing*] Oh, yes!

The right answers to such questions, of course, are to be found in the music itself, a chore in analysis of the materials collected by the ethnomusicologist. There is no need to confuse the musician with analytical questions that he probably has never considered.

Assuming that the student of ethnomusicology has absorbed all of the substantive knowledge of his subject that is available to him before going to the field, he most certainly will arrive there full of questions. How does he get the answers? Suppose through intensive examination of existing materials, through analytical and comparative methods, he has reached certain conclusions of reasonable probability. How does he get confirmation or denial of these conclusions from the musician?

Before my first trip to Java, I had completed a doctoral dissertation devoted to a study of the modal practices in Javanese gamelan.[4] All the findings and conclusions were based on two sources: an analysis of more than 100 orchestral pieces and an intensive reappraisal of everything written about Javanese music. One important conclusion was based entirely on the latter sources, the music manuscript giving no evidence one way or the other. It had to do with the assumption long held by Kunst and others that the Javanese sléndro tuning system was intended to be made up of five equidistant intervals. If this were true, it had important implications in modal practice. A reevaluation of pertinent sources indicated the highest probability that this was not so. And I became convinced that the intention, like the available evidence, was a nonequidistant five-tone system. After reading my arguments, Kunst agreed.

[4] Mantle Hood, *The Nuclear Theme as a Determinant of Paṭet in Javanese Music*, J. B. Wolters, Amsterdam, 1954.

220

When I arrived in Java at last, I was anxious to learn what the Javanese musicians themselves might have to say on the subject. But how to ask them without suggesting an answer? My first rebab teacher, Pak Tjokrowasito (now known as K.R.T. Wasitodipuro), as leader of the gamelan at the radio station and at the palace of the Paku Alam, was recognized as the outstanding musician in Djogjakarta. My high probability conclusion, for the most part, had been based on forty-six sléndro tunings published by Kunst.[5] These measurements were taken from the bronze keys of the one-octave demung.[6] From this evidence, not one of the gamelan measured had an equidistant tuning, although several approached it; and otherwise there seemed to be no consistency from one to another in the occurrence of large and small intervals. On this evidence, I could state with certainty that an equidistant sléndro did not exist. So much for one octave of bronze keys. But what was the *intention*? From this and other evidence, it could be said with high probability that the intention also was a nonequidistant tuning.

In my first lesson on the rebab, I was impatient to know what Djogja's leading musician could tell me about this. Should I ask him? I decided against it. I had a hunch that a rebab player, who could produce any pitch he wanted on the bowed strings of his instrument, might provide the answer as to the *intention* of the tuning system, whatever the pitches of bronze keys seemed to indicate. But I wanted to avoid suggesting an answer.

He showed me how to hold the loose-haired bow, how to balance the instrument before me as I sat cross-legged on the floor, how to articulate the fingers of the left hand in three fingering positions. My ears told me he was demonstrating a nonequidistant sléndro. Then he put the instrument aside, took paper and pencil, and drew two lines to represent the two strings of the rebab. Next he placed a number for each of the five sléndro pitches at the point on the string line where the fingers of the left hand stopped the string. Then he drew a bracket from the first pitch to the second, from the second to the third, and so forth, until all the pitches were bracketed. My heart missed a beat when he said, "They are all the same size. From pitch one to two is the same as pitch two to three." I sat there dumbfounded. Then he added, "Kunst explained this in his book." He picked up his rebab and played all the sléndro pitches from the lowest to the highest. It still sounded like a nonequidistant scale. He looked back at the paper and said again, "All of the spaces are the same size," adding, "but we don't play them that way. These two are always larger." And then he demonstrated.

[5] Jaap Kunst, *Music in Java: Its History, Its Theory and Its Technique*, 2 vols., 2d ed., Martinus Nijhoff, The Hague, 1949, pp. 574–575.
[6] We have learned since that no single octave of the gamelan can indicate the true intervallic nature of its six and a half–octave tuning pattern. See further Mantle Hood, "Sléndro and Pélog Redefined," *Selected Reports*, vol. 1, no. 1, Institute of Ethnomusicology, UCLA (1966), pp. 28–48.

A few months later, I went through nearly the same experience with my rebab teacher in the other major cultural center of Central Java, Surakarta or Solo. First a flat statement that sléndro was equidistant, then a demonstration to show that it was not. In both situations, if I had asked the direct question, would I have arrived at the same answer? Probably not. Both teachers knew that I was a former pupil of Kunst. Both respected the man's prodigious knowledge of their culture; and there was a real conflict between a certain awe for the prestige of European theoretical authority and their own practical knowledge. It is likely that if I asked, "Is sléndro equidistant?" they would simply have answered, "Yes." In the course of two years of study, I would eventually have got at the truth. But in this instance, the indirect method of approach certainly avoided a lot of confusion. It also encouraged both musicians in the course of future sessions to volunteer their own copious knowledge, whether or not it was in conflict with European theoretical concepts about Javanese music.

From that time on, I have always made it a practice to try to get the answers to specific questions by introducing only a general topic of discussion in the hope that the musician or musicians involved—with some inobvious guidance—will volunteer the information I seek. Most of the time, the answers emerge in the course of musical demonstration. If the musician does not get around to my unspoken questions or provides only part of the answers, I try again on another day with a different topic of discussion.

The method requires Fox Strangway's untiring patience, but it has much to recommend it. Some of the questions in the mind of the ethnomusicologist may lie outside the knowledge and experience of the musician with whom he is working. By this method, he will at least avoid getting the wrong answers to such questions. Some of his questions may not be valid. These too will have no wrong answers. There is another advantage. In the course of discussion, he may learn the answers to questions he has not yet posed in his own mind. I presume this approach in getting information is something like that of the psychologist or psychiatrist: Let the patient do the talking.

Such a relationship between ethnomusicologist and musician avoids the natural reservation and constraint that are likely to arise between the direct questioner and the respondent. There is no suggestion that the researcher knows more questions than the musician has answers to supply. The musician is completely at ease. He is never on the defensive. Moreover, as the person who apparently, though perhaps not actually, is leading the discussion he is likely to dredge his memory and experience for every detail that will demonstrate his devotion to and knowledge of the subject. Beyond this, two persons talking together and making music together are likely to establish a strong bond of confidence. They become good friends.

A few notes of caution. In much of his field work, the ethnomusicologist is likely to be living in a society other than his own. To the extent it is possible before visiting the field, he will have acquainted himself with the mores, sanctions, values, habits, etiquette, taboos, and other manifestations of the culture in question. If he has the knack of adjusting quickly to strange food, styles of habitation, and other aspects of living and can accept these uncritically as the necessary mode of his existence for some months to come, he will be on the way to acceptance by members of the society. However, as his circle of acquaintance and friendship increases, there is some danger that he may reach a false sense of security. This might come about in several ways.

Among the Javanese there is an elaborate etiquette. Some of its rules can be learned from the ethnological literature. Most of them must be learned from quick and perceptive observation. For a time and up to a point, the stranger will be forgiven breaches of correct demeanor. But the sooner he acquires these niceties and makes them habitual, the sooner he will be accepted in the sense that he is not attracting undue notice by offensive, albeit unconscious, behavior. A few examples: a person never takes a seat or touches a drink or food until invited to do so, even though refreshments may have been served ten or fifteen minutes before a verbal invitation is forthcoming. Even then it is polite to wait until the invitation is repeated. To stand with the hand on one hip or hands on both hips (almost a stereotype of American male posture in repose) or with the arms folded across the chest is considered coarse, if not vulgar. It is also regarded as a physical offense to touch someone's head. Traditionally, two persons are not introduced by a third party on meeting for the first time, but instead each mentions his own name. And there is a special way to do this. Rather than speaking in the clear ringing tones of an American salesman, "I am Tom Jones from Ohio," one nods and mumbles rather indistinctly something like this: "Tmjonsz." To pronounce the name clearly might be construed as a mark of conceit or arrogance. It is true, you never quite catch the name of the person you have just met, but if knowing the name becomes important, there are ways to find it out. Normally one does not knock at the door of a house (it is usually open) but calls out rather softly, "Kula nuwun…" ("If you please…"). If you must pass in front of someone, you bend low, hold one hand before you and mumble an apology for permission to pass, "Nuwun séwu…." Traditionally, food is eaten with the fingers, and there is a proper technique involved. If tableware is offered, a large spoon is held in the right hand and a fork in the left. Never serve anything to anyone with the left hand. It is reserved for the functions of personal hygiene. And so forth, and so forth.

These and other niceties of etiquette can quickly and comfortably become habitual. As the circle of friendship develops and the researcher becomes increas-

223

ingly relaxed in the company of the musicians with whom he is working, he may unconsciously begin to slip back into the more deeply ingrained habits of his own culture. Although in one sense such relaxation could be construed as a compliment to his friends, it is more likely that it will offend them. The ethnomusicologist can relax only to the extent that the habitude of the society permits.

On the other hand, the field worker should not "go native." He must learn to sense the fine line between living within local standards that will not attract undue attention and simulating local attitudes and customs to a point of ridicule. The latter could cost him the very respect he is trying to win. A doctoral candidate or a professor from a university is not to be equated with a peasant in the rice field. To behave like one in customs or' in dress would be regarded as absurd. Appreciation and respect for the customs of the peasant is quite another matter. On the proper occasion, especially when invited to do so, it may be appropriate to don the traditional dress of the society: perhaps on the occasion of a wedding, as a performing member of a local musical ensemble, in honor of a historical or religious ritual. Guidance in these circumstances is usually offered by one's friends. But an ethnomusicologist garbed in a sarong at a recording session, where even some of the performers may be wearing Western clothes, is rather silly. Relaxing in a sarong in his house or base camp is rather sensible, and this inobvious endorsement of comfortable dress will be appreciated.

To the experienced field worker, the importance of such considerations is well known. To the aspiring field worker they may seem to be a kind of finical nitpicking. They are not. The relative success of the beginner in the field will depend in part on his ability to cope with these personal details in establishing a working relationship with other human beings.

THE INTELLECTUAL ICEBERG

In part, the success of the ethnomusicologist will depend on his preparation in substantive matters. Before reaching the field, he should have acquired a thorough background in his subject. Let us assume that when he first arrives in the field he already has some knowledge of the regional language and that he is fairly bristling with facts, figures, theories, speculations, historical perspective, authoritative sources, myths, legends, and so forth. Let us also assume that he has managed some practical training in the performance of the traditional music to be researched. By virtue of such preparation, he might be regarded as a kind of "expert" before the fact.

A little bit of knowledge is a dangerous thing. And a great amount of knowledge—devoid of any contact with the subject in the field—can be more than a little bit dangerous.

The time lag between the dates of publications on which his bookish knowledge is based and his arrival in the field may represent a period of considerable cultural change. Some of his sources are likely to carry an outmoded bias. The chauvinistic attitude and political philosophy that unconsciously influenced early writers produced something less than objective description, analysis, history, documentation, speculations, and conclusions. His preparatory reading and an exposure to inevitable disciplinary bias—from the historian, the ethnologist, the linguist, the geographer, the agriculturist, and so forth—may have aggregated different points of view, which become confused when applied to the subject of music. The extent to which the ethnomusicologist may be aware of these inherent distortions of information can be tested only in the field. Altogether, the amount of accurate and pertinent facts he has acquired might actually constitute a little bit of knowledge.

But let us also assume that an ameliorative circumstance in his training was frequent contact with the appropriate center for area studies. In the interdisciplinary atmosphere of such a research unit, he has had the opportunity to mingle with scholars, recently returned from the field, whose fund of information and experience are current. Lectures and symposia sponsored by the center would have corrected some of the misinformation he might have acquired. Most important, however, is the opportunity for informal discussions. In this context, his questions, doubts, and reservations can be aired. He will also have had the chance to meet and talk with an assortment of political elites from the country of his subject interest who come to the center for short-term visits.

The ethnomusicologist can be reasonably sure that two aspects of his preparatory training represent current information and that they are completely relevant to his research: studies in musical performance and the regional language. His practical studies in musical performance are reliable if we can assume that he was taught by someone familiar with the tradition at first hand. Even limited experience in performance practices would have given him a critical basis for evaluating publications devoted to the subject of music per se. His studies of the regional language, unless his teacher has been too long removed from contact with the field, will also represent a currency of expression. As we shall see, these two modes of communication, speech and music, are the principal tools of his field work.

THE SPEECH MODE OF DISCOURSE   Whatever amount of current and pertinent information he may have amassed, the ethnomusicologist will soon realize in the field that this knowledge can work for or against him, depending on his skill in applying horse sense to speech-music modes of communication, once he understands some of the more subtle implications in such a task.

225

In considering the relationship between these two modes of discourse—speech (talking about music) and music itself (making music)—Charles Seeger has called attention to the fact that "the communicable contents of the two arts" are sometimes the same, sometimes similar, and sometimes different.[7] In the European tradition, the theorist is inclined to assume that the first two conditions obtain more frequently than the last; the performer is likely to believe the last two obtain more often than the first. Western theory, for the most part, is intended as an explanation of practice and as such usually involves a time lag. Theory tends to be a description or prescription of yesterday's musical practices. The practices of today form the basis of tomorrow's theories. When the theorist tries to project probable future developments, the performer subsequently might frustrate the projection by going off in quite a different direction.

In the Orient, the relationship between theory and practice is likely to be of a different order. In India, for example, the theorist appears to dwell in one realm of music and the performer in another. Almost as an intellectual, aesthetic, and philosophical exercise, the theorist has carried the classical possibilities of raga and tala, the foundations of melodic and rhythmic development, respectively, as far as possible—without concern for the extent to which these possibilities are not yet realized by the performer. The Indian performer respects this area of musical endeavor and is not too concerned that theoretical projections go far beyond actual practice; in the last few decades, he is also occupied with musical practices that lie outside this realm. In a direct confrontation between performer and theorist, there appears to be little if any foundation for communication of the type suggested by Seeger. Performer and theorist live and function within two quite different frames of reference.

Musical theory in some Oriental cultures includes philosophy, sociology, aesthetics, mysticism, superstition, historical reverence, and so forth. To the Western-trained observer, certain aspects of such broad-based theory seem to be unrelated to and at times in actual conflict with traditional practice. But apparent conflict between practice and theory does not mean that the performer in any way rejects these aspects of theory at the verbal level of communication. He seems to be able to separate his own musical practice from an appreciation for the speech realm of music.

I am suggesting that in some Oriental cultures the "contents" of these two modes of discourse, speech and music, may be regarded as representing a dichotomy, a division that might even have implications of the term as applied to logic: real and unreal. Which is to be considered real and which unreal will

[7] See further Charles Seeger, "On the Moods of a Music Logic," *Journal of the American Musicological Society*, vol. 13 (1960), pp. 224–261.

depend on who is making the evaluation, theorist or performer. Be that as it may, the performer can respect the art of speech relating to music and at the same time regard it as a realm separate from the art of making music. From such a vantage point, there is no conflict between theory and practice. They are accepted simply as two *different* "arts," in Seeger's terms, involved with the same subject, music.

As a scientist of music, the ethnomusicologist is committed forevermore to the problems of the speech-music syndrome delineated by Seeger in his reference to points of identity, similarity, and difference in communicable contents. At the same time, he must be aware that the musician with whom he is working is likely to have quite a different orientation to speech-music communication. The researcher, therefore, must know when to speak and when to be silent or noncommittal, whatever his actual knowledge of the subject.

In the course of instrumental or vocal lessons, a technique, a rhythmic phrase, a melodic ornament might be explained in one way and demonstrated in a different way. The demonstration might even be a direct contradiction of the verbalization. In this situation, there is no choice but to imitate what has been played or sung and after a successful imitation ask for the explanation again. It may be quite different on the second try. But subsequently so may another demonstration! It is important to remember that the musician doing the teaching is probably making an exceptional effort to furnish verbal explanations—if any are offered at all—and that his accustomed mode of teaching is essentially nonverbal. If explanations and demonstrations appear to be inconsistent or contradictory, the fault might lie in his eagerness to be informative under the duress of a situation that is foreign to him. Some inconsistencies in his performance might be due to a lack of skill in the approach of the researcher. And some of the contradictions between speech and musical performance might arise from his acceptance of theory and practice as two different arts.

With this background, we might reconsider the first rebab lesson and the question of nonequidistant sléndro. It would have served no purpose to invalidate the teacher's description of equidistance by saying, "But what you are playing is *not* equidistant!" In the first place, notwithstanding the brackets he drew on paper from pitch to pitch, can we assume that his description of the intervals as being "the same size" has the same meaning for him as it does for us? In the second place, his perception of the nonequidistant scale he played—in whatever terms he might define it—is sure to be keener than that of the researcher; to suggest that he is not hearing what he plays would be insulting. In the third place, to contradict what the musician has volunteered is not likely to encourage the flow of other information. And finally, from the point of view of someone who regards speech and music as two different arts embracing a common subject, there was

227

no *real* point of conflict between the teacher's verbalization and his demonstration.

The field worker should avoid direct questions, should accept uncritically at the time whatever is said or demonstrated, and should not react to inconsistencies in either explanation or demonstration by so much as the bat of an eyelash—let the musician do the talking and performing. However great the researcher's fund of knowledge, the performing musician is sure to know more about the subject in a practical sense. His verbalizations may not be to the point in the immediate discussion and still may have validity in a different context. The ethnomusicologist should develop the attitude of wait-and-see. His own knowledge should be reserved for the judicious moment when a comment or two may encourage further discussion. In most circumstances, his storehouse of information should be like an iceberg, just a little bit showing above the surface.

At this point, the seasoned researcher whose subject and field methods require a different orientation may feel inclined to say that the horse sense recommended in the speech-music modes of discourse sound to him more like nonsense. If you can't ask questions, can't point out obvious mistakes, and have to keep quiet about facts known to be true, what contact do you have with the informant? This appears to be a methodless method—and that is not horse sense but nonsense.

Reminding our critic that we are working with a musician rather than an informant, I will try to defend the approach by making a few other points, which he will surely want to add to his list of criticisms.

THE NOTEBOOK AND THE TAPE RECORDER   Three different forms of record keeping are useful in the field: the notebook, the log, and the tape recorder. We shall speak about the log further on when we consider some of the methods relating to technical know-how. The notebook and the tape recorder are germane to the present discussion.

In the course of a session involving the speech-music modes of communication with a performer, I seldom write down anything learned from the speech mode of discourse. Typical exceptions might be the correct spelling of an occasional term or the title of a piece; and these I jot down on one or two scraps of paper carried in my pocket for that purpose. The notation of music discourse is a different matter. This double mode of communication might occur when the field worker is personally involved in a lesson or performance or when he is observing other performers or when most of the discussion is verbal with perhaps an occasional musical demonstration. Significant musical points can be written out in an appropriate form of notation. If the performer is accustomed to an indigenous notation, which may or may not be used in actual performance, he will appreciate the fact that the field worker knows how to use it in dictation. If the culture has no form of music notation, the musician is likely to be even more impressed by the mystery of seeing music written down in whatever form, especially when the researcher "reads it back" to him by singing or playing what has been written. In all probability, the musician will want to learn how to do this himself.

Making notations of music discourse is likely to encourage further discussion. Extended note taking of speech discourse is likely to have the opposite effect. Even reliance on discussion rather than questions may not completely dispel the constraints associated with the "clinical" method of question and answer if the field worker is constantly writing down everything said, like an efficient court reporter. It is far better to rely on a few scraps of paper and some memory training in the retention of detail than to risk giving the impression of a local tax collector.

At the end of the day, the few scraps of paper and the memory are combined in a detailed entry in the notebook. Facts that may have emerged in random order during the course of discussion can be reorganized according to topic headings and entered in an essay style, which allows the ethnomusicologist free reign to make a tentative evaluation while the information is still fresh in his mind. He may challenge some of the information, speculate on meanings, note inconsistencies or contradictions, pose further questions for the morrow, and wind up with a summary of salient points. This method forces the field worker, no matter how tired he may be, to review, organize, and assess the day's work while impressions are still sharp in his memory. It obviates the tendency to allow extensive notes taken on the spot to accumulate without evaluation until the important impressions that were *not* written down have been forgotten.

Sometimes this method can be supplemented by tape recording the whole of a speech-music discussion—if it is certain that the principal discussant is perfectly at ease within the range of a live microphone. The recording should be a supplement rather than a substitute for the notebook. At the end of the work day, the material on the tape should be reorganized and evaluated in the form of the notebook entry discussed above. It is valuable to make periodic summaries of tentative findings and conclusions based on notebook entries and music notations. And twenty or thirty notebook entries are much more readily accessible for the purpose than their equivalent in tape recordings. The periodic summing up focuses attention on lacunae that otherwise might go unnoticed until an opportunity to fill them in has passed. It encourages constructive daydreaming and wide-swinging speculations that could open up new avenues for exploration while the investigator is still in the field.

Although the chores of detailed description and analysis can wait for the desk and the laboratory, the habit of summing up in the field can also help the ethnomusicologist anticipate the ultimate requirements of this phase of his work. Lessons in performance provide a sharp tool for ferreting out the musical norms on which descriptive and analytical studies must be based. Most of the information is communicated in the music mode of discourse.

If only the early researchers had included in their field methods the music mode of discourse through training in performance, what a mine of information would have opened up for them! And, of course, among those societies with a relatively low cultural resistance—whose arts were not strong enough to withstand the impact of foreign intrusion—much or all of this kind of information is irretrievably lost.[8]

The first formal program of training to include studies in the performance of non-Western music began as recently as 1954.[9] After the first few years, during which the skeptics were having their say, the results of field work based on an inclusion of such training demonstrated the advantages of being able to communicate in both the speech and music modes of discourse. Students of the program, and by now, students of former students, still constitute only a small corps of ethnomusicologists with such an orientation. It is encouraging to note that a number of other programs and individuals are emulating a similar approach.

If the critic of our methodless methods is still with us, he might want another chance to comment, perhaps something like this: "Granted that a little amateurish know-how in performance might be of value in winning acceptance from the informant, think of all the hours spent in endless lessons devoted to instrumental and vocal technique! You can never really get hold of it anyhow. Where's the payoff? The time and effort would be better spent in observation and getting the answers to some concrete questions!"

Our critic is persistent if not dogmatic in his use of terms and insistence on clinical methods. His reference to "a little amateurish know-how in performance" suggests a kind of dilettantism that should not be confused with either preparatory training in international musicianship or the dead-serious business of practical studies continued in the field. The student in training and the researcher in the field must aspire to performance standards worthy of himself as a musician

---

[8] See further Mantle Hood, "The Reliability of Oral Tradition," *ibid.*, vol. 12, nos. 2–3 (1959), pp. 201–209.

[9] The first performance group at UCLA was in Javanese gamelan; as student interest warranted it, the program was gradually expanded to include a number of other cultures of Asia, Africa, Europe, the Far East, and the Americas.

and equal to the expectations of the culture in which he is working. This amounts to considerably more than amateurish know-how.

It is true that such an objective requires a great many hours of study; and it is also true that the study of some instrumental and vocal styles could last a lifetime. But our critic's comment that "you can never really get hold of it" belies his acceptance of the myth—exploded long ago by the palace musicians of the imperial household in Tokyo—that a person must be native to the culture in order to perform its music. The Japanese musicians are not only masters of the gagaku tradition but also professionally competent in the performance of Western music of the classical period. Reversing this, a number of Western students and colleagues in ethnomusicology have acquired outstanding skill in the performance of various non-Western musical traditions.[10] The degree to which "you can get hold of it" simply depends on innate musicality and the amount of time devoted to study.[11]

As to the payoff, describing it is something like the problem of trying to describe the taste of a mango or a martini to someone who has never experienced either: the taste mode of communication. Unless our critic is willing to gamble the time and energy required in performance studies himself, it is unlikely that he will ever appreciate the unique significance of this aspect of music discourse or experience the direct channel of communication it represents.

At the time of my first rebab lesson, February, 1957, there were a number of references to and studies of this important instrument of the Javanese gamelan already in print. Most were based on the assumption that, since the instrument has no fingerboard but only a slender neck, it was played entirely in "harmonics," that is, not fundamental pitches produced by stopping the string but so-called partials produced on Western stringed instruments by lightly touching the string. The most significant reference was written by Kunst;[12] and although he remarked that "the sounds produced do not have the quality of the harmonics on the violin,"[13] his discussion closed with the cautious comment:

> That the last word about the rebab and rebab playing has not been spoken by a long way, should be clear from the article "Omtrent de rebab" ("About the rebab") by J. S. and A. Brandts Buys-van Zijp. As a matter of fact, nothing is known with certainty concerning the essential nature of its tone.[14]

[10] For example, *Music of the Venerable Dark Cloud*, LP recording, IE Records, Stereo IER 7501, Institute of Ethnomusicology, UCLA, 1967.

[11] See further Mantle Hood, "The Challenge of Bi-Musicality," *Ethnomusicology*, vol. 4, no. 2 (May, 1960), pp. 55–59.

[12] Kunst, *Music in Java, op. cit.*, pp. 220–229.

[13] *Ibid.*, p. 221.

[14] *Ibid.*, p. 229.

231

Within the first few minutes of an actual lesson on the instrument, it became clear that the rebab is not played in harmonics. And in the course of nearly two years of study, the true nature of technical and stylistic details that had been a source of speculation in earlier publications were communicated with great clarity in the music mode of discourse.[15]

For the field worker with a pragmatic turn of mind, there is great satisfaction in the "discovery" of techniques, ornamentation, and even the correct quality of sound itself when his own hands or voice have finally succeeded in producing them. Subsequently, this experience, whatever the modest limits of his own personal repertory, will enable him to perceive more accurately the musical sounds of his field recordings. Once he understands the specific musical requirements of his subject through his own studies in performance, the ethnomusicologist possesses the kind of knowledge essential to accurate description and analysis. His ultimate communication of the facts, therefore, through speech or writing, represents the constant interplay of the speech-music modes of discourse.

Practical studies in musical performance provide a unique advantage not only in discovering the technical and stylistic idiom of an individual instrument but also in "hearing," through actual participation, the precise requirements of certain norms of musical style that otherwise can be most elusive. Some practices common to the non-Western world of music are rare or even unknown in the European tradition—for example, interlocking parts, "filling-in," stratification, group improvisation, and true polyrhythm. We might consider a few illustrations of the advantage of studies in performance in recognizing the nature of such practices.

Interlocking parts shared by two or more players are a basic hallmark of style in Bali. A related practice is also known among some xylophone traditions of Africa. This should not be confused with hocketing, a practice of breaking up one melodic line through the performance of successive short fragments distributed among several players, a practice known in the late medieval literature of Europe. Hocketing, too, is common in Africa and Southeast Asia. But interlocking parts involve interdependent parts, the sum of which is greater than one melodic line.

One of the most appealing and complex traditions of Bali is the music performed by the quartet of instruments known as gendèr wajang. A principal role of this ensemble of metallophones (see Illustration 4-4) is its use in accompanying the shadow play based on the religious literature of the *Mahabharata* and the *Ramayana*. It has an important function in connection with wedding celebrations, tooth-filing ceremonies, temple festivals, cremations, and so forth.

[15] See further Mantle Hood, "The Javanese Rebab," *Hinrichsen's Musical Yearbook*, Proceedings of the First Congress of the Galpin Society, June 28-July 4, 1959, Cambridge, England, vol. II, 1961, pp. 220–226.

The instruments are tuned to one or another version of five-tone sléndro and have ten bronze keys suspended over bamboo resonators. The quartet consists of two pairs, one voiced an octave higher than the other, so that its lower octave is the same as the higher octave of the larger pair. The two instruments of each pair are tuned so that there is a difference in the pitch of their corresponding keys that amounts to 6–10 cps, depending on taste. This difference in pitch between pengisep (the higher instrument) and pengumbang (the lower) is known as pen-joreg, and the effect is a shimmering sound caused by the musical beats created between corresponding high-low keys. The principle of paired tuning is found among all types of Balinese gamelan as well.[16]

The player holds a disc-headed wooden panggul or beater in each hand, and his left and right hands perform highly independent parts requiring different physical techniques. The bronze keys are damped by the same hand that does the striking, stopping the sound with the back or outer edge of the hand or fingers.

[16] See further Hood, "Sléndro and Pélog Redefined," *op. cit.*, pp. 31–32 and fig. 1 on p. 38.

233

The technical and musical requirements of gendèr wajang are considered more difficult by the Balinese than those of any other genre of music in Bali. In fact, for some years there has been concern over the viability of the tradition because very few young men, although they may be expert performers in gamelan, have the patience and dedication needed to master this exacting art. Most of the performers of gendèr wajang in Bali today are old men.

The pengisep and the pengumbang play different parts, doubled at the octave (except for occasional slight deviations) by the smaller pair of instruments. Sometimes the higher-voiced pair may be omitted. The relationship between left and right hand of each part is quite variable in relative density, motion—parallel, oblique, contrary—rhythm, harmonic support, melodic importance, and relative independence. The two hands may collaborate momentarily in executing one lyrical line; or the right may perform a rapid ostinato while the left carries a melody; or this relationship may be inverted; or the two hands may move rapidly in parallel motion occasionally at the octave but more often at the interval of a sléndro fifth; or a staccato style may be used in one hand and a legato in the other; and so forth. Every imaginable compositional device and variable relationship between the two hands seem to be found in the repertory.

The relationship between the part played by pengisep and the one played by pengumbang is also as variable as the relationship between the two hands of one part. Sometimes the left hands of the two parts simply duplicate a lyrical line allowing the full shimmering quality of penjoreg tuning to come through. Sometimes they play quite independent polyphonic parts that have occasional points of agreement at the penjoreg unison, sléndro fifth, or sléndro octave. Sometimes they interlock in a rapid ostinato that may have rhythmic, harmonic, and even melodic importance. Halfway between this device and independent polyphony is the continual interlocking and separation of two melodies. The right hands of the two parts may have any of these relationships, but more often they play complementary interlocking parts having strong rhythmic cross accents, harmonic implications, and sometimes melodic importance as well. Either hand of pengisep or pengumbang may execute ephemeral clusters of grace notes. These may occur in only one hand of one part or be duplicated or complemented by the other hand or the other part in one or both hands.

This music, performed by eight hands covering three octaves of bronze keys, with the central octave duplicated in pitch, is a rich, vibrant, complicated web of sound to the ear. The homogeneity of quality of the four instruments makes it impossible to separate the eight parts by aural perception alone. A tape recording of the music is of little help in understanding the requirements and distribution of interlocking parts. The tradition of gendèr wajang is entirely oral, so the field worker has no guidelines to follow but his ears and—if he will take the time and has the patience—his hands. It is possible, with the close cooperation of the performers, to have one part played, fragment at a time, with many repetitions for purposes of dictation. It is a painstaking process that not only is fatiguing for performer and transcriber but also is likely to induce mistakes in performance, brief lapses of memory, and a degree of impatience when the player tries to perform in such an unfamiliar role. In my experience, transcription of music for gendèr wajang can be accomplished more quickly and much more accurately if the field worker will learn to play the parts himself. Subtleties in damping, rhythmic niceties, and the relationship of interlocking parts are highly resistant to observation and the artificiality of fragmentary dictation. These norms of musical style can be communicated with the greatest surety only through the music-making mode of discourse.

A different but related problem arises in connection with what I have termed "true polyrhythm" found in some African cultures. Transcriptions of African drumming ensembles made by Western-trained observers without experience in performance show differences in interpretation.[17] The same rhythmic pattern might be notated several different ways in terms of meter, bar lines, phrase structure, and so forth. It might not seem to matter, theoretically, which of several possibilities is chosen by the transcriber; for example, the same pattern might be transcribed in $\frac{3}{8}$, $\frac{6}{8}$ or $\frac{12}{8}$ meters or $\frac{2}{4}$, $\frac{4}{4}$ or $\frac{8}{8}$ meters. The real point of issue, it would seem, is where to place the bar line. Such a supposition, of course, is not valid. The question of meter is symptomatic of a more basic problem: How does the *African* hear his rhythms? Until this question is answered, African polyrhythm cannot be accurately transcribed.

In an ensemble of a dozen or more instruments performing a half dozen different rhythmic patterns, to what does each pattern relate? Do they all relate to the same thing? Can the matter be resolved simply by choosing the right meter? In the first place, the concept of the bar line is a development of the European tradition. In the second place, true polyrhythm is unknown in the tradition of European music. And in the third place, as a result, a Western-trained observer lacks a suitable precedent in his own system of notation and has no preparation in his background for perceiving true polyrhythm in the way it is heard and performed by an African. Let us consider a specific example.

In the fall of 1962, I was privileged to spend a couple of months launching the first graduate seminar in ethnomusicology at the University of Ghana. One of my objectives was to try to find better techniques in recording drumming

---

[17] A. M. Jones, "African Drumming," *Bantu Studies*, vol. 8, no. 1 (March 1934), pp. 1–16; also reprinted in "African Music in Northern Rhodesia and Some Other Places," Occasional Paper no. 4, Rhodes-Livingstone Museum, Livingstone, N. Rhodesia (Maramba, Zambia), 1949, *passim.*

235

ensembles. These will be considered in some detail presently; but for the moment a supporting activity, crowded into the schedule of teaching and recording, is pertinent to our present discussion. Immediately upon arrival, I engaged an Ewe master drummer, Robert Ayitee, to give me instrumental lessons. I had the hope that these studies would afford insight into some of the recording problems and reveal something about the nature of African polyrhythm.

The ensemble of instruments studied consisted of a master drum played with a stick in the right hand and the left hand bare, a hand drum, two stick drums, two or three gourd rattles, two or three metal rattles, two toquay (a short slit metal tube played with a metal rod), and two or three double bells. Lessons began not with the master drum, which interested me the most, but with one of the basic rhythmic patterns played by a double bell. Systematically, the pattern of each instrument was learned; and I noted that lessons on one instrument were always supported by volunteer performers on several of the other instruments. Finally, I graduated to the master drum. The rhythmic patterns of the other instruments were quite short and were repeated over and over with little variation. The master drum, by contrast, performed a variety of much more sophisticated patterns of greater length, their sequence and number of repetitions being improvised by the master drummer. The various patterns had direct relationship to different dance steps and were employed by the master drummer to guide the choreography of the dancers.

At night back in my quarters, I notated the patterns I learned during the working day. The next day these were performed for the master drummer to be sure they were correct. I found the task far easier than I had anticipated. The short patterns, in spite of a subtle asymmetry, offered no problem. The longer patterns of the master drum formed logical phrases that were easily recognizable. The next step in transcription, however, posed a number of questions. How did the different patterns relate to one another when arranged in score? Where did

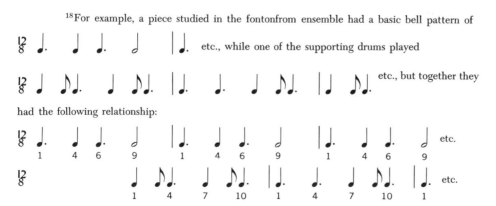

[18] For example, a piece studied in the fontonfrom ensemble had a basic bell pattern of
etc., while one of the supporting drums played
etc., but together they had the following relationship:

236

each pattern begin, that is, which beat of the pattern could be regarded as the downbeat, beat 1? Was there a common downbeat in this Ewe drumming? Or did different instruments have different beats 1 as in some Ashanti ensembles?[18] What was the correct meter? Did all patterns relate to the instrument I had learned first, the double bell? Or to the master drum?

The key to these questions could be found in the very teaching methods used by the master drummer. A summary of principal points noted in the course of the progressive studies will be enlightening at this point. (1) Despite my expressed interest in the role of the master drum, it was the last instrument studied. (2) The first thing learned was the pattern played by one of the double bells, sometimes called the master bell. (3) The study of each instrument always occurred in the context of patterns played on some of the other instruments but not always the same instruments—except for the inclusion of the master bell. (4) Lessons on the master drum always included the master bell and enough of the other instruments so that all the different patterns were represented. (5) A pattern duplicated by two different types of instruments was usually represented by only one of them in lessons on the master drum.

This sequence of lessons and the varying combinations they included made it clear that there were several levels of relationship to take into account. (1) All instruments related the the basic bell pattern. (2) However, the patterns of two similar instruments, for example, the two stick drums, related first to one another and then—as a pair or resultant pattern—to the master bell. (3) Different phrases of the master drum corresponded to different patterns of the ensemble, sometimes reinforcing only the pattern of the master bell, sometimes one or another patterns of the other instruments. (4) A consistent phrase length or multiples thereof for all patterns dictated logical bar lines. (5) This circumstance and the master drummer's absolute perception of the DR (density referent) made clear that the correct meter was:

Perhaps by now the critic of lessons in performance would like to try his hand at an experiment. First, he might listen to the recording of gendèr wajang on the accompanying LP, Side II, Band 1, and then, in whatever notation he finds comfortable, try to transcribe left- and right-hand parts of both pengisep and pengumbang. Second, he might listen to the example of Ewe drumming, Side II, Band 2, and then try transcribing the rhythms of this ensemble. When he is satisfied with his results or weary of the task, he can check his transcription by looking at Illustration 4-5, where he will find a portion of the gendèr wajang piece transcribed in cipher notation, and at Illustration 4-6, where part of the Ewe piece is transcribed in TUBS notation.[19]

Briefly we might consider three other norms of musical style mentioned earlier, practices that are most readily perceived by the field worker through his own participation in performance: "filling-in," stratification, and group improvisation. The large gamelan of Central Java employs all three and, to the best of my knowledge, in their most complex form. My term "filling-in" is a brief description of a practice found in many musical cultures of the non-Western world. It has sometimes been referred to as a cantus firmus technique,[20] a compositional device of the European tradition that can take a number of forms.[21] None of these, however, corresponds to the practice of filling in. In the Javanese gamelan, the fixed melody of the piece, the specific "tune" that makes it different from all other pieces, does not function like a cantus firmus. A melodic abstraction of the fixed melody, the balungan, serves as a modal guideline to the improvising instruments, which "fill-in" independent but interrelated polyphonic melodies. Depending on the relative density of the improvised part, these improvisations reflect in various ways the spirit and character of the fixed melody. At the higher densities of stratification, each improvisation spontaneously interacts also with the character of other improvised parts going on around it. Filling-in, stratification, and group improvisation, in this ensemble, are inseparable norms of style. The complete integration of these three practices at various levels of density can best be perceived and understood by performing on the variety of instruments representing different levels within the context of the complete gamelan.

A simpler, but no less subtle, example of filling-in came to my attention in Ghana. I made several recordings of a young xylophone player who taught in the Institute of African Studies. His instrumental technique was impressive, and I was curious to know what guided the rapid movement of his two hands. Was

---

[19] See further James Koetting, "The Analysis and Notation of West African Drum Ensemble Music," *Selected Reports*, vol. 1, no. 3, Institute of Ethnomusicology, UCLA (1970), pp. 115–146.

[20] Kunst, *Music in Java, op. cit.*, p. 167.

[21] See further Willi Apel, *Harvard Dictionary of Music*, 1st ed., Harvard University Press, Cambridge, Mass., 1965, pp. 117–118.

Gendèr

```
 I   ⎰R.H.   . . . 1̇ . . . 6  1̇ . 1̇ .  6 1̇ . 6  1̇ . 1̇ .  6 1̇ . 6  1̇ . 1̇ .  1̇ . 1̇ .
 &   ⎱
III   L.H.   . . . 1 . . . 6̣  . . . 1  . . . 6̣  . . . . .5̣ . .  .3̣ 5̣ 6̣  .5̣ .3̣


 II  ⎰R.H.   . . . 1̇ . . . 6  3 5 3 5  6 3 5 6  3 5 3 5  6 3 5 6  5 3 5 6  5 6 5 6
 &   ⎱
 IV   L.H.   . . . 1 . . . 6̣  . . . 1  . . . 6̣  . . . . .5̣ . .  .3̣ 5̣ 6̣  .5̣ .3̣


 I   ⎰R.H.   1̇ . 1̇ .  1̇ . 1̇ .  5 . 5 .  5 . 5 6  5 3 5 6  1̇ . 6 .  5 6 1̇ .  1̇ . 1̇ .
 &   ⎱
III   L.H.   . . . 1 . . . 6̣  . . . 1  . . . 6̣  . . . . .5̣ . .  .3̣ 5̣ 6̣  .5̣ .3̣


 II  ⎰R.H.   5 6 5 6  5 6 5 6  5 3 2 .  2 3 5 6  5 3 5 2  3 5 2 3  5 6 5 6  5 6 5 6
 &   ⎱
 IV   L.H.   . . . 1 . . . 6̣  . . . 1  . . . 6̣  . . . . .5̣ . .  .3̣ 5̣ 6̣  .5̣ .3̣


 I   ⎰R.H.   1̇ . 1̇ .  1̇ . 1̇ .  1̇ . 1̇ .  1̇ . 1̇ .  1̇ . 1̇ .  1̇ . . .  5 . 3 .  3 5 3 2
 &   ⎱
III   L.H.   . . . 2 . . . 3  . . . 5̣  . 3 . 2  . . . 6̣  . . . 5̣  . . . 3  . . . 2


 II  ⎰R.H.   5 6 5 6  5 6 5 6  5 6 5 6  5 6 5 6  5 6 5 6  5 6 . .  5 . 3 .  3 5 3 2
 &   ⎱
 IV   L.H.   . . . 2 . . . 3  . . . 5̣  . 3 . 2  . . . 6̣  . . . 5̣  . . . 3  . . . 2


 I   ⎰R.H.   6 . 6 .  6 . 6 .  6 . 6 .  5 6 . 5  6 . 6 .  5 6 . 5  6 . 6 .  6 . 6 .
 &   ⎱
III   L.H.   . . . 6̣ . . . 5̣  . . . 6̣  . . . 5̣  . . . . .3̣ . .  .2̣ 3̣ 5̣  .3̣ .2̣


 II  ⎰R.H.   3 5 3 5  3 5 3 5  2 3 2 3  5 2 3 5  2 3 2 3  5 2 3 5  3 2 3 5  3 5 3 5
 &   ⎱
 IV   L.H.   . . . 6̣ . . . 5̣  . . . 6̣  . . . 5̣  . . . . .3̣ . .  .2̣ 3̣ 5̣  .3̣ .2̣


 I   ⎰R.H.   6 . 6 .  6 . 6 .  3 . 3 .  3 . 3 .
 &   ⎱
III   L.H.   . . . 6̣ . . . 5̣  . . . 6̣  . . .


 II  ⎰R.H.   3 5 3 5  3 5 3 5  3 2 1 .  1 2 3
 &   ⎱
 IV   L.H.   . . . 6̣ . . . 5̣  . . . 6̣  . . .
```

Illustration 4-5
Cipher notation of "Selasah" showing the distribution of parts, paired between gendèr I and III and gendèr II and IV; gendèr I and II denote the larger pair of instruments; gendèr III and IV, the smaller pair, voiced an octave higher. Ciphers used in the notation indicate the central octave of the instrument; with the dot above, the upper octave; with the dot below, the lower octave.

239

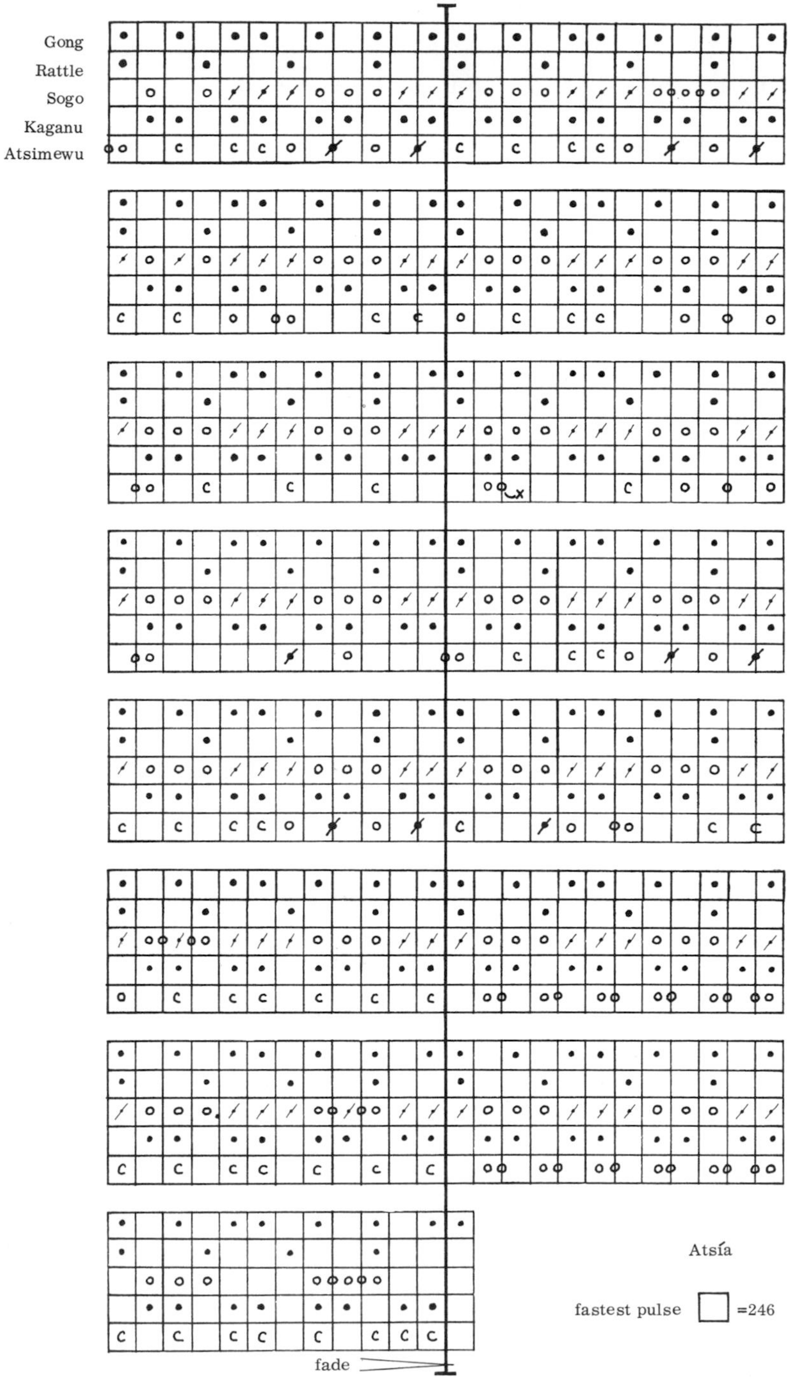

Illustration 4-6
Each box or tub represents the density referent, i.e., the fastest regularly occurring pulse. Occasional subdivisions of the density referent are indicated when a symbol occurs on the line. Different symbols indicate a variety of hand and stick techniques. (See further James Koetting, "The Analysis and Notation of West African Drum Ensemble Music," Selected Reports, vol. 1, no. 3, Institute of Ethnomusicology, UCLA (1970), pp. 115–146.)

Atsía

fastest pulse ☐ =246

fade

he playing a set piece that was handed down orally? Was he improvising? I was informed that most often two xylophones would perform interlocking parts in this tradition. I asked to be given some lessons on the instrument; and although the study was short-lived, it revealed a fascinating principle that governed the style. He began by playing for me the first piece he had learned. It was very simple. Then he showed me how the same piece was played at two successive stages in the learning process. To the observer, the three performances sounded like three different pieces, each more elaborate than the other. This suggested the process of filling-in; but I could not yet be sure—filling in what? Later, sitting next to him, trying to catch the manual technique required, I caught something far more essential to my question. As he played in his most brilliant style, he was humming a tune; and, compared to this simple melody, the xylophone part was indeed a type of filling-in. On Side II, Band 3, of the accompanying LP recording is an example of his xylophone style; Side II, Band 4, is a special recording in which his humming can be discerned along with the sound of the xylophone. (See Illustration 4-7.)

MUSICAL LITERACY It has been long recognized and accepted that the

Illustration 4-7
Lobi xylophone player.

241

Western musicologist concentrating on one or another musical style of the European tradition is competent to the extent that his background includes training in the skills of musicianship and performance. These constitute his ABCs of European musical literacy. By the same token, the ethnomusicologist researching one or another musical style of the non-Western world is competent only if he is trained in the pertinent skills of non-Western musicianship and performance. Such musical practices as filling-in, interlocking parts, true polyrhythm—or any other, for that matter—demand this kind of literacy if the field worker is to perceive and comprehend their peculiarities.

Musical literacy is the sine qua non of ethno*music*ology. A few decades ago, such a requirement was unrecognized except by one or two individuals—for example, Kirby, mentioned earlier. Today, proof of its absolute essentiality has been demonstrated in publications written by men with such an awareness. To the diehard, our critic of "amateurish know-how in performance," we can give little comfort. He must either retool his outmoded dogma or make peace with the inadequacy of his antiquated methods. Any publication in ethnomusicology that fails to take this requirement into account must be regarded with great reservation as to its perception, reliability, and significance.

THE VALUE EQUATION

Studies in performance also offer an advantage in the sociological approach to the subject of music. We have indicated that the speech-music modes of discourse, through the camaraderie realized in making music together, establish a basis of personal confidence. It is not simply that the ethnomusicologist is accepted as a fellow musician; it goes much deeper. His devotion to lessons and rehearsals is taken as evidence of the purest interest in the subject, a genuine appreciation of something of unique value to the society. And, of course, the sociological approach must transcend the mere consideration of function and usage by evaluating these in relation to the whole range of human values. Otherwise, it is likely to amount to little more than a dehumanized list of not-so-vital statistics. Unfortunately, in much of the literature to date, a concern for human values in the sociological approach is either ignored or, at best, given slight attention.

The ethnomusicologist who demonstrates sincerity of interest through studies in performance has a great advantage in his search for this vital type of information on which a true understanding of music in its social context must depend. What basic considerations are to guide his quest? Should his primary concern involve the whole of a society? A particular segment? An individual musician? The nature of his subject will offer some clues to these questions. In the Introduction we pointed out that beatle music has had a profound effect on many aspects of American society. The music of female puberty rites found in one tribe of West Africa may have no direct effect on the political entity known as Ghana. On the other hand, "the whole of society," in this instance, is the tribe in question; and its valuation of the music of female puberty rites may indeed have important implications on a comparative basis for the whole of Ghana or for all of West Africa.

How do we get at a social valuation? Let us suppose that we want to determine the social value of a specific piece of music or of all the music of one genre or of a whole tradition of music or of all the musical traditions of a society as well as the bundle of nonmusical traditions from which they are inseparable. Where do we start? If the field worker is taking lessons in performance, his teacher offers the best beginning With his help, the researcher can be led to the appropriate members of society to be consulted. He will try to learn, for example, what the composer's valuation is from specific piece to bundle of traditions. He must determine whether there are both professional and amateur performers of the music and in what terms they can be defined. How do their respective valuations compare? What about the user or consumer of the music? And how does his valuation compare with that of the nonuser? Is there a special social group involved, a hunters' association, a warriors' association, members of the royal family, a religious sect? How do their valuations compare with those of persons or other groups outside the special group? What is the value of a specific piece in relationship to the valuations of genre or tradition or bundle of traditions by these different members of society?

What percentage of the society is represented by each one of these categories: composer, professional, amateur, user, nonuser, special group? What is the social status of each of these? The economic status? How does the total percentage of musicians and users of the music and their valuation relate to that of the whole society? That is, if musicians and users represent 3 percent of society, how does the valuation of the other 97 percent compare with that of the group with a vested interest? Is this relationship the same or different in terms of economic rewards, social status, and so forth?

Assuming that these valuations are volunteered in the course of guided discussion rather than in response to suggestive questioning, in what terms are they expressed? Religious values? Philosophical concepts? Aesthetic standards? Perhaps value relates to superstition and magical propensity. Or maybe it involves personal property rights or sexual associations. Possibly it is to be measured in relation to social commentary as political satire or as a musical record of history or in connection with some venerated ritual or as a symbol of social status. Maybe its principal value is educational. Perhaps it is pure entertainment. Has it also a commercial value, and if so how does this relate to other categories of value?

243

Whatever the terms of valuation, it is also important to recognize the extent to which these judgments depend on reference to and inclusion of related arts, such as dance, puppetry, drama, prose and poetic literature, painting, sculpture. To what extent are value judgments associated with social institutions, such as various levels of government, the educational system, mass media of communication, the family unit, segments of the labor force, the military, and so forth? Is the relative age group of the valuer—the teen-ager, the child, the mature adult, the aged—a significant factor?

From the wide range of these questions, it is apparent that the researcher must have a very broad knowledge of the society in which he is working. His teacher in performance can provide entrée; but the greater the ethnomusicologist's general knowledge, acquired as part of his preparatory training, the more fully he will be able to seek out information relating to the social context of music. And as an invaluable complement to his general knowledge, the more he knows about musical practice the more readily he will be able to expand his contextual knowledge.

In addition to the sociological importance of such information, what insight can it provide in relation to the subject itself, music? Or is its worth, as it contributes to our understanding of the social context of music, to be measured only in extramusical terms? In my experience, these diverse social valuations of music can sometimes elucidate the relative importance of various musical principles which otherwise might be missed or misunderstood by the researcher.

It was suggested earlier that the polyphonic stratification practiced by the Javanese gamelan would seem to offer a musical correlation to the social and economic hierarchies that have dominated Javanese history. An economic valuation of the musical hierarchy of the gamelan can be determined by the pay scale of the professional musicians. In the Western orchestra, musicians who are paid above the union minimum are the conductor, soloists, and first-chair performers. The greatest financial rewards, therefore, are measured in terms of supply and demand as well as technical virtuosity. In the Javanese gamelan, the pay scale, for the most part, is governed by a different set of standards. The leader of the gamelan, of course, whether he plays the rebab or the drums, commands the highest salary. However, the pay scale is really a reflection of the musical requirements governing group improvisation. The standard has aesthetic significance because it is a measure of the relative importance assigned to an instrument in terms of the regulative principles of improvisation. Correspondence between pay scale and the requirements of technical virtuosity tends to be fortuitous. For example, the slenṭem, which requires a relatively simple technique in performance, is higher on the pay scale than the gendèr panerus, an instrument which demands great manual dexterity. The slenṭem carries or anticipates in long note values the tones of the fixed melody

244

of the piece and has, therefore, a major responsibility in supplying the pitches which guide filling-in and group improvisation. As a product of the oral tradition, the slenṭem player must carry in his head the fixed melodies of a large repertory; and his memory must never fail him. The player of the gendèr panerus, by contrast, performs at the very highest level of density of all the contributing strata, displaying real technical virtuosity in the course of his improvisation. But his *communal* responsibility in the context of group improvisation is not as great as that of the slenṭem player. Outranking both of these in pay is the player of the gendèr barung, which is played at about half the speed of the gendèr panerus, requires maximal technical skill, and above all carries a principal responsibility in polyphonic improvisation. The player of the large gong ageng, which sounds less often than any other instrument in the gamelan and requires a reasonably simple technique, rates higher on the pay scale than one who plays the relatively active saron barung, which performs the fixed melody or stylistic elaborations of it. The overriding responsibility of the large gong is its colotomic function of marking the longest melodic periods of the piece, a hallmark of musical form. The female soloist, in constant interplay with the rebab, supplies a line of improvisation that represents the freest melodic invention, a kind of distillation of group improvisation; and she is very near the top of the pay scale. The Javanese recognize the technical requirements of rebab playing as being more difficult than those of any other instrument. But it is at the top of the pay scale for a different reason. As the leader's instrument, it is responsible for controlling all the regulative principles of group improvisation, leading the female soloist, and passing along to the drummer and other instrumentalists various musical signals woven into the course of its singular improvisation.

This kind of economic valuation provides more than sociological insight. It correlates different levels of pay scale with different musical principles; and, consequently, it can serve as a guide for the researcher in the course of musical analysis. It can be used as an indicator in establishing the G-S line of improvisation. The signposts of pay scale, erected by the Javanese themselves, clearly mark the pathway of significant musical principles all the way from general concepts, such as mode and musical form, to the most specific requirements of group improvisation. Such a valuation is also a reliable referent in relating musical elements to the whole bundle of traditions that surround Javanese gamelan. For example, the large gong ageng, in addition to its principal function as a colotomic instrument, is often regarded as pusaka (having magic power) and is honored with the weekly burning of incense. The importance of the gendèr barung extends beyond its singular contribution to group improvisation to include a unique role in supporting the dalang, the puppeteer of the shadow play known as wajang kulit. And wajang kulit, in turn, represents a composite of all the performing arts and serves as a

245

kind of camera obscura of society, revealing within its frame of reference the whole bundle of Javanese traditions. The rebab and the kenḍang, too, have primary responsibilities in all forms of puppet and dance theater. And the poetic literature on which all forms of traditional theater are based has religious and/or historical significance.[22]

We have given an example of only one type of valuation, economic. In whatever terms value may be expressed, it can provide insight into many forms of cultural expression, all of which, to a greater or lesser degree, are inter-dependent. The ethnomusicologist, therefore, must negotiate a wide range of substantive considerations—nonart expressions of culture, all the art forms, the function and usage of music, musical practice itself—and meld these through a comprehension of the pertinent scale of human values.

If I have made clear the importance of the human equation in field work, we are ready to consider the requirements of technical know-how.

[22] See further Mantle Hood, "The Enduring Tradition: Music and Theater in Java and Bali," in Ruth T. McVey (ed.), *Indonesia*, Southeast Asia Studies, Yale University, by arrangement with HRAF Press, New Haven, Conn., 1963.

Chapter Five

FIELD METHODS
and the TECHNICAL EQUATION

IF BY NOW our budding ethnomusicologist is convinced that his personal relationship with other human beings and his substantive knowledge are of paramount importance, he is ready to be entrusted with the third interactive force of field work: technical know-how. Recording and photography, like language and musical performance, should begin as early as possible in the student's training. The mechanics of turning on a tape recorder or focusing a camera can be learned in a single session of coaching or in a careful reading of a book of instructions. After this initial briefing, experience becomes the teacher. Trial and error, objective self-criticism instead of excuses, and some common sense can produce a competent recordist and photographer. If meticulous attention to detail, a good ear, and a trained eye are included, the ethnomusicologist can become a professional in these media of documentation.

Anyone can operate a tape recorder or a camera. Not very many aspire to become professional. The ethnomusicologist should be one of the exceptions. It is rather surprising in a field of inquiry which depends on sound and sight that very few practitioners are really professional in their documentation. The majority are competent, some are inadequate. Technical know-how on the part of the research scholar has not kept pace with the marvels of technical development available to him. We shall touch on a few mechanical principles only in passing, since there are other spokesmen far more qualified than I in such a discussion. Instead, we shall concentrate our attention on some of the specific requirements of documentation in ethnomusicology, considerations that are not to be found in technical handbooks.

Perhaps it is more than coincidence that we speak of "shooting a picture," because a camera lens is something like a gun that is aimed at a target. So is a dynamic microphone with a cardioid-pattern pickup, the appropriate rugged weapon for field work. But unlike the rifle bullet, which either hits or misses, or the undifferentiated scatter pattern of a shotgun, the pickup of a cardioid mike and the focus of a lens are sharpest in the center and less sensitive toward the circumference of coverage. Constant awareness of this simple fact and a number of others related to it can make the difference between competence and inadequacy. But let us aspire to more than competence.

The foundation for professional handling of tape recorder and camera can begin with local field work guided in the critical context of the seminar. In the course of a semester or one or two quarters, each pair of graduate students, project director and silent assistant, should submit progressive examples of their documentation for evaluation by fellow students and faculty. It takes no expert to distinguish between a good recording and a bad one, a sharp, well-composed photograph and an indifferent snapshot. And the more experienced members of the seminar will be able to listen to the sound and look at the picture with a running diagnosis of strengths and weaknesses and suggest remedial techniques. With such evaluation, the two-man team will do better on the next attempt. And so the process continues throughout the course of the seminar until the lessons of practical experience have become an automatic reflex in the skills of documentation. It is imperative that such experience be accumulated before going to the field of ultimate choice. Deferment of constructive criticism until the collector returns from the field can be a costly postponement.

Good field equipment is expensive. A battery-operated, portable tape recorder of broadcast quality, at this writing, costs about $1,000. A microphone of comparable quality is another $200. Add to this a set of headphones, cable extensions, a battery recharger, mike stand, and so forth, and the package runs about $1,500. Below this standard is a wide range of brands that diminish in quality as they decrease in cost. The cost of camera equipment is analogous. The amateur may extol the virtues of a simple box camera: It is foolproof and it "takes good pictures." I suppose a hammer and chisel and a pair of pliers could suffice the needs of the dentist; I am rather glad they do not.

During his training, the student of ethnomusicology should have access to professional equipment. This is the appropriate time for him to learn how to handle the very best. At some point, however, he must decide what he is willing to purchase as a professional ethnomusicologist. It should be better than a hammer and chisel. It is true that usage of the finest equipment is no guarantee of professional results. But the limitations of inferior equipment certainly guarantee substandard quality in documentation. As part of the price of his education, the young M.D. expects to purchase the necessary medical implements. The self-employed, beginning businessman must furnish his office. The professional ethnomusicologist requires professional equipment. Let us consider some of the basic requirements in selecting equipment and then some suggestions for how to use it.

RECORDING

EQUIPMENT   In my experience with tape recorders, there is no equivalent to the Nagra for field work. But new brands and new models are constantly appearing. Some of the Japanese equipment bears watching. Whatever brand and model is finally selected, there are several basic prescriptions that should be taken into account. Field work is likely to be rugged work: bush roads, high humidity, low humidity, freezing or boiling temperatures, portage on horseback or donkey or oxcart, dust, wind, tropical rains—the variety of physical problems is infinite. So, the tape recorder chosen should be one that has been amply tested for its ruggedness. Its assembly should be convenient for purposes of maintenance and simple repair. It should be light enough to carry with a shoulder strap—and heavy enough to give assurance that it is strong and has all the components required to produce quality. It should be capable of operation on flashlight batteries, on battery pack (accumulators), and on electricity—all three. It should require the minimum power that will guarantee constant speed.

Music should never be recorded at a speed slower than 7½ ips (inches per second). It is incredible how much material in ethnomusicological collections has been recorded at 3¾ ips or even 1⅞ ips! These speeds are adequate for recording speech but not music. If the supply of tape and the length of example will permit, recording at 15 ips assures the very best quality. *All field recording should be done with battery power.* Electrical power is subject to "line surge," sudden changes in voltage, which affect the speed of the recorder. Electricity, if available in the field, is useful for playback and recharging batteries but never for recording. Type of electrical voltage is highly variable from country to country and even from one region to another within a country. A transformer and a variety of adapters for electrical sockets are part of the field worker's essential gear.

Different arguments can be advanced for buying a full-track tape recorder or a half-track machine or one that records in stereo. Full-track minimizes the effect of tape imperfections, half-track doubles the recording time of a reel of tape, stereo is popular for commercial reasons and permits some separation of sound that can be useful in aural analysis. Full- or half-track recordings made in the field can also be electronically reprocessed in the commercial studio to produce a high-low separation of sound that gives the effect of quasi-stereo and also has some advantage for purposes of analysis. The choice must be determined by the purposes of the collector. Personally, I am inclined toward full-track recording with the possibility of electronic reprocessing; the original product has the best quality and permits transformation to quasi-stereo. Besides, the problems of monaural recording in the field are already manifold, and stereophonic recording certainly compounds them. Eventually someone will develop a four-, eight-, or even sixteen-channel tape recorder for the field. It will never replace the full- or half-track machine; but, for analytical purposes, it offers the advantage of having different sections of a musical ensemble on different channels, which can be played back individually or mixed at various dynamic levels as a composite.

There are four types of microphones based on different design principles: dynamic, ribbon, crystal, and condenser mikes. Any one of the four may be useful for different purposes in the recording studio. For field work, the dynamic mike is the most reliable. It is reasonably rugged and the least affected by extremes of temperature and humidity. A good one has a wide range of response which, properly used, produces recordings of professional quality. The pattern of the dynamic cardioid mike is heart-shaped, and the vortex of the heart marks the center axis of the pattern which is the line of greatest sensitivity. This directional orientation is very critical in "aiming" the mike because a fractional difference in position, depending on its distance from the subject, can greatly alter the alignment of the axis. At a distance of 12–15 feet, $\frac{1}{4}$ inch of variance in the mike position may shift the axis several feet. If the mike is mounted on a floor stand, it is wise to sight over the "barrel" of the mike to be sure the major axis is directed precisely on target. If the mike is suspended overhead, the recordist should sight from the precise location of the target and adjust the angle of the mike until the major axis is pointed directly at him. There are other factors to consider in positioning the microphone, to which we shall return presently.

The spread of the cardioid pattern is another variable. For overall coverage of a large ensemble, a mike with a wide-angle pattern is necessary, otherwise the edges of the group are too far off axis. At the other extreme, for special purposes, "shotgun" microphones are available which have such a narrow pattern that they can pick out the voice of one singer in a chorus. Such a directional mike, of course, must be very carefully aimed. Between these two extremes, there is a great variety of choice in selecting a microphone. If the recordist can afford only one mike, it should be in the middle range. Too wide an angle, if used for small- or medium-sized ensembles, will pick up extraneous side noises; if the pattern is too directional it will not cover a medium-sized group adequately. Ideally, the field worker will carry two or three different types of microphones to serve different requirements.

If he can afford to double the cost of his equipment, the ethnomusicologist should add a playback system with a 10-inch or 12-inch speaker, a light field mixer, and a variety of mikes up to a total of five. Most good portable tape recorders have small built-in monitor speakers, but the size of such so limits the frequency response in playback that no fundamental pitches below about 150 cps can be heard. A good set of headphones, indispensable for establishing balance and dynamic level, is a better reproducer of the sound on the tape than a monitor speaker. Then why not settle for headphones and forget the added expense and portage involved in a separate playback system?

The most sensitive critics of a field recording are the musicians whose performance has been recorded. And without exception, quite understandably, the performers always want to hear the complete playback at the end of their performance. The monitor speaker will give them a very inadequate impression of the quality of the recording—not a very happy circumstance for a very critical audience! It behooves the recordist to provide a decent playback, not only as a courtesy to the performers, but also as an invaluable medium for the best critique he can obtain. On occasion, when I have not had access to a playback system with a sizable speaker, I have called on Fox Strangway's untiring patience while, one by one, twelve or fifteen players in an African drumming ensemble listened to a "take" through my set of headphones. To the beginning field worker, the added expense and bother of a separate playback may sound like a needless luxury. It is not. If we are aspiring to professional quality in recording, we need to provide an adequate reproduction system in order to enlist the valuable criticism of the performers.

It might be argued that the performer may never have heard a playback of a recording before. How could he do more than marvel and stand in awe of such a phenomenon! What kind of critic is this? Today it must be a very remote location not to have been exposed to the transistor radio and, in many improbable places, to the juke box. Neither of these audio instruments, it is true, provides quite the same experience as hearing one's own performance played back; but at least they do accomplish a certain conditioning to the idea of a musical box.

251

However, let us assume the extreme circumstance in which the field recording is the performer's first exposure to any kind of playback. In my experience, the novelty of the phenomenon wears off very quickly, and the performer accepts the products of electronic wizardry without much difficulty. There is a practical technique for assuring a rapid conditioning to the experience.

Let us imagine a typical recording session. We are not considering the one-shot festival or procession over which the field worker has no control. In this situation, criticism after the fact allows the recordist to make an honest appraisal of his recording, which may be of value the next time he records such an event; it will also allow him to point out faults and limitations of the recording in accompanying notes if it is released commercially. But it cannot improve the original product. The problems encountered in recording these spontaneous events challenge the most experienced collector for reasons which will be clear in our discussion of the controlled session.

SINGLE MIKE   While setting up his equipment, the recordist should be listening to the ensemble he is about to record, in order to predetermine which of several locations is likely to be the best for the microphone. If he is using only one mike, we can assume that there is one best location for it and one ideal alignment of the axis of sensitivity. Different types of instruments and/or voices in an ensemble have different degrees of what I have come to think of as carrying power (CP). This is not the same as loudness but instead is related to the quality of sound. For example, the double bell essential to many African ensembles usually has great carrying power (see Illustration 5-1). So have the rebab in Javanese (see Illustration 5-2) and Sundanese (see Illustration 5-3) gamelan and usually the kempli (see Illustration 5-4) and kadjar (see Illustration 5-5)—two small kettles in the Balinese gamelan that are damped as they are struck! In testing the dynamic level of an instrument, the view meter may show a fairly low level on the loudness scale, but the headphones will reveal the presence of CP. Such an instrument should be off axis in aligning the mike, the degree depending on the CP.

The sound characteristics of certain types of instruments are highly directional, that is, the sound waves tend to travel in straight lines rather than being diffused. Two examples are a drumhead and the vertical plane of a suspended gong, front or back. If the axis of the microphone forms a perpendicular to either one of these vibrating surfaces, the result is something like clapping your hands in front of the mike. The highly directional characteristics of drumheads and suspended gong surfaces, therefore, require that they also be somewhat off axis. Certain instruments in an ensemble may merit greater prominence than others because of their musical function—for example, the master drum in Africa. This must be taken into account in positioning the mike. When drumming ensembles

Illustration 5-1
The Ewe double bell.

Illustration 5-2
(Below, left)
The Javanese rebab.

Illustration 5-3
(Below, right)
The Sundanese rebab.

253

are combined with singers, the relative loudness of instruments compared to voices presents a problem.

Naturally, the greater the recordist's familiarity with the instruments he is recording—best of all through his own experience in playing them—the more easily he will be able to compromise these problems in determining the best location for the mike. Assuming some familiarity with the subject, the collector should make several diagrammatic sketches of the ensemble he intends to record, in advance of the actual session. On these sketches, from his previous experience and specific knowledge of the instruments, he can indicate several locations for the mike, knowing that each represents some sort of compromise. It will save much time if the various factors are sorted and analyzed on paper: the normal arrangement of the instruments, the relative CP of each, the directional qualities of each, the relative importance of the musical function of each—all balanced in terms

Illustration 5-4
The Balinese kempli.

254

of the angle of coverage of the cardioid pattern of his microphone. Except under rare circumstances, the physical arrangement of the ensemble should not be altered to accommodate the microphone.

Whether the recordist is facing an ensemble for the first time or following diagrammatic sketches based on previous experience, he will have to spend some time testing mike location, balance, and dynamic level. I make it a practice of recording all these tests, even though the headphones alone would be adequate for most of them, so that I have a record of trial and error for future reference. These tests are also invaluable in conditioning the performers to the phenomenon of the playback. By being presented with a variety of tests, they soon forget the astonishing experience of listening to a musical box and concentrate critically on the sounds coming out of it. If any one part is inaudible or obscure, the player

Illustration 5-5
The Balinese kadjar.

255

responsible for the part will make the fact clear. If the master drum is not sufficiently prominent, the master drummer will let you know it. In recording an ensemble for the first time, the recordist, no matter how confident he may be that his predetermined mike location is correct, should present several different test "takes" in playback for the performers, so that they have some comparative basis for critical judgment. It is even worth while to include one or two "bad" (but not ridiculous) locations of the mike as a check that the performers have enough confidence in their relationship with the recordist to be honest in their evaluations.

One might assume that a solo performance or a duo or trio offers no real problems. This is not true, of course. A singer accompanying himself on an instrument poses the same basic problems mentioned above, and the location and direction of the mike are just as critical. A Japanese singer accompanying himself on the shamisen is a case in point. There are three important factors to be taken into account: the voice, the percussive quality of the large plectrum, or bachi, as it hits the string and follows through with a sharp contact on the gut head, the left-hand pizzicato and glissando on the finger board. If the axis of the mike is directed at the singer, the subtleties of the left hand will be minimized or lost. If the axis is too near the percussive bachi, the directional quality of the gut head (for the moment a kind of drum) will be too strong. If the mike is directed toward the left hand, the singer will be too far off axis. The correct location must accommodate all three factors. In recording the unaccompanied solo voice, the "eye" or axis of the mike should not look down the singer's throat, otherwise all the noisy transients of syllabification will be overemphasized and the different degrees of carrying power of the singer's compass will be exaggerated. The eye of the mike should be looking at the singer's mouth but from an angle slightly above his head or to one side. If the shamisen is included, the mike should be located to the singer's left at an elevation just above his head with the axis directed a little below the mouth and at a distance that will allow the left hand to be heard slightly off axis and the bachi somewhat off axis. A few test "takes" will reveal the exact spot and direction.

Sometimes the solo performer may constitute a one-man band. In Indonesia, the musical tukang, a man who goes from door-to-door with a set of bamboo instruments slung over his shoulder on a bamboo pole, provides an interesting challenge in recording a mixture of shaken and struck bamboo, metal percussion plates, and a blown gong. This busy musician employs both hands, both feet, and his mouth (see Illustration 5-6). A sample of his performance recorded with a single microphone can be heard on Side II, Band 5 of the companion LPs.

It is worth the time and effort to research the recording characteristics of an important individual instrument in some detail. In preparation for filming

Atumpan, during the period the graduate students and I were developing a shooting script, we also made some preliminary tests in recording this master drum. It started with a question in the graduate seminar. I asked whether any of the students had ever recorded the atumpan and with what success. Several volunteered that they had made some good recordings of the instrument. When questioned about mike placement, they said it was located *behind* the pair of drums to catch the deep sounds that came out through the hollow feet of the two instruments. This, they explained, "gave a better sound" than recording in front. I went to the blackboard and drew two Xs for the pair of drums, indicating front

Illustration 5-6
The musical tukang of West Java.

257

and back; and then asked to see the precise location of the mike. Someone supplied the appropriate mark. Then I drew a large circle around the drums with one edge of the circumference cutting the mark. Next I drew four intersecting lines through the circle, so that it was divided into eight equal parts, and placed a number where each line cut the circumference of the circle, as in Illustration 5-7. Location numbers 1, 5, and 8 had a rear orientation; numbers 2, 6, and 7, a frontal orientation; and numbers 3 and 4, an extreme side location. I asked for opinions on the desirability of each location. The consensus was that it would not make very much difference where the mike was placed, except that locations with a rear orientation would have a deeper sound. I ventured the opinion that each location would produce a different result and suggested that we find the Ashanti master drummer who taught at the University in order to find out. Then I reproduced the diagram on a piece of paper, saying that I would add a ninth location, after the other eight were tested, which, considering all factors, should be the best.

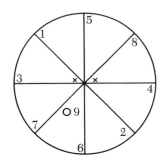

Illustration 5-7
Nine microphone placements used in testing the recording of the atumpan.

When the equipment was set up outside, one of the students placed the mike in location number 1, the customary spot for recording, at an elevation of about 5 feet; and we drew the circle on the ground around the drums and marked the other locations. The diameter of the circle was about 15 feet. The master drummer was asked to play a pattern about thirty seconds long. This was repeated for each of the eight locations. When the eight tests had been recorded, I moved the mike stand to location number 9 and elevated it about another 3 feet. I stood on a stool to sight carefully along the axis, and then indicated we were ready to check level and record the last example.

Back in the seminar room, we played the recording through two large speakers, and the students were asked to listen to each example in succession and on the replay to rate their order of preference. They were surprised that each example was indeed different and puzzled why number 9 was the best. Together we evaluated the factors that had to be taken into account. The lower-pitched drum of the pair, placed to the player's left, had greater CP than the higher pitched one. Therefore, the mike location had to favor the higher one slightly, thereby eliminating numbers 8, 4, and 6. Number 3 overemphasized the higher drum and was also ruled out. The drums had two basic sounds that required accommodation: the deep tones coming from the feet and the sharp impact of the sticks hitting the heads. The axis of a mike placement in the rear was shielded by the drummer's body from the sharp quality of the attack as well as the subtle damping with the sticks which is an important part of the style. A direct frontal placement was not good because the shells of the drums shielded the axis of the mike from the deep sounds coming out of the feet. Number 9 worked best because its location favored the high-pitched drum slightly; and the eye of the mike, at the increased elevation, looked down and a bit behind the drumheads, so that the sound coming out of the feet was no longer shielded by the shells of the drums as it had been at the lower elevation of the mike.

Proper elevation of the microphone increases in importance with the size and heterogeneity of the ensemble. Let us consider an extreme example. The problems of recording a complete Javanese gamelan with male chorus and female soloists are greater than those of any other ensemble I have encountered. It requires the very best equipment. The two large gong ageng are usually tuned to somewhere between 30 cps and 40 cps; and the pitches of the high partials or "overtones" of the bronze kettles and keys, which constitute the characteristic quality of the sound, stretch upward beyond the audible range. The drums, the large hanging gongs, and a dozen or fifteen smaller gongs suspended vertically are highly directional. A xylophone and several of the bronze keyed instruments are played with padded beaters that produce a fairly low dynamic level. The CP of each of the different instruments—made up of bronze, wood, plucked and bowed strings, flute—and that of the male chorus and the female soloists offer a worthy challenge to the recordist. The total floor space occupied by the ensemble may be as much as 35 feet deep and 40 feet wide. The normal acoustical environment is determined by the particular design of the pendopo, a pavilion open on three sides with a steeply hipped roof in the center and a tile, marble, or concrete floor.

I well remember the first time I faced the problems of recording the professional gamelan at the radio station in Djogjakarta. The "studio" in use in 1957 was a great rectangular room with a number of large windows on opposite sides that were always left open. The openings helped to compensate to some extent for the lack of a pavilion open on three sides. But extraneous sounds from playing children or roosters crowing were usually part of the environmental sound effects. The room had a very high ceiling which added an acoustical advantage. All the musicians were seated cross-legged on the floor; and for broadcasts the studio used four or five small microphones on low floor stands placed immediately in front of such key performers as the rebab, gendèr, sometimes the xylophone, female soloists, and male chorus. I had heard complaints and had observed myself that these radio broadcasts of gamelan performance were not too successful. The full sound of the gamelan was lost to an unnatural emphasis on a few important performers. And the fundamental pitches of the two gong ageng were never heard.

For some weeks, I had been attending broadcasts and other gamelan rehearsals as an observer (the slow beginning), trying to analyze all of the factors in deciding where to place a single microphone. When the day finally came and permission to record had been granted, I was rather unnerved by fact that there was no possibility for me to make any test runs. The first session, a recording of a two-hour live broadcast, had to be the test. I had been unable to obtain a Nagra on this first trip because of a long waiting list. So I was using a portable Ampex

259

601 with a matching playback unit Ampex 620, powered by a 32-volt set of truck batteries through a rotary converter which had a set of vibrating reeds that had to be monitored to be sure the power supply operated constantly at 60 cps. My single mike was an Electro-Voice 666.

I set up tape recorder and playback in a narrow alley beside the studio, the power supply being carried in the trunk of my car, 60 feet away. As I strung cable into the studio and mounted the microphone on a stand which, by means of flexible extensions, was elevated about 16 feet in the air, I could see the polite but dubious smiles of the musicians in the gamelan. It was clear that the whole operation looked very funny to these professionals accustomed to four or five floor mikes. The base of the stand was placed between the space occupied by the singers, who sat in front of the rectangle formed by the gamelan, and the front row of instruments made up of the rebab, two gendèr, xylophone, and slenṭem. The smiles were polite, but the source of amusement was unmistakable. I was quite certain that my mike placement would pick up the singers and soft-sounding instruments, but I was not sure that even with this elevation the EV 666 would do justice to the back row of gongs.

As the broadcast started, I was sitting out in the alley with my headphones on ready to adjust the dynamic level if necessary the moment the full gamelan would enter following a solo introduction by the gendèr; I could hear the gendèr quite clearly. At the close of the introduction came the deep pulsating throb of the large gong and the full sound of the gamelan. The balance was good. It really sounded like a Javanese gamelan. I sat there for the full two hours, changing reels during the break between numbers when the announcer came on. During one break, I took the time to rewind the first reel. And the moment the broadcast was finished, I put this on the tape recorder, turned the volume up on the playback, and went into the studio to begin packing up my gear while the rich sounds of gamelan on the first reel filled the narrow alley. When I came back a few minutes later, there sat all the performers around the speaker, listening intently. They were pleased and excited to be able to hear all of the parts—including the gong ageng. I was facing a different kind of smiles now. They sat through the whole half-hour reel. And I felt the great relief of knowing that the slow beginning was over. With this endorsement, I could really settle in and go to work.

Periodically, the radio station musicians in Djogjakarta broadcast from one of the princely residences where the royal gamelan is housed in a real pendopo. The acoustical environment had only one disadvantage in recording: a false ceiling that limited mike placement to an elevation of about 10 or 11 feet. After we have considered some of the advantages and added problems of recording with multiple microphones, I shall refer the reader to an excerpt of a recording made in this princely pendopo.

260

MULTIPLE MIKES   It is advisable for the recordist to accumulate a wide variety of experience in recording different performing media with a single mike before he tries his hand at recording with multiple microphones. Nagra makes a light field mixer that will accommodate four mikes, each with its own dynamic control; and with a fifth microphone plugged into the tape recorder, the field worker has quite a versatile setup. Therein lies a danger. The sound signals from all mikes go onto one full-track tape, a single channel. It is up to the recordist to balance these four or five signals properly, so that the composite gives the best simulation of the live sounds. If our discussion of single-microphone technique has made it clear that the recordist has a very powerful weapon in his hands which can badly distort or accurately simulate the sounds of live performance, it should be equally clear that four or five such weapons compound the problems and responsibility to the "nth" power.

It has been argued that recording with a single mike produces a truer representation of the original sound: the musical ensemble represents one source of sound, and the single microphone represents one source of perception. At one time I myself held this conviction. Some experimentation on my first field trip to Africa convinced me otherwise.

Prior to that time, recordings I had heard of African drumming ensembles combined with singing seemed to suffer from a common problem in recording with a single mike. The instrumental part could be heard quite well until the voices entered. At that point, as the recordist compensated for the difference in dynamic levels between vocalists and instrumentalists, the latter always faded into the background. Therefore, I decided to experiment with multiple mikes. In the course of these experiments, I realized that the argument for the single mike as the best simulation of reality had not taken into account one important factor. Recording with a single mike, in one sense, is like listening with only one ear. The human being has a natural stereophonic reception of sound with his two ears and his own cranial mixer. His perception of sound, therefore, is dependent on two axes of sensitivity, not one. In other words, so I reasoned, the aural impression in hearing a live performance by an African ensemble of singers and instrumentalists is quite different from that perceived from a recording made with a single mike. The moot point was whether one could properly mix the signals from several mikes, so that the composite would yield a better, not worse, simulation of reality. In recording Ewe, Ashanti, Fanti, Ga, and other ensembles I used up to four microphones, depending on the complexity of the group. One mike was reserved for singers, one for the master drum, and one or two for overall coverage. Sometimes I found that it was sufficient to use only one mike for master drum and the other instruments if the natural arrangement of the group permitted an advantageous placement of the mike.

261

Each instrument must be rated according to CP, its relative location in the ensemble, and its particular musical function. The same ratings are also necessary for the singers in order to accommodate soloists within a chorus, as well as individual voices, whatever their musical function, which have exceptionally high CP. The position, alignment, and dynamic level of each microphone must take into account all these factors. Because there is actually only one recording channel, each dynamic level must be established individually. After the dynamic level of each mike has been tentatively determined, it is usually necessary to make further adjustments when all these settings are turned up. For example, the level of mike 1, which, let us say, is picking up the master drum, may also be receiving a boost from the signal coming over mike 3 aimed at a supporting group of instruments, because its best position and alignment has placed the axis of sensitivity within range of the master drum. In this instance, the level of mike 1 should be lowered until the sound of the master drum balances the rest of the ensemble. In testing the level of each mike, the experienced recordist will perceive some of this tendency in overlapping of mike coverage. Overlapping is a desirable and, in fact, indispensable condition of recording with multiple mikes. After some experience, the recordist will know about how much to back off his initial setting. To pursue the example a bit further, let us assume that in listening through the headphones to mike 1, the recordist establishes a level of -6 db to cover the master drum. When he checks the level of mike 3, set at -5 db, he notices that the master drum has some prominence on the signal. After setting the other levels, he can try his first mix by backing off mike 1 to -7 db. Several examples of recording African ensembles with multiple mikes can be heard on the accompanying LP, Side III, Band 1.

There are so many variables in recording that no absolute prescriptions can be given. This should be encouraging to the ethnomusicologist who aspires to be a professional. If anybody who turns on a tape recorder could make good recordings, there would be little cause for pride in the profession. The recordist should be encouraged to experiment. He should remember that no one in the recording industry, presumably, is likely to have his intimate knowledge of subject, both practical and theoretical, needed to make the best recordings. And the truly professional recording engineer is always willing and anxious to learn from others. As an advisor to Columbia Masterworks and several motion-picture studios, I have been surprised and pleased to note that the best men in the industry are the first to admit that special requirements and the solutions required are virtually unlimited. A thorough knowledge of performance practice, an awareness of the peculiar nature of the instruments of his expertise, their CP, and relative musical function make the ethnomusicologist a qualified consultant in the industry when the music of his specialty is being recorded.

262

I have also experimented with the usage of two microphones for one instrument if its peculiar sound characteristics offered a problem for a single mike. Two mikes on the atumpan, with careful mixing, seem to produce a result closer to reality than one. Two mikes were used in recording the sound track of a film made of the Indian drummer Alla Rakha. The tabla and bayam, each with its own CP and style characteristics, are most difficult to accommodate with only one mike. An example from the sound track can be heard on Side III, Band 2. I have extended the experiment somewhat in recording the Japanese virtuoso Keiji Yagi on the koto by using our studio four-track Ampex 300-4SS recorder with one dynamic mike in the conventional placement above the instrument (channel A) and a second ribbon mike (channel B) placed about an inch off the floor to catch the sounds coming out of the sound hole in the bottom of the koto. With the artist's help, after the recording the two channels were mixed in the proportion of about 70 percent channel A and 30 percent channel B. The motivation for this experiment came from my experience with the atumpan: the sound heard as recorded by a single mike in the front of the drums was quite different from that recorded by one mike positioned in back of the instruments. The human ear perceives both of these sound qualities. I was intrigued with the notion that the koto, and other related instruments, had something in common with the atumpan: a characteristic top sound and a characteristic bottom sound, both of which are perceived in live performance but do not come through too well in a recording made with a single mike. In this experiment with the koto, I kept an open mind on the subject until after the recording; and then, without explaining to the artist the various manipulations being made with the volume controls of channels A and B, I asked him to choose the recorded sound that, in his judgment, came closest to reality. Channel A heard by itself he accepted as good; channel B heard alone he rejected completely; the mixture of 70-30 percent he approved as the very best. On Side III, Band 3, can be heard first a short excerpt from channel A, then the same excerpt from channel B and finally the 70-30 percent composite.[1]

Once the dynamic level has been established, whether recording with one or many mikes, the dials should not be touched. Riding the dials as the music gets louder and softer completely distorts the natural dynamic range of the ensemble. The contrast between solo passages and tutti must be preserved on the recording; cranking up the volume for the soloist will destroy it. This does not mean that the recordist can sit back and forget the volume controls, however, because in the field one must be constantly prepared for the unexpected. A minor adjustment in dynamic level may be imperative if an ensemble exceeds the level

[1]Tapes of these recording sessions are available in the archives of the Institute of Ethnomusicology, UCLA.

263

performed in testing or if, as often happens in West Africa, one or two drummers playing hourglass drums slung over their shoulders begin to move around too much. In recording drumming groups in Ghana, I have found that as the performance continues for some time the dynamic level gradually increases. Of course, when adjustment has to be made, it should be accomplished as smoothly as possible. In some situations, one setting of the dials not only preserves the great contrast between solo and tutti but also captures a sense of the "social context" of the performance. Two ancient and holy gamelan sekati in Surakata, Central Java, perform day and night throughout the Muslim Holy Week, Sekatèn, in two special pavilions located in a large square. Several thousand persons are jammed together in the festivities surrounding the location of the gamelan. The excerpt of gamelan sekati, Side IV, Band 1, made with one mike, the EV 666, and the Ampex 601, captures the crowd noises in the background during the solo introduction.

AUTOMATIC RECORD   At times, the problems of recording festivals and processions, during which the recordist can only react to rather than direct the action, become truly insurmountable. Without warning, a moving drummer may swing the head of his instrument so that its highly directional signal hits the eye of the mike squarely. Anyone, at any moment, may yell, scream, clap his hands, or fire a gun directly on axis of the mike. Under such extreme conditions, the recordist has little choice but to put the tape recorder on "automatic record" and hand-carry a microphone following the action. The automatic record on a tape recorder prevents extreme overload of the signal, often at the expense of frequency response and dynamic range. An example of automatic record made during a procession of several thousand persons in connection with a memorial funeral service among the Fanti can be heard on Side V, Band 1.

SPECIAL USES   The tape recorder is not only a mechanism for collecting music but also a tool for special research requirements. Still lacking the multi-channel field recorder, the ethnomusicologist can deliberately place off axis all but one principal element of an ensemble, thereby making a clear recording of one particular instrument by relegating the complex of the ensemble to the background. This technique applied to principal instruments in a group will provide excellent working tapes for purposes of transcription and analysis. A short excerpt of such a recording of the gendèr panerus with the rest of the Javanese gamelan in the background can be heard on Side V. Band 2, recorded with a single mike. For special reasons, an even more artificial separation can be made in which a principal instrument, with one or two supporting instruments, is recorded out of the context of the ensemble. For some years, I have been occupied with research of the practices of group improvisation in Javanese gamelan based on such a set of special recordings. On Side V, Band 3, the same short passage of one piece is heard four times, each selection being improvised by a different principal instrument. The barely distinguishable sound in the background of each example is the slenṭem playing the fixed melody on which the improvisation is based.

Keeping our discussion of single versus multiple microphones in mind, the reader may now wish to compare two excerpts found on Side VI, Band 1. The first was recorded with an EV 666 and an Ampex 601 in the Javanese princely residence referred to earlier. The second example is a continuation of the same piece with slightly different improvisation performed by the UCLA Javanese gamelan and recorded by Columbia Masterworks with thirteen microphones.[2] The former is played by professional Javanese musicians; the latter is a different gamelan, with slightly different tuning and sound characteristics, played by inter national students at UCLA. The former was recorded in the natural environment of the pendopo (but with the delimiting factor of a false ceiling)[3] and the latter in the CBS studios in Hollywood.[4]

SUPPLIES   I have frequently been asked how much tape one should take to the field, let us say, to accommodate one year of collecting. As a rule of thumb, I have found that for every half hour of finished (not testing) recordings, I spend an average of about three hours of work. The actual number of working hours devoted to recording only, in the course of a week, averages somewhere between twelve and fifteen hours. Applying the rule of thumb, this amounts to an average of four or five half-hour tapes a week. A year's supply, therefore, might run somewhere between 200 and 250 reels of tape. Under ideal circumstances, such a supply might be exhausted in half that time. But usually, if the collector avoids indiscriminate sampling and concentrates on a well-defined objective, the rule of thumb is fairly reliable. The researcher should purchase his supplies before going

[2] The engineering specifications are as follows: "This disc was recorded under ideal acoustic conditions in a large Hollywood studio. A sixteen-position multi-channel mixing console fed an Ampex 300-3 three-track, $\frac{1}{2}$-inch recorder. Thirteen microphones were used. Most of these were the Austrian AKG Model C-12 condensor microphone. Because of the extreme dynamic range of this music, the original was conservatively recorded, with peaks rarely exceeding -7 VU. This orchestration demanded a great deal of 'head room,' necessitating some sacrifice in signal-to-noise ratio. Scotch 111 tape was employed for the original and the dub-down. The reduction of the original three-track tape to the 2-track, $\frac{1}{4}$-inch master was on an Ampex 300-3 and an Ampex 350-2. Transfer from tape to lacquer master was made via an Ampex 350-2, a Westrex cutter, and a Scully lathe with automatic variable pitch. Mastering and pressing were by Columbia Custom." (Mantle Hood and Hardja Susilo, *Music of the Venerable Dark Cloud*, text accompanying the LP recording under the same title, IE Records, Stereo IER 7501, Institute of Ethnomusicology, UCLA, 1967, p. 42.)

[3] The complete recording can be heard in the archives of the Institute of Ethnomusicology, UCLA.

[4] Album and text are available from the Institute of Ethnomusicology, UCLA.

to the field, because availability and quality of tape are quite variable in different parts of the non-Western world. The most reliable type of tape for its durability under extreme climatic conditions is $1\frac{1}{2}$ mil Mylar. If field conditions are not likely to be too extreme, it may be worth the calculated risk of using 1 mil Mylar because of the additional recording time available on a 7-inch reel of the thinner tape. Reasonable caution is necessary to avoid stretching or breaking. All recorded tapes should be transported in special antimagnetic cases to prevent total or partial erasure from accidental exposure to magnetic fields in the course of shipment.[5]

THE LOG   Earlier, we mentioned the importance of systematic entries in a notebook during the course of field work. A companion to this type of documentation is the log, essential in both recording and photography. The log should contain complete information relating to each session: not only the usual logistics of time, place, performers' names, ages, backgrounds and so forth, but also a description of the acoustical environment, sketches showing the arrangement of the ensemble being recorded, dynamic levels of each take, CP ratings of instruments, mike placement, types of equipment and supplies used, and so forth. The physical aspects of the session should also be documented by supplementary photographs.

STILL PHOTOGRAPHY

The ethnomusicologist should aspire to a professional level of still photography. No eye is better qualified than his to concentrate on the details of his subject through a lens. It could be argued that the artist with a camera is born, not made. However, our concern is not with artistry but with documentation, and this should measure up to professional standards. Whether the ethnomusicologist is using colored slides in the course of a lecture, black and white photographs to illustrate a publication, or compiling a reference archive of graphic materials, his professional standing, in part, will be judged by his ability as a cameraman. Very often his subject is one that would make the professional photographer green with envy: colorful pageantry of musicians and dancers, mysterious rituals, picturesque villages, lush and exotic surroundings. Sometimes his subject is found on the bas-reliefs of ancient monuments, the carving on jewelry, the woven patterns of textiles, the engraving on weapons. It may be an old manuscript, detailed instrumental construction, techniques of performance, the expression on the face

[5] These boxes are made primarily of vacuum-process, high-purity iron with additional elements included to reduce shock sensitivity, for example, Primec 40, a proprietary alloy of Primec Corporation, 5057 W. Washington Blvd., Los Angeles, California, 90016.

266

of a listener in repose, music or dance lessons given a child. No photographic canvas is broader; and none more richly deserves the skill of a professional photographer than the performing arts of man depicted in their social milieu. Let us not settle for mere competence.

It is likely that the student will have had a more or less serious flirtation with a camera by the time he enters a graduate seminar in field and laboratory methods. Constructive criticism from his colleagues in the course of his local field work, directed toward a systematic approach to his subject, again is the best teacher. As in recording, technical mistakes in photography should be objectively appraised, so they become the stepping stones of professional camera work rather than the foundation for excuses.

The range of possible equipment and types of film is almost unlimited. Most requirements of the ethnomusicologist can be met with (1) a $2\frac{1}{4} \times 2\frac{1}{4}$ reflex camera for making black and white photographs for publications; (2) a 35 mm camera with normal lens, telephoto lens, and wide-angle lens for making colored slides or black and whites and extension rings for microfilming; (3) a good light meter; (4) a compact but sturdy elevator tripod with ball-and-socket head; (5) an inexpensive model of a polaroid camera. This amount of reasonably good equipment might cost in the neighborhood of $700 or $800. The polaroid camera is primarily an instrument of goodwill. It allows the field worker to hand to the musicians and dancers with whom he is working snapshots taken and developed on the spot as a memento of their collaboration. This means much more than the not-always-fulfilled promises of mailing back pictures at a later date. The polaroid camera can also serve for back-up duplication of especially important subjects filmed with one of the other cameras. There is more than one possible slip between opening the shutter and processing the film; better have a polaroid record than learn sometime later that a roll of film was lost in the mail or ruined by excessive humidity before it reached the processing lab.

The automatic camera, which requires only that the photographer frame and focus the subject, has limitations in common with the automatic-record switch of the tape recorder. The built-in light meter automatically determines the proper aperture or f stop in response to the amount of incident light coming in to it. Although this feature may be convenient in covering the rapidly shifting subjects of festivals and processions, it will prove too restrictive in exposures of subjects with more specialized requirements. Any dark subject with a light background requires a reading with a sensitive light meter and hand setting of the proper f stop. Sometimes it is desirable to give especial prominence to a detail, let us say the forked-fingering or half-holing technique on a bamboo flute; if a wide aperture is used with a good sharp focus, the surrounding background can be thrown out of focus and all attention concentrated on the subject of interest.

267

The great variety of types of film offers wide latitude. Slow film has very fine grain and will produce the sharpest enlargements. Very fast film is grainy but has the advantage of requiring the minimum light. Tropical locations or those surrounded by water or snow-covered terrain are very bright and would seem to obviate the usage of fast film. In my experience in the tropics, however, I have found both fast and moderately slow film types equally essential. Musicians and dancers performing in heat of the day are usually located under the roof of a pavilion or within the relatively cool environment of a bamboo and palm grove or some other situation that protects them from the sun. And although a tropical sun is very bright, tropical shadows are very dark and require fast film if the subject is to be clearly seen. Even with a film speed of 160 ASA, which out in the sunlight might require an aperture of $f22$ or more at a speed of $\frac{1}{120}$ of a second, tropical shadows may necessitate opening the lens to $f5.6$ or $f4.5$ at $\frac{1}{60}$ of a second. No matter what advice has been given by the experts back home—who may never have seen the environment and subject of concern—a meticulous reading with a sensitive light meter should be the ultimate guide to exposure. It is wise to experiment with the widest range of subjects and lighting conditions before going to the field, *always* with the meter reading as a guide. If in doubt, it is worth taking two or three shots of the same subject at different exposures; one of them will be the best.

In photographing the bas-reliefs of the Borobudur and Tjandi Prambanan in Central Java I found that the bright overhead sun produced very black shadows on the carvings. I experimented with the strobe light at half power, with aluminum foil reflectors, and with the technique called "painting" with the strobe light. All of the attempts caused the deep reliefs to "go flat." The sculpture appeared to be so designed that only the arc of the moving sun overhead produced the proper angle of light source. The best solution was short time exposures on a tripod in natural light. As a case in point, I have been told that the definitive photographic study of the Borobudur[6] required one year in the making, so that the photographers could literally follow the course of the sun around the monument.

Many performances take place at night, and a strobe light or flash gun may be a compromise solution to the problem of a very low-key lighting source such as oil lamps or torches or kerosene lanterns. The strobe light should be used only as a last resort. After several years of experience with the strobe, I no longer carry one to the field. In the first place, the bright illumination, of course, eradicates the low-keyed effect which is natural to the environment. In the second place, if the subject has a moderate to large depth of field—for example, a group of

[6] Nicolas Johannes Krom, *Borobudur: Archeological Description*, 3 vols., plates, Martinus Nijhoff, The Hague, 1927–1931.

dancers that occupy a space 20 or 30 feet deep—figures in the foreground will be overexposed and those in the background underexposed. In the third place, the blinding flash of a strobe quickly becomes an annoyance to performers and spectators alike. I believe it is better to preserve the naturalness of the subject by using extremely fast film which may even have to be "pushed" in processing, notwithstanding the grainy quality of the finished product.

Even though much field photography can be done by hand-holding the camera, there are numerous situations in which a tripod is essential, such as lighting conditions that require a speed slower than $\frac{1}{60}$ of a second, critical focus on the details of an art object or the details of instrumental construction, microfilming, and so forth. The elevator tripod with ball-and-socket head will accommodate all special requirements, and it should have enough rigidity so that wind or shutter action triggered by a cable release will not affect it.

For each photograph taken in the field, there should be a detailed entry in the log: type of film, speed of exposure, f setting, type of lens and camera, and the usual information relating to the subject. This technical record of photographic studies is the manual of experience which, with progressive evaluation, can lead the cameraman from mere competence to professionalism.

THE MOTION PICTURE

Although it is evident that the ethnomusicologist must aspire to professional standards as a recordist and still photographer, his position in relation to the documentary film is not yet clear. Neither has the role of the professional film maker been defined in the production of documentaries devoted to the performing arts. Most ethnomusicologists have no acquaintance with the basic requirements of making a film, and the film maker, understandably, has no familiarity with the needs of ethnomusicology. Yet the motion picture constitutes a unique and perhaps the most important form of documentation available to the ethnomusicologist. It has been badly neglected to date, not only because of the lack of qualified personnel, but also because of the expense involved. As they apply to the field of ethnomusicology, these two problems are closely related. But despite the initial cost of equipment, film, processing, editing, mixing, special effects, and so forth, the motion picture, in the long run, is actually the most economical form of documentation. It allows the ethnomusicologist to return to the field as often as he chooses, simply by threading a projector. And with the relatively new flickerless projector, he can slow down the film speed from 24 frames per second to 1 frame per second for purposes of visual analysis and description. The motion picture enables him to capture unlimited detail that the best memory or still photographic record cannot retain. It offers the possibility of placing music and related art forms in the natural environment of the society with which they are identified and which they in turn help to identify. Rerunning such a film for the hundredth time can reveal information that escaped the attention of the researcher during the ninety-nine previous showings, details that went unnoticed, needless to say, in the field itself. A piece of film with sound track can never capture a total record; but with sensitive usage it can come closer, in my opinion, than any other form of documentation.

It can also be badly misused. The reader will oblige me if he turns back now to pages 208–209 and reviews the principal conditions and limitations that are typical of its abuse.

Most films suffer from one or more of these nine basic faults. At one time it seemed to me that the ethnomusicologist had no other choice than to rely on the professional film maker to cover this important phase of his field work. Subsequently, a chain of fortuitous circumstances changed my mind. I believe there is a better solution. Both the professional film maker and the nonvisually oriented ethnomusicologist may quarrel with some of my arguments offered in support of a different solution. But a reply to each of them must be like the mango-martini rebuttal to the critic of studies in performance: until the film maker is willing to take the time to become something of an ethnomusicologist or the ethnomusicologist something of a film maker, he is not a qualified contender. To make my own position perfectly clear, I claim, at most, amateur standing in the brotherhood of film makers. But trial and error and the school of hard knocks have afforded a modest practical know-how and a great deal of insight into the nature of the problem. It also has suggested the direction toward a solution.

Only a few ethnomusicologists and even fewer film makers have given any serious attention to the problem. And most of these, in my judgment, have placed the cart before the horse by launching forth into a project before the basic problem and their specific objectives were clearly defined. The flexibility possible in using a camera offers an unlimited number of approaches to the subject. But the best approach or approaches for a given objective usually comprise a fairly narrow range within these theoretical possibilities. Who is to make the choice? I suppose the ethnomusicologist tends to be overawed by the technical apparatus and know-how required in putting together a motion picture. And, of course, it is understandable that the film maker emphasizes these aspects of his trade in his collaboration with the ethnomusicologist. But the responsibility of choice belongs to the ethnomusicologist. And in this he is sadly derelict.

Where is he to find appropriate models? For many years anthropologists have been aiming cameras at every imaginable subject in the field. Colleagues in anthropology have said that scattered throughout the community of academic institutions there is an overwhelming quantity of footage shot in the field, most of it lying unedited and much of it, from the film maker's viewpoint, uneditable. At the top of this mountain of celluloid, however, are a number of excellent documentary films in the field of anthropology. Some of these are worth the attention of the ethnomusicologist. But from the outset, both he and the film maker must recognize the fact that the various models of anthropological films, models that change as anthropological theories change, fulfill a different set of requirements from those encountered in filming the performing arts. Until the ethnomusicologist has defined his specific requirements, neither he nor the film maker nor a collaboration between the two is likely to produce very many model films in ethnomusicology.

What is the first step? In the past few years at ethnomusicological gatherings there is sometimes a program of films included. With an occasional exception, these films "document" the nine basic faults more than their purported subjects. Aside from their too-often dull and monotonous reportage, such amateur showings could be invaluable if they were presented with the primary purpose of evoking discussion and constructive evaluation of the extent to which the films serve the needs of their subjects. But alas! There seems never to be time for such preoccupation. One comes away from these programs with the gnawing conviction that the ethnomusicological halt are leading the ethnomusicological blind. On the rare occasion when a film maker is called in, he is not given the role of cinematic critic but is used as an expert on technical equipment and supplies.

The first step, yet to be taken, is the initiation of continuing discussion and definition among ethnomusicologists of what they want a motion picture to do for them. The task is too large for one man or even a five-man committee. It requires systematic exploration by specialists whose subjects vary all the way from music of the Australian aborigines to the rock beat of the metropolitan grottos. No objective has more immediate or long-range urgency. As a start, it might well be the total concern of an international ethnomusicological congress.

By default, therefore, I want to venture a few guidelines which I hope will provoke a wide exchange among students and colleagues who are beginning to recognize the singular importance of this medium of documentation.

THE NARRATIVE, THE DOCUMENTARY, THE DOCUMENTARY-NARRATIVE   Many different films can be edited from the same footage, providing the coverage has taken this possibility into account. Although the degree of emphasis on one or another aspect of an ethnomusicological subject is almost infinite, there appear to be three basic types of film addressed to different purposes and audiences: the narrative film, the documentary film, and the documentary-narrative film. The first type is organized around a central theme and has the greatest appeal for a general audience. The second features some technical aspect of the subject for a specialized

271

audience. The third combines elements of both other types and is proper fare for a mixed audience.

As an illustration of the first type, I might mention a narrative film made at UCLA while the Indian virtuoso Ravi Shankar was in residence as Regents' Lecturer in 1966. The film is not concerned with Shankar's great artistry or the technical requirements of playing the sitar but has as its theme the depiction of the impact of the artist as a teacher on general university students and the reciprocal impact on the artist of various non-Western performance groups found in the environment of the Institute of Ethnomusicology. The point of view expressed in this film, therefore, establishes a musical context for showing the interaction among artist, students, and environment. As an illustration of the second type, the documentary film, Alla Rakha, the virtuoso on the tabla, is shown as a teacher in three stages of the learning process: teaching the beginning student, the intermediate student, the advanced student. Although this is a technical film devoted to three levels of lessons on the tabla, the intimate approach used in filming gives it an appeal beyond the specialized audience for which it was intended. No English is spoken in the course of the film, except for an occasional exclamation from the teacher; and yet it manages to communicate with a mixed audience without any added narration.

The third type of film, the documentary-narrative, contains elements of both other types. In some ways, it is the most difficult to manage. The narrative film and the documentary film might be compared to the short story in literature: each is driving toward a single point illustrated in a variety of scenes. The documentary-narrative, on the other hand, might be compared to the novel. There is a "hero" or central subject with a cast of supporting characters. It too drives home a principal point but one that includes subplots and subordinate characterizations to support it. *Atumpan,* discussed in Chapter Four, is such a film. The footage shot in the field was edited to show how this Ashanti master drum is manufactured, how it is played, how it functions within the ancient traditions of the society, how it has been adapted to the needs of modern Africa, how it relates to other forms of cultural expression, and how it is valued by society. It would be possible to edit the same footage as a true documentary by concentrating exclusively on the details of manufacture or the varied requirements of instrumental technique or the role of the atumpan in three modes of drumming: signal, speech, and dance modes. The same footage could also yield a narrative film with a central theme depicting the role of the drum as a status symbol valued in different ways by various segments, types of individuals, and special groups in the society as well as by the society as a whole. If the coverage of the original footage had been slightly expanded, it could also yield several films with varying emphasis on dance. For the researcher, unedited work prints of all the footage may have a variety of uses.

The nature of the subject and the specific objectives of the researcher will determine which of these three basic types of film is appropriate. Each type is sufficiently broad to accommodate an emphasis that may, to some extent, overlap one of the other types. But it is advisable for the field worker to have clearly in mind the primary purposes and audience his film is to serve.

After his subject has been thoroughly researched and the ethnomusicologist has determined which basic type of film is appropriate, he must develop a shooting script. Useful models of the shooting script can be found in a number of standard references on the motion picture.[7] The script should be prepared in as much detail as possible prior to any filming, even though field conditions and previously unknown aspects of the subject are bound to require revision of the script during the shooting. A detailed log, similar to that kept in tape recording and still photography, should document all details that are not found in the final revision of the shooting script.

As an illustration of some of the special requirements of the ethnomusicological point of view in the treatment of a subject and the development of a shooting script, we might consider further the so-called documentary, the technical film. This type of film is in constant demand in industry, business, military training, and so forth. For example, the subject of such a film might be the process of manufacturing jalousie windows or fishhooks or automatic toasters; or sales methods used in training vendors of vacuum cleaners or yachts or real estate; or the steps in dissassembly, cleaning, and reassembly of a rifle; or the techniques of infiltration behind enemy lines. In each instance, the subject, its function, and its audience are quite clear. Now let us consider the manufacture of a drum. If we show only how it is made, the subject, its function, and its audience may not be sufficiently defined. Let us suppose that the materials of the drum can be got only in the context of a tree-felling ceremony, including entreaties addressed to the spirit of the tree and the pouring of libations. In the technical sense of "manufacture" these are not important; from the ethnomusicological point of view, they are an essential aspect of manufacture. The function of a jalousie window,

[7] Joseph V. Mascelli, *The Five C's of Cinematography*, Cine/Grafic Publications, Hollywood, 1966; Joseph V. Mascelli and Arthur Miller (eds.), *American Cinematographer Manual*, 2d ed., American Society of Cinematographers, Hollywood, 1966; W. Hugh Baddeley, *The Technique of Documentary Film Production*, with preface by Paul Rotha, Communication Arts Books, Hastings House, New York, 1968; Karel Reisz and Gavin Miller, *The Technique of Film Editing*, Communication Art Books, Hastings House, New York, 1968; Raymond Spottiswoode, *Film and Its Techniques*, University of California Press, Berkeley, 1968.

a fishhook, or a toaster is widely known. The function of a drum, how it relates to other musical instruments and to various social institutions is not, strictly speaking, a consideration in the process of manufacture; but the inclusion of such information greatly enhances the treatment of the subject and increases the audience potential of the film. From the ethnomusicological point of view, it might also be important to depict the social status of the drum maker, including a glimpse of his family life, his personal frustrations and obligations, as a means of revealing pride of workmanship and the value he and others place on the drum. Music, the subject of ethnomusicology, is made and used and valued by human beings. And the cinematic treatment of a musical subject, however narrowly circumscribed, requires some cognizance of the people who have made it part of their identity.

The residents of Honolulu, Manila, and Kumasi will know how to operate the louvers of a jalousie window, bait a fishhook, and put bread in an automatic toaster. But only the resident of Kumasi will know and value the function of the atumpan. A technical film devoted to the manufacture of a drum must be different from one devoted to fishhooks. I am not suggesting that only the documentary-narrative film can express the ethnomusicological point of view; but I am insisting that within each of the three basic types of film, social context and human values deserve some inclusion.

In summary, the ethnomusicological point of view can be expressed in three different degrees of emphasis: (1) in the narrative film, a number of heterogeneous aspects of the subject are unified by a central theme, such as social or musical function, usage, value, and so forth; (2) in the documentary film, some technical aspect of the subject is featured with enough contextual support to make clear its function and value; (3) in the documentary-narrative film, a comprehensive treatment of technical aspects of the subject is presented in a broad cultural frame of reference.

The advanced student of ethnomusicology, without being aware of the fact, already has acquired the most important aspects of technical know-how before he ever touches a motion-picture camera. It is true he must learn how to load an external magazine, read a light meter, frame his subject, focus, and so forth. These mechanical requirements, like those of tape recording and still photography, can be quickly learned. But from the very beginning, he has the all-important advantage of knowing his subject thoroughly, of being sensitive to vital details through his training in performance, of understanding function and value in relation to cultural environment. When he looks through the lens, there is little question in his mind about the best angle of coverage, because he knows what is important to be shown. His previous training and experience will quickly tell him whether in a given scene his subject must be framed in a tight close-up or a long shot. For the objectives of the ethnomusicologist, *technical* know-how relates to the proper coverage of the subject; and *mechanical* know-how comes with a surprisingly little amount of doing. This does not mean that he will become a film maker overnight. He will need the help of the professional at various stages between initial shooting and finished film. But his training in observation, in performance, in ethnographic detail, in relating to other human beings, and even his bookish knowledge as background—all these provide the firmest foundation for technical know-how in making a film that expresses the ethnomusicological point of view.

Some film makers are quite vocal about the difference in requirements between still photography and motion pictures. No one can deny that there is a difference. But at the rather simple level of the ethnomusicologist's requirements there are some basic similarities that should be comforting to the beginner. A practiced eye in still photography, in framing, composition, and specialized treatment of subject already has experience basic to good motion-picture camera work. One might point out the obvious by saying the inert subject is appropriate for still photography and the moving subject for the motion picture. But this is an oversimplification. Inert subjects can be made to "move" in the motion picture by a sequence of very short scenes shot from different angles, and a moving subject can be "frozen" in still photography by using a short exposure time or even made to simulate motion by blurring the subject slightly with a longer exposure. But without dwelling on similarities and differences between these two forms of documentation, let me simply state that as an amateur film maker I am grateful for a rather considerable experience as a still photographer.

EDITING   How long should a film be? The film maker would probably answer without hesitation: "Shorter than you think!" The ultimate art of motion picture is in the editing. Good footage badly edited will not make a very good film. Not very good footage with skillful editing can make an acceptable film. Good footage edited with sensitivity to the subject and with imagination can produce a winner in a film festival. Even though we are not competing for Oscars, we should have in mind some of the essential requirements of editing before exposing a lot of film. The film maker likes to shoot at a minimum ratio of 6:1 or 7:1, better 10:1, or even greater if the budget will permit. That is, every 7,000 feet of footage will be edited to a finished 1,000 feet. This may sound like a lot of shrinkage to the beginner, but such a ratio allows the editor needed flexibility in applying his skill, sensitivity to overall form, and imagination. The beginner will do well, whenever possible, to work closely with an experienced film editor. In learning the basic requirements of good editing, he will be learning much about the requirements of good filming. And if the collaboration involves his own

275

beginning efforts with a motion-picture camera, the following vignette may be of some value.

The total footage shot in the field for the film *Atumpan* was about 7,500 feet. I engaged an experienced graduate student in the Motion Picture Division of the Department of Theater Arts at UCLA as an editor. He has since become well established as a professional film maker. His talents in this field are exceptional; and his convictions, as a film maker, are exceptionally strong. After he had seen work prints of most of the footage, we had a very interesting discussion, one that I think highlights the principal difficulties faced by the ethnomusicologist in collaborating with the film maker. I shall try to report the gist of the interview with a minimum of bias.

When he came into the office and sat down, I could see by the uncomfortable expression on his face that he was far from ecstatic about the work prints he had run through the moviola. We chatted about nothing in particular while the secretary served us coffee. I felt as though I were waiting for an ultimate prognosis: would the celluloid brainchild live or die? From the commercial lab where the color film had been processed and the black and white work prints made, the footage had elicited praise for the excellence of its lighting exposures under some very difficult field conditions. But an appraisal from the young man I hoped to work with as an editor would be directed toward other considerations. Finally I asked, "Do you think we have enough usable footage to make a film?" He considered his answer for a moment and then said, "Maybe—if we cut it to about ten minutes."

Now ten minutes of film at 24 frames per second is about 400 feet long—not a very good batting average out of 7,500 feet of film! At least I admired his candor. I asked him what the principal difficulties were. "Well," he said, "most of it all looks alike. Just a lot of people shuffling around. The camera work is old-fashioned. Not enough close-ups." The work prints of 50-foot, 100-foot and 400-foot segments had been assembled in random order on 2,000-foot reels. I had been through the material several times, and even knowing the shooting script by heart had not prevented some confusion in viewing this random assemblage. I told him there was more to the footage than a lot of people shuffling around and briefly explained the story line of the film, saying I would give him a copy of the shooting script. He nodded, but without very much conviction. I reminded him that this was my first attempt at filming and agreed that there could have been more close-ups. While we talked, I was struggling to see the raw footage through his eyes. I was not unfamiliar with some of the latest camera techniques in which close-ups were so tight that one eye and part of a nostril would fill the screen or in which a hand-held camera was shaken to produce the effect of frenzy or a pushing crowd or in which the camera was turned upside down or revolved

276

from side to side, and so forth. I have sometimes referred to these tricky camera techniques as "armpit photography": the coverage is so close you can almost smell the perspiration. But the young editor was telling me about his efforts at editing some material for a professor in the field of anthropology. He concluded his point by saying he had finally given up the attempt. The anthropologist's footage had ranged indiscriminately over a wide field of unrelated subjects, and there was no way to tie them together in any kind of film. I realized he was drawing an analogy and shifted uncomfortably in my chair wondering whether, as a point of professional pride, he was trying to tell me politely that I would have to find another editor. In retrospect, I am sure he was. But he had come highly recommended, and I was anxious to engage his interest in the project. So I, too, tried a story by analogy.

The story related to the composer, Ernst Toch. He told me once about a commission he had received from bereaved parents who had lost their teen-age son. The boy had written a melody, and Toch's commission was to use this as the basis of a composition. I explained to my young editor that the composer was obligated by the commission to create a composition in a style that would complement the given melody rather than dominate it or obscure it or even, in effect, obliterate it. Certainly, the melody was one that Toch himself would not have created. But the success of his commission was actually a test of his skill as a composer and orchestrator. The taste, intuition, and experience of Ernst Toch the composer was not allowed to override the ingenuous quality of the tune in the finished three-movement suite he composed in fulfillment of his commission.

I suggested to the film editor that I was asking him to orchestrate a simple cinematic tune, the story of a drum. It appeared he was not entirely convinced. So I tried another story by way of illustration, my first lesson in orchestration. Toch had handed me the Mozart Piano Sonata in F Major (K 332), telling me to set the first movement for orchestra. I asked him for some guidelines in the assignment, but he smiled and shook his head saying, "Use any instruments you think are appropriate." A few weeks later he read through the elaborate and heavy-handed score I had prepared during many hours of hard work. He read in silence to the very end and then said, "How I wish you could hear this performed—it is so very bad! You have completely destroyed the transparency and economy of line that is the hallmark of Mozart's style." My orchestration was more Wagnerian than Mozartian. It demonstrated a fair knowledge of the instruments of the orchestra, but at the expense of the Sonata in F Major.

The film editor and I talked on in this vein for perhaps two hours until finally he seemed to understand the requirements of the ethnomusicological point of view. To make sure, I put it in these terms. The composer, like the film maker, strives to express himself through his creations. But as an orchestrator he has the primary obligation of allowing the subject to express itself. And in the field of ethnomusicology, the nature of the subject, even if it includes "a lot of people shuffling around," has priority over cinematic artistry except where this complements and serves the subject.

The point was clear, and subsequently we went to work. The finished film runs forty-two minutes, about 1,400 feet in length. It is a fine example of not-very-good footage skillfully edited as a quite acceptable finished film. The success of the film has greatly exceeded expectations based on its cinematic quality. But this is to be expected of ethnomusicological subjects. The subject itself in its colorful social context sustains the interest of specialist and general audience alike, notwithstanding the minimal competence of filming techniques. There could be more close-ups, stopping short of armpit photography; but the saving factor is simply that the camera is always looking at the right place at the right time. As the most amateurish of cameramen, I was professional in two critical aspects of technical know-how: an intimate knowledge of subject and an ethnomusicological point of view.

My intention in telling this fortuitous success story has been to stress the importance of good editing and to assure the advanced student of ethnomusicology that he already possesses the most important assets in relation to technical know-how.

THE SUPER 8   Among the institutions offering a seminar in field and lab methods few, if any, will have enough 16 mm cameras, tape recorders for synchronized sound, and editing facilities to service a dozen or fifteen graduate students in ethnomusicology in the limited duration of the seminar. The multiple costs of making 16 mm motion pictures also complicate the problem. As a compromise solution to these practical problems, I have required students to document their local field work with an inexpensive model of the 8 mm or super 8 mm motion-picture camera, regarded as a "home-movie" camera without sync sound. They are also asked to produce a tape recording of the subject filmed that matches the action, with allowance by fellow critics in the seminar for the lack of lip sync. The cost of super 8 mm film and processing is minimal, and the experience, notwithstanding the limitations of the equipment, is invaluable. By concentrating strenuous efforts on the preparation of the shooting script, we manage to bring the normal editing requirements down to the vanishing point. Each project requires a finished film of at least four minutes' duration, about the length of film on the super 8 mm cassette. At the student's option, he can use a 16 mm camera with a 100-foot reel, three minutes long as the finished product. It is surprising how much information in the ethnomusicological frame of reference can be presented in three or four minutes if each step in the filming has been carefully evaluated beforehand. In other words, for purposes of preliminary training, the student is encouraged to shoot on a 1:1 ratio. At his discretion, this ratio may be increased if he can locate editing facilities on his own initiative. The 1:1 ratio, unthinkable in serious film making, forces the student to "edit" before the fact. It teaches him much about editing and minimizes the expense of film and processing. When all the short projects are complete, one long session of the seminar is devoted to constructive criticism. The first time this procedure was used in the seminar, the results went far beyond my expectations. In spite of awkward camera techniques, every film managed significant documentation because the student had chosen a subject he knew intimately and had followed a shooting script written from the ethnomusicological point of view.

Before we dismiss the super 8 as an instrument of the home movie, it should be noted that some professionals are using the best models of the super 8, which have a pressure plate as well as sync sound, to make films that are subsequently blown up to the commercial standard of 16 mm or even 35 mm. It may be that such equipment holds the best promise for the ethnomusicologist in the field. It is light, economical, and steadily being improved in quality.

THE SINGLE-SYSTEM SOUND CAMERA   One type of super 8 mm camera has its own sound system built into the camera, so that picture and sound are recorded at the same time by the same apparatus. It is practically impossible to edit such a film, and the quality of sound falls far below broadcast quality. There is, of course, no flexibility in mike placement. Better quality is available either in certain brands of single-system 16 mm cameras or in the new portable videotape recorder.

Any one of these three types of cameras offers the ethnomusicologist the possibility of making what we might call analytical documentary studies to aid him in the detailed examination of instrumental techniques, dance movement, ritual, and so forth. Such studies, which can be of great value to the researcher in relation to a particular objective, are similar in purpose to some of the special uses of the tape recorder for analytical purposes mentioned earlier. But two limitations prevent them from being considered documentary motion pictures: (1) inferior quality and control of sound and (2) the fact that the film or tape cannot be edited. In making such studies, the cameraman has no choice but to let the camera "bake" on a tripod.

This limitation introduces a fundamental difference of opinion held by proponents of two diametrically opposed techniques in filming ethnomusicological subjects. One we might refer to as the technique of the Cyclops Era (a term well known to the student of motion pictures) and the other the technique of the Contemporary Era.

In the infancy of the motion picture industry, a camera was mounted

279

on a tripod and the actors performed in front of it. Sometime around the first decade of the twentieth century, the whole industry was revolutionized when someone for the first time moved the camera to different locations to allow different distances from and angles of exposure to the subject. This development was based on the reasoning that a camera has only one eye which films the subject in a flat, two-dimensional plane. A human being has two eyes, and with them he can see a subject in three dimensions. Moving the camera or using several cameras at different angles and distances opened up the possibility of editing the reels of film so that the composite, with its changes of angle, simulated the three-dimensional perspective of human vision. This technique became a basic law of the motion picture. The finished product is a composite of many, many short scenes. Over the years of development, experience indicated that an average scene or angle should last only six or seven seconds; a duration of twenty seconds before a change of angle is considered a long scene. For special purposes and special effects, there is considerable latitude on either side of these averages.

Proponents in ethnomusicology of the Cyclops Era have rolled back the motion picture to its earliest infancy. They mount one camera on a tripod and let it run while the subject does its stuff. Their arguments in support of a one-eyed technique are based on the mistaken assumption that a continuous camera run, which eliminates the decision making required in editing, produces a pristine-pure record. The product of such a method, no matter how much the subject moves, is very static, because the viewer is never allowed to see with more than one eye. I have stated before that even the most professional recording and filming represents only a selective simulation of reality. The Cyclops Era goes as far as possible in the opposite direction by putting a patch over one eye of the viewer— which is a far cry from a pristine-pure record! The procedure certainly simplifies the problems of the film maker. But no film maker would want to be accused of using a technique that predates the Contemporary Era.

The Cyclops Era also obviates the ethnomusicological point of view. With only one camera running continuously, there is no possibility of relating the subject to its environment, to members of society with which it is involved, to value indicators. Even for the specialist, whose attention may be riveted to details of performance, such a film is as static as grandmother's tintype. If the ethnomusicologist is to present the ethnomusicological point of view, he must learn something about camera angles and the ultimate decisions which only he is qualified to make in editing.

Ideal shooting in the field requires three cameras. The first camera is mounted on a tripod and runs continuously, or nearly so, framing the complete subject. The second camera, sometimes on a tripod, sometimes hand-held, runs intermittently to cover different angles and distances and concentrates its framing on tighter shots of the subject—for example, on first one and then another part of an ensemble of musicians or group of dancers. The third camera is hand-held and concentrates on details of performance, spectator reactions, and so forth in tight close-ups. The first camera, in sync with the tape recorder, is the Cyclops of the team and produces the main line of coverage into which are cut the various angles and concentrated details filmed by the second and third cameras. In the most sophisticated setup, all three cameras are in sync with one another and with sound; otherwise, cutting scenes from the second and third cameras requires exacting efforts to put them in sync during the editing. Sometimes the second camera takes over the main coverage while the first camera changes from a normal lens to a wide angle or a telephoto lens or changes magazines.

THE ZOOM LENS   These three lenses can be replaced by one zoom lens. Although the zoom lens is not as sharp throughout its range as the single lens, it offers the advantage of an infinite number of lens sizes as well as quick changes in framing. The amateur must remember that actual zooming with a zoom lens should be used very sparingly. The zoom also permits a quasi-dolly shot in the field; that is, instead of having a camera with a fixed lens mounted on a dolly that can be rolled back and forth to keep the proper frame as the subject moves, sensitive and almost imperceptible movement of the zoom will maintain proper framing. This is not a real dolly shot because it involves a continuous change of lens size; but in rough terrain encountered in the field, it is a practical substitute.

THE CREW   How big a crew is required? Textbooks on the motion picture indicate that eight or nine persons is the minimal number for professional results: one for each camera, a recordist, a mike man who may have to follow the movement of dialogue with an overhead boom, a script girl responsible for entering final revisions in the shooting script, perhaps a still photographer, a unit manager, and the director. The ethnomusicologist can manage if he takes two persons with him and hires a guide in the field. This four-man team might distribute responsibilities in the following way: The ethnomusicologist acts as director, first camera-man, and supervises recording; the second member of the team is responsible for second camera and the shooting script; the third person handles the third camera and still photography; the guide serves as the all-important unit manager and turns on and off tape recorder or occasionally a fixed camera. The unit manager is responsible for all arrangements prior to actual shooting. He must make sure that all the subjects to be filmed are on location at the right time, wearing the proper clothing, that the crew has housing with a source of power for recharging batteries, that all props and appurtenances are on hand for a scene, and so forth. The guide is the only man qualified for such a responsibility because he knows local conditions

281

intimately. The ethnomusicologist must be responsible for preliminary testing of sound level and balance, for the location of each camera and the type lens used for each shot, for light-meter readings and adjustment of aperture, and so forth. Even though some of these chores are delegated to other members of the crew, it is wise for him to check the details before shooting.

He must also be the director. Now, in Hollywood the director is king of all he surveys, which is simply a way of saying that he must be knowledgeable in all requirements. Recently a famous Hollywood director told me that his success in large part was due to the fact that he personally checked the framing of every camera for every scene before shooting. This is not a matter of distrusting the judgment of other cameramen in the crew but rather that the director must be able to conceive in his mind something approaching the finished film. And it is important to check every detail against this total conception.

In the role of director the ethnomusicologist must be careful not to overdirect his subject. If he walks and talks the performers through a scene in a casual way, suggesting the principal line of action rather than too many details, the naturalness of the scene will be preserved. After the "walk-through," the performers then go through a camera rehearsal for checking angles, framing, and panning. In my experience, most subjects in the field are natural actors; after all, their profession is performance. Frequently, therefore, following these two initial run-throughs, the first actual "take" with the cameras running is good. The drum carver in *Atumpan* was such a natural actor that numerous times he volunteered bits of business during a "take" that added clarity to the intention of the scene.

Some scenes, of course, such as processions, sacred rituals, the actual carving of a drum, cannot be rehearsed because they can occur only once. Before these one-shot "takes," the director must have the fullest description of the action and must do his best to visualize the appropriate filming techniques. One-shot scenes should be covered as fully as possible by all three cameras to allow the greatest selection in editing.

The ethnomusicologist can reduce his crew from four to three if he settles for two cameras. If he goes to the field alone, he and the guide can still accomplish good coverage with two cameras and a tape recorder by instructing the guide in some of the simple techniques of the second camera. I suppose one camera is better than none at all. But without a second camera, the ethnomusicologist must either operate a continuously running Cyclops or develop a keen sense of pre-editing and strive to achieve the theoretical ratio of 1:1. Changes of angle must be calculated to coincide with sectional changes of the musical sound track, otherwise picture and sound cannot be cut to preserve musical continuity. To do this he must know the musical form thoroughly.

Operating two or three 16 mm cameras in the field, I have found that an average day of following a shooting script from 10:00 A.M. to 4:00 P.M. requires about 400 feet of film. Selective coverage of one-shot "takes" might quadruple this amount to permit flexibility in editing. Depending on the basic type of finished film, a two-hour procession, representing only one of many contextual uses of the subject, might be represented adequately by two or three minutes of edited film. The ratio of 1,600 feet of film edited to a length of 100 feet is high; but the unpredictable aspects of the one-shot "take" justify extended coverage.

Commercial color film has a slow speed. In the tropics, this is ideal for subjects lighted by direct sunlight. But as in still photography, the fact that most subjects prefer to perform in the protective shadows of a grove of trees or in a pavilion requires very fast color film as well. In the tropics, all film should be sent out for processing as quickly as possible after exposure or the latent image will be affected by excessive humidity. The basic supply of film in the field should be stored in a cool, dry environment. It is worth driving 100 miles every few days if the supply can be located in air-conditioned storage.

Before going to the field and after returning, the ethnomusicologist should be in touch with a professional film maker. If he is lucky enough to find one who will accompany him to the field—and who is sympathetic to the necessities of the ethnomusicological point of view—then he will have established the basis of a promising collaboration. The open-minded film maker will not misunderstand the directorial responsibilities of the ethnomusicologist in the field, even his persistence in checking the framing of every camera before shooting a scene. Once back from the field, such a film maker and the ethnomusicologist should make the ideal team of editors.

This form of collaboration, I am convinced, can produce the very best models of ethnomusicological films. It will remain a utopian dream, however, until the brotherhood of ethnomusicologists sits down and defines its requirements of the motion picture for the edification of the brotherhood of film makers.

Chapters 4 and 5 have attempted to illustrate one recurring point: The ethnomusicologist must do his own field work because only he can satisfy the manifold requirements of the ethnomusicological point of view. Having done so, he is ready for the laboratory and the writing desk.

Chapter Six

QUEST for the NORMS of STYLE

ONE OF THE most dramatic moments in the puppet plays of Java and Bali occurs in various episodes from the *Bharatayudda*, the *Götterdammerung* of the *Mahabharata*, during the scene that follows the violent death of a beloved hero. The tragic expression of bereavement is accompanied by a song known as "Tlutur." The style of the piece, the style of the musical ensemble, the style of the puppets, the style of the production, the style of the puppeteer's singing, the style of the language, the style of the empathic audience, the style of the environment—this bundle of traditions is remarkably different in a comparison of the Sundanese of West Java, the Javanese of Central and East Java, the Balinese of Bali. The emotions are the same, the function and usage of the dramatic vehicle are quite similar—but the norms that regulate style are different. Each of the three societies has long since refashioned the Indian literature on which the puppet play is based to reflect its own, its unique, cultural image; and this composite art form represents the purest distillation of cultural heritage. Comprehension of the norms of musical style in this context requires an understanding of the norms of style that govern the whole bundle of traditions. Each segment of the bundle, as it touches and affects other parts to which it is bound, offers unique insight into human behavior.

I am not suggesting that the ethnomusicologist is essentially a behavioral scientist, however the term may be defined; but his particular sphere of expertise can contribute much to a knowledge of human behavior. In almost every phase of his endeavor, he is involved in media of communications which, by their very nature, are most difficult of access to his colleagues in other disciplines. I have pointed out several times that the ethnomusicological approach requires the collaboration of the psychologist, the linguist, the ethnologist, the archeologist, the physiologist, the historian, and others. At this point, it is pertinent to state unequivocally the converse relationship: the psychologist, the linguist, the ethnologist, the archeologist, the physiologist, the historian, and others require the collaboration of the ethnomusicologist.

The impetus for reciprocal collaboration must come from the ethnomusicologist. On him lies the burden of proof. Unless he is able to relate the norms of musical style to the bundle of traditions surrounding music, the significance of his description, analysis, comparison, and criticism will remain inscrutable for scholars in other disciplines.

Music is inseparable from its cultural context—as distinct from its social context—and it both affects and is affected by that context. Beatle music in the United States, whatever its value to different segments of the society, is what it is—*can only be what it is*—because of its cultural context. And that context makes it different from beatle music in Africa or Indonesia or Europe. In turn, beatle music has affected not only its social context, as suggested in the Introduction, but also, more importantly, its cultural context. Domination of television commercials by the beatle-style rock beat, for example, is an illustration of its effect on the style of communications. On the other side of the coin, the specific requirements of the TV commercial, *its* norms of style, have also affected the style of rock music. And the norms that govern each are indicators of human behavior, of communications, of values, of "generation gap," of a whole bundle of traditions in the making. They should be of profound interest to the "ologists" referred to above.

If the bundle of traditions surrounding TV and rock music, if a bundle of such recent vintage, has something to tell the scholars of various disciplines, then what a rich source of information is available in the thousand-year-old bundle surrounding the puppet play of Java and Bali!

285

When the ethnomusicologist returns from the field to his laboratory and writing desk and prepares his specimens for the vivisection of analysis and comparison, he should not lose sight of the bundle of traditions to which they belong. Let us put the little piece "Tlutur," the musical essence of tragic expression in the puppet play, on the operating table for a moment and see what our surgical instruments reveal in Sunda, Java, and Bali. The basic stuff of which it is made is five-tone sléndro. Additional vocal tones are supplied by the song of the ḍalang (puppeteer) and, in Sunda and Java, perhaps by the rebab. The piece is quite short and may be tacked onto the end of another piece. Musical poignancy is probably achieved primarily by the peculiar way in which the vocal tones are employed, although in Bali the accompanying pair or quartet of metallophones, even though limited to only the five sléndro pitches, also seems to contribute to this effect. The emotions portrayed by the piece are the same in all three societies, but the musical character of each is quite distinctive. The function and usage of the music relate to dominant or residual religious practices, to calendrical rites, and entertainment. Risking a slightly subjective conclusion, we might say that an extraordinary musical pathos is created within a surprising economy of means.[1] (For an example of the rebab part only, hear Side VI, Band 2.)

Documenting the revelations of our vivisection, of course, are a series of detailed Melograms, statistical summaries of the various pitches used, tables showing the relationship between the hierarchy of tones in this piece and other pieces in the repertory, intervallic measurements, rhythmic idioms, and so forth, all neatly tabulated in a comparison with norms of musical style that regulate the whole musical tradition.

Keeping in mind the need for reciprocal collaboration with scholars in other disciplines, we must say that the vivisection was impeccable, the operation a success—but the patient died. Let us try the bundle of traditions surrounding "Tlutur" as a resuscitator. Let us see the extent to which these other norms of style may give life to the distinctive human behavior of each of the three societies and permit us to glimpse the living musical expression of the puppet play within its cultural context.

THE PUPPET PLAY IN JAVA AND BALI

Although historically the origin of the puppet play in Indonesia is subject to some difference of opinion, there is general agreement among scholars that it is at least a thousand years old. In addition to the autochthonous stories of the

[1]For transcriptions of three versions, see Jaap Kunst, *Music in Java: Its History, Its Theory and Its Technique*, 2 vols., 2d ed., Martinus Nijhoff, The Hague, 1949, pp. 509–510.

286

culture hero Pandji,[2] poetic literature based on the Indian *Mahabharata* and *Ramayana* began to develop during the late tenth and early eleventh centuries in East Java and subsequently spread throughout Java and Bali. Sometime early in this development, it is probable that the religious literature and style of puppetry, as well as musical instruments, tuning systems, scales, modes, performance practice, and so forth, were closely related among the Sundanese of West Java, the Javanese of Central and East Java, and the Balinese of Bali. Each of these three societies had adapted Indian Hinduism to regional beliefs in animism and ancestor worship. But over a span of centuries, the norms of style surrounding the puppet play developed differences in response to the ever-changing cultural and social context of each society and in response to external forces as well.

Today, a comparative perspective reveals that the emotions are the same, the function and usage of the dramatic vehicle are quite similar. The sociologist would contend that in each of the three societies the puppet play has the same social meaning. But the fact remains that in each society the norms that regulate style are different.

Proper approach to the subject carries the implication of social meaning far beyond the sociologist's interest in ritual, in mere function and usage. It includes definitive information relating to human behavior, human values, social interaction, codes of morality, standards of taste, and, in historical perspective, even a capsulated account of social evolution. These, too, of course, are of profound interest to the sociologist. But unless he is prepared to negotiate not only speech discourse but also music discourse and dance discourse—traditional dance styles are based on the movements of the puppets—unless he acquires expertise in modes of communication that are exclusive to the arts, he will have access to little beyond the superficial description of function and usage. And on this basis alone, as we have indicated, there is little apparent difference among the three quite different societies.

In comparative terms, let us consider briefly some of these differences as they are reflected in the style of puppet theater. The most ancient form of the puppet play, probably originating in East Java, has been retained in Bali. The musical ensemble consists of a pair or quartet of ten-keyed metallophones tuned to five-tone sléndro and known as gendèr wajang. Although Jaap Kunst was persuaded on the basis of ethnological evidence that seven-tone pélog represents the older tuning system in Java,[3] there is recent evidence that five-tone sléndro

[2] For a definitive study, see Willem Huibert Rassers, *Pandji, the Culture Hero: A Structural Study of Religion in Java*, Martinus Nijhoff, The Hague, 1949; or, in the original Dutch, *De Pandji-roman*, D. de Vos-van Kleef, Antwerpen, 1934.

[3] Kunst, *Music in Java, op. cit.*, pp. 18–24.

287

predates the seven-tone system by as much as eight centuries.[4] The ten-keyed metallophone itself represents an ancient form of the gendèr, which in more recent times has fourteen or fifteen keys and is one of the principal improvising instruments in the large Javanese gamelan. It is also worth noting that in Balinese gendèr wajang there is no improvisation.

The Javanese and Balinese leather puppets are supported by a central rod; both arms articulate at the elbow and shoulder, and some of the Balinese humorous characters have articulated jaws. The Balinese style of the flat leather puppets is more realistic than that of the Javanese counterpart—evidence, according to some scholars, that the more abstract style of puppet developed in Java after the advent of Islam with its prohibition of making graven images.[5] Wajang figures found on the bas reliefs of temples built in East Java prior to the encroachment of Islam support this theory; they are quite similar in style to the wajang puppets found in Bali today. It is remarkable the extent to which under the skilled hands of the puppeteer all these puppets come to life, especially viewed from the shadow side of the screen where the flickering rays of the oil lamp add to the illusion of breathing and other subtle movement. The puppeteer is also skilled in handling several puppets, separate weapons, and possibly horses or a chariot in action-packed battles, which are very popular.

As a principal carrier of the religious literature of Balinese Hinduism, the shadow play is an essential part of the ritual of temple festivals and rites of passage. For all three societies, the puppet play is also a form of entertainment. It is filled with humor, wit, tragedy, topical satire, adventure, battles, philosophy, sex, morals, manners, ethics, history—the full gamut of human and godly experience. And, as we shall see, even though the Sundanese and the Javanese were converted to Islam more than three centuries ago, the deeper social meaning of the literature still derives from the socio-cultural configuration achieved during the period of the East Javanese Empires from the tenth to the sixteenth centuries.

In Bali, where the external force of Islam never gained a foothold, Balinese Hinduism has become a way of life. In spite of its organic function as an expression of religious devotion—or more probably because of it—on some occasions the Balinese might seem to have a rather casual regard for the shadow play. Actually, such an interpretation is quite misleading. It is difficult to find an analogy in Western societies. Perhaps to some degree it is like the difference between the relatively formal attitude of the Catholic in the United States toward the regular

[4] Mantle Hood, "The Effect of Medieval Technology on Musical Style in the Orient," paper read in 1962 at a meeting of the Royal Anthropological Institute for Great Britain and Northern Ireland, London; *Selected Reports*, vol. 1, no. 3, Institute of Ethnomusicology, UCLA (1970), pp. 147–170.

[5] Frits A. Wagner, *Indonesia, the Art of an Island Group*, trans. by Ann E. Keep, Art of the World Series, Crown Publishers, Inc., New York, 1959, p. 127.

rituals of his church compared to the more matter-of-fact acceptance of trappings of church dogma characteristic of Catholic countries like Italy and Spain. Neither attitude indicates a greater or lesser religious devotion; but the governing norms of style, developed in response to their respective cultural contexts, are different. On most occasions, however, no more rapt audience for theater could be found than the Balinese watching the shadow play. Two performances held in connection with two different temple festivals will illustrate the range of audience response. The first was staged inside the temple and the second outside the temple.

During the summer of 1967, I was invited by the officiating priest, Ida Bagus Njana, and his son, Ida Bagus Tilem, to attend a local temple festival in the village of Mas in southern Bali. After a sumptuous evening meal, which had its own memorable norms of style, Tilem and I walked some distance through a gathering crowd to the temple gates. A Balinese temple is a walled-in, open courtyard containing various kinds of balé or small pavilions and small shrines. From some distance, we had heard the light, delicate sounds of gamelan angklung; and now, as we entered the temple and came in view of the balé in which about twenty musicians were performing, the sounds seemed suddenly brighter. Several other small pavilions contained colorful offerings; and in another sat the officiating priest singing kekawin and, from time to time, ringing an ornate silver bell. Opposite this balé, was a tiny pavilion in which the puppeteer was busy arranging his cast of characters. Behind him were two gendèr wajang ready to provide accompaniment for the shadow play. The screen in front of him, against which the shadows of the puppets would be cast by an overhanging oil lamp, was facing the priest. A short distance from the gamelan angklung, the instruments of the large gamelan gong kebyar had been arranged to form a sizable rectangle on the ground as a dance area. At one end, a bamboo frame supported a curtain through which the dancers would make their entrance. Near a balé filled with offerings on the other side of the gamelan angklung, a number of kneeling women were singing. A second priest stood before them with a container of holy water.

For a few minutes, I remained close to the gamelan angklung listening to the rapid interplay of kotekan, watching the rise and fall of the musicians' hammers as they coordinated interlocking parts. Suddenly I nearly jumped out of my skin when the large gamelan behind me rocked the night air with the loud opening chord of their first piece. While the gamelan angklung continued to play, I stood transfixed for some time between the sound of four-tone sléndro on one side and the powerful five-tone pélog of the large gamelan on the other. Moments later, I noticed that the two performers of gendèr wajang, with their instruments tuned to five-tone sléndro, had also begun to play. The dalang was beginning the shadow play. An abrupt change of tempo and dynamics brought my attention back to the large gamelan; one of the dancers was about to enter.

It was an unforgettable evening. Sometimes everything was going at once: four-tone sléndro, five-tone sléndro, five-tone pélog, dancers, the singing of the ḍalang, the action of the puppets, the singing women, two priests in their ritual. Like a very busy bee, more than an ethnomusicologist, I found myself drawn from one flower of activity to another. Sometimes I just stood in the middle of it all listening and watching in a kind of psychedelic trance. Most of the crowd gathered round the large gamelan and the dance area. The performance of the ḍalang and the gendèr wajang continued through it all, but it seemed to be almost forgotten except for a cluster of small children who watched the shadowy movements of the puppets with complete absorption. For a time, I sat on the edge of the tiny pavilion close to the ḍalang listening to his voice and watching his skillful manipulation of the puppets. It struck me that this miniature theater with its miniature audience had a quality of sacred devotion not unlike that of the kneeling women singing nearby, receiving the blessings of the priest. And in a very real sense the puppeteer himself performed in the devoted spirit of a priest. I could imagine that the crowd of spectators surrounding the dance area were continuously aware, even though their attention was directed elsewhere, that the priest of the puppet play was in his place and that all the devotional forms of the temple festival were being fulfilled. And throughout the evening, whether I was concentrating on gamelan angklung or gong kebyar or the dance, I found that I, too, was aware of the presence of the kneeling women, the priests, and the miniature theater of the shadow play, whose characters are believed to be reenacting the stories of Balinese ancestry.

A few nights later I attended a performance of wajang kulit in another village. The occasion was a week-long temple festival, and this whole evening was devoted to the shadow play. A large bamboo pavilion had been erected for the purpose, and when I arrived near midnight there was only standing room at the outer edges of the structure. The attention of the tightly packed audience was absorbed by the antics of the shadowy figures of the clowns and their ribald humor. For the next hour, I spent as much time watching the faces of the audience from different vantage points as I did watching the performance. They seemed to respond like one person. The priest of the puppet play was in his place, in the context of a temple festival; and he had his audience with him every moment, for every nuance of action and wit. Communication that night was immediate and direct. His was both the voice of the ancestors and the voice of the people. And the quartet of gendèr wajang supporting him was part of its timbre. Sometimes it served as a musical foil for his virtuosity, sometimes as his musical partner, sometimes as the sole commentary on the action. There was no place in this episode for the tragic tenderness and musical fragility of "Tlutur"—but in response to the paradoxically kindred emotion of humor the empathy of the audience was just as intense.

In this society, where the religion of Balinese Hinduism is a way of life, where the very essence of religious devotion is expressed through music, dance, poetry, puppetry—in this society, audience and performer, carver and beholder, priest and parishioner, composer and instrumentalist, temple offerings and the shrine have a common identity. Each facet of this identity, each segment of its bundle of traditions, offers unique insight into human behavior: the style of communications, the style of political fervor, of individual and communal responsibilities, of taste, of loyalties, prejudices, discrimination.

With this brief glimpse of Balinese audience and environment serving as a point of departure, let us consider the Javanese and Sundanese equivalents as well as other norms of style which constitute significant aspects of the tradition.

More than three centuries have passed since the Javanese and the Sundanese were converted to a mystical form of Islam. Even though (with rare exception)[6] music is not part of Muslim religious festivities, the deep roots of Hinduism, animism, and ancestor worship are curiously entwined in the continuing function and usage of the performing arts. On a variety of specified occasions, particular styles of gamelan, dance, and puppetry are performed in the palaces of the sultan, the Mangkunegara, and other titular designees continued from earlier days of social and religious hierarchies. In Javanese society, the puppet play is featured in celebration of weddings, circumcisions, and other calendrical rites. It is considered an indispensable panacea for pestilence and disease and the alleviation of calamity and disaster. It is also a form of entertainment.

The formal attitude of the Javanese toward wajang kulit, compared to the more casual acceptance of the shadow play by the Balinese, may be slightly analogous to our earlier comparison of the American Catholic and the Italian Catholic. In part, this difference can be ascribed to the overall pattern of Javanese behavior so elegantly expressed in the cultivation of prijaji ideals of formality;[7] in part it can be attributed to the constraints of Islam which apparently have affected even the shape and stylization of the puppets. Whatever the multiple explanations for the difference in behavior, the Javanese take the performance of wajang kulit quite seriously. The restraints of Javanese etiquette and sense of refinement permit only the subtlest show of emotional response. There is no raucous laughter when the clowns are doing their stuff; but the smiles and polite

[6]Gamelan sekati being a principal exception; see further pp. 346–347.

[7]See further Hildred Geertz, "Indonesian Culture and Communities," in Ruth T. McVey (ed.), *Indonesia*, Southeast Asia Studies, Yale University, by arrangement with HRAF Press, New Haven, Conn., 1963, pp. 42 ff.

291

giggles of the audience make clear the depth of emotion even though the norms of style require a markedly different response from that of the Balinese. Evidence of the high percentage of saturation of the tradition in Javanese society can be seen in the regular broadcasts of wajang kulit from the radio stations of Central Java. The listening audience is so familiar with the theatrical elements of the shadow play that it can visualize all of the dramatic action through the narration and singing of the ḍalang and the music of the supporting gamelan—a literal example of tele-vision. On the rare occasion when the complete series of episodes that comprise the *Bharatajudda* has been performed in Central Java, Javanese from many miles' distance have made a pilgrimage to Djogjakarta to witness the performances.[8]

The environment and, in some instances, the physical arrangement of the audience also tend to be more formal than in Bali. In the towns and larger villages, a performance of wajang kulit is usually staged in the pendopo—the pavilion that is the entry to the house proper in a princely residence or the home of a wealthy businessman. It is here that the head of the household entertains male guests on the formal occasion of the celebration of a wedding or other rites of passage. Female guests are accommodated within the house proper. The screen is set up in the pringgitan, the entry bridging the pendopo and the house, with the ḍalang and the gamelan facing it from the pendopo, so that the shadow of the puppets may be seen only from the house. Some scholars believe that in former times wajang kulit may have been a form of male initiation rite which allowed only the men and adolescent males to see the actual puppets and the ḍalang functioning in the role of priest, while the women and children, watching from the other side of the screen, saw only the shadows.[9] Although today in many places, either sex of any age may sit on either side of the screen, in some regions the older tradition still obtains.[10] In Bali, although there appear to be no prohibitions of this kind, the entire audience, except for a few youths who perhaps themselves aspire to be ḍalangs one day, sits on the shadow side of the screen. In fact, in Bali the puppet play is physically staged so there is no room for an audience on the ḍalang's side of the screen.

Javanese wajang kulit may also be performed in a public building or even in a bamboo pavilion temporarily attached to a private house in connection with rites of passage. In the small village, the environment may be extremely simple.

[8] See further Mantle Hood, "The Enduring Tradition: Music and Theater in Java and Bali," in McVey (ed.), *Indonesia, op. cit.*, pp. 444–445.

[9] Compare R. L. Mellema, *Wayang Puppets, Carving, Colouring, Symbolism*, trans., by Mantle Hood, Koninklijk Instituut voor de Tropen, Amsterdam, 1954.

[10] For example, in princely residences in Djogjakarta and also, according to an oral communication from Max Harrell, in Tjeribon in 1962.

However the puppet play is staged, there is always an air of formality with the occasion.

The style of the production in Java is also quite formal. The musical accompaniment is provided by a large gamelan sléndro in contrast to the pair or quartet of gendèr wajang used in Bali. The Javanese performance begins about seven-thirty in the evening with an overture by the orchestra that may last a half hour or forty-five minutes. The play begins shortly after 8:00 P.M. and has a structure divided into three time periods: the first ending around midnight, the second about 3:00 A.M. and the third at 6:00 A.M. It is a very long production without intermission. In Bali, by comparison, the starting time of the overture by gendèr wajang is quite variable, and the total production lasts less than five hours.

An indication of the special regard of the Javanese for wajang kulit and the high value they place on it can be seen in their frequent philosophical and sociological interpretations of the shadow play.[11] Comparison is made between the three time periods of the wajang night and the time periods of the life cycle: youth, maturity, and old age. Mystical interpretations of various passages in the poetic texts and symbolism ascribed to the many characterizations represented in the dramatis personae could, in themselves, comprise a sizable body of literature.

Above all, the Javanese, like the Balinese, accept the stories of wajang kulit as the story of their own ancestry. It does not matter that some of the principal characters and some of the story line derive from India; some of the characters and some of the story line are purely Javanese. The technical terms of the puppet apparatus are Javanese, the style of the music, the instruments, the singing, the style of the puppeteer, the language are all Javanese. The poetic forms of the texts have long since been Javanese. The rich mixture of religious and superstitious beliefs and the complex fabric of prijaji ideals, which stem from the ancient kingdoms of the East Javanese empires, are Javanese. Yes, it is true: This bundle of traditions, these cultural norms of style are indeed the story of Javanese ancestry.

In West Java, the Sundanese version of the *Mahabharata* is performed in a kind of puppet play known as wajang golêk. Unlike the stylized puppets of the Javanese, which are delicately carved from buffalo hide and meticulously painted, or the more realistic leather puppets of Bali, those found in Sunda are round wooden figures. (For a comparison of the three kind of puppets see Illustrations 6-1 and 6-2.) These, of course, are not shadow puppets; so, although they may perform within the boundaries of a frame, the screen is omitted. Wajang golêk

---

[11] See, for example, K. G. P. A. A. Mangkunegara VII, *On the Wayang Kulit (purwa) and its Symbolic and Mystical Elements*, trans. by Claire Holt, Cornell University Press, Ithaca, N.Y., 1957; also see Hood, "The Enduring Tradition," *op. cit.*, pp. 438–445.

Illustration 6-1
From left to right, the Sun-
danese wajang golêk, Java-
nese wajang kulit, and
Balinese wajang kulit repre-
sentations of Ardjuna.

Illustration 6-2
The same three figures
showing the two leather
puppets in silhouette.

294

is also found in Central and East Java, but it is never used for the literature of the *Mahabharata* and *Ramayana*, nor has it the great popularity known in Sunda. (For examples of Central and East Javanese wajang golêk see Illustration 6-3.)

The style of Sundanese audience behavior and typical environment are somewhere between those of the Javanese and the Balinese, less formal than the first and more formal than the second. Sometime during my residence in Central Java during 1957–1958, I heard that there would be an evening performance of Sundanese wajang golêk in the large public building in the square south of the sultan's palace. I was genuinely surprised to learn that there was enough interest here in the heartland of Javanese culture to support a performance of Sundanese wajang golêk. That night in the middle of the performance, I walked to the back of the room and joined several Javanese friends for coffee while we continued to watch the production. All evening long, I had been amazed at the overt display of changing emotions in the audience. I turned to my Javanese companions and said that in the context of a wajang performance I had never heard a Javanese

Illustration 6-3
Wajang golêk figures of Central Java (left) and East Java (right).

audience so boisterous in their laughter or so openly demonstrative in their enthusiasm for a female singer, a special feature of the Sundanese production. One of the Javanese sipping coffee put down his glass, looked at me smiling, and said, "This is not a Javanese audience. These are Sundanese people living here in Djogja."

Sundanese wajang golêk is a younger form of puppetry than wajang kulit. Not only do the arms of the round wooden puppets articulate but the head also turns from side to side and the trunk moves up and down and rotates partially. The figures are gowned in traditional Sundanese dress, often including a long scarf important in the dance. And one of the delights of wajang golêk is the realistic manner in which the puppets perform traditional dances. Realism reaches a marked credibility at the conclusion of a vigorous dance when the puppet's chest rises and falls in response to the exertion and gradually comes to a point of repose as he catches his breath once again.

The Sundanese gamelan which accompanies wajang golêk is much smaller than its Javanese equivalent used for wajang kulit. It is located behind the ḍalang, and the audience sees only the puppets in action, the puppeteer and the musicians being relegated to the dim background. In the performance of "Tlutur," the ḍalang is joined by the rebab and the gambang, a xylophone, instead of gendèr. The function and usage of wajang golêk are similar to those of Javanese wajang kulit; but increasingly, especially in the larger towns, wajang golêk often functions purely as entertainment.

There is no less concern among the Sundanese than among the Javanese for the mystical and symbolic interpretations of the literature. In both societies, various characters of the wajang serve as stereotypes in designating the character of living personalities. Each physical, spiritual, moral, and ethical attribute of every wajang character is well known, and these constitute a simple and direct reference in describing the traits of human beings. If a man is likened to Bima or Ardjuna or Gatakatja, the characterization is understood immediately. *Wajang characterization forms one of the principal norms of style in communication.*

This thumbnail sketch of three bundles of traditions (see Illustrations 6-4, 6-5, and 6-6), each of which could comprise the subject of a book, has been necessarily brief. But like the respiratory exercise of the dancing golêk, it is an illustration of the living and breathing norms of style required in understanding the life force of a little piece like "Tlutur."

MUSICAL STYLE

If it is clear that a true comprehension of musical style is dependent on an understanding of its cultural context, it must be equally clear that a primary

296

Illustration 6-4
A performance of Balinese
wajang kulit.

Illustration 6-5
A performance of Javanese
wajang kulit.

297

Illustration 6-6
A performance of Sundanese *wajang golêk.*

298

responsibility of the ethnomusicologist is the quest for norms that regulate musical style. The word "style" is applied to music in many different contexts by musicians, and by consensus they seem to understand what it means. Yet, no one has offered a definition. Rather there tends to be scholarly concentration on one or another aspect of style. In part, this may be due to the nature of salient features of a given music under study, in part the natural result of a particular scholar's bias, and in part the inherent weakness or relative isolation of any kind of one-man definition. Be that as it may, musicians spend a lot of time talking and writing about style. Let us consider some of the problems encountered in such pre-occupation, in an attempt to gain perspective on this responsibility of the ethno-musicologist.

It is not generally recognized that the educative processes surrounding the Western musician provide him with a set of "trade terms," extending into jargon, which by consensus allows him to communicate with other musicians at the verbal level. These tend to be accepted uncritically as necessary tools of the trade, and are perpetuated through teaching and publication. Not infrequently, in the Western world of parlance, reviewer and author of a scholarly publication come to a bitter exchange of viewpoints, which, if the altercation is dispassionately assessed, may be founded on a misunderstanding of terms. In this instance, the reviewer's terms refer to one consensus and those of the author to another. Within his respective circle of consensus, either reviewer or author would be understood. Said another way, musical terms of reference are embedded in an oral tradition; and, somewhat like folk songs, they are known in a number of variant applications.

A study of music outside the European art tradition but researched and talked about in the vocabulary of Western parlance compounds the problem of oral variants. Also, as suggested in several places in this book, the application of Western musical concepts, in whatever terms they may be expressed, is some-times inappropriate. And this compounds the problem further. We shall have something to say about communications in Chapter Eight; but, for the moment, let us merely be aware that Western musical terms of reference are known in variant applications, each of which merits specific definition.

As a case in point, we have made frequent reference to one or another kind of G-S line, from the General to the Specific. In philosophical terms, this might be more correctly designated as the G-P line, from the General to the Particular, or the V-S line, from the Vague to the Specific. But oral tradition in the Wednesday Seminar at UCLA has endorsed "G-S," perhaps because "GP" has the musical connotation of Grand Pause. At any rate, there is nothing "vague" intended by the General, and the Specific can be as "particular" as you like. Earlier, we mentioned a laboratory device that gives a gross numerical index of tone quality (actually timbre). For obvious reasons, we called this measurement the QI rather than the IQ of sound. So much for the whimsy of oral tradition surrounding musical terms of reference.

Let us keep all this in mind in examining the chart on page 303, given as one possible orientation in the quest for the norms of musical style.[12] Quite different terms could be substituted in a number of places, but if I can make clear the application of those offered, perhaps they will serve our present purpose. The chart is intended as a reminder that any aspect of musical style must be considered in relation to two or more G-S lines; that is, two or more continua, which in turn relate to other continua outside musical practice. All research problems in musical style can and should be identified with some such orientation in mind. Let us discuss the chart and then try a few illustrations.

The bold G-S line at the top of the page and the bold vertical G-S line running down the center of the page are movable. The horizontal G-S line may be superimposed over any of those below it on the page. The vertical G-S line may be moved to the right or to the left to intersect any segment of the horizontal G-S line. The segments of each G-S line have been connected by a meandering dotted line to suggest that the proportions of the segmentation are somewhat arbitrary and that not only contiguous but also separated segments tend to impinge on one another. The segmentation of the horizontal G-S line indicates that a concentration on the whole tradition of a given music is a more general consideration than a study of one or another style period within the tradition. A study of one genre is more particular (or more specific!) than a study of one style period, and a concentration on individual pieces is even more particular. A concern for the style of the individual performer is the most particular segment of the G-S line.

THE CONSENSUS MAKERS OF MUSIC   The vertical G-S line and all its segments are referred to on the left side of the page as the MUSICAL CONSENSUS, which is in constant interaction with the CULTURAL CONSENSUS and the SOCIAL CONSENSUS. The MUSICAL CONSENSUS includes the interaction of performers and/or composers with teachers, theoreticians, critics, users or audiences, patrons, and others involved in the processes of music making. The musical consensus is affected by, and also affects, the CULTURAL CONSENSUS made up of the consensus of dancers, of puppeteers, of storytellers, of native speakers of the language involved, of the literati, of religious devotees, of any group involved in the processes of cultural expression outside music making per se. Both the musical consensus and the cultural consensus are affected by, and to some extent also affect,

[12] Compare Mantle Hood, "The Quest for Norms in Ethnomusicology," *Inter-American Music Bulletin*, no. 35, Pan-American Union, Washington, D.C. (May, 1963), pp. 1–5.

300

the SOCIAL CONSENSUS consisting of special interest groups and institutions, such as economic segments of society, the organized church, the military, the local and national government, political elites, the hierarchy of social status, and so forth. These three consensuses are subject to a variety of intrinsic and extrinsic forces. The importation of beatle music into Africa, Indonesia, or the United States is an example of one kind of extrinsic cultural force. The European Common Market, NATO, SEATO, the Warsaw Pact, Communism, Capitalism, Islam, Buddhism, Christianity, and similar alliances are examples of extrinsic forces which affect the total socio-cultural consensus of each member of the alliance. The extent to which extrinsic forces may affect a society depends on the relative strength of its own musico-socio-cultural consensus, its viability in terms of rejection, acculturation, and assimilation or ultimate loss of identity. Sometimes the extrinsic and intrinsic forces exerted on the socio-cultural consensus may have a very direct effect on the MUSICAL CONSENSUS, which establishes the norms of musical style. For example, an artist in my circle of acquaintance who spent the summer of 1968 in one of the countries of the Warsaw Pact informed me that not only painters and sculptors but also composers in that country enjoy the privileges of the highest economic bracket. They live in villas, have chauffeured automobiles at their disposal and generally receive social and economic recognition beyond that of academicians and medical doctors. In return, they must maintain a quantitative output to meet the demands of frequent exhibitions and public concerts. Quality in this regulated creativity is not lacking, but neither is it given primary consideration. In this instance, both extrinsic and intrinsic forces accepted by the socio-cultural consensus combine in a form of governmental subsidy that exerts a direct influence on the musical consensus governing the norms of musical style. A study of the musical style of this country, however general or particular the intersecting segments of our two G-S lines, must take into account these forces exerted on the MUSICAL CONSENSUS.

THE MUSICAL CONSENSUS   Let us return to the chart and examine the vertical G-S line. The first three segments—Tuning Systems, Scales, Modes—have been grouped under a subheading of the MUSICAL CONSENSUS labeled *Tonal Stuff*, for want of a better term. The subheading *Ensemble* refers to the segment Orchestration, which here is meant to indicate not only instrumental and vocal groupings or solo performance but also, when appropriate, inclusion of interrelated arts such as puppetry, dance, ritual, recitation, choric reading, and so forth. The subheading *Formatives* requires some explanation. In one sense, all the segments of the vertical G-S line could be designated as *Formatives*. But in the grouping chosen, I have been influenced to some extent by the composer Ernst Toch, who was careful to distinguish between "form" in lowercase letters, for example, rondo or sonata

301

allegro, and "ꜰᴏʀᴍ" in capital letters, by which he meant all the formatives that distinguish a musical piece from a musical exercise.[13] Such a concept of ꜰᴏʀᴍ might well include the niceties of Orchestration and even *Ensemble*, in the sense in which I have used the term. But for the purpose of a kind of generative G-S line, I have chosen to make this arbitrary division.

For the moment, we need not comment further on the segments under *Tonal Stuff* and *Ensemble*, but the segments under *Formatives* deserve some attention. Form is meant to designate Toch's usage of the term in lowercase letters. Text, which might well require its own G-S line, is considered here for its importance in relation to the overall organization of music (form) on one side and the broad implications of the next segment, namely Rhythmic Design, Melodic Contour, and Harmonic Outline. Rhythmic Design might include such basic concepts as relative or "perfect" time, gradations or plateaus of tempo, divisive or additive rhythms, relative or saturation density, mixtures of any of these, patterns of change within the design, and so forth. Melodic Contour, as the term implies, is simply the predominant configuration of melody such as the contour of an arch, ⌒ ; a bow, ⌒ or ⌣ ; or inversions of the bow or arch; or the rise and fall of the saw tooth, ∧∧ ; or diagonal lines, ＼ or ／ ; or undulations, ∿ ; or combinations or variants of these; and so forth. Harmonic Outline might include the scheme of key relationships or principal chordal relationships; modal relationships or transpositions within a mode; the implied harmony of melodic outline; harmonic clusters; predominant rudimentary intervals; harmonic color, that is, the use of simultaneous, different pitches as an organizational feature within the flow of successive pitches; and so forth.

The next segment of the vertical G-S line is more particular in its concern with the character of the three elements rhythm, melody, and harmony, and also includes loudness. The specific terms in which the character of these elements is considered might be quite variable. Depending on the music under study, a comparative evaluation might be in order. As an example, let us consider the Ashanti musical grouping of Ghana known as Adowa. For a start we could point out that the *Ensemble*, which consists of drums, rattles, bells, chorus (male, female, or mixed), and dancers, has a *predominant* Rhythmic Character, an *important* Melodic Character, a *secondary* Harmonic Character, and essentially one level of loudness as an *undifferentiated* Dynamic Character. In further defining Rhythmic Character, we should take note that the resultant rhythmic patterns of the ensemble, but no individual parts, reach saturation density and observe that the sustained driving character of the rhythm is punctuated by outbursts from the

---

[13]Compare Ernst Toch, *The Shaping Forces in Music: An Inquiry into Harmony, Melody, Counterpoint, Form*, Criterion Music Corp., New York, 1948, pp. 153 ff.

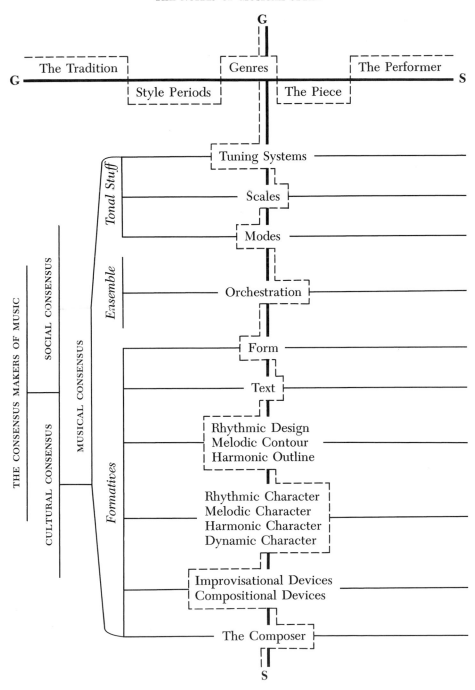

master drum performing in the extramusical speech and signal modes of drumming. A deeper understanding of the Rhythmic Character would require comparison of the patterns played by the various instruments, including a hierarchical arrangement of the different parts to show the relative importance of each in establishing the overall rhythmic character. Melodic Character might include a more particular examination of orchestration in terms of solo passages in relation to chorus, leader response, or antiphonal effects. Range, tessitura, and "frequency tones"—those dwelt on most often—would further define Melodic Character. Tone quality, styles of attack and release, extramusical poetic terms such as "lively," "animated," "lyrical," "martial," "sentimental," and so forth, would add more particulars to this segment of musical style. In approaching Harmonic Character, we should take our cue from the Ashanti himself, who describes his harmony not in terms of European medieval organum, to which it is sometimes compared, but as being essentially the duplication and reduplication of the melody beginning on different pitches.[14] With his more particular (that is to say, Ashanti) approach to a comprehension of Harmonic Character, we might want to reconsider our rudimentary interpretation of the Harmonic Outline. Dynamic Character we must describe as essentially one level of loudness, which varies only as the total number of performers varies at any one time in the *Ensemble*.

The penultimate segment of the vertical G-S line is concerned with the details of musical style which we have called Devices in Improvisation and Composition. Sometimes the researcher exhibits a disproportionate concern over this segment of the G-S line to the partial or gross neglect of other segments. Any segment of concentration along these lines may frame the objectives of a given research project. But to coin a phrase, it is a wise ethnomusicologist who plays both ends against the middle and the middle against the ends. The details of musical practice should never be allowed to obscure the broad outlines, nor can the broad outlines be sketched in without some comprehension of the supporting details. The Improvisational Devices and Compositional Devices may be as particular as the "queer twists and pranks" of the Negro singing voice described by Metfessel[15] or as stereotyped as the "melodicules" mentioned by Curt Sachs.[16] It is this level of particularity, *viewed in the total context of both the horizontal and vertical continua (G-S lines)*, that can provide great insight not only as to

[14] J. H. Kwabena Nketia, *African Music in Ghana*, Longmans, Green and Co., Ltd., Accra, 1962, p. 54.

[15] Milton Franklin Metfessel, *Phonophotography in Folk Music: American Negro Songs in New Notation*, with an Introduction by C. E. Seashore, The University of North Carolina Press, Chapel Hill, 1928, p. 20.

[16] Curt Sachs, *Our Musical Heritage: A Short History of Music*, Prentice-Hall, Inc., Englewood Cliffs, N.J., 1948, p. 23.

the niceties of similarity and difference in the norms of musical style between two Traditions, Style Periods, Genres, Pieces, or Performers but also as to the similarities and differences in the norms of cultural style—human behavior—between two societies. How far we have yet to travel before we are ready to practice the *vergleichende Musikwissenschaft* preached in the 1890s!

The most particular segment on the vertical G-S line, situated like his counterpart on the horizontal G-S line, The Performer, is The Composer. And norms of his musical style are likely to require attention to all segments of both continua. And, of course, the closer we get to the "S" end of both G-S lines the more nearly they coincide. One might advance the argument that on the horizontal G-S line an additional segment, labeled The Composer, should be inserted between The Piece and The Performer. And that The Performer should be added as the final segment of the vertical continuum. I have no objection to such an argument but have opted for the present arrangement by rationalizing that a study of The Composer may or may not extend to the particular practices of The Performer.

THE SEGMENT AND THE CONSENSUS Perhaps we are ready now to test the usefulness of the chart as a means of organizing our quest for the norms of the musical style of "Tlutur" as it is performed in Central Java. Although our ultimate attention will be on The Piece, we shall consider first The Tradition segment of the horizontal G-S line and the middle of the G-S line of MUSICAL CONSENSUS. The *Ensemble* of The Tradition includes the full gamelan sléndro, the apparatus and literature of the puppet play known as wajang kulit, and the dalang or puppeteer. Being aware that this total *Ensemble* is a vital force in the style of communications in Javanese society, we had better consider briefly the MUSICAL CONSENSUS in relation to the SOCIO-CULTURAL CONSENSUS. We must take into account historical depth, which reveals a number of extrinsic and intrinsic forces that have shaped the SOCIO-CULTURAL CONSENSUS. The result of these forces has been the infusion of various forms of cultural expression that have affected The Tradition surrounding "Tlutur"—for example, several religious overlays; poetic literature; a code governing ethics, morality, manners, and etiquette; civilian and military models of behavior; the philosophical good and bad; economic sanctions; and so forth. Historical depth also reveals two primary orders of extrinsic forces that have affected the society: one that has been essentially compatible with the indigenous socio-cultural entity, deriving from India, and one that has been basically incompatible with the autochthonous identity, stemming from European cultures.[17] The viability of The Tradition, measured against the incompatible force,

[17] See further Mantle Hood, "The Reliability of Oral Tradition," *Journal of the American Musicological Society*, vol. 12, nos. 2–3 (1959), pp. 201–209.

has not been affected except for the practice of radio broadcasts, the occasional use of the public address system, and sometimes the electric light bulb in lieu of the blèntjong, or oil lamp. To some extent, the incompatible force has enriched the poetic literature as the butt of satire and topical humor. In most recent times, The Tradition, unlike some other musico-dramatic traditions in the society, has also withstood an attempted "takeover" by the extrinsic and intrinsic forces of communist propaganda.

Having established the depth and viability of The Tradition in relation to the SOCIO-CULTURAL CONSENSUS, we can return to the middle of the G-S line of MUSICAL CONSENSUS and consider the intersection of The Piece, "Tlutur," with the vertical segment Orchestration. The dalang, the rebab, flute, xylophone, and the gendèr (an instrument with bronze keys resonated by bamboo or metal tubes), are the only performers of The Piece; the rest of the gamelan is tacit. Sometimes even the rebab is omitted. The Form is quite free but is guided by the Text and is related somewhat to the paṭetan, a short prelude or postlude which intones and elaborates the melodic formulas of the Modes. The Scale employed is usually in the Mode known as paṭet sanga belonging to the five-tone tuning system called sléndro. The complete Scale, however, may include up to five additional sléndro vocal tones and possibly one pitch borrowed from the seven-tone pélog tuning system.

Returning now to the *Formatives* of the MUSICAL CONSENSUS we might note that not only is Form determined by Text but also, to some extent, are Rhythmic Design, Melodic Contour, and Harmonic Outline. The Rhythmic Design is unmeasured; that is, it has no regular meter. It is marked by two orders of durational units: long note values or reiterations of the same pitch which are typical values of the principal tones of the modal hierarchy; and clusters of ornamental pitches, occurring between these principal tones, which approach saturation density. The overall Melodic Contour resembles a kind of bow, ⌒, with infixed deformations that mix several other contours. The Harmonic Outline, underscored by the harmonic intervals of the two-handed gendèr, gives stress to the principal tones of the modal hierarchy that form the primary and secondary intervals of the sléndro fifth as well as the sléndro octave, namely, the intervals 2–5, 5–1, and the octaves of these pitches. The interval 6–2 sounded occasionally by the open strings of the rebab is not essential to the Harmonic Outline but is idiomatic to the instrument in all sléndro modes.

The Rhythmic Character might be described as rhapsodic, the Melodic Character as tragic, the Harmonic Character as supportive of the principal intervals of the mode, the Dynamic Character as one undifferentiated level. In comparative terms, we might say that the Melodic Character is *predominant;* the free Rhythmic Character, *important;* the Harmonic Character, *secondary;* the Dynamic

Character, *undifferentiated.* A deeper understanding of Rhythmic Character requires reference to the fact that The Tradition is based on the practice of absolute or "precise" time, and that even though The Piece is in free rhythm, the dalang and the supporting musicians—by the processes of the precise-time concept of the MUSICAL CONSENSUS—perceive the occurrence of principal tones of the mode simultaneously, notwithstanding the highly individual flow of free rhythms characteristic of each part between these points of concordance. The ultimate niceties of Rhythmic Character are revealed in a detailed study of the manner in which the rubato or rhythmic freedom of each part, each in its own idiomatic expression—voice, bronze keys, wooden keys, bowed strings, flute—complements the tragic character of the Text. A deeper understanding of the Melodic Character requires a detailed examination of the employment of vocal tones by the dalang, the rebab, and the flute, the shifts of tessitura, control of tone quality, styles of attack and release—all in relation to the meaning of the Text. A full understanding of the Harmonic Character must take into account a certain ambiguity created by the excessive occurrence of vocal tones, which is controlled within the modal frame of reference by the octave or fifth reinforcement of principal tones. Although the Dynamic Character of The Piece is undifferentiated, it takes on a different meaning when considered in relation to the whole *Ensemble,* which includes the full gamelan. In this context, the Dynamic Character, established by only a few performers instead of twenty-five or more, represents a tiny plateau of low-level loudness that is appropriate to the dramatic situation and the Text.

Improvisational Devices used in The Piece must be referred to The Performer of the horizontal G-S line. The individual performer has great latitude in the number and occurrence of vocal and borrowed tones employed, the relative density of his improvisation, the duration of principal modal tones, and relative independence in relation to the other performers. Compositional Devices can be described in terms of the basic melodic formulas essential to mode as well as the melismatic, rhythmic, and melodic configurations occurring as ornamental elaborations between principal tones of the mode used to heighten the effect of the tragic melodic character.

The Piece is in the oral tradition and has no known Composer.

THE UNTALKABLES Before proceeding to a discussion of some of the laboratory methods required to give concrete reality to the approach suggested by our chart in the quest for the norms of musical style, I want to call attention once more to the G-S line of MUSICAL CONSENSUS. The segments listed under the subheadings *Tonal Stuff, Ensemble,* and *Formatives* are typical of the verbal referents used by musicians in talking about music. We have already indicated that they are known in variant applications, and we have tried to show in a cursory fashion their application in our chart. These and similar terms, however they may be defined in specific applications, we might call the "talkables" of MUSICAL CONSENSUS. But I have the haunting suspicion that the consensus of music makers, *the* MUSICAL CONSENSUS, also includes a great number of "untalkables," those aspects of musical style that resist the most diligent scientific methods. Take, for example, one extreme of the G-S line: Tuning Systems; let us speculate on the extent to which this rather general talkable might include the untalkable.

We pointed out that "Tlutur" is performed in the five-tone sléndro tuning system and that up to five vocal tones and perhaps one pitch borrowed from seven-tone pélog may be used by the ḍalang, the rebab, and the flute. Now, of course, there are almost an infinite number of different five-tone sléndro tunings; so let us assume that our study is based on a *particular* gamelan sléndro (the G-S line of gamelan sléndro) and that we have measured precisely the intervallic structure of all six and a half octaves of the gamelan. We know the ranges of the ḍalang's voice and of the supporting instruments, so we can be quite precise in describing the intervallic portion of the total compass of the gamelan actually being used. Our sure referent is the bronze keys of the two and a half–octave gendèr. And we can show how this compass compares with the complete tuning pattern of the gamelan. It appears probable that the particular tuning pattern (the stretching and compression of octaves) of a gamelan, together with the quality of the bronze keys, are primary factors in establishing the character, reputation, and relative fame of a given gamelan. If our research problem were centered on tuning systems per se, these details would be important for comparative purposes. But here we are interested in Tuning System as it may have direct bearing on the norms of style that regulate The Piece, "Tlutur." Earlier, we mentioned vocal tones in connection with the complete Scale under *Tonal Stuff*: five sléndro pitches (Tuning System), up to five additional vocal tones, perhaps the addition of one pélog pitch. The precise intervallic size of the vocal pitches and a pitch borrowed from a different tuning system is quite difficult to determine. We must refer to The Performer segment of the horizontal G-S line. Quite a few Javanese musicians in my acquaintance have what Western musicians term perfect pitch. But the perfect pitch of a Javanese musician relates to *one* particular gamelan and the tuning pattern of its total compass, since there is no absolute standard pitch or standard intervallic scheme underlying the tuning system. The dalang may be accustomed to singing with one gamelan more than any other, but frequently he must perform with whatever gamelan is provided for the presentation of wajang kulit. The extent to which he must adjust or is capable of adjusting to less familiar sléndro pitches is probably one of the untalkables. The rebab player, as a regular member of the gamelan, will reinforce the pitches of the gendèr, and this is probably helpful to the dalang. But to what extent may

308

this difference between accustomed and less familiar sléndro pitches influence the usage and intervallic relationship of *vocal* tones? Is their occurrence less frequent if the sléndro pitches are quite different from those known to the ḍalang? Is the distance from sléndro pitch to vocal tone affected? How? More untalkables. We must also bear in mind that "Tlutur" is performed in one or another version by different ḍalangs and necessarily accommodated by rebab, flute, xylophone, and genḍèr. To what extent is the interaction among sensitive musicians responsible for a greater or lesser employment of vocal tones, intentional or accidental disagreement in pitch, inspired performance to achieve the desired poignancy of tragic melodic character or mere adequacy in support of a dramatic moment in the play? All of them untalkables. Beyond the interaction of these musicians, what is to account for the difference between an inspired performance and mere adequacy by any one of them? A good harvest from the rice fields? A quarrel with the wife? A good dinner? Indigestion? The very particular mixture of rich partials arising from the ancient bronze of a particularly fine gamelan? More untalkables.

We might ask, "What have these illusive variables, these finical details, to do with the *norms* of musical style? Are we being unduly fussy when we should be sticking to the talkables of concrete rules and regulations governing style?" I believe not. I think it is quite likely that some of the most important norms of musical style are formed in those submerged layers of the MUSICAL CONSENSUS that we have termed the untalkables. Every performing musician, whether improvising or reading music from a printed page, knows in his own experience the difference between an inspired performance and an indifferent one. And so do sensitive members of his audience. Undoubtedly, the difference must be attributed to many interrelated and unrelated factors. But I am willing to bet my bottom dollar that most of them dwell in the realm of the untalkables and are totally resistant to the most meticulous scientific methods.

As a case in point, the following passage from the seventeenth-century *Tjenṭini* not only contains a variety of readily apparent norms of musical and extramusical style but also suggests a universe of untalkables that underlies the musical norms:

5. Jayèngraga, with an elegant gesture, took up the rebab. It was well-shaped. The neck was pontang [made of ivory and buffalo horn]; the bow was ornamented with carving and gilded; the sound-box provided with an embroidered covering (*jamangan*).
6. The *nem*-string [pitch 6] was plucked; when bowed, its tone was evidently quite in accordance with the *nem* of both genḍèr and gambang [xylophone]. The *nem* of the suling [flute], too, harmonized. Jayèngraga settled himself; his attitude was humble, as was his nature.

309

7. He bowed a few times up and down, to test the instrument. The bridge was cut from teakwood; the tension of the skin [rebab head] was firm; in short, everything was perfectly well finished. He then intoned *paṭet sanga*. His fingers vibrated, touching the strings now and then,

8. ...like the scorpion getting ready its sting. Pressing down the string was done accurately; the tips of the fingers pressed the resilient string down, searching for a *wilet* and a *chengkok* [melodic phrase segment], in rapid tone-figures. The sliding to and fro of the hand caused the strings to bend through. Every now and then the exact pitch of the tone was deviated from, so as to heighten the charm.

9. The middle finger was conspicuous in its movements; the index was like the sprig of a young fern; the little and ring-finger looked very much like spider's feet. The fingers were placed skillfully on the strings, each in its turn. The bow was used in quite a natural manner, from the nut to the point; whenever the tempo accelerated, the bowing adjusted itself to this without any hesitation.

10. *Ngechek, ngekik, ngelik* and *ngungkung* [registers and bowing techniques] were done in accordance with gendèr, gambang and suling. The enchantment was perfect. Garlands of tones twirled round the (hearer's) heart. The play of the strings harmonized with the tones of the nuclear melody; it was distinct, regular and suitable.

11. On close examination of Jayèngraga's rebab playing one had to acknowledge that it was full of devotion, well-finished and clever. Sometimes he slightly moved his thighs; that was a habit of his and is, after all, not annoying. It was not the same this time as on previous occasions; the playing this day excelled everything.

12. The other players were in ecstasy (lit.: had no heart left); not a single niyaga [musician] had any remark to make; they all sat dumbfounded while watching Jayèngraga; they simply sat perplexed, looking at him in dumb admiration.

13. The *sendon* was finished; *sarayuda* followed immediately after and was wound up with a drumbeat *bem* and a beat on the gong that gave one a feeling of satisfaction. After the *paṭetan*, Jayèngraga gave a critical look at the rebab.

14. The host, Kidang Wirachapa, laughed heartily and said: "Bless me, wasn't it lovely. It would cure a sick man!"[18]

SCIENTIFIC METHODS   The musicology of European art traditions is sometimes referred to as historical musicology; the early stages of ethnomusicology were formed under the banner of comparative musicology. Such designations are inept. Both historical and comparative methods are likely to be applicable to nearly every phase of research, whether our momentary concentration is descriptive, analytical, or synthetic. And, conversely, if our research objective is concerned primarily with historical depth or with comparative study, description, analysis, and synthesis are essential to the approach.

[18] Canto 276, stanzas 5–14, Vol. VII/VIII. Cited by Jaap Kunst in English translation in *Music in Java, op. cit.,* pp. 224–225.

Beyond the universe of untalkables suggested by the descriptive poetic stanzas cited above from the *Tjentini*, what manner of scientific method might be required in understanding this literary source? Stanza 5 is descriptive of the rebab and also indicates something about the norms of human movement: the player took up the rebab with an elegant gesture. In stanza 6 we have a description of tuning practice; plucking, then bowing with the information that the "tone was evidently quite in accordance with [the pitch nem of gendèr, gambang, and suling]...." The phrase "evidently quite in accordance" is a free translation of "wus pekolih."[19] In modern practice, the nem (pitch 6) and the djangga (pitch 2) of the two rebab strings are tuned ever so slightly sharp in sléndro, whereas in pélog they are perfectly pleng (in tune).[20] In stanza 7 we are told that Jayèn-graga "intoned *patet sanga*," one of the sléndro modes. From our practical knowledge of tuning and playing the rebab, we can improve the translation of "wus pekolih" by describing the pitch nem of the rebab as having "the proper relationship" to the nem of the other three instruments, an example of *comparative* method applied to the translation of a *historical* literary source in order to assure a slightly more accurate *description*. In the closing line of stanza 6, we find another indication of the norms of human behavior dictated by one of the prijaji ideals: "his attitude was humble, as was his nature." Understanding of the full implications of this literary description requires comparison with an ancient historical code governing the refinements of human behavior. Stanza 7 continues the description of tuning practice: the additional bowing "to test the instrument" is a final check to be sure the delicate tuning pegs, which in the initial process of tuning have a tendency to slip, are holding fast. This is followed by further description of certain hallmarks of a fine instrument, and then, continuing into the next few stanzas, a description of performance practice in playing a modal prelude in patet sanga. In stanza 8, the last sentence indicates another norm of style: "Every now and then the exact pitch of the tone was deviated from," followed by a critical justification, "so as to heighten the charm." Both observations relate to the untalk-able layers of the MUSICAL CONSENSUS.

[19] Stanza 6: kawat tinenteng nemipun
                sinenggrèng ngèk wus pekolih
                lan neming gendèr myang gambang
                eneming suling nyamlengi
                Jèngraga miragèng rebab
                pachak jatmika amanjing
[20] See further Mantle Hood, "The Javanese Rebab," *Hinrichsen's Musical Yearbook*, Proceedings of the First Congress of the Galpin Society, June 28-July 4, 1959, Cambridge, England, vol. II, 1961, p. 223.

Stanza 9 begins with a description of instrumental techniques. As an amateur performer on the rebab, I can attest to the nicety of the poetic similes used to depict the articulation of the four fingers of the player's left hand. The importance of long strokes from the bow hand is suggested in the next sentence; and the adjustment of bowing "without any hesitation" to an acceleration of tempo is a reference to the norms of precise or absolute time that regulate the group improvisation of four performers involved in the free rhythm of the modal prelude.

Stanza 10 begins with a reference to the norms that govern melodic and rhythmic invention in group improvisation. And then follows a poetic description of the performance including the value judgment that the rebab part "was distinct, regular and suitable."

Except for a comment on human movement in stanza 11—the habit of slightly moving the thighs, still in vogue among good rebab players today—the remaining stanzas are devoted to the description of a truly inspired performance.

Although we can say that the entire citation is *descriptive*, we must be aware that it is a *historical* document, albeit a poem, from the seventeenth century, which for proper understanding requires the application of *comparative* and *analytical* methods. We should be aware that much of the description depends on the exercise of *critical* methods. And presently we shall see how *synthetic* method can be applied to the passage. By now it should also be apparent that the application of various scientific methods in the interpretation of such a source can be greatly facilitated if based on a performing knowledge of the rebab itself. And finally, we might point out that the whole passage is an attempt to describe the kind of inspired performance that is governed by those norms of musical style that spring from the universe of the untalkables, the unutterable laws of the MUSICAL CONSENSUS.

Our quest for the norms of style must include the application of scientific methods in the laboratory.

Chapter Seven

SCIENTIFIC METHODS
and the LABORATORY

IF OUR COMPREHENSION of musical style is bound on the one hand to an understanding of the bundle of traditions surrounding music and on the other to a vague universe of untalkables, to what extent can our quest for the norms of musical style be guided by specific laboratory methods? Is precise measurement of the intervallic structure of a tuning system important? Is a scale made up of fixed pitches and variable vocal pitches only a theoretical scale, or does it have some practical value? Are the percentages of various melodic intervals of a piece significant? Do the percentages of different pitches used tell us anything about style? Is a modal hierarchy merely the product of a theorist's imagination? What good is precise description and analysis if the norms of style are subject to the forces of other cultural norms, a musical and an extramusical consensus—both of which are constantly in flux—and a universe of untalkables? Is the tedium of laboratory methods an unreal world of abstraction that has little to do with the here-and-now world of the music makers, the consensus ultimately responsible for the norms of musical style? Should we simply settle for making music, knowing its cultural bundle of traditions, speculating on the universe of untalkables?

Well, for some musicologists, who have been too long wedded to the laboratory and the stacks of the library, such a solution might provide a much-needed catharsis. But we are concerned with the ethnomusicologist; and he had better know what the stacks and the laboratory can contribute to his quest.

Remembering that historical and comparative methods are likely to be in constant interplay in the course of our research, let us review the nature of the materials we have brought back from the field that will be useful in description, analysis, and synthesis. And with these materials and scientific methods in mind, we shall also want to reconsider the segments of the vertical G-S line governed by the MUSICAL CONSENSUS.

We have on hand a field notebook filled with information based on discussions with musicians, dancers, puppeteers, and others actively involved with the performing arts. And beyond these circles of overlapping consensus makers, it contains information gathered from persons who shape the SOCIO-CULTURAL CONSENSUS, both users and nonusers of the arts. In addition, we find the speculations and musings of the ethnomusicologist, tentative conclusions, unanswered questions, and whatever else inspired him or provoked his curiosity in the course of his daily summaries and periodic summary of summaries. It also includes pertinent transcriptions of musical examples set down in one or another form of notation, the relative accuracy of which has been checked with the performer in the field. Incorporated within the notebook or as an adjunct to it is the written record of the ethnomusicologist's own studies in performance.

The field log provides a host of technical and environmental details, biographical sketches, and other specific information about music recorded and subjects photographed and filmed.

The notebook, the log, and a treasure chest of tape recordings, photographs, slides, and motion-picture footage, considered together, are something like an araki—a native plant dug up from some lofty crag in the mountains of Japan—which under skilled hands using special tools is slowly to be transformed into a bonsai, a living miniature tree. With the special tools of the laboratory and scientific methods, the ethnomusicologist must transform his field materials into a representative microcosm of the musical culture under study.

Like the araki, some of our source materials may need pruning and reshaping, the conglomerate soil and small rock cleaned from roots, the root hairs and the tap root trimmed in proportion to the eventual size of the finished bonsai,

314

the leaves pruned, and the limbs properly wired to represent in miniature the natural configurations of a strong living tradition of music and its interrelated arts. Our laboratory tools must be sharp enough to prevent bruising the tender araki. What is the preliminary task in this transplant?

DESCRIPTION

Accurate descriptive method is essential to other scientific methods. Assuming our laboratory tools are reasonably sharp, if we are to be accurate in our description, we had better first have a clear understanding of precisely what we are describing. Continuing our simile a bit further, we might say that music in its socio-cultural context is like a native plant in the natural environment of a mountain fastness, its growth and development subject to the continual change of sun and rain, heat and cold, wind and ice, accumulating compost, and barren rock. And by way of metaphor, the processes of defoliating and leafing, developing new limbs, a constantly changing conformation, a greater root system—these natural processes of change and growth in the musical tradition are subject to the forces of its socio-cultural context. The rate of growth will depend on whether the environment is congenial or hostile; but in either circumstance *the musical tradition is constantly changing.*

Our musical araki, by contrast, has been removed from its natural environment. The sounds on our tape recording represent a frozen historical moment in the processes of musical change. The scholarly delays between field recording and the publication of research often represent a considerable time lag. Whether we are working with a collection of "fixed" pieces or improvisations, we can be sure that the moment of recording is already in the historical past of musical style. The notebook, the log, the treasure chest of sound and pictures represent an arrestment in the processes of continual change. And this arrested moment, this musical araki, can be transformed into a musical bonsai only if it is precisely described with constant reference to the historical past, to the analytical and comparative present, to the synthetic and critical future.

For descriptive purposes, our field materials will yield (1) pertinent information about the bundle of traditions surrounding music, (2) the function and usage of music qualified by its place in the scale of human values, (3) physical and acoustical description of musical instruments and voices, (4) physical aspects of instrumental and vocal techniques, and (5) transcriptions of music and text.

Accurate description under items 1 and 2 requires comparison with published sources drawn from ethnology, art history, dance, theater, religion and philosophy, folklore, and so forth. The research of scholars in these allied and interrelated fields will indicate collectively something about the rate of change

315

and growth of the tradition which is necessary to place the ethnomusicologist's information in proper perspective. In turn, the two modes of discourse, speech and music, on which his field materials are based have probably provided the ethnomusicologist with new descriptive information that will enhance the knowledge of scholars in other disciplines. It is not unlikely that the directness of his field methods will have revealed information that justifies some correction of publications based on less direct modes of communication.

Item 3 (physical and acoustical description of musical instruments and voices) requires special laboratory equipment and some anticipation of its requirements while the researcher is still in the field. Physical description of an instrument, insofar as possible, can be based on the elements of the organograms discussed in Chapter Three. Documented by good photographs, the physical description should include complete measurements and details of construction, types of materials, internal and external shape, methods of manufacture, tuning, and so forth. Ratings on the Hardness Scales for Materials, Techniques, Finish, Motif, and Value discussed in Chapter Three should be included in organogram notation along with the symbolic representation of socio-cultural information relating to ritual, special groups, the instrument maker, and so forth.

By "physical description of voices" is meant a description of a singer's posture, body attitudes, gestures, facial expressions, and other features that resist capture by the photograph. Good motion pictures, slowed down in projection, are essential to this kind of description. For the notation of these physical attributes of the singer, we can borrow from the dance world its enviable descriptive tool, Labanotation. Imagine, for the sake of comparison, a record in Labanotation of the differences in physical movement and mannerisms of a singer in West Africa, in Iran, in Java, in Japan, in the Metropolitan Opera, in the hills of Tennessee! Ultimately, the significance of such comparison must be determined in conjunction with other scientific methods such as acoustical description, analysis, and synthesis. Aside from some gross observations insufficiently supported by complementary scientific methods, little attention has been paid to this aspect of vocal style. In time, when enough studies of different vocal styles have included this kind of description, the physical attributes of singing may prove to be important for comparative purposes, not only as one measure of culturally determined human movement as an aspect of behavior but also as one indicator of culturally determined styles of singing. If such information, properly supported by acoustical description, analysis, and synthesis, were available now, we might be able to add a supplement to Chapter Three composed of organograms based on culturally determined types of human movement which could serve as a notation for singing styles!

What I have termed "acoustical description of instruments and voices"

316

involves field recordings made with the special requirements of several laboratory instruments in mind. Earlier we posed a rhetorical question regarding the value of precise measurements of tuning system and scale. Assuming that they may or may not be important, we must at least admit that there is no way of judging the significance of such measurements unless they are precise. And judgment must wait on our discussion of analysis and synthesis.

An essential tool in the laboratory of the ethnomusicologist is the Stroboconn. Operating on the standard that the pitch A equals 440 cps, this instrument can be used to measure pitch to an accuracy of plus or minus 1 cent, that is, $\frac{1}{100}$ of a tempered Western semitone. The technique of operation is quite simple; and the readings are given as, for example, A minus 42 cents, C♯ plus 22 cents, and so forth, in other words, up to plus or minus 50 cents of the standard tempered Western semitone. On this scale, B *plus* 50 cents represents the same pitch as C *minus* 50 cents, since the tempered B and C are a semitone (100 cents) apart. With the aid of a table,[1] these figures can be converted quickly to cycles per second. Or, if the principal interest is intervallic structure expressed in cents, it is simple to remember that A at 440 cps has the number 446 in the conversion table, and using this number all other intervals can be computed directly from the Stroboconn readings to intervallic measurements expressed in cents. For example, let us say that the first key of a metallophone reads A plus 20 cents, the second key B plus 15 cents, the third key D minus 27 cents, the fourth key E minus 23 cents, and so forth. First, let us determine the intervallic structure in cents directly from these readings. The interval between A plus 20 cents and B plus 15 cents is 195 cents—that is, 5 cents less than a tempered whole step (200 cents) from A plus 20 cents to B plus 20 cents. The second, from B plus 15 cents to D minus 27 cents, is 258 cents—that is, 42 cents less than one and a half tempered whole steps (300 cents) from B plus 15 cents to D plus 15 cents. By the same methods, we find the interval from D minus 27 cents to E minus 23 cents is 204 cents—that is, 4 cents greater than a tempered whole step from D minus 27 to E minus 27 cents. The three intervals formed by the first four keys of the metallophone would be:

$$I \underset{195 \text{ cents}}{\rule{3cm}{0.4pt}} II \underset{258 \text{ cents}}{\rule{4cm}{0.4pt}} III \underset{204 \text{ cents}}{\rule{3cm}{0.4pt}} IV$$

Second, to determine the pitch of each key in cycles per second, we consult the conversion table and find that A at 440 cps is represented by the number 446 on the table. A plus 20 cents, our first Stroboconn measurement, equals

[1] Prepared by Erich von Hornbostel, and published by Jaap Kunst, *Ethnomusicology*, 3rd ed., Martinus Nijhoff, The Hague, 1959, p. 232.

446 plus 20 or 466, which on the conversion table corresponds to 445 cps, the pitch of the first key. The cycles per second of the second key, 195 cents higher than the first, can be determined by adding 195 to 466 to get 661 which, in conversion, is 498 cps. The third key, 258 cents higher, is 661 plus 258 or 919 converted as 578 cps. The fourth key, 204 cents higher, is 204 plus 919 or 1123 converted as 651 cps. In summary, key I is 445 cps; key II, 498 cps; key III, 578 cps; and key IV, 651 cps.

These measurements could represent a portion of a sléndro tuning in Java or, coincidentally, a five-tone xylophone tuning in West Africa. We shall have more to say about this coincidence presently.

Whenever possible, Stroboconn readings should be taken directly from the musical instrument itself. If the tuning system must be determined from a tape recording of the instrument, several variables may be introduced. The speed of the best field tape recorder, not to mention lesser models, is not perfectly constant. And a change of speed between the recording of two pitches will result in a change of pitch. Recording tape itself is subject to slight stretching or shrinkage, which also affects pitch. Two solutions are possible in the field to minimize the effect of these conditions. The simplest and least expensive method is to sound a tuning fork, let us say with the pitch 440 cps, frequently during the recording of pitches to be measured. This standard referent can be checked in the laboratory with the Stroboconn for variations in speed or tape. The second method is more convenient but rather expensive: a crystal designed at a fixed frequency can be used to record, on a second channel of the tape recorder, a continuous record of the tape recorder's speed. In the laboratory, this same crystal can then be used to govern the speed during playback. This method effectively eliminates errors due to tape speed variation in the field and those due to possible stretching of the tape.[2] Nagra IV incorporates such a feature.

Why not carry a Stroboconn to the field? There are two models available, but the smaller one is not sufficiently precise for the needs of the ethnomusicologist. The larger one is rather delicate and is designed for the laboratory rather than for the rugged conditions of field work. Adequate battery power is also something of a problem. The greatest difficulty, however, arises from the fact that the Stroboconn is on a security list as a precision instrument and is, therefore, difficult to export, an interesting twist in marketing a laboratory tool originally designed by the Conn Company to teach student performers to play "in tune" (tempered tuning, that is!).

It takes a little practice to develop a reliable technique on the Stroboconn to measure the pitch of wood or bamboo keys which have a very rapid decay.

[2] Suggested by Michael Moore, recording technician, UCLA Institute of Ethnomusicology.

A similar challenge must be met in capturing the precise pitch of vocal tones of very short duration. But both problems respond to experience on the part of the operator.

The most reliable measurement of vocal or instrumental pitch can be made on the Seeger Melograph or one of its near equivalents. Melograph C "samples" the pitch line 250 times per second. What appears on the Melogram can be considered an accurate representation of Metfessel's queer pranks and twists of the pitch line. The Melogram also displays loudness and duration, that is, rhythm, measured against time. The most promising feature of Melograph Model C is the display of tone quality in a form something like that of the sonogram used in linguistics, except for the clear advantage that it gives a continuous display instead of being restricted to short tape loops. At the present writing, this laboratory instrument, more than any other, affords the maximum descriptive information about the pitch line. The extent to which sampling 250 times per second is necessary or even desirable is a question we shall consider in due time.

Descriptive information provided by the Stroboconn, the Melograph, or its near equivalent, and, if possible, the decibel meter used in the field can establish the Hardness Scales for Loudness, Pitch, Quality, and Density.

In summary, item 3 (the acoustical description of musical instruments and voices) should include (a) precise measurement of fixed and/or principal pitches expressed in cycles per second, (b) intervallic structure expressed in cents, (c) ornamental and vocal tones graphically displayed and measured against fixed or principal pitches by intervals expressed in cycles per second and cents, (d) the graphic measurement of time (i.e., duration = rhythm), (e) the graphic measurement of loudness (supplemented if possible by readings on a decibel meter in the field), and (f) the graphic measurement of tone quality (i.e., the spectrum of partials or overtones, including the envelope: attack, decay, and release).

Item 4 (physical aspects of instrumental and vocal techniques) requires a combination of several kinds of field materials: observation, the ethnomusicologist's own studies in performance, and detailed documentation on motion-picture film. For purposes of written description of instrumental and vocal techniques, the researcher's own studies in performance are the most reliable. The "feel" of the technique and the "look" of the technique are sometimes surprisingly different; the latter can be quite deceptive. On the other hand, good motion pictures, slowed down in projection, can reveal details of movement that may lead to the proper "feel" of the technique in execution. Detailed observation, of course, is requisite to both study in performance and to filming.

Item 5 (transcriptions of music and text) requires precise methods. We stated earlier that accurate descriptive method is essential to other scientific methods; and this aspect of description, the transcription of music, must be as

319

accurate as laboratory instruments can make it. Insofar as possible, a transcription should represent the actual performance of instrumental and vocal music. As we learned from Metfessel many years ago, only some form of objective, graphic display will suffice. The conditioned hearing of the personal transcriber, regardless of the form of notation he elects to use, disqualifies him in the requirements of objectivity. Whatever the ultimate purpose for transcribing a piece of music, the *initial* transcription must be accurate and detailed. Then, as suggested earlier, some of the details may be simplified or even eliminated altogether, depending on the specific research requirements at hand and the audience for which publication is intended. But unless the initial transcription is complete and objective, there is no reliable basis for the selection of greater or lesser details. Said another way, wherever we may decide to stop on the G-S line of musical description, the process must begin with the most specific and detailed transcription possible.

The transcription of text, in addition to its musical setting, may involve several steps. If the language in question has no written form, then it must be set down in the phonetic symbols established for it by the linguist. If it is a written language in something other than Latin script, then the original should be given with an accepted transliteration. If translation is required, it too can be considered essential to the description of text, since a textual analysis will be understood by the intended reader only if he understands the meaning of the text.

ANALYSIS

Some anthropologists believe that musicology is the science of counting notes. Some musicologists believe that anthropology is the science of ferreting out who-sleeps-with-whom and in what kinds of houses. Ignoring such stereotypes, let us try to make clear that the ethnomusicologist is neither an anthropologist nor a musicologist—nor, in my belief, is he a combination of the two. This whole while we have not been talking about "anthro-musicology" or "musico-anthropology." Risking two more simplistic labels, we must point out that our concern has not been limited to "the science of man" or "the science of music" or to some combination of the two "sciences." Instead, in our approach to the study of music, we have often had occasion to refer to ethnology, art history, dance, theater, religion, and so forth; we have also found it necessary to refer to archeology, geography, psychology, physiology, acoustics, physics, and so forth. We have spent much of our time talking about music within the framework of a very large socio-cultural context. Perhaps labels, as such, are of little consequence. But sometimes I think it would be convenient, and more accurate, if our approach to the study of music—the ethnomusicological approach—were to be labeled "museology." Certainly all nine of the Greek Muses must sit on the shoulder of the struggling ethnomusicologist all of the time.

With the help of Euterpe, goddess of music, and the assistance of her poetic and scientific sisters, let us peer into some of the inner workings of music, the fascinating pursuit known as analysis.

To a considerable extent, analytical method applied to music is determined by a particular point of view. Depending on the background and interest of the researcher, musical analysis may amount to little more than a table of statistics at one extreme or a complete musical grammar at the other. In the Introduction, the reader was forewarned of a certain prejudice and inevitable bias in the process of molding literary flesh to the skeleton of this book. It is my belief that the most desirable point of view for purposes of musical analysis is that held by the mature and articulate composer. More than any other of the different practitioners in the field of music—performers, theorists, educators, critics—the composer, in his training, his attitude, and his practice, is constantly involved with the inner workings of music. If his training has been thorough, whatever he knows to be true about musical practice is based on the habitual process of analysis. Over the years, he will have discovered that even within the limits of a specific tradition, style period, genre, piece, or improvisation by the performer, there are almost an infinite number of ways of moving from pitch 1 to pitch 5. This wonder of musical creativity he accepts without difficulty while, at the same time, he seeks to understand a particular passage within the rules of the musical grammar that generated it. More than any other kind of musician, he is capable of keeping one eye on the forest while he makes a microscopic examination of the tree. Aware that not only Euterpe but also her eight sisters have vested interests in our quest, let us apply the composer's analytical point of view in our search for the norms of musical style.

Musical analysis requires a special kind of slide rule with two G-S lines running in opposite directions, either of which can be rotated 180 degrees. It is necessary to slide quickly up and down the segments outlined by the meandering dotted lines on the horizontal and vertical G-S lines of our chart. At any moment, the vertical segment Mode may have to be aligned with the horizontal segment Genre or The Tradition or The Performer. And Mode may have to be lined up with its own neighboring segments such as The Composer, Tuning System, or Text. In fact, any segment, either vertical or horizontal, may serve as a starting point for reaching any other segment. In addition, a concentration on one segment may require reference outside the MUSICAL CONSENSUS to the DANCE CONSENSUS or THEATER CONSENSUS or POETRY CONSENSUS. Or even to the total SOCIO-CULTURAL CONSENSUS affected by the extrinsic force of its membership in NATO, SEATO, or the Warsaw Pact.

321

Yes, such requirements are considerably in excess of the composer's point of view in musical analysis. But they are a necessary reminder that we are borrowing his point of view and adapting it to the needs of the ethnomusicological approach. Now let us take a brief look at some of the things he does that have been simplistically described as counting notes.

TUNING SYSTEM   From the composer's point of view, he might want to start with the most basic stuff of which music is made, what has been labeled *Tonal Stuff* in our vertical G-S line: Tuning System, Scale, Mode. Assuming that our descriptive methods have been accurate, let us hand him the measurements of a five-tone sléndro tuning of a particular Javanese gamelan. We shall also supply information to the effect that this is a unique example. since no two gamelan are tuned precisely the same. To test his reaction, we might add that similar tunings can be found among the xylophone traditions of West Africa.

For someone conditioned to the tempered tuning of the piano, this information will be rather disquieting. Our composer may have some questions. If sléndro tuning is so arbitrary, why bother with the precise measurements we have handed him? From what we have told him, how can he be sure it is really Javanese? Maybe it's African. Come to think of it, there are anhemitonic (no semitones) pentatonic tunings found all over the world. Are we kidding him? These measurements don't mean a thing! With a little rounding off, they could even represent the black keys of the piano, which are also anhemitonic pentatonic: C♯, D♯, F♯, G♯, A♯!

This conversion of the Western composer's analytical point of view to the ethnomusicological approach may take longer than we thought. Of course, looking at one octave of the gamelan measurements, we must say that he is quite right. They really do not mean very much if, with a little rounding off, they might apply to the black keys of the piano or the Scottish bagpipe or an African xylophone. But our composer is still in a temporary state of cultural shock; he has not yet looked closely at the whole compass of the measurements, which cover a range of nearly seven octaves. On closer inspection, we find that there are no perfect octaves; that is, for example, the interval between the lowest pitch 1 and its "octave" is not 1,200 cents—twelve tempered semitones times 100 cents—the so-called perfect octave of tempered tuning which has the ratio of 2:1 expressed in cycles per second. If pitch 1 is 120 cps, its *perfect* octave must be 240 cps. But our measurements show that these octaves of pitch 1 are somewhat larger or smaller than 1,200 cents; depending on which part of the total compass of the gamelan we are looking at, the "octave" intervals vary from 1,162 cents to 1,240 cents.

Now comes a critical moment. Unless we can answer our composer's next question, we may lose his interest altogether. If there are no true octaves—and after all, isn't an octave an octave?—doesn't that indicate that the Javanese aren't very careful about tuning their gamelan? Another argument for ignoring our finical measurements! Well, at least he stated the matter in the form of a question. We still have his attention.

When he is informed that our measurements are based not on a series of single instruments in each octave but on every bronze key and gong of all instruments in the gamelan, his interest begins to pick up. We tell him further that the accuracy of the measurement of a single pitch in one register of the gamelan has been confirmed by its duplication on the keys of as many as seven or eight different instruments. Whatever our conditioned Western notion of the octave, we can be sure that the Javanese responsible for the tuning of this particular gamelan wanted it just the way it is! Looking further, we find that the five different pitches of sléndro have different degrees of compression and expansion of the octave. If octaves of pitch 1 show compression in the lower compass of the gamelan and expansion in the upper registers, the octaves of pitch 2 may show just the opposite relationship. This compression and expansion of the octaves of the different sléndro pitches we have termed the tuning pattern of the gamelan; and this tuning practice, when it is understood from a large enough sampling of gamelan sléndro, may prove to be extremely important in classifying our particular gamelan under one of the nine different species of sléndro tunings which today are only vaguely and somewhat residually recognized by the Javanese themselves. There is a Javanese name for each species; when our samplings are adequate, precise descriptive methods based on the Stroboconn and the Melograph may help us to comprehend the character of each species.[3]

Before leaving this most general consideration of *Tonal Stuff*, Tuning System, we should take note that historical evidence of the evolution of tuning systems in Java and Bali is quite clear among the different types of extant gamelan, some of them very ancient, still in usage; namely, three-tone, four-tone, five-tone sléndro and three-tone, four-tone, five-tone, six-tone, seven-tone pélog, as well as some recent derivatives of these found in West Java. The lack of standard tuning systems and the absence of a concept of an absolute standard of pitch may be disquieting from a Western point of view. But if our analysis of Javanese music is to mean anything, it must proceed with the full realization that the Javanese MUSICAL CONSENSUS has made this segment of Javanese *Tonal Stuff* precisely what

---

[3] See further Mantle Hood, "Sléndro and Pélog Redefined," *Selected Reports*, vol. 1, no. 1, Institute of Ethnomusicology, UCLA, 1966.

it is, no more and no less. Western theories based on gross averages of gamelan tunings or African xylophone tunings have little to do with the norms of Javanese or African musical style.[4]

SCALE   Consideration of Scale requires a distinction between the pitches included in a *theoretical* Scale and those actually used in a particular piece or genre or those available on a particular instrument. All five sléndro pitches are represented by the bronze keys of the saron; but the fixed melody of some pieces played by the saron may involve only four of these pitches. In a piece like "Tlutur," on the other hand, the rebab may add up to five additional vocal tones to the five sléndro pitches and perhaps a tone borrowed from pélog. In pélog, a seven-tone system, an instrument like the gendèr or the gambang includes only five of the seven pitches. In considering Scale, therefore, it is necessary to distinguish between the total number of pitches included within the system and the actual number appearing in a particular piece as performed by a particular instrument or the voice. Such an approach may require reference to several segments of our meandering dotted lines: Tuning System, Mode, Orchestration (perhaps even *Ensemble*), Genre, The Piece, and possibly The Performer. The theoretical Scale consists of all pitches available within the system; the practical Scale is made up of those pitches that are used within a specific set of circumstances. Both considerations of Scale are essential to understanding the norms of style.

MODE   We might hazard the guess that most musical traditions in the world are modal. Earlier, in a discussion of Mode, we indicated that this segment of the G-S line of MUSICAL CONSENSUS must itself be defined in terms of a continuum, the G-S line of Mode. And if the subject of study is a musical tradition based on Mode, then all other segments of the G-S line of MUSICAL CONSENSUS, to some extent, require an understanding of their relationship to Mode. What are some of the features we might expect to find in the course of analysis?

Basic features of Mode seem to include the following: (1) a gapped scale, that is, a scale made up of both small and large intervals; (2) a hierarchy of principal pitches; (3) the usage of vocal or ornamental pitches; and (4) extramusical associations with the seasons, hours of the day or night, and so forth. In addition, modal practice might involve the usage of special registers, for example, low, middle, and high; rhythmic requirements including unmeasured "silence" following points of melodic repose (modal cadences); regulation of the *quality* of sound; special associations with language and/or text; particular requirements in connec-

---

[4] Compare A. M. Jones, *Africa and Indonesia: The Evidence of the Xylophone and Other Musican and Cultural Factors*, E. J. Brill, Leiden, 1964; but also, see further M. Hood, Review of Jones, *Africa and Indonesia, Man*, vol. 65, nos. 110–112 (July–August, 1965), pp. 124–125.

tion with interrelated arts such as dance or puppetry; special practices governed by the requirements of ritual or religion; and so forth. Examples of most of these modal practices can be found in the musical traditions of such cultures as India and Indonesia; other cultures may have only residual elements of mode. The major and minor modes of Western music, for example, have retained only a gapped scale and a minimal hierarchy of principal tones.

The composer's analytical point of view must be free of the natural prejudice of prolonged conditioning to the harmonic practices of the West. He must assume that the structural features of the piece he is looking at have a horizontal orientation rather than vertical, that the primary generative force is melodic, and that harmonic elements derived from this melodic force are secondary. He must even keep an open mind on something as fundamental as Scale, and be prepared to accept the word of the MUSICAL CONSENSUS that pieces in a given mode should be performed only between the hours of 8:00 P.M. and midnight. In other words, he will discover that his exposure to the European church modes—considering our present knowledge of the subject—affords him little preparation for an objective understanding of mode in other parts of the world. Still, the composer's point of view is quite open-minded. Assuming he is capable of transcending his own musical conditioning, we can expect him to be fascinated by the niceties of modal practices awaiting him in the non-Western world.

Let us look more closely at the four basic features of mode.

1. *Gapped scale*. The theoretical Scale might be based on a tempered tuning system like the equidistant intervals of the twelve white and black keys of the piano octave; but the practical scale on which mode is based must be nonequidistant. The major and minor modes of Western music are made up of whole steps (two semitones) and half steps consisting of the following arrangements of L(arge) and S(mall) intervals:

		L	L	S	L	L	L	S	
Major Mode:	C	D	E	F	G	A	B	C′	

	L	S	L	L	S	L	L	
Minor Mode: A	B	C	D	E	F	G	A′

Both modes use the same seven pitches, but the starting point of the scale determines a characteristic gapped structure, L L S L L L S for the first and L S L L S L L for the second.

Five-tone sléndro and seven-tone pélog are *not* tempered tuning systems, so their theoretical scale structure is gapped; and the relative size of S(mall) and L(arge) intervals is variable. In pélog, several modes are realized by selecting five

325

of the seven pitches. The mode known as pélog paṭet nem, for example, is based on pitches as follows:

$$
\begin{array}{ccccccc}
 & \text{S} & \text{S} & \text{L} & \text{S} & \text{L} & \\
\text{Pélog paṭet nem:} & 1 & 2 & 3 & 5 & 6 & \dot{1}
\end{array}
$$

The omission of pitches 4 and 7 creates a sizable gap between 3 and 5 and between 6 and $\dot{1}$. The matter is complicated by the fact that in this mode, pitches 4 and 7 may be introduced occasionally as passing or nonessential tones or as so-called exchange tones substituting for one of the original pitches to accomplish a transposition to one of the auxiliary gapped scales of pélog paṭet nem. Whatever conditions obtain in a given instance, the scale of the mode is always gapped.

In sléndro, three different modes, based on the same five pitches, are known. But for the Western-oriented analyst, the gapped structure of sléndro presents another kind of problem. A comparison of different gamelan sléndro tunings reveals that there is no standardized arrangement of large and small intervals making up the gapped scale of the tuning system. Kunst's comparison of sléndro tunings based on one octave of forty-six gamelan measured shows little consistency in structure,[5] for example, Gamelan 1: S L S S (?) L; Gamelan 2: L S L S L; Gamelan 3: S (?) L S L S; Gamelan 37: L S S L L; and so forth. The question mark in Gamelan 1 and 3 indicates that S could be considered large—or perhaps medium? The difficulty in interpreting these measurements lies in the fact that only *one* octave of each gamelan has been measured. The tuning pattern of gamelan mentioned earlier causes a shift of large and small intervallic relationships from one octave to another in the total compass of the gamelan.[6]

In the Western church modes a *particular* gapped structure seems to be a hallmark of Mode—Ionian (major) Mode: L L S L L L S; Aeolian (minor) Mode: L S L L S L L. If a piece in a sléndro mode is played on two different gamelan which have different gapped scale structures, has it changed modes in the process? The Javanese MUSICAL CONSENSUS says it has not. Our discussion of the next basic feature of Mode will throw some light on the subject.

2. *Hierarchy of principal pitches*. Even a cursory examination of various musical cultures in the non-Western world indicates that the inner workings of most modal music depends on the recognition of a hierarchy of pitches far more developed than that of the church Modes—unless, sometime in the future, a broader analytical approach to medieval and Renaissance music adds to our present knowledge of the European tradition. In the Javanese modes each principal pitch

[5] See further Jaap Kunst, *Music in Java: Its History, Its Theory and Its Technique*, 2 vols., 2d ed., Martinus Nijhoff, The Hague, 1949, pp. 574–575.
[6] See further Hood, "Sléndro and Pélog Redefined," *op. cit.*, pp. 45–46.

326

has a particular role, which governs not only the basic structure of a piece but also the various strata of the improvising parts. These requirements are well understood in practice, if not at the conscious verbal level, by the composer and performing musicians.

Mozart, because of his genius and a secure knowledge of the harmonic tradition in which he wrote, avoided the obvious musical solutions and the "tyranny of the bar line." He had masterly control of those formatives of style that differentiate a piece of music from a musical exercise. In a similar way, the Javanese composer or performer, because of his genius and a secure knowledge of the modal tradition, especially the modal hierarchy that governs his music, is a master at manipulating the laws of the hierarchy. We cannot take time to examine the formatives of his artistry[7] but must be content with a few of the basic laws within which he works.

A primary law in either a harmonic tradition or a modal tradition is the set of rules governing points of repose, harmonic or melodic resolution, the cadence. In the study of modal music, this law has often been misunderstood and oversimplified by attaching undue importance to the pitch on which a piece or a section of a piece ends, the so-called finalis and con finalis of the church Modes. Melodic or modal resolution in Javanese music is accomplished by sounding the two pitches that form the principal interval of the sléndro or pélog fifth in a given mode. They might occur at the very end of the piece as a harmonic interval formed by the two pitches; or they might occur successively as a melodic interval with one of them, usually the lower, as the final pitch of the piece; or there may be a number of intervening pitches sounded successively between the two; or, *after* this interval has occurred in any of these several possibilities, the melodic line may be *extended* to end finally on any other pitch of the modal hierarchy. The nature of the extension and the closing pitch of the piece are far from arbitrary, however; they are determined by the individual character of the piece itself, that is, germinal or thematic aspects of the melody that have been featured in some way.

In each mode, it is possible to identify simple melodic formulas underlying these cadential practices. The ways in which the basic formulas may be expanded, contracted, elided, anticipated, extended, elaborated, or ornamented are determined by the individual roles of the hierarchy of pitches and the genius of the composer and the performer. Whatever artistic devices may be employed within

[7] But see further Mantle Hood and Hardja Susilo, text accompanying the LP recording, *Music of the Venerable Dark Cloud*, IE Records, Stereo IER 7501, Institute of Ethnomusicology, UCLA, 1967. Consider especially the finesse of the fixed melody in such pieces as "Gangsaran—Bima Kurda—Gangsaran," Side I, Band 1, text, pp. 29–31; "Sriredjeki," Side II, Band 1, text pp. 35–37; "Ajak–Ajak, Srepegan, Sampak, Gara-gara," Side II, Band 3, text pp. 38–41.

327

the norms of this practice—including momentary objectives based on a desire for ambiguity in melodic movement[8]—ultimately the outline of the basic melodic formula is perceived by the Javanese listener. This recognition of melodic pattern, however it may be elaborated or elided, is as essential to the workings of modal music as the recognition of harmonic cadences in a Beethoven symphony to the workings of harmonic music. *Melodic pattern* constitutes a fundamental norm of modal style not only in relation to the cadence but also as a framework for melodic development itself. The fixed melody of the Javanese orchestral piece is sounded by the family of one-octave instruments known as the saron and by the one-octave slentem, a relative of the gendèr. The limitation of one octave together with the behavior of the hierarchy of pitches establish different melodic patterns characteristic of the different modes.[9] One of the primary ways of identifying a mode, therefore, is the recognition of its characteristic melodic patterns.

It is this sensitivity to *pattern*, rather than a particular *gapped scale*, that causes the Javanese MUSICAL CONSENSUS to say that a piece played on two different gamelan with different intervallic structures is still in the same mode. Sometime over the span of the past twenty years of listening to and performing Javanese music, I came to agree with the consensus. But it took a long time and a lot of personal involvement to reach this vantage point of perception.

3. *Ornamental pitches.* What I have called vocal or ornamental pitches in relation to Mode refers primarily to function and only secondarily to the specifics of cycles per second and intervals expressed in cents. At this point, we might want to distinguish four orders of pitch found in most musical cultures: (a) fixed pitches, such as those sounded on the keys of a xylophone or metallophone, gongs and bells, sonorous stone, tuned drums, or determined by the fixed length, size, and tension of "open" or unstopped strings on such instruments as the piano, the cymbalum, the koto, as well as stringed instruments with fixed frets like the guitar; (b) relatively fixed pitches, which depend on the performer to play "in tune" with the system, heard on such instruments as clarinets, trumpets, oboes, and others with pitches relatively determined by the momentary length of a vibrating air column; (c) variable pitches, performed by the voice and a group of instruments which are also capable of realizing relatively fixed pitches, for example, the violin, the rebab, the Indian sitar—the arched frets of which are designed to allow the performer to pull the string to one side to alter pitch—simple flutes and oboes without keys, springs, and pads; (d) indeterminate pitches, found on instruments like wood blocks, rattles, and many other idiophones.

[8] See, for example, the analysis of "Gangsaran—Bima Kurda—Gangsaran" in Hood and Susilo, *Music of the Venerable Dark Cloud, op. cit.,* pp. 29–31.

[9] See further Mantle Hood, *The Nuclear Theme as a Determinant of Paṭet in Javanese Music,* J. B. Wolters, Amsterdam, 1954, *passim.*

Our momentary concern is with the variable pitches used in ornamentation; but we should note in passing that, in a musical culture like that of West Java, the Sundanese may substitute a "vocal" tone, therefore a variable pitch not found on instruments with fixed pitches, for one of the principal tones of the mode in a complicated practice known as surupan.[10] We shall also want to make a distinction between *discrete* variable pitches and *continuous* or connected variable pitches functioning as ornaments.

After sufficient ear training in international musicianship, the ethnomusicologist can manage a rather keen perception of discrete variable pitch, something that is often referred to as a microtone, a pitch when compared to its neighbor that forms an interval smaller than a tempered Western semitone, 100 cents. Perhaps it is worth noting that the designation "microtone," long since in common usage, by inference refers to *any* interval smaller than the smallest interval recognized in Western practice. There is a certain bias suggested by the designation, which obviates concern with the particular size of a microtonal interval. Earlier, we indicated that one of the basic differences between the phonemic and phonetic approaches to transcription centered on their relative interest, or lack of it, in either discrete or continuous ornamental pitches. It is the discrete variable pitch, measured against a principal tone of the mode, that forms a microtonal interval. An important feature of most modal musical cultures is the way in which these discrete variable pitches, these microtones, are used—individually or in various *patterned* clusters—in relation to the different tones of the modal hierarchy. One aspect of modal analysis, therefore, must be concerned with the question "Which discrete variable pitches, in what kinds of ornamental configurations, are associated with which principal tones of the hierarchy?" Needless to say, to answer this compound question we need some form of objective display like the Melogram.

Continuous or connected variable pitches used as an ornamental device in the attack or release of different tones of the modal hierarchy constitute another norm of musical style. The ear perceives this type of ornamentation as a more or less articulated slide up or down in the attack or release of a principal pitch or as a controlled variation of vibrato functioning as an ornamental device. The Melogram is essential to any systematic analysis of the types and particular functions of this kind of ornamental practice in relation to mode.

Finally, we should consider an area of ornamental pitch about which very little is yet known: the extent to which in some musical cultures the control of the quality of sound itself—timbre, attack, decay, release—may have an ornamental function. Listen to a good blues singer; or to Side I, Band 1, of the accompanying LP once more. Perhaps in time Melograph Model C can furnish an answer.

---

[10] Although the concept of surupan requires much more study, for one theoretical explanation, see further Kunst, *Music in Java, op. cit.*, pp. 51 ff.

A secondary concern of ornamental pitches in relation to Mode brings us to the question "What are the actual sizes of the microtonal intervals employed?" Within a few cents, is a given interval used in association with a given principal tone of the hierarchy in a given structural location always the same size in a particular piece sung by a particular singer? Is the size of the interval the same in a different performance of the same piece by the same singer? By a different singer? In a different piece?

Someone has said that the threshold of pitch perception stops at an interval of about 20 cents; someone else once told me that it was more like 12 or 13 cents. In my own experience, *depending on the musical context*, I believe it may be significantly smaller than either of these pronouncements suggests. Be that as it may, pitch perception by the professional musician practicing his art somewhere in the Greater Orient is far keener, as his consistency in performance bears out, than we are able to accommodate within the presently gross reference to microtones as being smaller than a half tone—or even a quarter tone.

Unless our analysis is based on an objective and minutely detailed display of the pitch line, these niceties of Mode will be missed. Assuming that some ornamental intervals may be 80 cents, some 22 cents, and some 56 cents—let us say, within a predictable variation of plus or minus three cents—we had better ascertain the particular function of the different size microtones in relation to the different tones of the modal hierarchy. A difficult task? Not really, not if our descriptive method has been sufficiently precise.

Here is a speculative note that might be of interest to the Western musicologist researching the European art tradition. For the sake of argument, let us assume that in medieval times, during the Renaissance, and even into the Baroque period of Western music the concept of Mode included the kind of discrete and continuous variable pitches we have been discussing, used as ornamental devices well understood in the oral tradition on which the written music depended. Sometime after the birth of opera, when the rapid encroachment of a harmonic orientation engulfed the niceties of modal practice, the oral knowledge of this kind of ornamentation was lost. Indeed, with the development of the modern orchestra, beginning with the Mannheim School, there was no longer an Orchestration or *Ensemble*, thinking of our G-S chart, that could accommodate such niceties of style. Could it be that the slipping and sliding around on pitch, the portamentos, the expressivos, the rubatos, the "artistic license" practiced by the best Western performers is residual evidence that this aspect of early modal practice is reluctant to die? That it still survives in an untutored, unlettered form that is reminiscent of some ancient forgotten language, fragments of which continue in bastardized, unintelligible form? Is it possible that a comparison of these remnants with the norms of modal practice in the Orient might yield a greater comprehension of the church Modes?

4. *Extramusical associations.* In many musical cultures, mode is considered an aspect of the cosmos that may be associated with the seasons, directions, times of the day and night, and so forth. We need the help of the ethnopsychologist to understand the processes of musical conditioning that support such associations. There is no question that they exist; understanding them is another matter.

From 1958 to 1960, it was my pleasure and privilege to be responsible for a program of study undertaken at UCLA by the well-known Indian virtuoso on the flute, Tanjore Viswanathan. During the course of his first year of residence, I became especially fond of a particular evening raga which he played on a number of occasions in my home or some other equally intimate environment so important to the atmosphere of the performance of Indian music. One morning while he was demonstrating various requirements of raga and tala to a class of general university students, I asked him, somewhat impulsively and against my better judgment, whether he would consent to play my favorite evening raga. Quickly and graciously, he agreed to do so. It was an unfair request, one I regretted making the very moment it was asked. I turned to the class and explained that we would be hearing the raga at the wrong time of day, that on second thought perhaps a morning raga would be better. But the harm had been done. The faces confronting me showed a mixture of incredulity and curiosity, not to mention an understandable amusement at my embarrassment and discomfort. Nothing would do but the evening raga.

Viswa performed in the style of the true virtuoso that he is. And the class was most appreciative. Even with my limited exposure to Indian music, I had no difficulty in distinguishing this performance of the raga from all others played at the proper time by the artist. The improvisation was fluent, the articulation immaculate, but the realization of the raga lacked deep involvement by the artist, the inspired kind of performance that rises from the universe of the untalkables. For the first time, through an empathy established while he played, I began to understand to what extent the artistry of the performer related to the strength of association between this raga and the nocturnal atmosphere of the evening hours. Later, when I apologized for the thoughtlessness of the request, he admitted that it had been an uncomfortable and forced performance.

If we are to enlist the interest and assistance of the ethnopsychologist, what kind of musical analysis must we furnish for the extramusical associations characteristic of mode? All pieces grouped under whatever cultural term of reference—time of the day, season, or what have you—must be compared as to tuning system and scale, hierarchy of pitches, ornamental pitches, rhythmic

331

practices, melodic range, special relationships to language and/or text, interrelated arts, and so forth. Other segments of our vertical G-S may also be critical, for example, Orchestration and *Ensemble*, Form, Text, the general and particular features of rhythm, melody, harmony and loudness, particular devices in composition and improvisation. In short, any aspect of music, the MUSICAL CONSENSUS, The Tradition and its segments, even the SOCIO-CULTURAL CONSENSUS, may have to be taken into account in order to identify the bundle of traditions that through association relates a given mode to morning hours rather than evening or to early evening rather than the late hours of the night. It is the responsibility of the ethnomusicologist to make this thorough identification. Then, in collaboration with the ethnopsychologist, perhaps someday it will be possible to understand the psychological bases responsible for the distinguishing features of each mode in relation to extramusical associations. At the moment, we can say that the psychological bases of such associations are culturally conditioned. It is possible, however, that some of these may be based on a response to certain universal aspects of musical style which in turn come to have a culturally determined association or that, if even someone outside the culture becomes sufficiently conditioned to the laws of Indian *musical* grammar, for example, he may readily make an association between a particular raga and the euphoria of the evening hours in India. It is also possible that a particular segment of the bundle of traditions surrounding music and certain universal aspects of musical grammar together are responsible for such associations.[11]

By way of summary, our analysis of this aspect of mode should be based on a compound question, such as, for example, "What common musical features and surrounding bundle of traditions distinguish all early evening ragas from morning ragas?" With these answers at hand, then let us confer with the ethnopsychologist as to their meaning and with the specialist in Javanese or Sundanese music as to their significance in comparative studies directed toward a search for universal practices in music.

ENSEMBLE   Although thus far our objectives in analysis have been centered on *Tonal Stuff*—Tuning System, Scale, Mode—it should be clear by now that we had to make constant reference to the segments of our vertical G-S line labeled *Ensemble* and *Formatives*. If our analytical point of view had been limited to the objective of a table of statistics, we have already gone too far; if our objective is to be guided by the composer's point of view, we have not yet gone far enough

---

[11] For a tentative indication in relation to the Javanese puppet play, see further Hood, *The Nuclear Theme, op. cit.*, pp. 128–129.

to establish the rules of musical grammar. Consideration of modal practice must also include the possibility of characteristic Orchestration and *Ensemble*. For example, the *literature* of Javanese wajang kulit, the *Mahabharata*, and the *style* of puppets used for the play are accompanied by gamelan *sléndro*—sléndro tuning, sléndro scales, sléndro modes with their definitive requirements, sléndro instruments. The literature of Javanese wajang geḍog, the Pandji cycle, and the style of puppets used for the play (which to the untrained eye look very much like those of wajang kulit) are accompanied by gamelan *pélog*—with all that implies. If our ultimate objective is understanding the rules of musical grammar, we shall have to comprehend their generative force in both sléndro and pélog.

FORMATIVES   Each element of the *Formatives* of musical style deserves analytical attention. But as we travel farther down the G-S line, the different segments become increasingly difficult to consider in isolation. Of course, they should not be so considered. Beginning near the middle of our grouping of segments under *Formatives* we might note that although Rhythmic Design is partly determined by Form and influenced by Text it can achieve some individuality when considered in relation to The Piece. This individuality will be further defined by its specific Rhythmic Character established through Compositional and Improvisational Devices. A comparison with other pieces will reveal which characteristics at these levels of segmentation comprise the rules of grammar for all pieces in one Genre. Depending on our ultimate objective, we may then have to consider other Genres, other Style Periods, and finally The Tradition.

The composer's analytical point of view—keeping one eye on the forest while making a minute examination of the tree—is especially important in considering these *Formatives*. Analytical methods appropriate to each segment and relating it to other segments might well comprise a separate manual devoted to stylistic analysis. In the scope of this essay we shall have to limit ourselves to a few observations.

Analytical responsibility in relation to Text deserves special consideration. The relationship of Text to the norms of musical style will be determined in large part by the nature of the language in question. If the Text is cast in one of the tone languages of Africa or the Orient, the kindredship between the rules of speech grammar and the rules of music grammar may be very close. Melodic Contour and Melodic Character may be governed by the rules of speech grammar. Rhythmic Design and Rhythmic Character are also likely to be similarly controlled. Relative pitch levels of speech (e.g., low, medium, and high) and the relative duration of vowel sounds may determine the course of melodic and rhythmic development. But we must not forget that the genius of the composer or the

333

performer, operating within this sphere of regulation, will be directed at shaping the *Formatives* of musical style so that the obvious solutions are avoided—the kind of genius that creates music rather than musical exercises. He not only has considerable choice in the variety of melodic and rhythmic detail employed within these rules but also can count on such familiarity with The Tradition on the part of his listeners that he can be sure they will understand momentary exceptions to the rules and deliberate parody of them. If the ethnomusicologist is to catch these subtleties—and they are likely to constitute a hallmark of style—he must not only have a thorough knowledge of the language in question but also enlist the help of the linguist and the native speaker in obtaining an analysis of the text itself, which should include structure, style, and meaning. Needless to say, this kind of analysis is also essential in relation to the Text of languages not based on tone but on polysyllabic words that are inflected to affect meaning.

Improvisational and Compositional Devices, accustomed quarry for the practiced eye of the composer, constitute the specific vocabulary employed within the rules of musical grammar. And like the words of a spoken language, they may be combined in an endless variety of ways to create musical sentences. Analysis at this microscopic level of the MUSICAL CONSENSUS must proceed with constant awareness of less detailed segments of the G-S line. Let us say that we are attempting to determine the range of different configurations in which discrete variable pitches may appear as ornaments. These rules of musical grammar must be established in relation to, for example, the sléndro tuning system, the practical scales determined by instruments like the gendèr, gambang, suling, rebab, and the voice, to sléndro paṭet sanga (Mode), and to the hierarchy of principal pitches; all of which, in turn, must be considered in relation to the structural requirements of Form, associations with Text, Rhythmic Design, Melodic Contour, and so forth. Within this broad orientation, therefore, we try to understand the rules of musical grammar that generate x number of ornamental stereotypes, each of which has the potential of particular variations.

In certain applications, even counting notes may have some limited value. But tables of statistics, in themselves, tell us very little; in fact, they are more likely to deceive rather than enlighten the researcher unless the figures and percentages are carefully weighted according to the implications of other segments of our special G-S slide rule. For example, the *number of times* pitch 1 occurs in a piece may have little significance compared to *where* it occurs. Or, another example, the predominant interval used may be some kind of major second (slightly greater or smaller than 200 cents); but the significant question in relation to the generative rules of grammar may be where do *larger* intervals occur and between *which* pitches?

Whether the objective in analysis is centered on a group of solo songs, the repertory of a small instrumental ensemble, or a body of orchestral music including dance, song, and mime, the researcher is attempting to discover the rules of musical grammar responsible for the norms of musical style. Once the analysis is complete, how can he check his results? What is the relative importance of the various rules he has discovered? Let us say that in a given mode he finds that the usage of pitch 3 is generally avoided and that when it appears it is in a weak structural location or is used as a passing tone. Let us call this the rule governing the "enemy tone."[12] But there are those occasional pieces in this mode in which pitch 3 is given melodic prominence; and in a few rare instances a piece even ends on pitch 3! Are these exceptions to be ignored? Should they be considered exceptions which prove the rule? If they are to be explained as products of the composer's inventive genius, evidence of his ability to create music rather than musical exercises, what details of Melodic Contour, Melodic Character, and Compositional Devices combine to justify these exceptions? Are there qualifying regulations in the operation of the rule of the enemy tone?

I well remember the first day of class in one of the courses I took in Western musical analysis as an undergraduate. The instructor announced that by the end of the semester each student must have written an original composition, in any style, using sonata form. For the few of us interested in composition, this kind of term project had especial appeal. Other members in the class were not so enthusiastic. In answer to their protests, the instructor explained that there was no better way to test their studies in analysis than such a concrete demonstration of the extent to which they understood the rules of musical grammar. Of the compositions submitted by the end of the semester, a few demonstrated that their composers still had little knowledge of the musical grammar under study, the majority ranged from acceptable to excellent exercises illustrating the rules learned in the course of analysis, and some were respectable pieces of music. In the last category, several compositions had been written by students with no training in composition but who had gained a masterly control of the processes of analysis.

The processes of analysis involve taking things apart. The thoroughness with which this has been accomplished is best tested by putting them back together again, the processes of synthesis. If only the basic rules of musical grammar have been isolated, then the synthetic product will probably sound like a gawky exercise. If the rules of musical grammar have been thoroughly exposed, attempts at

[12] See further *ibid.*, pp. 245–246.

synthesis will probably vary between acceptable and excellent musical exercises. Can the processes of synthesis yield a piece of music, something more than a correct exercise? Perhaps. In the class in Western musical analysis, a few of the noncomposers produced very musical pieces. Is this merely evidence that they had been more thorough in their analyses than their classmates who wrote excellent exercises? Possibly. But something else must be taken into account. These few highly successful students, although they were untrained in composition, were nonetheless *carriers* of the musical tradition in which they wrote. Certainly, to some extent the reason they were able to transcend the quality of a musical exercise was due to their unconscious or semiconscious awareness of the universe of untalkables that was part of the MUSICAL CONSENSUS governing the norms of musical style.

Let us ask the question again. Can synthetic method produce a piece of music? Insofar as synthesis is employed to test the rules of musical grammar, it need not produce a piece of music. If the end result is a good or excellent musical exercise, it will have proved as much as most theory classes in Western music are able to prove, namely, a thorough comprehension of the rules of musical grammar. But synthetic method could, in fact, lead to the creation of a piece of music *if*—and it is a big "if"—the researcher, whether or not he is a carrier of the tradition, a member of the SOCIO-CULTURAL CONSENSUS, has managed to identify with the universe of untalkables. By definition, these formatives of musical consensus resist scientific and laboratory methods. For want of a better explanation, shall we say that with sufficient exposure in depth, as a student of performance, as a researcher, the ethnomusicologist may develop an almost intuitive sensibility to the universe of the untalkables? This need not be his objective in applying synthetic method to test his analysis; but if it happens, it is a reassuring bonus in the expectations of analysis.

Synthetic method need not be limited in application to testing musical analysis. A practical example comes to mind in relation to the seventeenth-century verses from the *Tjenṭini* cited earlier.

In that context, I mentioned that as an amateur performer on the rebab I could attest to the aptness of the poetic similes used to describe instrumental techniques. Actually, the nicety of this poetic description was tested through synthetic method a number of years ago.

Before I had had the opportunity to study rebab, one of the students in our extracurricular performance group in Javanese gamelan asked whether I could help him learn to play the instrument. He was a cellist. I told him I had never studied rebab, in fact, at that time, had never even seen it played. But if he was willing, we could try; his technique as a cellist, I warned him, might prove to be either an advantage or disadvantage. Together we studied pictures of rebab players, listened to recordings, and spent a number of hours trying to discover the physical techniques that would produce something approaching the sounds we heard in recordings. As I recall, we were rather close to giving up the attempt, when one day I suggested we sit down and reread pertinent passages from the *Tjentini*. Using his accustomed fingering technique, the cellist had had no success in producing a proper sound when stopping the string with his index finger. Fingering with the little and ring fingers was only slightly better. I read the passage aloud: "The middle finger was conspicuous in its movements; the index was like the sprig of a young fern; the little and ring-finger looked very much like spider's feet." Now, the index finger of a cellist in action looks like anything but the sprig of a young fern! I told him to make his finger look like the description. He did so, pressed it against the string, drew the bow, and for the first time out came a strong and clear rebab sound. A discussion of the movement of spider's feet, through some poetic power of suggestion, improved the technique of the little and ring fingers. (See Illustrations 7-1, 7-2, and 7-3.)

The student was unable to continue our program of self-study long enough to become a good rebab player. But in the course of our rather unusual application of synthetic method, we both had gained a sense of respect for the powers of poetic description.

The validity of the synthetic product itself should be tested by comparison with particular pieces of music and, whenever possible, subjected to criticism by musicians native to the tradition being studied. We shall have more to say about critical and comparative methods after a brief consideration of historical method.

HISTORICAL SOURCES

Almost any subject of research in music, even the most contemporary, can be related in some manner to the historical past. And the sources of history are virtually unlimited. Annals, chronicles, literature, artifacts, monuments, bas reliefs, sculpture, painting, illuminated manuscripts, the technology of agriculture, of metalwork, of pottery, of architecture, and so forth, together furnish the historian with the bits and pieces of evidence that constitute the factual skeleton of his narrative reconstruction. Through induction, inference, and imagination he attempts to recreate the probable past. Differences in interpretation of these diverse types of evidence sometimes produce rather diverse reconstructions from one historian to another. In seeking to understand the cultural history of a given society, therefore, the ethnomusicologist may find himself caught up in the finical debate of the scholarly arena. How does he evaluate the differing opinions? Annals, chronicles, and early literature and histories, it is well known, are subject to a patent chauvinism. Is this likely to be true, to some extent, of histories written

337

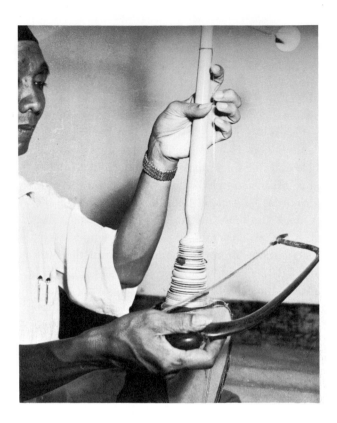

today by scholars who are descendants of the subject society? Which scholar can be cited as the authority? Given relatively few facts and a plethora of inferences, what can be said with certainty that relates to music in its socio-cultural milieu?

Exposure to the vagaries of differing histories is, in itself, enlightening. But it is to the sources of history relating to music that the ethnomusicologist must turn. Interpretation of these particular bits and pieces of evidence falls clearly in his sphere of expertise, and such an enterprise not only may furnish helpful clues to the historian but also may contribute much to the research objectives of the ethnomusicologist. Whether the source is poetic literature, like the passage cited from the *Tjentini*, or any of the other diverse sources suggested above, the scholar with a knowledge of The Tradition of music is uniquely qualified to interpret their meaning.

A particular kind of historical source not uncommon in ethnomusicological research deserves special mention. In many musical cultures of Asia, ancient types of musical ensembles are still in usage, so that the historical past of music, to some degree, has managed an unbroken continuity to the present. The extent to which

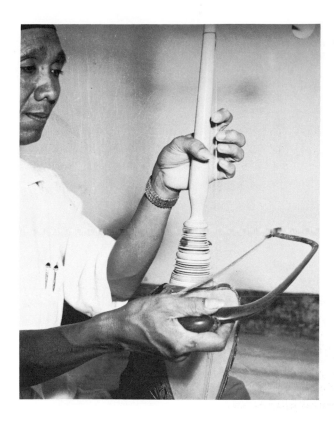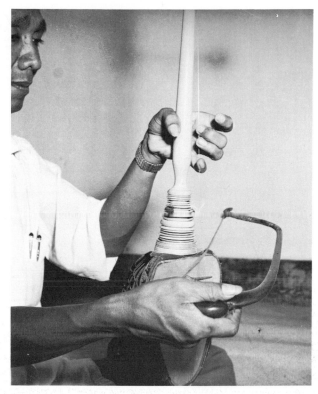

the musical style and instrumentation of such an ensemble may have changed through the centuries is, of course, a question that must be posed. But the viability of such ensembles is usually ensured through their association with religious and/or secular ritual which itself is highly resistant to change. Often, therefore, the ethnomusicologist has the good fortune to be able to work in the here and now within a kind of living laboratory of the historical past of music. In Indonesia, for example, there are extant performing ensembles that document the probable evolution of tuning systems covering a period of nearly 2,000 years.[13] Other types of evidence such as the bas reliefs on the Borobudur (see Illustrations 7-4 through 7-8) or terracotta figurines (see Illustrations 7-9 through 7-12) dating from the Majapahit Empire (A.D. 1293–1525) in East Java indicate other ensembles and individual instruments imported from India that have not survived in Indonesia. These sources, together with other forms of documentation provided by the

[13] Mantle Hood, "The Effect of Medieval Technology on Musical Style in the Orient," paper read in 1962 at a meeting of the Royal Anthropological Institute for Great Britain and Northern Ireland, London; *Selected Reports*, vol. 1, no. 3, Institute of Ethnomusicology, UCLA (1970), pp. 147–170.

Illustration 7-4
Bas-relief on the Borobudur
depicting dancers and
musicians.

Illustration 7-5
A detail from Illustration
7-4.

Illustration 7-6
The dancer's pose in the upper left-hand corner is reminiscent of a style still found in Thailand today, but not in Indonesia. In the central portion of the relief, the blown conch shell on the right and the short barrel drum on the left have disappeared, but the central small drum resembles the present-day Javanese keṭipung.

Illustration 7-7
The drums in the upper half of this relief are still found in Indonesia today, the pair of drums on the left in Bali, the drum in the center in Central Java; the Indian instruments in the lower half of the relief have disappeared.

Illustration 7-8
A remarkable tree laden with various types of drums.

historian, constitute the factual skeleton of the ethnomusicologist's narrative reconstruction and furnish invaluable insight into the norms of style that govern various types of gamelan orchestras in use today.

COMPARISON AND CRITICISM

Comparative and critical methods are continually involved in the course of description, analysis, synthesis, and the processes of historical reconstruction. The habit of comparison and the exercise of critical judgment tend to become an almost automatic response to certain kinds of research problems. And, of course, either comparison or criticism may become an end in itself.

I cannot agree with those who maintain that the *principal* concern of ethnomusicology is comparative musicology. On the other hand, comparative studies at various levels of concentration can be identified among the important objectives of the ethnomusicologist, *when sufficient knowledge of the musical cultures being compared is at hand.* The tendency toward premature emphasis on cross-cultural comparison has been pointed out elsewhere.[14]

Assuming sufficient knowledge of the things being compared, what are

[14] See further Mantle Hood, "Music, The Unknown," in Frank Ll. Harrison, Mantle Hood, and Claude V. Palisca, *Musicology*, Prentice-Hall, Inc., Englewood Cliffs, N.J., 1963, pp. 217–239.

some of the levels of concentration that might have especial significance? If a study centers on the Compositional Devices of The Composer or the Improvisational Devices of The Performer, for example, it is likely to have greater significance if it includes comparison with the practices of other contemporary composers or performers in The Tradition. The implications are even greater if it extends to include comparison in historical depth. In the same way, the study of a collection of Pieces or a Genre will be enhanced if it includes comparison with other kinds of pieces or genres within The Tradition.

Assuming sufficient knowledge, a comparative study of two different but related musical cultures (e.g., Javanese and Sundanese) may yield not only distinguishing and similar characteristics but also added knowledge of each culture considered in depth. Today, we have a basic understanding of the concept of patet (modal practices) operating in Javanese music. When we have reached a clearer understanding of the Sundanese concept of papatet and surupan, a comparison of these practices in Java and Sunda may well reveal further details important in each of these concepts as well as points of similarity and difference between the two.

Comparative methods may tell us something about the processes of acculturation and assimilation through a study of two contiguous or interpenetrated, but culturally unrelated, societies, for example, displaced Javanese residing as enclaves in Sumatra. Or to take advantage of greater historical depth, comparison might be concentrated on areas of early colonization by the Javanese of Borneo (Kalimantan) among the Dyaks. We might learn something in addition about the rate of acculturation and the relative importance of environment and modes of employment—on one hand, the fairly recent importation of Javanese labor to work the rubber plantations in Sumatra and, on the other, early colonization of South Borneo—by making both comparisons and then comparing the results of the studies. A comparative study of two unrelated societies sharing common features of cultural heritage (e.g., the cultures of Java and south India) would yield a different order of acculturation and assimilation from that mentioned above and would also be invaluable for purposes of historical reconstruction.

Comparison of two or more isolated cultures (e.g., the Balinese of Indonesia and the Ashanti of Ghana) might prove or lay to rest the seemingly fanciful thesis entertained by some scholars who believe that some time in the first six centuries A.D., West Africa was colonized by Indonesians who sailed around the Cape.[15] Or the objective of such a study might be directed at the exploration of possible universals in musical practices among those cultures that use some form of stratification.

[15] Jones, *op. cit.*

343

Illustration 7-9
An ensemble of musicians
depicted in terra cotta.

Illustration 7-10
A plucked lute.

344

Illustration 7-11
Frame drums.

Illustration 7-12
Two gendèr in foreground.

Perhaps it is the last objective mentioned—the search for universals in musical practice—that causes some scholars to insist that the proper concern of ethnomusicology is comparative musicology. It is certainly not an improper concern—when comparative methods are applied to subjects which are sufficiently understood. Of course, the moot point comes down to the question "What kinds of universals have significance?"

And this question requires consideration of critical methods.

It is understood that the exercise of critical judgment is one of the constants in the habitude of research. When all the available facts have been marshalled, it is the critical faculty in operation that discerns their proper ordering. But in what applications may critical method become an end in itself?

Let us begin with a little vignette. An incident that provided me with privileged access to the collection of music housed in the palace of the sultan of Djogjakarta and, subsequently, a chance observation during a gamelan rehearsal in the palace give some indication of the critical standards maintained by the Javanese MUSICAL CONSENSUS.

I had been invited, along with two or three other Westerners residing in Djogjakarta, to the opening ceremonies and performance of the two gamelan sekati, the sixteenth-century holy gamelan that play during Sekatèn, Muslim Holy Week in Java. The ceremony begins about eight o'clock on the first evening of Sekatèn in an open square within the palace walls. The two sacred gamelan are placed in a special pavilion located before the inner main gates of the palace proper. By the time the opening piece, "Rambu," [16] is begun by one of the gamelan, hundreds of men, women, and children are jammed into the square waiting for the moment the sultan or an appointed substitute (one of his brothers) will appear to scatter saffron rice and coins to the crowd. A person lucky enough to catch one of the coins is blessed with the assurance of good health and good fortune.

I was seated cross-legged on the platform close to the gamelan. When the long formal introduction to the piece was concluded by solo bonang, an instrument with large, horizontally suspended bronze kettles, I brought out a notebook and pencil and began to transcribe the fixed melody of "Rambu" in cipher notation. After a time, someone touched me politely on the arm. I looked up to see the head of the court musicians, K. R. T. Madukusuma, smiling broadly and holding in his outstretched hands a large open volume of kraton (court) or "checkered script" notation. He laid it before me and pointed to the passage being played at that moment by the gamelan. I put away my notebook and followed

[16] An excerpt already referred to is located on Side IV, Band 1, of the accompanying LPs.

346

the kraton notation for the rest of the evening, until at midnight the massive gamelan were moved to two special small pavilions near the mosque where they would continue to perform during the whole of Sekatèn week. Formerly, the two gamelan played alternately day and night around the clock. In recent times, they are silent between midnight and six o'clock in the morning.

During the evening, I had deduced that the sacred nature of the repertory and its infrequent performance put the musicians' memories to a severe test, even with the head of palace ceremonies standing by with the written record, which, of course, is never used directly in either rehearsal or performance. I also learned that in addition to the volume of Sekatèn repertory there were six other volumes of notation in the palace. When I had explained the importance of such a collection in terms of the research I had undertaken, without hesitation Madukusuma gave me permission to microfilm the manuscript.

Many months later, after I had attended countless gamelan rehearsals and performances, both within and outside the palace, and had gained some familiarity with the palace repertory, I set up a schedule of microfilming three hours each morning. A work table was placed for me adjacent to the pendopo where the palace musicians rehearsed. One morning, with my attention divided as usual between the details of photography and the absorbing sounds of the gamelan rehearsing close by, I stopped in the process of adjusting focus to listen more intently. Unlike the skillfully wrought pieces I had come to associate with the repertory of the palace gamelan, this piece seemed to have a somewhat awkward melodic line that struck me as a kind of fragmentary pastiche. It was not in the style of the "modern" pieces or novelties that were becoming popular with some of the gamelan outside the palace; but the longer I listened the more curious I became to know its history.

When the piece was finished, I approached the leader of the gamelan and asked whether he could help me locate it in the kraton manuscript, so that I could study its construction in some detail. I volunteered the opinion that the piece seemed different from others I had heard performed by his gamelan. He looked at me rather quizzically, then turned to the other musicians and began speaking rapidly in a level of the Javanese language I could not follow. Suddenly it seemed everyone was talking at once. Some of the musicians shook their heads vigorously, others nodded as though resigned—to what, I had no idea. All of them, it seemed to me, were casting glances in my direction. In a few minutes, the leader turned back with an explanation. He said the piece had been composed rather recently, but he did not indicate by whom. The gamelan had rehearsed it a number of times but had never included it in a performance. It was not part of the kraton collection, and the consensus of the musicians suggested it never would be. He

347

assured me that new pieces were added to the collection only after a considerable test of time and a strong consensus of approval.

There are several different implications of critical method suggested by these two incidents. It is significant that the Javanese were sufficiently concerned about standards in the performance of the sacred Sekatèn repertory to want the head of palace ceremonies close by reading score. In this context, whether the motivation was prompted purely by musical standards or by ritualistic standards or, more probably, by a combination of the two, is not of immediate interest. But the conscious effort to maintain the best performance standards is a clear application of critical method by the Javanese MUSICAL CONSENSUS. The fortuitous audition of a piece that did not measure up to the standards of the palace repertory, reinforced by the gamelan leader's explanation, is a different kind of application of critical method by the Javanese MUSICAL CONSENSUS.

Subsequently, close study of the extensive introduction to the seven volumes of kraton manuscript disclosed numerous and varied applications of critical methods operative in The Tradition of the palace gamelan. In the course of his field work and in the perusal of documents, the ethnomusicologist must be alert to evidence of critical methods—in both music and speech modes of discourse—as they are applied at various levels of communication within the MUSICAL CONSENSUS. Whether or not the culture under study tends toward verbal theorizing, evidences of critical standards—by word or gesture, by acceptance or rejection, by praise or noncommital apathy—constitute one of the most significant sources of information about the *Formatives* of the MUSICAL CONSENSUS.

There is one more point in connection with the second incident. The leader of the gamelan as well as his musicians were surprised and possibly even startled that a Westerner detected, on first hearing, a gamelan piece that the consensus had virtually rejected for inclusion in the kraton manuscript. At the time, I was surprised and startled myself when I learned that I had somehow singled out this substandard piece. In retrospect, I continue to be a bit surprised, considering that my exposure to the palace repertory at that time was less than two years; but I no longer consider the incident startling. I believe there are several possible, tangible explanations other than the several mystical interpretations of the incident accepted by the Javanese.

One possible explanation might be the fact that, almost continuously for six years prior to this incident, I had been occupied with an intensive study of the fixed melodies of Javanese gamelan pieces, first, in connection with modal practices and, second, in connection with mode and group improvisation. In other words, I had spent a great many hours studying the movement of Javanese melody.

Another explanation, not necessarily exclusive of the first, might be that during the span of nearly two years of studies in performance, playing with a number of different gamelan on a variety of instruments, I had to some slight extent—perhaps the barest minimum—been able to touch the realm of the untalkables, which provided an "instinctive feeling" about the "rightness" of a gamelan piece suitable for the palace repertory.

But I think there is possibly a third explanation, which might or might not be interdependent on either or both of the other two. In my very early study of the movement of Javanese melody, long before I had ever heard live gamelan or visited Java, I was often struck by the logic, the inevitability of many of the fixed melodies. There were momentary deceptions, delayed cadences, the wide range of compositional devices known to any composer—augmentation, diminution, inversion, retrograde, extension, condensation, fragmentation, elaboration—but often, almost always, the kind of inevitable logic characteristic of a Mozart or a Bach. Yes, these were pieces in sléndro or pélog rather than in the well-tempered keyboard tuning of Western music. And yet, given the difference of the milieu of their tuning system, they exhibited the musical integrity of any masterpiece in the West.

THE UNIVERSE OF MUSIC

I am suggesting one explanation based on the assumption that there may indeed be universals in music that ought to be of concern to the ethnomusicologist. And I am convinced that the gross generalities that have confused and confounded comparative studies in the past or the vague descriptive habits too often substituted for precise laboratory methods or tables of statistics in lieu of composer-oriented analysis will never expose these elusive universals of music.

I am convinced that only through the application of the most precise scientific methods, all of them—historical, descriptive, analytical, synthetic, comparative, critical—can we hope to understand the universals of music. Comparative musicology? I no longer understand the term. We shall need the closest cooperation from the psychologist and the physiologist, the humanist and the physicist, the philosopher and the aesthetician.

We shall have to turn to one meaning of the word "universe" borrowed from the astronomer: not a closed system, but rather *the totality of the observed or postulated physical* (substitute *musical*) *whole*. And this calls for a much more conscious and braver application of critical method than has been in evidence thus far in the field of ethnomusicology.

349

Elsewhere I have mentioned at some length the importance of considering the intrinsic value of individual pieces of music viewed in relation to such a universe of music.[17] And the determination of intrinsic value through the application of critical method is, in fact, the exercise of value judgment. For more than fifteen years, I have had the responsibility of presenting concerts of various musical cultures of the non-Western world to Western audiences. Countless individual members of those audiences have sought me out to express their personal reaction to this or that kind of music. By now it is a well-established fact that persons *outside* a given musical culture, who may lack any specific knowledge of the culture, may be deeply moved by the beauty—however defined by the listener—of a *particular piece of music* within that musical tradition. Why?

The *who* that he is—the total limitations and capacities, the environment and conditioning that have made him *what* he is—responds to a particular cluster of purely musical factors, virtually unlimited in number, that make up the universe of music. Are we speaking about a special, universal realm of the untalkables? Not necessarily, although such a possibility may have to be taken into account.

Let us try a formal statement published some time earlier, offered here with slight modification and expansion:[18]

We may postulate a universe of music with the hypothesis (1) that a particular piece of music within its own society may or may not have extramusical associations for members of the society, that it operates within a certain range of musical predictability determined by The Tradition, and that it may produce varied emotional responses; (2) that the same piece may evoke the same, different, or no extramusical associations in nonmembers of the society, that perception by the nonmember may vary according to the length of exposure to the initially unfamiliar idiom, according to the natural limitations and capacities of the individual, and according to the similarity or difference between his cultural background and that of the society carrying the tradition; and (3) that individual aesthetic responses to the piece—by either a member or nonmember of the society—is evidence of value judgment, of critical method, expressed in terms of beauty, depth of feeling, or however defined, and that such responses, independent of extramusical associations, indicate the *existence* of a universe of music.

Although postulate 3 is independent of postulates 1 and 2, an explanation for such aesthetic responses that would lead to a comprehension of the universals in music might ultimately have to be based on a thorough exploration of the conditions of postulates 1 and 2.

[17] See Hood, "Music, The Unknown," *op. cit.*, p. 264 and pp. 279–289.
[18] *Ibid.*

350

To make doubly sure that the formality of language has not obscured my meaning, let me restate the facts: The intrinsic value of a piece of music, regardless of its tradition, may be appreciated by an individual, regardless of his background or prior lack of exposure to The Tradition, through the unconscious application of critical method. This response might apply to no more than a single piece in a whole tradition or to most of the pieces in the tradition.

It is in such a universe of music that the music mode of discourse achieves the essence of communication.

Chapter Eight

COMMUNICATIONS

THE VERY CONCEPTION of a universe of music, defined as the totality of the observed or postulated musical whole, requires some comprehension of its complex system of communications. In various contexts, thus far, we have stressed the peculiar significance of both the speech and music modes of discourse. Let us reconsider them briefly, along with other modes of communication, in relation to our postulated universe of music.

SPEECH-MUSIC MODES

The ethnomusicologist utilizes speech in a public lecture, in a paper read, in an encyclopedia entry, in a monograph, in a classroom, in an essay, in a proposal for research funds directed to a foundation or governmental agency, in talking with musicians and dancers, with scholars in other disciplines, with deans and chancellors, with members of the community at large, with the political elite of foreign countries. His ability to communicate at the different levels required by these different audiences demands more than a conscious shifting from technical to popular vocabulary. It demands more than a knowledge of the bundle of traditions surrounding music. It requires some cognizance of the universe of music.

It has been said that the relative success of a teacher can be measured by his ability to anticipate the problems the student will encounter in the learning process. In one sense, in facing these different audiences in the speech mode of discourse, the ethnomusicologist is a teacher. He is quite literally "professing" his devotion to subject. And he will be able to anticipate the problems in the learning process peculiar to each audience to the extent that he is aware of and sensitive to the universe of music. Each member of these several audiences is himself a carrier of a musical tradition. Whether he belongs to the SOCIO-CULTURAL CONSENSUS or the MUSICAL CONSENSUS or to those of the interrelated arts, he is the carrier of a musical tradition. It is incumbent on the ethnomusicologist in the speech mode of discourse to try to anticipate those universals of music on which communication can be based.

We have postulated the existence of a universe of music on the ample evidence that individual pieces of music, in the music mode of discourse, do establish some kind of extracultural communication. This observation centers on the S end of the G-S line of the universe of music: nothing could be more particular in such a universe than a particular piece of music. But our definition of the universe of music—the totality of the observed or postulated musical whole—encompasses all the bundles of traditions surrounding the musics of the world: the other end of the G-S line. It is an awareness of the G-S line of the universe of music—the G-S line of the totality of the observed or postulated musical whole—on which communication depends in the speech mode of discourse directed to various kinds of audiences.

By way of illustration, let us consider a current worldwide problem. Increasingly, universities and governmental agencies are devoting time and energy to population problems. Interdisciplinary teams are occupied with such problems as birth control, agricultural practices, sanitation and public health, economic development, and so forth. In almost every instance, remedies to halt the acceleration of population growth depend on the successful communication of ideas to those peoples directly affected. In large part, therefore, the problems of overpopulation must be resolved by tackling pertinent problems in communications. No matter how thorough the research or how imaginative or practical the proposed solutions to the problems, unless the message gets across to the people, the growth of population will continue to accelerate.

How do population problems relate to the universe of music?

In the summer of 1967, I was informed by a knowledgeable Indonesian that the principal mode of communication for 90 percent of the population of Java, where more than two-thirds of the total population of Indonesia resides, was not the newspaper, not the radio, not recently imported television, but the local ḍalang—the puppeteer of one or another form of puppet play. To the best of my present knowledge, this medium of communication, the puppet play, has never been considered as a potential mode of education in relation to the problems of overpopulation. Why not?[1]

For the past two decades, private foundations and federal agencies of the United States, as well as those of other countries, have supplied millions of dollars for support of health, education, welfare, economic development, agriculture, and so forth in Indonesia. Such areas of support are directly related to population problems. Nonetheless, the growth of population continues to accelerate at an alarming rate. The same set of circumstances obtain in India, in some parts of Africa, in Southeast Asia, in many parts of the non-Western world. And like Indonesia, in most of these societies the medium of communication for the majority is likely to be the puppet play, the clown shows, the singer of histories and chronicles, or other ages-old genres of the performing arts. Why are these viable channels of direct communication generally ignored by the very agencies whose objectives they could serve so well?

Such agencies are directed and supervised by individuals—mere human beings, despite the staggering budgets for which they have responsibility. In the United States, these individuals are *carriers* of a tradition in which the puppet play today functions as *entertainment for children*. Furthermore, these puppet plays of the Western world, for the most part, are not experienced directly by their children but through the impersonal eye of the television tube, which is *the medium* of communication. Farther down the chain of command in private foundations and agencies of the federal government are all those individuals who make specific proposals for solutions to the population problem. And these individuals, too, are carriers of the same, nearly puppetless, tradition. Perhaps vaguely they are aware

[1] James R. Brandon has called attention to the great emphasis on the usage of various forms of theater throughout Southeast Asia for purposes of moral education in his book *Theater in Southeast Asia*, Harvard University Press, Cambridge, Massachusetts, 1967; in Java, other forms of theater such as the clown shows, known as dagelan, and folk plays, called ketoprak, were dominated for some time by communist players and propaganda; ludruk, a popular form of theater especially favored in East Java, has been studied in terms of communication dynamics by James G. Peacock, *Rites of Modernization*, University of Chicago Press, Chicago, 1968.

354

of the power of even this watered-down, impersonal form of puppetry via television when they respond to the demands of their youngsters in buying a particular brand of breakfast cereal or hot dog. But such parental indulgence is practiced as part of the game, kid's stuff of the children's world. World problems of overpopulation are another matter. This is serious stuff. If posters, newsprint, radio, and television get the message across in the United States, the same media ought to work in Indonesia or in India. But the fact is that such media of communication are *not* getting the message across to some 90 percent of the population. And the 10 percent being reached is likely to be already reasonably informed about such matters.

The chains of command in foundations and federal agencies are dedicated to philanthropic objectives. Individuals responsible for such programs have eyes but they do not see, ears but they do not hear. They are unaware of the universe of music, the totality of the observed or postulated musical whole, which includes puppetry. They have forgotten that many years ago in their *own* tradition the principal mode of communication was the singing bard who traveled from castle to castle, from feudal estate to feudal estate, informing their ancestors in much the same manner as that of the dalang. The norms of style were different; but, in the universe of music, the mode of communication was the same.

Megacycles and television tubes, newsprint and tricky posters have nearly blotted out the memory and experience of the power of the live voice getting the message across in person.

But let us give our critic a chance to speak. He is demanding the use of the microphone. I think he is going to begin with a brief introduction, something like this: "I am a student of Indonesian culture. I know something about the importance of the puppet play in Java. Do you mean to tell me that you are serious in suggesting that the dalang talk about contraceptives and the pill or toilet training and hepatitis in the middle of religious stories associated with the ancestors? You haven't got a chance of sticking in that kind of propaganda. I agree with your point about the puppet play in the universe of music. But you have to be practical. The dalang isn't the answer. The problem is too big. Do you know that there are reported to be more than 5,000 dalangs in Java?"

I had better turn off the microphone and collect my thoughts.

In the first place, any serious student of Indonesian culture knows that, during the clown episodes and dialogue of minor supporting characters, topics of current interest are likely to appear in the puppet play. The viability of the tradition, in part, depends on the dalang's skill and wit in handling hot topics of immediate currency. In the course of the antics and ribald humor of the clowns, I suggest that the dalang could handle the realities of the pill and toilet training with great conviction. A dalang is an educated man. It would not be difficult to

355

extend his education to the high purposes and objectives underlying the solutions to population problems. And far from desecrating the memory of the ancestors, he would be ensuring the survival of his society. A big job to so educate 5,000 dalangs? Not really, considering that the population of Indonesia has already pushed well past the 100 million mark.

Not long ago, I mentioned this idea to a Javanese friend of mine. Aware of the formal atmosphere that surrounds the style of Javanese wajang kulit, I was not too surprised at his reaction. Although he readily understood the importance of such communications, he said the puppet play was not the appropriate vehicle because the mention of such matters would embarrass the audience. Then he suggested that dagelan, earthy clown shows that for some years have been purveyors of communist propaganda, might serve the purpose. We are close friends, so I felt free to press the point. The formality of wajang kulit and the fundamentally serious nature of the religious literature on which it is based, I argued, was precisely the kind of context needed to ensure that the audience would accept these matters with the serious intent they deserved. Dagelan and the characteristic level of humor it generates would likely have exactly the opposite effect.

Then I told him about a lecture I had attended a few days before, given by a young colleague recently returned from a year of field work in India. At one point, she had discussed the use of the bhajan for family planning, a subject of real concern in India for some years. I believe my Javanese friend was convinced when he heard the gist of the following particulars which I later asked the lecturer to set down for me:

> The bhajan is a song genre of India which has as its text religious thought characteristic of the bhakti movement from which it sprang. Bhajans are sung by Indians from all levels of society, from wandering folk musicians to the finest artists of classical music, and thus are rendered in many different styles.
>
> Recently the Government of India, Ministry of Information and Broadcast, Song and Drama Division has adopted the bhajan as a means of communicating the urgency of family planning among the rural population. Six units tour the countryside, singing bhajans whose lyrics have been composed specifically to promote family planning.[2]

Perhaps it seems rather fanciful that the board of directors meeting on one of the upper floors of a high-rise building in New York City or the planning and operations team tucked away in some nook or cranny of the Pentagon might someday devote a plenary session to discussion of the puppet play. But the possibility seems as realistic as recent deliberations designed to land a man on Mars and beyond.

On one occasion or another, for a greater or lesser purpose than professing

[2] A written communication generously furnished at my request by Bonnie Wade.

356

knowledge of the puppet play, the ethnomusicologist must rely on the speech mode of discourse in establishing communication with such a board of directors or any other particular audience. It is not enough to recognize and understand the significance of the puppet play as a potential educative medium in relation to population problems. He must also anticipate those factors in the background of his audience that are likely to inhibit his own speech communication. And the critical factors to be identified exist somewhere in the universe of music.

Our illustration has touched on two different examples of getting the message across within the system of communications of the universe of music: (1) speech directed to a particular audience and (2) music making (the talking-singing ḍalang) directed to a particular audience. Both of these, talking about music and making music, inclusive of the surrounding bundle of traditions, are universal modes of communication operating within the observed or postulated musical whole, the universe of music. And like any two branches of a network of communications, they can be connected with or disconnected from one another as occasion demands.

HUMAN MOVEMENT

Let us turn to an entirely different kind of universal in music making; human movement as an indicator or set of signals evolved by the MUSICAL CONSENSUS and influenced by the SOCIO-CULTURAL CONSENSUS. A few years ago, I made a comparison of two documentary films of the same subject, an ensemble of musicians playing keti, a group of instruments used to accompany dance among the Ashanti. The two films were nearly identical, the same drums, rattles and bells, the same piece of music played at the same tempo, both filmed outdoors. The soundtracks of the two films could easily be accepted as two nearly identical versions of the same piece. There was one notable difference between the visual images of the two documentary films: the performers in one were Ashanti and in the other were international students in the Institute at UCLA. There was a marked difference in the movements of the Ashanti musicians compared with those of the UCLA performers. I believe we do not yet understand the extent to which the refinements of musical style may depend on the complex of human movements evolved by the MUSICAL CONSENSUS. But there is little question that these gestures, reflex responses, facial expressions, large and small bodily movements, absence of movement, tension, relaxation, together form a complicated network in the system of communications utilized in music making. I have noticed that the longer the student of ethnomusicology studies the performance of a particular idiom of non-Western music the more of these human movements native to the tradition he begins to take on.

357

There has been insufficient study of this aspect of musical style. But based on casual observation, I would hazard the guess that the more nearly the *movements* of the performer conform to the patterned movements established by the CONSENSUS the closer he comes to realizing proper *sounds* of the musical style. Watch the movements of any virtuoso on the piano, the extramusical signals employed by a fine string quartet, the string section of a symphony orchestra, the fourteen or sixteen players in the gangsa section of a Balinese gamelan gong kebyar, the byplay between the sitar and the tabla players improvising in North India. Yes, the movements of each example are different; they are culturally determined to be sure. Within that culture, they may also be further determined by Style Period, by Genre, and perhaps even local conditions reflecting the attitudes of the SOCIO-CULTURAL CONSENSUS.

In 1953, I witnessed a performance given by an excellent troop of musicians and dancers from Spain in the context of an international festival in Biarritz. A few days later, I had the privilege of seeing the same group perform for a Spanish audience of 10,000. The quality of the two performances was quite different. The Spanish SOCIO-CULTURAL CONSENSUS present at the performance in Pamplona was clearly a vital force in the system of communications operative in Spanish music making and dance.

Let us merely note in passing that culturally determined human movement forms an important part of the system of communications in the universe of music. Recognition of this fact, hopefully, will lead to systematic studies to increase our understanding of its role in communications and its effect on the norms of style. It, too, might land, one day, in a plenary session of the board determined to get a message across.

IMPACT OF THE ETHNOMUSICOLOGIST

A study of communications in the universe of music is a chapter that is barely begun in the field of ethnomusicology. There is one area of concern, however, that demands immediate attention. The fact that it seems not to have been given particular attention by political scientists or anthropologists or archeologists or others working in the far-flung corners of the earth should not excuse the ethnomusicologist from looking at the problem squarely.

Increasingly since World War II, a variety of self-styled ethnomusicologists, representing all shades of convictions and approaches, have been turned loose all over the world to ply their trade for whatever individual purposes and objectives may motivate them. Little attention has been paid to the effects of this onslaught on the various musical cultures under study. Sometimes they have been harmful; sometimes they have been beneficial. But always, *in every instance*, there

358

has been some kind of effect on the subject of study. In considering the universe of music, the ethnomusicologist must recognize that whatever his personal objectives and motivations, his overt interest in and study of a given musical culture—*this in itself*—affects his subject directly. Let us consider a few illustrations drawn from personal observation and experience.

The first example that comes to mind represents a segment of the bundle of traditions surrounding music in Bali: the graphic arts. Traditional Balinese paintings on cloth or canvas lack any realization of perspective. They are representational rather than abstract and are often devoted to subjects from the *Mahabharata* and the *Ramayana*—gods, heroes, demons, and animals rendered in highly stylized forms. The composition tends to be very tight and is filled with meticulous detail that requires close reading to be appreciated. The usual medium is tempera.

Beginning in the 1920s, contact with individual European painters who came to live in Bali gradually introduced the concept of perspective, designed spatial relationships in composition, realistic human figures, oil as a medium, and finally, in more recent times, most of the trends in abstraction found in the Western world.

As a student in Holland, I had been able to observe evidence of some of these changes in the paintings in the collection of the Royal Tropical Institute in Amsterdam. A few years later, during my first trip to Bali, I found that contemporary styles, not represented in the collection in Amsterdam, which dated from the period prior to World War II, were being followed by the younger painters anxious to enter the international art market. I also discovered that there was still a small number of painters working in traditional styles.

One traditional type, the so-called wajang paintings used to decorate the ceilings of the palaces and princely residences, showed no evidence of European influence. (See Illustrations 8-1, 8-2, and 8-3.) I also noticed that most of these paintings, through years of exposure to humidity and heat circulating through the pavilions in which they hung, bore marks of the ravages of time and needed to be replaced with new ones. This was 1957. When I inquired discreetly about such a possibility, it was only to learn that there were very few painters still alive who were masters of the art. And, of course, a threadbare economy in the country had affected the splendor of the royal residences. There was simply no money for such refurbishment and consequently no incentive for young painters to apprentice in this ancient style of painting. There was some limited market for *old* wajang paintings among Western tourists for whom the primary value of art seemed to be its age. Small, cheap imitations of the style, rendered by unskilled hands, were also offered to the tourist trade. The fact that they were new and badly done limited their traffic.

359

Over a two-year period of residence in Java I made several subsequent trips to Bali. Really good traditional painting and sculpture became increasingly difficult to find.

Ten years later, in the summer of 1967, I stayed in a guest pavilion at the Puri, or palace, in Ubud. I noticed that some of the old wajang paintings had disappeared; they had been given to various Western friends by the generous Tjokorda Gdé Agung Soekawati. One evening on the veranda of the princely residence, I sat staring up at the tattered remnants of the few paintings remaining. I turned to my host and asked whether there were any painters living today who could still produce such quality. Tjokorda Agung followed my gaze and said, "Yes, there is one old man living in a village near Klungkung who can paint in the best wajang tradition."

The next morning the Tjokorda's nephew, Tjokorda Mas, and I set off by car for the village. Finally the road stopped, and we went on by foot. The

Illustration 8-1
(Below, left)
The left upper portion of a traditional wajang painting.

Illustration 8-2
(Below, right)
The right upper portion.

360

mighty volcanic eruption of Gunung Agung a few years before had filled a deep gorge with lava flow; and the last stage of the journey was barefoot through the rushing waters of a wide stream with a bed of sharp lava rocks. My non-Balinese feet were lacerated by the time we gained the other side of the stream and the edge of the village.

We inquired for the house of the old man, only to learn that he had died a few months before.

"But," we were told, "he had an apprentice. Would you like to meet him?"

A few minutes later, we stood in the modest quarters of the apprentice. In the Balinese language, Tjokorda Mas explained that we had come to see his master, that I was interested in wajang paintings. Did the apprentice have any to show us?

Illustration 8-3
A detail of the central upper portion.

361

As he listened, the young painter's eyes betrayed his pride of profession; but his manner was shy, if not humble. He mentioned that no Westerner had ever visited his house before.

He brought out a number of paintings of different sizes to spread them out on a mat. I held my breath while the first one was unrolled. It was good. Very good! Perhaps not quite up to the standard of his teacher. But very close. I found myself struggling with a mixture of emotions and reactions.

As he exposed the paintings, one by one, I felt a great sense of relief. The tradition was not dead; and the painter was still a young man. For no tangible reason I could account for then or now, I also felt that whatever reaction I showed overtly might be terribly important. I said nothing until all the paintings were on display. At one point, I had glanced at Tjokorda Mas for confirmation of my unexpressed enthusiasm. He certainly knew much more than I about the wajang tradition. He had nodded and said in English, "They are very good!" For some time I went from one painting to another, studying the details.

Finally, I turned to Tjokorda Mas and asked him to translate as precisely as possible. I said that out of respect and love for the work of the apprentice's teacher I would buy all the paintings he had displayed; that I hoped he would continue to emulate his master's work until he had not only equalled it but surpassed it. Then, looking at the young man, I added, "You, yourself, are nearly a master. These are excellent."

When my words were translated, his smile and that of his wife, who had joined us, I shall never forget. But while they were rolling up the paintings, I had another concern. One such purchase could hardly ensure the survival of a tradition. How could other young painters be inspired to follow the apprentice's example? Suddenly, I noticed another painting rolled up at one edge of the platform in the little pavilion in which he worked. I asked to see it. As he spread it out before me, he explained that it was unfinished. It was one of my favorite scenes from the *Ramayana*. I asked how long it would take him to complete it. He said about three days. I told him that, if he could deliver it to me at the Puri in Ubud at six o'clock on the morning of the fourth day, I would buy it before catching a plane for Java. He agreed to try.

Somehow, the trip back across the lava bed, with the painter and his wife accompanying us to the car, seemed much less difficult. We waved good-bye and went on with our busy schedule.

Later, back in the Puri, I had a long talk with Tjokorda Agung. An idea had been born while I looked at the apprentice's unfinished painting, but I needed Tjokorda Agung's approval and consent. The Puri in Ubud is visited by a great many VIPs from the Western world. When the Tjokorda heard my plan and understood its intention, he gave his consent. My last day in Bali, at six o'clock

362

in the morning, when the young painter arrived with the finished painting, I commissioned him to refurbish the Puri in Ubud with new wajang paintings.

Back in Djakarta, I told my story to various individuals working in the American embassy, showed them the wajang paintings I had purchased, and, I believe, aroused considerable interest among them in the work of this young master of the wajang tradition.

I have chosen this first example from the graphic arts because it so clearly shows the effect of Western influence on all forms of Balinese painting, an influence with emphasis on commercial marketing that has brought traditional styles of painting to the very brink of extinction. And, among them, the wajang style is very much a part of the bundle of traditions surrounding our universe of music. An attempt by one individual to assure continuity of the tradition, no matter how futile it may ultimately prove to be, also has had *some* direct effect on the tradition. I hope a postive one.

Let us try another example of the effect of the ethnomusicologist's interest on his subject, this one pertaining to the very heart of the tradition of Javanese gamelan: the art of making the great gong ageng.

In a discussion of the manufacture of gong ageng in the second edition of *Music in Java*, 1949, Kunst wrote:

> It is indeed a great pity that this industry, which, although carried on in an incomparably primitive manner, achieves the highest results in its own fields, is now on the verge of ruin. The demand for good instruments is getting steadily smaller. The principal—i.e., the Semarang—gongsmithies, for example, which, in 1907, still numbered seven, and at present only two, hardly, if at all, train any pupils now, so that it is probable that this beautiful craft, so full of ancient tradition, will die with the present generation, unless, in some way or other, a helping hand is offered in the nick of time.[3]

And then as an addendum to this passage, bound as a separate page in the back of Volume I, we find:

> The sad news reached me—too late for its inclusion in the text—that there is not now a single gongsmithy left in Semarang. As a result, owners of gamelans in both Java and Bali, knowing the replacement of their gongs to have become impossible, are giving greater care than ever to their maintenance.
>
> This information was given me orally by His Excellency Anak Agung, Prime Minister of the Republic East Indonesia.
>
> Thus, an unrivaled craft was lost before our very eyes in a single generation. For shame![4]

---

[3] Jaap Kunst, *Music in Java: Its History, Its Theory and Its Techniques*, 2 vols, 2d ed., Martinus Nijhoff, The Hague, 1949, pp. 139–140.

[4] *Ibid.*, following p. 410.

363

I still remember, with the same sense of shock and deep personal loss, the first time I read these words as a student in 1950—several years before I began to find my own life increasingly enmeshed with the manifold studies of gamelan tradition. Although at that time I had heard only recordings of gamelan, the sound of the gong ageng to my composer-trained ears was a unique source of beauty in the universe of music. Apparently Kunst's last sentence stuck with me at the subconscious level through the years, because when I first landed in Java in 1957—after two years of study with Kunst and nearly three years of additional research and practical studies with my own small gamelan—my first burning question was whether Anak Agung's information had been correct. Was the art of making the gong ageng really lost? For the first month, I received conflicting answers. Finally, in an audience with the sultan of Djogjakarta I had confirmation that the last family of gong makers capable of fabricating the gong ageng had disappeared from Semarang some time during World War II. He informed me that small gongs, up to 75 cm in diameter, were still manufactured; but the art of making the large ones had vanished.

Several years earlier, I had come across an old publication which described in detail the manufacture of gongs and included a number of excellent photographs.[5] At the time, it had occurred to me that if a diligent search were made, it might be possible to find men who had assisted in the making of a large gong as well as those who were still making small ones. With this book and the proper encouragement, they might be able to recover what appeared to be lost. There was no doubt that a book could not capture the skilled and coordinated movements of four men wielding hammers and a fifth man, the principal smith, handling the long tongs with which the cherry-red disk of bronze was turned as it was slowly forged into shape. Still, it seemed to me, it was worth a try.

Earlier in Djakarta, I had mentioned this possibility to representatives of several different ministries. They all agreed that it was a tragic cultural loss and that every effort should be made to recover the ancient craft. But when I tried to press on for specific assurance that something would be done about it, my discussants became rather vague and retreated with smiles into more general talk about gamelan and the arts. At least, it had been reassuring that everyone with whom I spoke seemed deeply concerned. It also occurred to me that perhaps I was being rather presumptuous—a well-meaning American, still an amateur of Javanese culture, suggesting to the connoisseur ways and means of recovering a lost art.

Hesitantly, I mentioned my idea to the sultan. He looked at me for a

[5] Edward Jacobson and J. H. van Hasselt, *De Gong-fabrikatie te Semarang*, E. J. Brill, Leiden, 1907.

364

moment and then said, "It would not be possible. Different gongsmiths hear differently." He affirmed that he was referring to the different number of ombak, or musical beats, found in different gongs. I explained that the ombak were predictable, that they were produced by the manner in which the boss and the surrounding flat surface of the gong were tuned. If they were the same pitch, there were no ombak. The greater the difference in cycles per second between the two the greater the number of ombak. I suggested that if someone of his eminence requested a certain number of ombak, the gongsmiths would quickly settle their "differences" or taste in hearing. He shook his head and smiled. "No, I am afraid it would not succeed."

During the following months, while I was busily engaged in study and research centered on the art of improvisation, I continued whenever an opportunity offered to talk with musicians, gamelan smiths, and anyone else who would listen to my idea. I was troubled by one subtle reservation in my otherwise resolute determination to launch a gong project. It had to do with the peculiar aura of mystery and the mystical that had always surrounded the manufacture of gong ageng.

Traditionally, the smith who made the large gong was in effect entrusted with a dangerous responsibility. He was a man of great spiritual development; and he fasted for three days before beginning his sacred task. His art was numbered among the excellences and virtues of Pandji, the culture hero; and, for this reason, during working hours he and his assistants took the name of Pandji Sepuh (Pandji the Old One) and his half brothers, servants, clowns, and so forth.[6]

> Just as was the case in mediaeval Europe, the Javanese smiths are not mere craftsmen like the others; an atmosphere of mystery surrounds their labours— more especially those of the gamelan smiths—and their activities can flourish only under the special patronage of the higher powers. More than all other mortals they are exposed, during their work, to the cunning artifices of evil spirits.
>
> In order to ward off any disasters the gamelan smiths, therefore, adopt other names during their labour than those they bear in daily life. These names they borrow from various personages from the Pandji-stories. One may wonder why it should be precisely from this cycle of stories that they choose their adopted names. In regard to this, Rassers arrived at some remarkable conclusions. He discovered, in fact, that the identification of the prince or tribal hero (for that is what Pandji, after all, appears to be) with the smith has been carried to such an extent that the two are, at times, almost indistinguishable. The art of gong-forging is thereby elevated to a sacred act, heavily charged with magic, on the part of the king-priest.[7]

[6] See further Kunst, *op. cit.*, p. 138.
[7] *Ibid.*, pp. 137–138.

This background, I finally concluded, was responsible for the reluctance with which gamelan smiths would even discuss the possibility of making the gong ageng. Several times I thought I had found a man who would be willing to attempt the experiment only to be told, after much deliberation that sometimes extended over a span of weeks, that he was not sufficiently skilled for such an undertaking.

A second problem in connection with the gong project was the high cost involved. High quality bronze and tin were very dear; even the price of charcoal—required in large quantity—was becoming increasingly expensive. I had to find a foundation or a private donor who would understand the importance of a project for which I had not yet located the "principal investigator"—if, indeed, such a gamelan smith existed at all.

The following year, 1958, the Asia Foundation gave me the money needed to begin. And the search for the right gongsmith continued.

A strong ally who believed in my idea was one of Central Java's leading musicians, Pak Tjokrowasita (now known as K. R. T. Wasitodipuro). The day before I was to leave Central Java, he appeared at my door early in the morning saying that he had heard about a smith in a small village near Solo. Was I willing to try again?

Two hours later, we stood in the dim, dark smithy watching a lean, wiry man and his assistant in the final stages of forging a large kenong. He had merely glanced over at us as we entered the smithy without pausing for a moment in the important task at hand. When the instrument was finished, he left us in order to wash up; and we were escorted to the house by his wife and were served tea. We spent several hours in discussion with him before revealing the real purpose of our visit. It was apparent in examining instruments he had made, including gongs up to 75 cm in diameter, that he had prodigious skill as a gamelan smith. We learned that three times on his own initiative he had tried to make a large gong; but each time, he told us, because of the size of the required fires, he had nearly burned down his smithy. He added that he was saving his money to build a larger smithy before trying again. By this time I was convinced that he had the right "heart" for the job. So I explained at length the reason we had come and laid out a suggested plan of procedure. We would provide the money for one gong about 80 cm in diameter. When this was made, Pak Tjokrowasita would judge the quality of the instrument, and if it was as good as those he had already made of smaller size, we would place an order for another gong 80 cm in size. If the first try was not of good quality, it was to be melted down and another attempt made with the understanding that he would be paid for his work anyhow. After he succeeded in making several gongs 80 cm in diameter, we would then commission him to make one 85 cm in diameter. This order, too, would carry the stipulations of the first. Our plan, therefore, was to try to increase his and his assistants' skill and experience, little by little, very slowly approaching the goal of 90 cm and larger.

I also asked him to promise that he would train his assistants, so that he would not be the only one who knew the art of gong making. He agreed to this, and the next day I departed for the United States.

After some months, I learned that the ceremony for completion of the new and enlarged smithy was to be delayed until the proper hour and day designated by the forecast of the astrologer-numerologist consulted. Some time after that date, I received word that the project had begun. About a year and a half after leaving Java, I was sent a letter describing with great jubilation the news that the gong ageng had been completed and that dignitaries from all over Java had come to the humble village in honor of the occasion. I was also told that there were customers waiting to buy the gong; could the smith sell it to someone else? I answered that our only objective was to keep him busy—by all means he should meet the needs of the local consumer. In the following months and years, I heard from time to time about the continued success of the project. I also learned that there was resentment in some quarters that American dollars were responsible for the recovery of this ancient art. I was also told that the success of the project and the attention it received was partly responsible for a decision on the part of the Indonesian government to open a gamelan factory in Solo. This spirit of competition, almost in the tradition of free enterprise, was a rather ironic development during the days that communism was rapidly gaining power in and considerable control of the central government.

Actually the critics of American dollar support were never fully aware of the facts. I had left instructions that when a gong had been purchased with funds from our project, it was to be given to a needy gamelan club or one of the public schools, at the discretion of those persons responsible for cultural affairs in Central Java. But a curious twist that developed in this simple plan makes one wonder whether the gods who watch over cultural matters are not rather sophisticated in the workings of supply and demand. Although from the beginning, project funds were used time after time to commission the making of a gong, the fact is we never really managed to purchase a single gong. Each time, a waiting customer brought it out from under us (with our blessings), and we went on to commission another. In other words, the project fund served to underwrite or guarantee the commercial manufacture of gongs. In time, with several successive devaluations of currency ordered by the government, our bank account dwindled to nothing. But by then the trade was firmly reestablished.

Or so I thought, until my visit to the smithy in 1967.

It was a warm reunion after an absence of nearly ten years, and the gongsmith and his wife told me with pride and a rekindled sense of excitement

367

about the honors that had come to the smithy. There was the time the president asked the two of them to visit him in his palace at Bogor. When they arrived, it was to learn that the president wanted the gongsmith to move his smithy to Bogor, possibly with the idea that this location was very much more accessible to foreign visitors and that it would become a kind of unique showcase. The gongsmith is a very sincere, uncomplicated person who is only completely happy when he is plying his trade. He and his wife considered the request, but the thought of leaving their village and the smithy of which they were so proud was not very attractive. The president bought a gong for the palace, and the gongsmith and his wife returned home.

The gongsmith had also been urged to join the gamelan factory at Solo. And although he continues to supply them with large gongs when needed, he prefers to remain independent. He told me that true to his promise he had trained five other men in the art of making the gong ageng, although he was still the only one who could accomplish the delicate task of the final tuning.

Even though I had dropped in to see him unannounced, I was understandably disappointed not to find him and his assistants at work on a large gong. I had never witnessed the actual operation itself. My disappointment turned to alarm when I learned that the fires of the smithy had been black for more than eight months and that his assistants had gone back to work in the rice fields. He explained that the times were so difficult economically that there were no buyers. He had on hand several finished gongs which I tried and found excellent. Ten years earlier, when the gong project was only an idea, I had stressed the point, to those with whom I spoke, that even if we were to succeed in recapturing the lost art, it would most certainly die out again unless an adequate market were maintained. Now, the threat was before us. When I mentioned the possibility of finding foreign markets, he told me that it was impossible to fill new orders because he could not obtain copper and tin.

The gongsmith and his assistants are reasonably young men, so that I do not anticipate the likelihood of a last-minute addendum to this book like the tragic news that Kunst sadly added to his warning. It is disquieting, nonetheless, within the ten-year cycle of loss and recovery, to find it necessary once more to warn the peoples of Indonesia and other owners of gamelan that the art and craft of the gong ageng is in very real danger.

Sometimes the effect of one's interest in subject is not so readily apparent. During that same summer of 1967, a specially appointed committee representing all the performing arts of West Java organized an eight-day tour designed to show me the great variety of Sundanese traditions. From seven in the morning until nearly midnight every day, there was a constant round of unforgettable performances in one village or town after another. On one of these days, filled with music, dance, and theater, we spent an afternoon in a village renowned for its old traditions. Typical of our stopover, everyone in the surrounding area had turned out for the special performances. Some hundreds of persons were squeezed into the one public building in the village where the performances took place. Outside, listening and viewing as best they could, were perhaps another 2,000 persons. We were welcomed by an ancient type of Sundanese gamelan I had read about but had never seen before. In the course of the afternoon, there was a variety of different styles of traditional music and dance, the latter performed by young people in their teens and twenties. There had been a number of formal speeches of welcome and explanations about the different traditions offered. I knew that my turn would come at the end of the program, so I had been collecting my thoughts for the effort. The moment seemed to have arrived for me to go to the microphone of the public address system. And then, quite spontaneously, three old men, clad partly in Western dress but wearing the long dance scarf, made their way out to the open space in front of one of the gamelan. Everyone settled back again respectfully, but it seemed to me with a slightly indulgent attitude.

For the next twenty minutes, I sat enthralled with the dance performance of these three old men. It was a style, I learned later, that had gone out of fashion thirty or forty years before. Their movements had the refinement and disciplined style that I associated with the very best of the court traditions of Sundanese dance—a quality that had not been sufficiently in evidence earlier in the program in the movements of the young dancers schooled in the court style. This particular tradition had originated as a deliberate blend of court and village dance styles.

When the three men had finished, without waiting for the microphone and the formal speech of thanks expected of me, I went immediately to the elderly dancers and wrung their hands one by one in traditional Sundanese style. I thanked them profusely with whatever words I could find. There was little doubt I had succeeded in establishing communication of my deep admiration for their art.

Then I went to the microphone and made my speech.

After we were back in the car headed for a banquet in the residency at Sumedang and an evening performance to follow, I turned to my host and told him how much I had enjoyed the afternoon, especially the dances of the three old men. I added that I wished there had been some way for me to express my gratitude to them. My host looked at me with a long, steady smile. "Do you know what you have done?" he asked. "With a handshake and a few words for those old men who are practically forgotten members of the village you have given them and their style of dance great status in the whole community. You could not have done more!"

369

If my host was right, and I suppose he may have been, the young people of the village have probably begun to study the old style of dance again—I hope so.

Sometimes the system of communications in the universe of music requires the application of critical method: an attempt to evaluate probable effect before initiating cause. We might consider two types of illustration, one that might have an immediacy of effect, the other long range.

During my first period of residence in Java, I was asked a number of times by professional musicians and several Javanese composers whether I had any suggestions to make about "improving" gamelan practice. From a knowledge of Western music and an acquaintance with Javanese gamelan, what innovations could I recommend? Well, the truth is, as a composer, I had a number of ideas that I really wanted very much to try out within the potentials, yet unrealized, of traditional gamelan.

But each time, remembering the effects of the introduction of Western techniques in Balinese painting—which not only has resulted in a threat to the very existence of traditional forms but also has not produced very many master-pieces in the international art world—each time, with this in mind, I said that I preferred not to make any suggestions. It was not a matter of whether gamelan would or should change in style. There was plenty of evidence that it had been doing just that for centuries. When an art form no longer involves change, it is likely to die. But stylistic changes in Javanese gamelan over the centuries have occurred as a result of the intrusion and influence of compatible, if not kindred, styles of music within the universe of music. And the changes have been wrought by the Javanese themselves. This American composer, whatever his high ideals and purposes, could not lightly undertake responsibility for such change. It should come from the Javanese, I argued with myself.

The argument was sound in principle; yet when I considered the naiveté and primitive descriptive and programmatic effects that were beginning to appear in contemporary gamelan pieces, my resolve would waver. But even to this day, through the years of working with countless students in the study of Javanese gamelan at UCLA, I have refrained from the composer's impulse of "improving" gamelan practice. Students and I have written a number of Javanese pieces in the best traditional style possible to be sure we understood the rules of musical grammar. A few of these exercises might even qualify as pieces of music. But there has been no experimentation. This is a task for the Javanese.

And this thought introduces a different set of long-range problems peculiar to the complicated network of communications in the universe of music—those relating to the exposure and/or training abroad of the Javanese or the Sundanese or the Ashanti or the Japanese or the Indian musician. Let us consider several types of illustration.

RECIPROCITY

It was indicated near the beginning of this book that the activities and positive propaganda of the ethnomusicologist have helped stimulate a widespread interest among educational institutions in the United States in the musical cultures of the non-Western world. Programs of training and research are being initiated in universities and colleges as rapidly as budget and available personnel permit. Private academies devoted exclusively to training in the performance of non-Western music and dance are also beginning to appear. The teaching staff of such academies as well as some universities and colleges include performing musicians and dancers from various musical cultures of the non-Western world.

What happens to these performers in the course of their residence in the United States? During a two- or three-month summer institute, during one or two years of residence, working alongside performers from alien and/or kindred cultures, what kind of influences are transmitted through the speech-music modes of discourse in this particular aggregate within the universe of music? Does the Ashanti master drummer begin to borrow from the Ewe or the Yoruba musician? From the Indian tabla player? Is history beginning to repeat itself in this special environment if the Japanese musician borrows from the Korean? And both of them from the Chinese virtuoso? Are these centers of international performance studies likely to become cultural melting pots in which the tints and shades that distinguish different traditions begin to mix?

Have the interest and best intentions of the ethnomusicologist opened a Pandora's box in the realm of the performing arts? Unwittingly has he violated his Hipkinatic oath?

Part of this melee in the arena of the performing arts are the various national troops of musicians and dancers who tour the United States. Recently, after a rousing performance by the national troupe from Mali in Royce Hall at UCLA, I spent some time backstage watching a fascinating exchange. It occurred in the context of a reception honoring the performers. To be more precise, it occurred at the edge of the reception.

A long table holding bowls of punch and other refreshments had been set up center stage; the bulk of the crowd of guests and hosts was clustered before it. In the wings, on the floor, were the musical instruments that had been used in the performance. At one point, I observed that two UCLA students, Americans who are exceptionally sophisticated and accomplished in several drumming styles

371

of Ghana, were admiring the drums. Two Mali drummers and the two students were not making very much headway conversing in French. They turned from the speech mode to the music mode of discourse. The two Americans sat down to a pair of drums and the two Malinese to another pair. The Americans tested a few strokes on the drums and then launched into a complicated interlocking rhythmic pattern. I watched the faces of the two Mali drummers. Their initial surprise at hearing two American students break forth with West African rhythms wore off quickly. Tentatively, each Mali drummer tried to find the underlying pulse, tried to imitate the patterns. They were different from those of Mali. What a wondrous play of emotions crossed their faces: first surprise, then curiosity, frustration, admiration, good humor! The exchange only lasted three or four minutes; it never became a quartet of drumming. But the desire for communication in the music mode of discourse was clear. No master drummer is ever content with his vocabulary; he wants to increase it. Given enough time, how many Ghanaian rhythms might have been introduced into Mali culture? And, we should ask, vice versa? No, not through the American students. Oh, they were ready enough to learn all the Mali rhythms time would permit. But only as rhythmic patterns in Mali tradition, not something to be mixed up and blended with Ghanaian traditions.

This incident is offered as a reminder of a particular responsibility that must be borne by the ethnomusicologist involved with a program of training and research that includes performance teachers from the non-Western world. In my judgment, based on some twelve years of experience with such a program, the critical factor is the length of exposure. The shorter the exposure the more likely the performer is to carry back to his own culture superficial imitation of other traditions which he has not had time to comprehend in sufficient depth. A few minutes or a few hours backstage in Royce Hall are of little consequence in themselves. But the episode points to the natural appetite of the performer for extending his skill and knowledge. Only if he has an exposure of one or two years, even longer if possible, is it likely that he will gain proper perspective.

During an extended period of residence, with more than a little guidance from the ethnomusicologist, the performer from the non-Western world gains an enviable perspective about his own musical culture in relation to the universe of music. For the first time, in the atmosphere of international music making, through the speech-music modes of discourse, he will come to appreciate the unique identity of his own culture within the universe of music. In such an environment, I have seen a fine musician and dancer from the imperial household in Tokyo become a skilled performer in the traditions of Mexico and Bali; I have watched him become acquainted at first hand with the traditions of Korea and

China; and I have noted with relief and great satisfaction his increased pride in the traditions of Japanese gagaku and bugaku.

Several years ago, a fine master drummer came to UCLA from Ghana. He was truly outstanding in the traditions of his own tribe and, as a teacher in the Institute of African Studies at the University of Ghana, had learned the traditions of several other tribes as well. Each of these musical traditions he taught with equal devotion. Near the end of his stay he told me he had been "composing." Now, one does not usually think of a master drummer as a composer. I listened to his compositions—which were designed for a kind of one-man band playing drums, bells, rattles, and singing all at the same time—with more than passing interest. They were a kind of synthesis of different tribal traditions. Before he left, he presented me with a tape of these pieces. We spent a long evening together at dinner the night before he flew back to Ghana. We talked about Ghanaian traditions and his new compositions. By the time he departed, I was satisfied that in his conception these were two distinctly separate things, that as a teacher from Ghana his first responsibility was the accurate representation of Ghanaian traditions.

Ideally, in such a program, the performer from the non-Western world is both a teacher of his own traditions and a student of others. The extent to which the ideal may obtain varies with the interests and attitude of the individual. Through the years of working with nearly fifty such teachers, I have never found one who was not anxious to learn something about notation and music dictation. From this minimal interest in the universe of music, there have been the exceptions whose objective became a strong desire to be thoroughly trained as ethnomusicologists.

And this brings us to the concluding consideration of this volume: training in the Western world of the non-Western musician-dancer. Within the system of communications in the universe of music, it should be of vital concern to the ethnomusicologist.

We might begin with a question that in a slightly different context was intimated in the Introduction: "Can the Japanese musician researching the music of Japan or the Javanese musician researching the music of Java or the Ashanti musician researching the music of Ghana be thought of as an ethnomusicologist? Can the American musician researching rock music or Negro spirituals or jazz or contemporary compositions of the avant garde be considered an ethnomusicologist?"

I hope, by now, the answer has become obvious: He can be called an ethnomusicologist if he does what an ethnomusicologist is supposed to do—if he uses the ethnomusicological approach to his subject. This, we have tried to dem-

373

onstrate, is different from the musicological approach, different from the anthropological or ethnological approach.

If it is clear that a Chinese ethnomusicologist can apply such an approach to Chinese, Japanese, Indian, or any other kind of music, let us ask what implications this prospect holds for the field of ethnomusicology?

Early in my first field work in Indonesia, it became apparent that there were enormous problems threatening the continuation of some forms of the traditional arts.[8] This condition seemed all the more critical because in the aftermath of revolution and economic chaos in Indonesia, in the turbulence of confrontation with Western technology, few Indonesians were even aware of these cultural problems. And there was little sensitivity to the need for assistance in the fields of Indonesian music, dance, and theater within the purview of American foundations and agencies of the federal government. When I tried to communicate my concern to professional musicians and dancers, I found that there was no common basis in the realm of speech on which comprehension of my concern could be established. It occurred to me that the most direct way, certainly the ultimate and best way, to head off degeneration in the traditional arts would be to educate Indonesian musicians and dancers in the language of scientific methods developed in the West. One notable success story in this effort has been told elsewhere.[9] Very recently I have seen the beginning of several more such successes. Foundations and governmental agencies of both American and Indonesian sources have been very slow to comprehend the urgency for such training. There are a few indications that perhaps this condition is beginning to change.

What is the ultimate significance of this reciprocal training and research as it may affect communications in the universe of music?

Let us make a few assumptions. Let us assume that the American or French or British ethnomusicologist because of *who* he is—that is to say, what he has succeeded in becoming through years of training in scientific methods applied in various ways discussed in this essay—is capable of insights and evaluations, as a transmitter of a non-Western music, which no Javanese, even with training abroad in Western methods, could ever duplicate. But let us also assume that the Javanese, with adequate training abroad, as a *carrier* of his own tradition, is also capable of insights and evaluations that can never be duplicated by his Western colleague.

I have long been convinced that accurate communication in the universe of music about *a particular musical tradition* within that universe must depend

---

[8] See further Mantle Hood, "Changing Patterns in the Arts of Java," *Bulletin of the Institute of Traditional Cultures*, Madras, 1959, pp. 199–209.

[9] Mantle Hood, "Music, the Unknown," in Frank Ll. Harrison, Mantle Hood, and Claude V. Palisca, *Musicology*, Prentice-Hall, Inc., Englewood Cliffs, N.J., 1963.

374

on the efforts of both the carrier of Western scientific methods and the carrier of the musical tradition who has also been trained in scientific methods. I am suggesting that every ethnomusicologist who is a *transmitter* of a particular musical tradition accept the responsibility of ensuring that some *carriers* of the tradition become ethnomusicologists of their culture.

It is a difficult task. At present, as I have suggested, there is little interest in funding such objectives. Beyond this, the non-Western musician-dancer, like the American student of ethnomusicology, must be guided through the shoals of ethnocentricity. I am referring to a point mentioned much earlier in this book: the tendency of an American student concentrating on, for example, Indian music to see all other kinds of music through the prism of Indian music. Both he and the Javanese musician-dancer—who as a budding ethnomusicologist is likely to develop an exaggerated ethnocentric bias in terms of his own objectively rediscovered traditions—both of them must be reminded of the place of Indian and Javanese music within the universe of music if they are to establish accurate communication.

I have had the deep and abiding personal satisfaction of watching one such line of communication develop. There seem to be others in the offing. The observed or postulated musical whole—the universe of music—demands this order of reciprocity from the ethnomusicologist.

INDEX

The Recordings

Side I, *Band 1 (4:03)*   Brief excerpts of a demonstration by five Sundanese female singers recorded by Mr. Moehtar and made available through the courtesy of Mr. Oejeng Soewargana. The performers and the pieces sung appear in the following order: Tuti, "Tjangkurileung" (:44); Atjih, "Doblang naik Sinjur" (:40); Ratnasih, "Gawil Kabatjangan" (:31); Iar, "Modjang Priangan" (a Sundanese version of "Dark Eyes") (:40); Tati, "Titil-Kombinasi" (1:13)

2:01 { *Band 2*   A brief excerpt of a Matjapat sung by Njai Bei Mardoesari (:11) and then repeated at half speed (:20). The fragment of text is "tan kabélan Narapati" which in translation means "not attracted by the king"

Band 3 (:09)   Kakko played by Suenobu Togi

Band 4 (1:12)   Brief illustrations of the following instruments: the Western oboe, the Indian shanai, the Thai pi-nai, the Korean piri, the Japanese hichiriki, the Chinese so-na, the Indian nagaswaram.

Side II, *Band 1 (:37)*   The beginning of the piece for gendèr wajang entitled "Selasah"

Band 2 (:40)   An Ewe ensemble playing atsía

Band 3 (1:19)   A portion of a Lobi Fetish piece entitled "Boobene" played on the xylophone by Kakraba Lobi

Band 4 (:45)   Special placement of the microphone to reveal the same performer humming while he plays the xylophone

Band 5 (:55)   An itinerant musician performing as a one-man band in Djakarta, Indonesia

Side III, *Band 1 (3:43)*   Yoruba royal drummers belonging to the Court of the Timi of Ede in Nigeria (:58); the Globemasters Dance Band in Accra, Ghana (:53); Ashanti adowa ensemble in Accra, Ghana (1:01); an Ijaw dance ensemble from Eastern Nigeria residing in Legon, Ghana (:43)

Band 2 (:36)   An excerpt of drumming by Alla Rakha

Band 3 (1:23)   An excerpt from "Godan Ginuta" played on the koto by Keiji Yagi: microphone on Channel A, microphone on Channel B, composite of the two

Side IV, *Band 1 (6:02)*   The opening and close of "Rambu" played by gamelan sekati in Surakarta, Java

Side V, *Band 1 (:40)*   Fanti drumming recorded in Ghana during a procession celebrating a memorial service

Band 2 (1:05)   An analytical recording with special microphone placement emphasizing gendèr panerus

Band 3 (1:42)   Analytical recording of: rebab (:23); gambang (:23); gendèr (:23); tjèlempung (:29); playing the same brief excerpt from the piece "Ladrang Retnananingsih" (Background noises are the sound of the neighbor's children taking a bucket bath.)

Side VI, *Band 1 (3:07)*   "Gondjang-Gandjing" recorded with one microphone in Djogjakarta, Java (1:57); a continuation of the same piece recorded with 13 microphones by Columbia Masterworks in the CBS Studio in Hollywood, California (1:10)

Band 2 (1:23)   The "Sendon Tlutur" played on the rebab by Pak Pontjopangrawit, preceded by a tjulikan (a traditional testing of the open strings) and a paṭetan djugag (a modal prelude)